Dreaming in the Classroom

SUNY series in Dream Studies

Robert L. Van de Castle, editor

Dreaming in the Classroom

Practices, Methods, and Resources
in Dream Education

Philip King
Kelly Bulkeley
Bernard Welt

KH

Cover image courtesy of Justin Knight.

Published by State University of New York Press, Albany

© 2011 State University of New York

All rights reserved

Printed in the United States of America

For information, contact State University of New York Press, Albany, NY
www.sunypress.edu

Production by Eileen Meehan
Marketing by Anne Valentine

Library of Congress Cataloging-in-Publication Data

King, Philip,
   Dreaming in the classroom : practices, methods, and resources in dream
education / Philip King, Kelly Bulkeley, Bernard Welt.
        p. cm. — (Suny series in dream studies)
   Includes bibliographical references (p.) and index.
   ISBN 978-1-4384-3687-6 (hardcover : alk. paper)
   ISBN 978-1-4384-3686-9 (pbk. : alk. paper)
   1. Dreams—Study and teaching (Higher)   I. Bulkeley, Kelly, 1962–   II. Welt,
Bernard, 1952–   III. Title.

   BF1078.K56 2011
   154.6'3071—dc22   2011000769

10 9 8 7 6 5 4 3 2 1

10/17/11

Contents

Preface

There are many excellent books on dream theory, research, and practice. This volume is not an effort to add directly to that impressive body of literature. Rather we approach the topic one level removed: in the foothills looking down at the plain, discerning activities, patterns, trends, and opportunities in how dream knowledge is taught broadly throughout the society. We look at classroom courses and efforts outside academia in the community, considering teaching methods and vehicles and all target audiences from children to the elderly. We describe different educative approaches and activities and try to note their uses and potentials accurately and fairly.

Some words about the domain and purpose of this book: It is neither a history nor an encyclopedia of persons, practices, and programs in dream education, although we would welcome such a valuable contribution written by others. Our goals in this effort are both more modest than that, and more ambitious in other ways: We have written a resource book for dream educators—a description and evaluation of educational practice in the field, and an exploration of associated pedagogical and epistemological questions. The book is for current and aspiring dreams teachers, as well as for dreamers everywhere and persons interested in new trends and methods in education, particularly interdisciplinary approaches, the integration of the sciences and humanities, and the use of the Internet and other public media.

Our writing stems from our many years of dream teaching and the experiences of other dream teachers. As such, it is our subjective (although carefully thought-through) "take" on the field; we make no claim to comprehensiveness. For example, we emphasize dream courses in conventional university programs of study because this is our particular professional focus (and the place where aspiring dream teachers are most likely to find opportunities). Other writers would have other emphases. The reader can think of this volume as a team-taught tutorial on dream pedagogy, subject to the authors' biases as well as profiting from our insights.

We undertook the writing of this book at this crucial juncture of human and planetary history in which a widespread valuing of dreams may become ever more important. The macro-problem of overpopulation, resource depletion and environmental degradation and attendant social instability and injustice presents unprecedented challenges as well as opportunities for positive change. We are hopeful that an increased attention to dreams will contribute, if modestly, to the breadth of vision needed to deal cooperatively, selflessly, and creatively with these global issues.

Dreams are universal, a fundamental experience in all places and times. Dreams also are unique to each person, distinguishing us even as they put us in relation. Dreams connect and integrate unconscious process with conscious waking choice and action. We believe that dreams can connect persons within local communities and across cultural and national boundaries, and that increased attention to dreams could contribute to human progress. The potential of dreams therefore is social as well as personal.

As authors, we have profited from the ideas, inspiration, and direct helpfulness of many in the international community of dreams scholars and practitioners. We try to acknowledge them specifically for their contributions. However, we undoubtedly have absorbed some ideas and points of view the sources of which we have forgotten. We apologize for any failures of attribution and credit. The dreams community is characterized by generous spirits who readily share ideas that are taken on, developed, and modified by others. We continue that practice in deep appreciation of our contemporaries, those who came before and those who will assuredly come after.

Acknowledgments

This book owes much to the many persons in the dream education community who filled out surveys, granted us interviews, responded to our questions, provided course materials, and generally impressed us with their creativity and innovation in dream education. Our collective thanks go to Kate Adams, Sheila Asato, Deirdre Barrett, Paula Berggren, Barbara Bishop, Fariba Bogzaran, Bob Coalson, Betsy Davids, Mary Dombeck, Bill Domhoff, Christopher Dreisbach, Rita Dwyer, Michele Ferrante, Nicole Gratton, Mike Grady, Jody Grundy, Olaf Hansen, Michael Hewett, Iris Maria Heller, Deborah Hickey, Clara Hill, Robert Hoss, Don Houston, Tracey Kahan, Johanna King, Roger Knudson, Cynthia Kuhn, Don Kuiken, Stanley Krippner, Justina Lasley, Ruth Lingford, Susan Locke, Athena Lou, Tom Maddox, Laurel McCabe, Don Middendorf, Jim Pagel, Victoria Rabinowe, Henry Reed, Sara Ridberg, Stephen David Ross, Michael Schredl, Maxine Skuba, Carl C. Smith, Charles Stewart, Allucquere Rosanne Stone, Peter Struck, Jeremy Taylor, Jason Tougaw, and Richard Wilkerson. Thanks to Jane Bunker, Nancy Ellegate, and Eileen Meehan of SUNY Press, and to Robert Van de Castle, editor of the SUNY series in Dream Studies, all of whom were most helpful in shepherding the book from its inception through the publication process.

We are grateful to Laura Lamp of Harvard Divinity School, whose dream inspired a walking labyrinth in the back courtyard of the campus in Cambridge, Massachusetts, which is featured on our book's cover in a photograph by Justin Knight.

Phil King thanks Hawaii Pacific University for funding his attendance at numerous professional dream conferences, and for hosting a regional conference on dreams and holistic health. He also thanks his students and colleagues, and family and friends for their support and for sharing their dreams with him.

Kelly Bulkeley would like to acknowledge his colleagues and students at the Graduate Theological Union, Santa Clara University, John F. Kennedy University, the University of Chicago, and the other schools where he has had the opportunity to engage in dream education. He also thanks his family, both human (Hilary, Dylan, Maya, Conor) and feline (Lightning, Thunder, Levi, Strauss), for their support and companionship.

Bernard Welt wishes to acknowledge with gratitude the Corcoran College of Art and Design and Dean Kirk Pillow for a faculty-development course release for research, and the Artist House at St. Mary's College of Maryland for residencies during which he wrote some of the text of this book. He thanks his students at the Corcoran College of Art and Design and at St. Mary's College of Maryland, and colleagues in faculty, administration, and library staff, including Jennifer Cognard-Black, Nan Fry, Michael S. Glaser, Andrew Hudson, Sue Johnson, Beth Baruch Joselow, Doug Lang, Joe Lucchesi, Martha McWilliams, and Casey Smith; and Colby Caldwell, Dr. Michael S. Hammond, Dr. Timothy Price, Dr. Thomas Qualey, and always, most of all, Arthur.

Kelly Bulkeley and Bernard Welt would like to acknowledge Phil King's leadership, initiative, patience, and sage advice throughout the development, writing, and editing of this book.

Introduction

This book is probably not the first book you have read about dreams. There are many fine treatments of the subject, which we identify and discuss throughout, and list in a bibliography. This is primarily for dream educators and others who want to extend and deepen their knowledge by involving themselves in dream education as teachers and/or as advanced learners. The relative newcomer to dreams also will find this book, supplemented by other resources, to be a useful guide.

We acknowledge that it might sound strange to speak of "educating" people about dreams. Isn't dreaming something you just do, without needing anyone to teach you how? Yes, and no! Yes, dreaming is a natural process of the imagination that does not require any conscious effort or training; it simply happens, automatically, all through our lives. Indeed, the capacity to dream seems to be inherent in the evolved neural architecture of the human brain. We are truly a dreaming species, born to a lifelong cycling of waking and sleeping modes of consciousness. At the same time, we do learn how to view and use our dreams. Every culture through history has developed its own traditions of dream belief and practice and has passed them on (i.e., taught them) to the next generation. People learn about dreams from their families, their religious or spiritual leaders, their healers, and their teachers. Cumulatively, these influences have a tangible impact on the frequency and content of people's remembered dreams. Dream education is, by any reasonable standard of cross-cultural comparison, a universal practice in human societies. So, no, it shouldn't seem strange to engage the different ways people teach each other about dreaming. What is strange is how rarely these practices have been discussed in the contemporary Western academic context.

The purpose of this book is to examine current activities and issues in dream education, giving our sense of emerging possibilities that will shape teaching practices in the coming decades. The book is a resource guide for practitioners at all educational levels, in a wide variety of disciplines. In addition to our many years of experience teaching our own courses on dreams, we have spent the past several years gathering information—convening panels and symposia on the subject of dream education, listening to teachers from many different disciplines describe their approaches and experiences, and surveying the curricula of colleges, universities, and graduate institutes. Thanks to the far-ranging scholarly network spawned by the International Association for the Study of Dreams (IASD), we have gained a broad overview of what is actually happening in contemporary Western dream education. At the most basic level, this book holds up a mirror to present-day society, reflecting back a lively but little-known collectivity of educational practices revolving around the universal human experience of dreaming.

We do not believe any one culture or tradition has a monopoly on how best to do dream education. Our major emphasis is on teaching practices in Western higher education because that is where we work and what we know best. However, we are well aware of and deeply respectful toward venerable non-Western dream perspectives, and dream education outside conventional university environments. In this era of the Internet and instantaneous worldwide communication, information of all kinds is increasingly flowing over national, cultural, and institutional divides. We see this happening in dream education, and we view this book as one contribution to that broader process of emerging cross-cultural dialogue.

We recognize that for some persons dreams are associated with superstitious beliefs and fringe activities like astrology, channeling, and alien abductions. We have noticed, too, that the reactions of many persons typically combine doubtfulness about the value of dreams in general and their fittingness as objects of study with a fascination about their *own* dreams. Experience has taught us that people possess an innate curiosity about dreaming, but they are wary of exaggerated claims and dubious theories. In this respect, we address our book and its arguments not just to people already interested in dream education, but also to the wider public. We devote considerable attention to questions of intellectual integrity in the study of dreams, with the goal of establishing a sound, reasonable basis for making valid claims about the origins and functions of dreaming and the meanings of dreams. Dreams always will be viewed by some people with skepticism, even disdain, but that should not stop dream scholars from continuing to develop theory, gather evidence, and promote dream practices that meet the highest standards of academic quality. We believe the best, most effective, and most enjoyable dream education practices are grounded in precisely that kind of knowledge.

Once beyond questions about the value and meaningfulness of dreams, an even more formidable challenge presents itself to anyone who wants to learn about the subject. What is the best disciplinary perspective for studying dreams? The first answer that comes to mind (from a contemporary Western perspective) is psychology. To be sure, more courses and program units on dreams are taught in psychology departments than anywhere else. But as we show in the coming pages, there are teachers in many disciplines other than psychology who are making valuable contributions to our efforts to understand the nature and potentiality of dreaming. This may seem to complicate matters, but in our view it is simply a reflection of the pluralism of dreaming itself. An honest appraisal of human dreams reveals them as complex, multifaceted, and nearly infinite in their diversity and possible meanings. The study of dreams therefore embraces many scholarly disciplines, bringing together the arts, humanities, and social and natural sciences. Complementary approaches from all these fields are required for a full understanding of dreams, with direct implications for all forms of dream education. In this regard, we embrace multidisciplinary and interdisciplinary teaching, with critical, self-reflective dialogue across disciplines helping us sort out what is and is not useful and trustworthy.

Our discussions in this volume range from thoughts on the best ways to teach and learn about dreams in particular subject contexts, to epistemological arguments about why dream studies are an appropriate and important part of study in various academic fields. For example, in the chapter on psychology, a field where dream studies are relatively well established, we give greater weight to pedagogy, whereas in the chapters on humanities and writing, where dream studies are less prevalent and less well known, we emphasize the reasons for their educational importance and curricular inclusion.

Although courses on dreams are relatively scarce, a number of schools and teachers are working to develop not only single courses but also broad-based curricular enterprises. We look forward to the benefits that emerge as students are able not just to take one course on dreams but are also able to immerse themselves in programs of multiple courses involving ongoing interaction with a community of faculty and students who share their interests.

The Authors' Perspectives: A Dreams Primer

We want readers of this book to know the beliefs and attitudes that we hold about dreams, as they informed our choices about what topics to include and what to write about them. To this end we present the following "dream primer," summarizing our view of dreams.

This section doubles as a brief but densely packed introduction to the field for educators who want to incorporate dreams into their teaching and want to expand their existing knowledge. In Appendix A, we discuss books that we have found particularly enriching in learning and teaching about dreams. This can serve as a reading list, both for those with little or no previous background in the subject, and those more experienced in the field for whom the books may provide a helpful review, extension of their knowledge, and possibilities for student reading assignments.

We encourage you to reflect on the contents of this volume and other works on dreams and incorporate into your own understanding those ideas that resonate most meaningfully and prove to be most useful. Which theories, perspectives, and approaches hold up best to tests of logic, experience, practice, and empirical confirmation? Teaching is more effective when teachers personally embrace the material they are using, having considered and selected it carefully.

The three of us come from varied academic disciplines (general humanities, literature, and film studies for Welt; religious studies, philosophy, and psychology for Bulkeley; and psychology, political science, and research methodology for King) and have different dream interests, yet agree broadly about their nature and use, the differences among us being largely ones of emphasis.

What about dreams intrigues us enough to devote much of our careers to their contemplation? It is their intense and meaningful quality, first encountered in our childhoods, which drew us as adults into their study. We believe that work in dreams is usually grounded in and motivated by one's own dreams, at least initially. We agree with Gordon Globus that those working with dreams need to honor their own dreams.[1] The experience of dreams and their personal significance is vital for the best possible dream teaching, scholarship, and clinical practice. Eventually, of course, working with dreams may range far from one's personal dreams. Researching and teaching about sleeping and dreaming patterns, dream content, and studying and creating literature or art derived from dreams all can extend well beyond the scholar's own dream experience.

Dreams are emotion-laden stories that our minds create during sleep. They may be complete or fragmentary, coherent or confusing, joyful or troubling, recalled on waking or forgotten. We found in surveying more than 1,000 of our students that on the average, they report remembering between two and three dreams per week, although some recall dreams rarely or never and some recall many dreams most mornings. Dreamers can strengthen recall with intention, focus, and practice. A remembered dream, once recorded, becomes a text that we can engage to understand and develop its meanings. A dream, or (better) a series of dreams for a person becomes a narrative of that dreamer's life concerns.

The dreaming person most often experiences being a participating character in the dream, although sometimes the dreamer is only an observer. The dreamer usually takes the events of the dream as "real," which is to say as if they were occurring as in waking life. Only on waking, does the realization dawn that "it was only a dream." An exception to this is the "lucid" dream, in which the dreamer realizes that he or she is dreaming even as the dream takes place. Lucid dreams are rare as a percentage of all dreams but are experienced at one time or another by a majority of people who remember their dreams.

Everyone dreams every night, although biological depressants or brain injury can reduce dreaming activity. In a typical night's sleep, some mentation may be occurring all along, from forms of thinking to storylike dreams with a plot and visual contents. Dreams have much in common with films: Both primarily are visual experiences with other sensory and emotional content. Dreaming can occur in any of the cyclic stages of sleep.

Dreams range from the mundane to the sublime and powerful. All dreams can inform the dreamer's life in some way. Each dream is unique in the variety and subtlety of its emotions and meanings. Remembered dreams overall tend to be slightly more negative than positive in their emotional tone. However, even so-called "bad" dreams (nightmares) can be "good" in their deepening of experience and insight, and we believe it is important to experience and understand "bad" dreams, and not flee from them. Repeated or recurrent dreams indicate ongoing concerns or issues that have yet to be resolved.

Dreams can bypass defense mechanisms that inhibit deep experience in waking. Therefore, dreams often are more sensorially vivid, emotional, and meaning-laden than is much of waking life. Therein lie much of their appeal and fascination. Dreams remove blinders and we can experience our lives and ourselves in fresh and revealing ways, particularly if later we consciously consider what meanings our dreams hold. What we do in waking with dream experiences, if anything, is up to us.

Dreams may even be a conduit to paranormal experience. Thousands of persons claim to have had telepathic, clairvoyant, and precognitive (predictive) dreams. Although the cumulative weight of these reports is impressive, it has been difficult to prove their existence to scientific standards. We believe in staying open to the possibility of such anomalous dream experiences and respectful of dreamers' claims, without becoming unduly credulous. We advocate carefully assessing the evidence and considering alternative explanations.

Dreams are lodged in sleep processes, grounded in the neurology of the brain. As is true with all experience, dreaming events are produced by and filtered through neural mechanisms. We know this because injury to these mechanisms results in corresponding deficiency of dream imagery or affect. This does not mean, however, that dreams are "nothing but" neurological products. Brain could be viewed as the vehicle through which mind manifests itself—we do not believe that mind necessarily can be reduced to brain. Many qualities of dreams cannot be linked empirically to specific neural structures or events. Mental processes (including dreams) have functional autonomy. We leave open the *possibility* that there is consciousness independent of brain activity, and thus prior to it and transcending the individual human being. This means that dreams may have spiritual dimensions in terms of personal meanings and perhaps as conduits for exogenous spiritual influences.

Dreams as recalled and written down as narratives can be analyzed using methods of the natural and human sciences, philosophy and the humanities, and can serve as material and inspiration for new creations and modes of expression and engagement. We can analyze dream content statistically to extract meaningful patterns and regularities. We can interpret dream stories in terms of the psychology of the dreamer or larger social, philosophical, spiritual, literary, historical, and political categories. Dreams can reveal the meanings and concerns of the person or the community. We believe that the more vivid and striking the dream, the more it speaks to the dreamer's deepest existential concerns. Dreams and dream processes can be a window into phenomena of sleep and brain functioning in waking and sleeping. Therefore, the study of dreams is inherently multidisciplinary, and the constituent disciplines of the sciences and humanities, separately and in concert, may lay claim to the subject. Dream studies are primed for new, *inter*disciplinary approaches that combine the analytical rigor of the sciences with the imaginative creativity of the humanities.

What do dreams mean? How should we interpret them? Is there an automatic function, or more than one function, that they serve? Additionally, what purposes or uses can we place on dreams as a matter of choice? We do not hold any one stance about these questions, and we caution the reader not to adhere to any particular perspective for adherence or theory's sake. Theories and methods are lodged in particular cultural contexts, their use contingent on the users' purposes, which tend to reflect and support extant worldviews. We see theories as devices that are helpful in clarifying aspects of reality, dream reality in this instance. They are tools in our analytical toolbox. In practice, we view theories as useful or not useful, rather than true or false. (Although we admit that some theories illuminate some aspects of dreams so brilliantly at times that they do seem true as well as useful.) We have found all approaches to dreams valuable in clarifying some aspects of the phenomenon, but none sufficient by itself.

Dream pioneers Sigmund Freud and Carl Jung emphasize, respectively, dreams as reflecting the past and giving guidance for the future. We like this complementary focus, and believe that much, even most of *psychological* theory about dreams consists of extensions and modifications of Jung and Freud. We find Freud's view that dreams are primarily disguised sexual wishes and Jung's belief that dreams can manifest inherited tendencies to express archetypical ideas interesting and heuristically valuable but of questionable general validity.

We share the perspective of Harry Hunt that there may be multiple types of dreams with different sources, functions, uses, and meanings.[2] Dreams may be primarily about the dreamer's psyche or body, or the dreamer's immediate community or society. They may reflect the past or present, preview the future, give voice and form to unconscious conflicts, spur and express creativity, solve problems, reveal the divine, or even cull unneeded cognitive material. Dreams, including religious dreams, may speak directly and clearly to personal concerns, or be metaphors that sidle up to issues and their meanings in cleverly disguised ways. Although dream content varies in terms of demographic factors such as the age, gender, and culture of the dreamer, these aggregate differences become less salient the deeper one delves into particular dreams of specific persons.

Dream theories tend to be self-fulfilling as dreams themselves reflect waking perceptions and attitudes. People who believe in Freudian, or Jungian, or paranormal explanations of dreams will tend to have dreams that corroborate their beliefs. Although dreams always retain the ability to tap one on the shoulder, so to speak, and impart a new perspective, they sometimes will simply confirm one's extant positions. Homicidal terrorists perhaps are more likely to have dreams justifying their worldview than they are to have dreams that challenge it. Dreams are not necessarily more moral than the waking consciousness of the dreamer. They *can* express existing but latent, repressed or incompletely developed positive qualities and views.

There is no consensus about the functions of dreaming. We believe that dreaming even without recall may serve to regulate emotions by completing experience and expression of feeling and, as Ernest Hartmann argues, by absorbing traumas and lesser emotional events into existing contexts of meaning.[3] Remembering dreams and evaluating their significance, however, go an important step beyond any automatic regulatory function of dreaming. A conscious assessment of one's dreams, including discussing them with other people, can be a kind of self-therapy, a spur to personal psychological and spiritual growth. A consideration of dreams offers the potential of discovering previously unexplored aspects of self and of the world.

We urge the reader of this book to learn about dreams and dream education with an open mind and open heart, while retaining a critical eye regarding evidence adduced in support of any claim or theory. Anecdotes, historical accounts, and case studies are fascinating and great springboards for reflection and theorizing, but do not constitute proof of assertions. Where the point is empirical, scientific criteria of verification, reliability and validity apply. Where the point is philosophical, logical criteria apply. Where the point is aesthetic, subjective and consensual criteria apply. Where the point is about one's own life, the "a-ha" of recognition and the ongoing consequences of the insight are major criteria for meaningfulness. It helps us to remind ourselves that at the core of learning about dreams for the dreams teacher is an exploration and sharing of one's own dreams. This grounds all other endeavors.

We are truly and perpetually fascinated with dreams, and continue to study them, teach about them, and use them as material for self-understanding and creativity. We enjoy being part of a widespread community of dreamers and dream scholars who share ideas, friendship, and support. Still we caution against giving dreams more than their due. This is an occupational hazard, as dreams are beguiling and awe inspiring, and communicating one's dreams can be grounding and nurturing. Dreams celebrate our triumphs and our ongoing expansions of self; they will not hesitate to show us our contractions of self and failures at seizing the moments of possibility that come to us. An attention to dreams can enrich life. However, there is little redemptive quality per se to dreams; they "only" illuminate experience and possibility. The redemption is in the waking act and thought—the role of the dream is to chronicle, goad, inspire and celebrate.

Following this introduction, *Dreaming in the Classroom* is organized into 11 chapters. The first, "Practical Guidelines for Dream Education," outlines the major considerations involved in virtually any kind of enterprise in dream education. These themes include the institutional setting of the course, the backgrounds of the students, the range and depth of course content, logistical issues of class size and course schedule, and practices of dream sharing in the classroom. In this chapter, we lay out the broad pedagogical terrain of dream education.

In the following six chapters we treat six distinct subject areas in higher education, beginning with fundamental preparation in academic skills. Writing is foundational to academic work, to literacy, the life of the mind, and success in all academic pursuits. In Chapter 2 we discuss how creative writing courses can incorporate dreaming as a topic and a resource. We also argue that dream study has exciting potential for development in visual studies and electronic media in contemporary technologies of education and communication.

Chapter 3 looks at psychology, traditionally the preeminent source of Western academic knowledge about dreaming. Certainly, since the early 20th century, dreams have been regarded first and foremost as psychological phenomena. Naturally, this has led to a history of dream courses in college and university psychology departments, and we examine some of the most creative and successful of these courses and their teachers. Included in this chapter is a discussion of psychology offerings that combine the study of dreams with the study of sleeping and dreaming processes. Psychology courses bring scientific methods into the discussion, a fundamental dimension in dream pedagogy.

Chapter 4 focuses on the discipline of anthropology, which also has a colorful history of interest in dreaming reaching back to its founding researchers and theorists. Although long influenced by developments in psychology, anthropologists have developed their own distinctive way of exploring the cultural dynamics of dreaming, and their educational practices reflect this more-than-psychological perspective on the origin, function, and meaning of dreams.

Chapter 5 examines dream education practices in the disciplines of philosophy and religious studies. These fields have a historically important influence on ideas about dreaming, and remain the locus for some of the most radical questions that should be posed in dream education. Virtually every known religious tradition in the world looks to dreaming as a means of communicating with sacred powers and realities, and most major philosophers in Western and Eastern traditions have devoted at least some attention to the epistemological and metaphysical dimensions of human dream experience. We discuss courses that have been inspired in these disciplines.

The sixth chapter surveys the practices of dream educators in general humanities courses, including literature and the arts. These teachers have developed a host of robust, theoretically sophisticated understandings of human dreaming.

Indeed, courses taught by teachers in these fields feature some of the most creative interdisciplinary practices we have found in dream education.

Films are perhaps the human creation closest to dreams in both process and content, and the reciprocal relevance of dream studies and film studies is the subject of Chapter 7. It has been widely noted that many basic film techniques seem to derive from the subjective experience dreaming, with its highly variable focus, sudden shifts of scene, slowing of action, alternation of clarity and obscurity, and so on. The cinematic dream sequence often is scrutinized in courses on dreams and dreaming. Here, however, we suggest that beyond the immediate relevance of the dream–film analogy, the most fundamental questions addressed by contemporary dream theory are deeply meaningful for understanding cinema, and that film theory's accounts of narrative and of the hallucinatory experience of watching movies may offer provocative new ideas to students of dreaming.

Chapter 8 draws on our previous discussions of psychology as well as other disciplines in a consideration of dreams as a topic in the training of clinicians, including psychiatrists, psychotherapists, counseling psychologists, nurses, and pastoral counselors. It is perplexing that despite the *prima facie* value of dreams as a therapeutic tool and source of clinical data, dream education is largely absent from graduate clinical training. We examine some reasons for this state of affairs, while highlighting notable exceptions of clinical educators doing sophisticated and important work.

In Chapter 9 we venture outside the ivory tower and its traditional departmental structures and programs to review dream education in the community, where there is a creative burgeoning of innovative and flexible dream teaching. We look at alternative dream institutes and training programs, the work of several individual practitioner-educators, and lay dream discussion groups. We consider the evident advantages and possible disadvantages of dream education freed from the institutional constraints of conventional universities. Learning about dreams needn't (and doesn't) begin and end with college studies.

We take a developmental turn in Chapter 10, in which we discuss dream education in primary, intermediate and secondary schools, and the implicit learning that occurs when dreams are discussed in the family. Children and teenagers have a natural curiosity about their dreams, and some teachers have responded to this by bringing dreams into their classrooms in a variety of contexts. However, for a variety of reasons, very few primary or secondary schools will have anything to do with dreams! We examine this general situation with the aim of highlighting the best current practices, responding to common objections, and pointing in the most promising directions for future progress.

Chapter 11 concludes with reflections on dream education's current status and future prospects. The teachers, courses, and activities we describe are part of a broader trend in Western educational practice in which old boundaries are crumbling and new interdisciplinary alliances are being forged, all in the midst of cultural ferment and rapid social and technological change. The current state of dream education for lay students and professionals alike offers promising opportunities to bridge the gaps between disciplines, theories, and schools of thought. Significant movement in this direction has already begun. Freudians, Jungians, neurobiologists, psychologists, practitioners of meditation, religious mystics, artists, doctors and others have finally started talking to each other about dreams, seeking to transcend the limitations of existing models in understanding consciousness, mind, and imagination. There has never been a better time to focus attention on dream education from kindergarten to graduate school, as well as in adult and senior education, across a variety of disciplines and fields. We believe the accumulated experiences of contemporary dream teachers can serve as a model for educational practices that incorporate critical thought, creative imagination, and authentic human interaction in the classroom.

Also in our concluding chapter we speculate about future trends and possibilities. We discuss the promise and the possible perils of the Internet and related electronic technologies as vehicles for dream teaching. We take a fresh look at the perplexing question of teaching dream interpretation: What are the proper bases for interpretation? How can we know if an interpretation is valid? We ponder the forms that interdisciplinary dream education might take, and offer a template for an evolved hybrid course on dreams.

Although we attempt in the book to give examples of and discuss all types of contemporary dream education, our coverage is not exhaustive, but rather representative. There are many worthy dream teachers doing excellent work that we do not get to or mention only in passing; this does not diminish their importance. Also, because this is a book about teaching, we discuss only in a pedagogical context the work of the many brilliant and dedicated scholars who supply educators with new material in their theories, scientific findings, approaches to working with dreams, and creative products. In places we are prescriptive, as well as descriptive. Although we try for detachment, we are passionate about dreams—in both their substance and teaching—and have strong points of view grounded in our experience. These opinions will come through; we invite you to consider them and agree or take issue, as you will.

Dreaming in the Classroom includes a number of appendices to enhance its practical usefulness for educators. Appendix A contains a brief discussion of books and other resources that have influenced us and that we recommend as useful in developing a strong background in dream, theory, scholarship, and educational practice.

Appendix B provides sample syllabi and assignments, including those that have proven their usefulness in actual teaching experience. Appendix C treats community dream discussion groups—their establishment and operation. Appendix D gives guidance for one-shot presentations on dreams to various groups.

Appendix E discusses the DreamBank—a repository of dream reports and tools for systematic analyses of dream content. In Appendix F we describe a college class project that melded quantitative content analysis with an exploration of dream themes. Appendix G presents a template for interdisciplinary dreams teaching. In Appendix H we give tips for proposing a course on dreaming. In Appendix I we consider assessment and evaluation of the effectiveness of dream teaching: How can we know what students learned, and if they learned what we intended? Finally, Appendix J presents an essay by Barbara Bishop, "Why I Teach Dreams in Freshman Composition." The appendices *in toto* will give readers access to abundant resources for creating new dream education models and/or augmenting existing courses and programs.

The book is enriched throughout by the views, opinions, and insights of many dream educators whom we interviewed for this project or have otherwise spoken with over the years. Where no endnote is present, the information is from the interview or exchange with the person mentioned. Written and other sources are noted in the usual manner.

Let us start our exploration in the following chapter with a look at some fundamental questions and issues in dreams courses in general, across disciplines. Then we consider discipline-specific course contents and teaching approaches, target groups, and learning environments.

Chapter 1

Practical Guidelines for Dream Education

There are a number of issues to address in teaching about dreams, whether the instruction is in formal academic settings or in less-structured community environments. In this chapter, we explore the "nuts and bolts" and surrounding questions and concerns of dream education in the college classroom, and beyond. Our comments in this chapter apply in a broad, cross-disciplinary way. Subsequent chapters address specific academic fields, target audiences, and educational settings.

Dream education encompasses much more than dream interpretation. The study of dreaming leads us beyond finding meaning in the dreams of individuals to theories of mind, models of culture, and accounts of imagination and creativity. Although we focus primarily on college-level courses, the same basic principles also apply to dream education in professional training (e.g., psychotherapy, counseling, or pastoral training programs), in freestanding dream institutes, and in nonacademic community settings.

First we look at the environments in which dreams education takes place. These provide both opportunities and constraints. Any course on dreams is located in nested contexts, from its outer cultural and institutional environments inward to the course structure, content, and students at the center. The largest context is the dominant cultural attitude toward dreams, which in the West is a mixture of indifference, dismissal, and fear counterbalanced by a persistent interest, sense of value, and fascination. Our culture is ambivalent about dreams, to say the least. Important contexts are the educational culture and the wherewithal of the institution housing the course. In colleges and universities we find a wide range of resources, programs of study, academic standards, and student abilities. Expectations for student performance differ greatly. Students will be variously well or ill prepared, motivated, and focused. For these reasons, we need to consider the surrounding academic culture in proposing and teaching courses on dreams. Although you can always do more with better-prepared students and more lavish resources, it is possible to teach rich and meaningful courses on dreams almost anywhere. Instructor commitment, skill, and enthusiasm can make the difference.

Also to be considered in putting together a course on dreams is the type of college or university. In the United States this would include 2-year (community) colleges offering the associate of arts or sciences degree; 4-year colleges offering a bachelor's degree; colleges or universities offering bachelor's, master's, and perhaps professional degrees; and full-fledged research universities offering doctoral degrees. If you are proposing a course on dreams from outside the institution, you will have a greater chance of its acceptance at colleges having a high percentage of adjunct instructors. These tend to be community colleges and 4-year colleges with fewer resources. It is easier to get a new course accepted if you are a member of the regular faculty. Faculties guard their curricula, and take their responsibilities seriously. If you are not on the inside, finding a faculty or administrative ally who will champion your course will be helpful and may be necessary. One option is to volunteer as a guest speaker on dreams in an existing course, hoping thereby to generate interest in having an entire course on dreams.

There are also noncredit continuing education and adult-enrichment programs offered in otherwise degree-granting institutions. These often look for innovative courses appealing to segments of the public, such as retirees. They may have a lesser bureaucratic gauntlet to run, employ instructors from the outside, and may be more receptive to proposals for courses on dreams. Noncredit courses also are spared required assignments and products, exams, and grades.

Requirements will be even less stringent in nonacademic community institutions, especially when one offers the course on a noncompensated or minimally compensated basis. Although this does not relieve the instructor from the obligation to be well prepared and to follow ethical guidelines, it is easier to get permission to offer dream education in nonacademic settings. One of our colleagues in dream education, Athena Lou, started by teaching about dreams in a community center and on the radio, moved on to assist Phil King by leading dream discussion groups in an undergraduate course, and has since done her own workshops in IASD dream conferences and taught about dreams to clients in her management training company.

Educational expectations, including resource considerations, also are at play in dream teaching set in secondary or primary schools, and in institutions such as churches, community centers, prisons, and libraries. The questions to ask as a prospective dreams educator in these various environments are what resources the organization can provide, what by the instructor, and what limits resource constraints place on the kinds of activities that constitute the course.

Another significant context for dream courses is the institutional perception of a subject matter still viewed by some as exotic or even vaguely disreputable.

This is especially important in universities and colleges, as academics view themselves (quite properly) as arbiters of scholarly legitimacy. We have found a mixed attitude among professors and administrators, reflecting the ambivalence most people feel about dreams. On the one hand, you will find a sincere interest. On the other hand, there will be skepticism and discomfort with, even fear of, the subject (perhaps in part because of its potential to reveal, even in the most benign and helpful way, workings of the unconscious and its relation to waking life). There also may be an implicit, although incorrect, view that the subject of dreams is insufficiently grounded in scholarship. We hope this book helps to dispel that particular assumption. Be prepared to offer evidence supporting the legitimacy of taking dreams seriously as an object of academic study.

Your task as the advocate of the prospective college dreams course is to convince the department faculty, chairperson, or other decision makers to let the course go forward. Although this may be easier for a full-time faculty member than for an adjunct or outsider, there still may be significant impediments to course approval. Almost all colleges require a formal statement of any proposed course's goals, objectives, relevance, planned topics, and activities, along with ethical safeguards and the instructor's qualifications and experience. It is understandable if the standard is higher for innovative courses in areas that are unfamiliar to the administrators and faculty committees charged with curricular oversight. We recommend that the prospective instructor cite similar courses taught by him or herself and others, and that he or she obtain endorsements from previous satisfied learners, dream experts, and responsible authorities at the institution where the course was taught. In Appendix G we suggest further strategies and tactics for getting approval for your proposed course.

In college settings, once the course is approved the next context on which to focus is the set of majors, minors, programs of study, and prerequisite course requirements within which the course is lodged. Your undergraduate course is likely to be an elective fulfilling a distribution requirement within the liberal arts or perhaps a specific major, depending on the course's disciplinary home. You could propose an upper division course, with a set of prerequisites. For example, in psychology departments prerequisites may include personality theory, psychological development, counseling and/or psychotherapy, research methods, and statistics. Alternatively, your course could be a lower-division survey course, which would have few or no prerequisites other than adequate writing and perhaps mathematical skills, depending on the subject area and course focus. Our experience is that substantial prerequisites unduly limit the number of interested students who are eligible to enroll in the course and who could benefit by taking it. In lieu of prerequisites, one can teach necessary background knowledge and skills within the course itself.

An interesting innovation in course structure is one taught by two or more professors from different disciplines (or from different theoretical perspectives within one discipline) focusing on a topic or theme. For example, there could be a course on movement taught by a dance historian, a physiologist, and a film studies professor. A curriculum at Antioch College included such courses, taught by three professors and comprising first-year students' entire course schedule for a term. Such a team-taught course structure could work well with dreams and dreaming. We look forward to an undergraduate "mega-course" on dreams, sleep and dreaming, and applaud in advance the intrepid group that pulls it off. (We have more to say about interdisciplinary dream course possibilities in Chapter 11.)

If you are preparing a course on dreams for the first time—or even with considerable experience—you probably have a lot of questions. What will be the class size and schedule? Are the students lower or upper division, or graduate students? What is their range of majors, and the courses they have taken? What skills needed for the course (e.g., empathic, analytical, compositional, introspective) do they have, and to what degree? What are their intellectual levels, ages, and life experiences? What are the gender and nationality compositions, and how do the international and domestic students' abilities compare? Answers to these questions guide the choice of course activities, assignments, and the degree of depth and rigor that you build into the course. Let us look at them one by one.

Class Size

Engaging and effective dream education can be accomplished with class sizes as small as a solitary student and as large as 100 or more. Instructional dynamics and strategies change with class size. Lectures, individual exercises, and small-group interactions not needing moment-to-moment instructor monitoring work well with large classes, and dream sharing with feedback works best with smaller ones. The key is to provide meaningful individual participation within a critical mass of group energy and interest. The authors have found 12 to 18 students optimal for purposes of discussion, dream sharing, and individual and small-group research projects.

Although smaller classes may be preferable for some course activities, instructors should be excited and not dismayed if they should happen upon a large group of students. Group energy, the inherently fascinating nature of dreams as a subject, and instructor skill and commitment produce effective learning in large groups. Montague Ullman has effectively taught dream group leadership skills to groups of 30 and more, and Kelly Bulkeley has had success teaching dream theory and interpretation skills in classes of up to 200 students.

Class Schedule

Typically a college course involves between 40 and 50 class "contact" hours spread over 10 to 15 weeks. Some courses are offered in shorter terms of 4 to

6 weeks. Courses taught over the duration of a traditional quarter or semester term (10 to 15 weeks) make possible a gradual development of skills, particularly in dream discussion and interpretation, which is more difficult to do in a shorter course format.

The educational institution rather than the instructor generally will determine length of class meetings, so teachers should be ready to configure their planned class activities accordingly. For standard three-credit undergraduate courses, we find that two meetings per week of 90 minutes each allow for significant time devoted to discussion of students' dreams at some sessions. Three-hour classes can be fatiguing, and sap energy and focus. Shorter meetings often don't permit sufficient time to get into the spirit and flow of dream sharing or lively discussion.

Dream teaching in settings other than dedicated dreams courses ranges from one short talk or demonstration, some as short as 30 minutes, some 1 or 2 hours, to a focused series of lectures, weekend workshops, or ongoing open-ended dream discussion groups. Obviously, what teachers can offer and accomplish varies tremendously according to how much time is available. We have found even a single presentation on dreams to be invaluable in communicating essential information and in sparking interest in further exposure to the subject.

Another element in college course scheduling is the time of day that the course meets. There are no hard and fast guidelines for the best time. Mid- to late morning has been a good time in our experience, as students seem most alert then. With regard to dream sharing, mornings have the advantage of being proximate to the previous night's sleeping and dreaming. Mid-afternoon classes tend to compete with a low point in the diurnal cycle when students need naps. However, many students nowadays keep late hours and may not fully waken until midday, so afternoon may be best for them. The same applies to evening classes, which may have the added advantage of attracting mature students who work full time (or those who sleep through the day). Of course, the instructor may not have control over the course scheduling and will need to adapt accordingly. Similar considerations apply to teaching in nonacademic settings.

Student Class Level and Age

Because of the universality and fascination of dreams, in some ways student level in college courses is not a concern (it certainly is not a concern in nonacademic settings). Students at all ages within the traditional undergraduate age range of 17 to 23 are equally likely to possess qualities of psychological mindedness and self-awareness, and all can relate well to their dreams. Dream students older than traditional college age generally are more self-reflective and may have more interest in their own dreams. This isn't surprising, as the extra years of life experience and existential bumps and bruises tend to guide their attention inward.

Our experience is that students entering or returning to college after some years of adult living—often women in their 30s and 40s—get the most from our courses. Younger students who benefit significantly tend to experience the course more as a personal awakening, an early orientation to their internal psychological life.

Dream education for children and adolescents is age-dependent, with distinct approaches and modalities appropriate for different age groups. (We address dream education for preschool and elementary through high school students in Chapter 10.) Where college students' level and age do make a difference is in activities that require academic skills unlikely to have been learned in high school, or a personal perspective that only can be gained from years of adult living. The importance of particular academic skills will vary depending on the course's pedagogic home and its focus. In psychology and other sciences, skills involving research design, data collection and analysis, writing research reports, and reading them with understanding may be crucial. In the humanities, a background in literature, cultural studies, and essay writing may be the most needed (although as we argue in Chapters 2 and 6, dream studies is an excellent topic for the teaching of writing and for introducing fundamental questions in the humanities). Self-knowledge, intellectual curiosity, and the ability and willingness to examine one's experience and connect it to theory are important in courses that involve the students' own dreams.

Besides deepening self-understanding, some students find that studying dreams sparks interest in research, writing, and other applications, such as artistic creativity, in their fields of study. Not infrequently in our teaching experience, dream courses provide impetus toward future careers—for example, in teaching, counseling, psychosocial nursing, and film studies.

Student Majors

Students from a variety of academic majors may take a college dream course, and bring to it different strengths and weaknesses. For example, pre-med students, although well educated in the sciences, may be less skilled in research design. Nursing majors may be more empathic but less analytical, literature majors stronger in narrative analysis but weaker in quantitative reasoning. Heterogeneity in the majors of students in a class should affect course design in the choice of reading assignments, class activities, and student projects. Instructors can address this by (a) simplifying the subject matter and activities to the point that all students can succeed; (b) requiring prerequisite courses; or (c) building necessary skills and teaching theory within the course itself. On balance, we recommend the last alternative. In psychology courses we have had success in teaching previously inexperienced students to access collections of dreams for quantitative analysis via the Internet; to code and measure dream elements; to analyze the data so generated using statistical software; and to write the methods, results, and conclusions using appropriate paper organization and format.

Instructor Skills

A great thing about dream education is the variety of disciplines, skills, and overall educational backgrounds needed for a comprehensive understanding of the subject, and the challenges and opportunities this provides for the instructor and for the pedagogy of higher education. Many fields (psychology, art, history, literature, biology, philosophy, theology, film studies, anthropology) can be used to reflect and develop the richness of the subject matter. For example, in his dreams psychology course, King uses excerpts from films—Akira Kurosawa's *Dreams*, and Hirokazu Koreeda's *After Life*. In his humanities course in dreams, Welt uses material from psychological theorists, including Freud and Jung. So we encourage not only multidisciplinary teaching, but also efforts to develop integrative *inter*disciplinary approaches. We caution, however, that when treading outside their fields, instructors should proceed carefully. We all have our areas of expertise, but as dream scholars, we constantly find ourselves in unfamiliar territory. One needs to maintain a humble attitude, as we all are perpetual students in this field. This is a blessing in disguise, as we are constantly refreshed with the discovery of new perspectives and challenged to develop new abilities. The sense of surprise and wonder we find in encountering our dreams therefore has a parallel in our experiences in dream scholarship and teaching.

Student Qualities

Dreams courses call on a wide range of student qualities and abilities. These include general intellectual and analytical ability to understand, question, and propose changes to theory; methodological and quantitative skills to produce and understand research findings; writing and speaking skills to articulate views; artistic and technical skills to develop aesthetic dimensions of dreams and create artistic products; and capacities of self-reflection, imagination, and empathy to delve into one's own and others' dreams. In clinical training programs, dream education adds to the professional ability of the psychologist, counselor, pastor, social worker or nurse in several ways. It deepens self-understanding, provides tools for engaging and working with clients, and offers a window into clients' unconscious processes and life concerns. Dream knowledge provides both a mode of understanding and a set of techniques for clinicians. Chapter 8 presents a longer discussion of dreams in clinical training.

Outside the academy, the educational experience of students may be enhanced simply because they have freely chosen to study the subject. They are there because they want to learn about dreams, not because of convenience of class schedule or other extrinsic reasons. Instructors would do well simply to develop students' understanding of dreams from where they were when they started. Gaining a prescribed level of academic attainment is neither the point nor the goal.

Students' and Instructors' Life (and Dream) Experiences

Although one can analyze, generalize about, and abstract dreams in interesting and useful ways, they are, first and primarily, immediately experienced phenomena. We believe in giving participants' dreams an important place in both academic and nonacademic courses, although this should not be the sole focus. How one may do this is an important and somewhat complicated matter, which is addressed later in this chapter.

Historically, dream experiences have grounded dream theory building. The two preeminent dream theorists of the 20th century, Freud and Jung, both used their own dreams as foundations of their theories. Although this led to overgeneralizations based on their individual personalities, cultural milieus, and circumstances, the brilliance and heuristic value of their insights is unquestionable. It was an interest in their personal dreams and the insights they revealed that prompted their efforts. Work of contemporary dream theorists and scientists, as well, has been motivated in part by their own dreams even as they have moved beyond their individual experiences to consider dreams in a broader way.

Therefore, instructors would do well to follow historical precedent in attending to their own and their students' dreams in bringing theory alive. The point is to recall and articulate dreams and then to step back and reflect on them in light of their intersection with theory and the particulars of the dreamer's life. Students' dreams can become touchstones of class activity. Teachers can integrate the theoretical with the personal, the head with the heart. They can use their own dreams to illustrate theoretical points and (importantly) to model both self-disclosure and a sense of ease in discussing dream experiences.

Gender Distribution

Psychology, nursing, social work, and humanities students nowadays are predominantly female, and women in general seem to be more interested in dreams. The upshot of this is that the students in college dream courses are mainly women. Don't be surprised if this is the case in your course! Although we wish for more male students, it is not a problem to have mostly (in one of our classes, *all*) female students. We do believe that in general female and male sensibilities and orientations differ, if often subtly, and that the presence of men adds some complementary strengths to those that women bring. When classes are divided into subgroups, for example in sharing dreams or doing projects, you might consider balancing gender distribution by dividing the (relatively few) men proportionally among the subgroups.

Outside the university, particularly in one-shot guest lectures, the proportion of males may be substantially higher. There were more men than women in dream talks given by King to groups of Jaycees and credit union employees.

Student Nationality

Does the college class include international students, and if so how do their abilities compare with those of the domestic students? In our experience, the abilities of international students' compared with most Americans often will be either significantly better, or significantly worse. For example, many British and European students have been educated more rigorously, and will tend to have superior analytical skills compared with American students at most institutions. In one of our dreams psychology classes, only the one student from Sweden knew how to use statistical software and was familiar with research report protocol. Other international students may have more difficulty with English. Of course, these are generalizations, and individuals and classes will differ. Communities in most parts of the United States (and other countries) increasingly are heterogeneous. Dream learners may be from many different nations, cultures, and linguistic backgrounds. The teacher should ascertain this and tailor the approach to the particular audience accordingly, for example, by treating as a topic cultural differences in attitudes toward dreams, or allowing dream journal entries to be written in the student's first language.

Course Content

In addition to standard texts, films, works of art and literature, and online and other electronic resources, courses can use dream reports both of the students and others. Such reports reflect the dreamer's waking experience in psychological, social, and cultural contexts. They contain discernable elements that students can measure and quantify. They are aesthetic productions. They use plotting and presentational forms akin to those in stage drama and film.

Therefore (as noted in the introduction to this volume), dream courses can draw on the biological sciences, social and behavioral sciences, humanities, arts, and psychology. There is always a tug toward the recognition that the study of dreams is multidisciplinary, even though the thrust and organization of any particular course may reflect primarily one field of study. One can take a multidisciplinary approach without compromising unduly the disciplinary focus of the course. For example, brief forays into dreams in history, anthropology, art, literature, or film can be a valuable part of a psychology course. The current or aspiring dreams course instructor will want to consider elements from a number of disciplines to suit the goals of the particular course.

Course activities include work in class and outside. In class, lectures, discussions, small-group project work, and dream-sharing groups are primary activities. The instructor can lecture and can bring in guest lecturers. Lectures and discussions are best for imparting and clarifying theory, in conjunction with reading assignments. Small-group work can be a valuable part of a dreams course, both to discuss dreams and for other course activities. We have had success with students conducting research projects in groups of three to five, with the instructor as a guide and resource.

Course content will differ depending on the level of the course and the academic background of the students. Lower-division courses will presume little or no background beyond high school in the subject area framing the dream content. For example, and as noted earlier, a humanities course emphasizing dreams in literature or film may assume no particular college studies background in literature or film per se. The dream course itself will be an introduction to these subjects. Upper-division undergraduate courses will assume some back-ground, and the instructor can expect that students will bring to the course previous academic learning that will serve as a context and referent for the dreams material.

Dream Journals and Dream Discussion Groups

People have been writing down their dreams for thousands of years, and dream scholars in many times and places have encouraged this activity. Keeping a dream journal has many benefits, and we recommend it highly as a course compo-nent, as well as an individual practice. As a solitary endeavor, it contributes to dream attention and recall, lends itself to spiritual self-scrutiny and practice, and enables a tracing over time of existential themes as they wax, wane, evolve, and transform. A dream journal has the quality of a private but psychologically astute personal diary. Journal keepers are safe from outside scrutiny as they ponder the evolving record of their dream lives. Much as movies viewed for a second or third time, recorded dreams are there for the dreamer to appreciate anew. Reading and reconsidering recorded dreams often re-evokes the feelings of the dream and brings new perspectives and understandings. Dream journals in the aggregate also provide a "history of psyche" in different cultures, places, and times, and information about how social milieus penetrate the workings of the unconscious mind.

Both the individual and social perspectives can be tacks taken in using dream journals in course settings, as students can view their dreams as state-ments of their unique personhood or as emblematic of their cohort experience. Dream journals are a great way to include students' dreams in the course while providing privacy protection ranging from complete to partial. Students can share dreams with no one, with the instructor only, or with the instructor for grading purposes only (with the instructor perhaps not even reading the dreams). The instructor can be the conduit for anonymous sharing in class of dreams from student' journals, for content or thematic analyses. On the public sharing end of the continuum, students can relate their recalled dreams selectively in dream discussion groups.

One caution in having students keep dream journals is that typically, dream recall will vary widely, from students who remember multiple dreams most nights to those who remember just a few—or sometimes even no—dreams over an entire semester. The "low recallers" can become frustrated. Our teaching experience has shown that most students with low recall will improve their recall over the span of the course.

Some students with high or even very high recall will encounter dry spells (as their defense mechanisms kick in from a sense of increased exposure). There likely will be something of a leveling process——a regression to the mean. However, it is still advisable to mitigate the large variation in students' dream recall by broadening the scope and purpose of the journal. Among the elements that teachers could include are reflections on the class activities and course assignments, comments on others' dreams (e.g., from dream-sharing groups or literary or historical examples), dreams the student would like to have, descriptions of waking events as if they were dreams, drawings of dreams, and so on. These inclusions will augment the journal and may help stimulate remembering dreams for the low recallers. King tells his students that it is possible to remember no dreams at all and still get an "A" on the journal component of the course, by a healthy inclusion of these other elements.

Instructors will need to make choices about the stance they will teach students to take toward their dream recall and journals, and the structured processes, if any, that students should use in making sense of their dreams. With regard to the former, we recommend an alert but relaxed focus and attention, akin to that which produces the best golf shots or baseball batting averages. One should not grip the golf club, Louisville Slugger, or dream journal pen too tightly! One should, however, pick them up, practice, and use them regularly.

We believe that students should write in their dream journal consistently— several times per week. However, they should not try to write in them every day, or write down every recalled dream. It should not become an arduous task. As with exercise programs and other skill-building activities, persistence is good, compulsiveness not so. Some dreams more than others are worth writing down.

Buying and using an attractive blank page journal lends an importance and focus to dream journaling that is absent when using a computer word processing program, so we advocate the former.

There are many systems and schemes for analyzing or otherwise processing one's recalled and written dreams. Many of these are dream interpretation systems that the dreamer can use as an individual activity. To mention just three: Julia and Derek Parker suggest considering major themes, focusing on the separate dream images, using word association techniques, and consulting a thesaurus (which they provide) of *possible* meanings of dream themes.[1] Gayle Delaney provides a well-elaborated "dream interview" procedure, elements of which could be modified for individual journal use.[2] Robert Moss offers a helpful, moderate position in his guidelines for using dream journals when he encourages dreamers to note feelings and immediate associations, recurring themes and locales, and correspondences between dreams and waking events.[3] Instructors can teach any scheme of the many available for students to use with their recorded dreams. Any may work and have value. We agree by analogy with Jeffrey Kottler in his analysis of the myriad theories and forms of psychotherapy that many different approaches can get similarly beneficial results.[4] Using *any* reasonable system, especially for neophytes, is more significant, in our opinion, than which system one uses. Instructors should experiment and find what works best with their students in their courses. The potential danger lies in over elaboration and in rigidity of application.

On balance, we take a naturalistic view toward how students should relate to their dream journals. We believe that the recording over time and subsequent reading and contemplation of one's dreams is most important. What percentage of people even does this? Subsequent systematic processing can be useful but runs the risk, when overdone, for losing the dream in a thicket of interpretative concepts and processes. We agree with Medard Boss that the dream speaks for itself and that superimposing theoretical or procedural structures can have an obscurant effect.[5] First recording and then contemplating (and sharing) recorded dreams trump in importance particular theories and systems of dream processing and interpretation.

Students can work with their dreams individually outside class time through various homework assignments. They also can work with their dreams interactively in class through dream discussion groups and other projects using dreams as sources of data. We find that teaching people how to work with their own dreams brings higher student engagement, and usually is rewarding for instructors and students alike. Sharing dreams is fascinating and fun, and we learn more about ourselves from the process.

Certain considerations and cautions apply in working with dreams in a group setting. One is that a trained leader should be present. Another is that there should be opportunity for students to be able to relate their dreams and respond to dreams of others. Eight to 10 students is an ideal size for dream discussion groups, about half the ideal size of an optimal overall enrollment for a course emphasizing active student participation in class. Having more than 10 students in a "dream group" is somewhat problematic in that the chances of getting to relate a dream and possibilities of direct communication between any one "responder" and the dreamer are reduced. Fortunately, one can learn much from another person's dream, particularly if one can participate by responding to the dream "as if it were (your) dream." Welt conducts dream discussion in two concentric circles; at the end, students in the outer circle report what they observed about the comments and questions raised by the active inner circle. Vicarious participation through observation, and inward exercises guided by the teacher are possible and valuable no matter what the group size. Therefore, larger dream-sharing groups can be valuable for all members. It remains, however, that as group size increases the immediacy and intensity of interaction is diluted. Doubling the size means that each member will be able to present and discuss only half as much.

Attempting to achieve the greater yield per student of smaller dream discussion groups can pose a practical problem for the instructor who wishes that a trained leader be present. King has handled this in two ways: first, by meeting an extra session, with the class divided into two separate dream discussion groups. This necessitated some extra work. Second, by finding a qualified co-leader, and having the instructor and co-leader meet with the two groups alternately, with the two leaders debriefing one another after the sessions. It also is possible, but not recommended, for the instructor to split time between two dream groups meeting at the same time. This can work when the groups are more experienced and able to function well on their own. It provides some leader presence and monitoring, but at the cost of losing continuity. On balance, the most prudent policy is to be there when group dream sharing is taking place.

One important concern is that the ways we treat students' dreams in the group context are energetic and focused enough to gain and hold their interest, without being overly disruptive to their psychological equilibrium. We provide information *and* experience but stop well short of clinical intervention, wanting students to swim in new waters but not too far from shore. The conscious projection technique developed and popularized by Montague Ullman and Jeremy Taylor (and used by many others) is ideally suited for the kinds of moderate effects sought in a course context. The key element in this approach is that *projection*, which easily can be a confusion in clinical work or normal interpersonal dialogue, becomes a virtue in dream groups when prefaced by "If it were my dream . . ." The verbal formula both indicates to the dreamer and reminds the responder-projector that the comment to follow is (only) the responder's "take" on the dream, something to be considered by the dreamer as possibly useful, but possibly *not* useful. (See Appendix C for a modification of the Ullman–Taylor approach, which allows typically for a dream to be rather thoroughly processed in 30 to 40 minutes.)

Coming down quite deliberately on the side of caution, we take a somewhat conservative stance about the techniques best suited for classroom use.

We have tried stronger techniques, such as Gestalt processes, as (optional) alternatives to the Ullman–Taylor procedures. One thing for certain is that Gestalt techniques evoke emotion more than do conscious projections from group members. Some of the small numbers of our students who have tried a Gestalt rendering of their dreams have liked it; a few have found it uncomfortable. Gestalt approaches and other stronger methods can go at least half a step too far for most classroom applications—an exception being practicum graduate training for clinicians.

Instructors should choose carefully the dream-processing activities best suited to instructional purpose and context, including the psychological strengths and weaknesses of the students. Our impression and that of some teaching colleagues is that more students are psychologically troubled than was the case in former decades. The key is to find the approach that yields the greatest benefit for students while keeping risk acceptably low.

There is a cumulative benefit to working with one's own dreams on a regular basis over a semester's time. We have found that in a psychology of dreams course, having about 10 "dream group" sessions spread over a 14-week semester—up to 40% of the course contact hours—has consistently resulted in students becoming skillful in understanding their own dreams and helping others with their dreams. We note, however, that some instructors may want to put less emphasis on dream sharing, even relegating it to a demonstration basis, in order to free class time for other topics and activities.

A larger issue is whether students' dreams should be included at all in a dreams course, and if so, to what extent and in what manner. At first glance, it would seem obvious that the course should deal directly and forthrightly with the basic datum—the dream, as experienced by the students. Our experience has led us to appreciate the fundamental importance and value of engaging students' dreams.

Ullman has (with Nan Zimmerman) argued persuasively that there is great value in attending to one's dreams and the personal psychological issues and growth opportunities that they embody.[6] However, Ullman and Zimmerman were speaking about people in general, not about students in college courses, who are our main concern here. And their precept was based on working with self-selected groups of adults whose purpose was precisely to work with their own dreams. One can infer that Ullman's dream group participants were indeed ready and eager to tackle their own dreams. But does Ullman's recommendation apply equally to students in college courses?

Roger Knudson, recent director of Miami University's graduate clinical psychology PhD program, has questioned whether it is wise to expect undergraduate psychology students routinely to encounter their own dreams in a group-sharing context. Perhaps some of them—albeit a small minority—are too psychologically vulnerable for the experience to be positive rather than harmful. Knudson notes as an example the increasing numbers of combat veterans returning to college who are encumbered to some degree by posttraumatic stress disorder.[7] On the other hand, many courses—literature, philosophy, and biology—and the overall college experience itself could be troubling to vulnerable students. In Ullman and Zimmerman's phrase, "working on dreams is as dangerous as thinking."[8] But is it fair to single out as dangerous courses in which students discuss their dreams?

We take Knudson's concerns seriously. A college course in dreams is a special case because of the multiple reasons for students to enroll in the course. Some students may be seeking precisely to encounter and understand their own dreams; for them the motive is the same as for those seeking out a "dream group" in a workshop or other community context. (See Chapter 9.) These students have a good sense of what they are getting into. Other students will have a variety of reasons for showing up. They may have a mild curiosity about dreams without expecting to recall, record, relate, or understand their own dreams. Others may be there to fill an academic requirement, because they expect an easy or quirky course, or for reasons as casual as the days and times the course meets. In short, not all students will be expecting to look at the emotion-laden concerns that propel and fill dreams.

The issue is both ethical (what do the students expect when they sign up for the course?) and clinical (will the experience be psychologically helpful or damaging?) Encountering one's own dreams is overwhelmingly positive for the vast majority of students. However, it may not be an appropriate practice to have dream sharing as a routine part of the course without screening, informed consent, and/or providing alternative learning activities. Simply put, not all students in dreams courses are necessarily looking for quasi-therapeutic experiences. And make no mistake; dream-sharing groups *are* therapeutic (as in therapy with a small "t"). Dealing with one's dreams nudges and sometimes shoves one toward experienced emotion and self-reflection.

Our perception is that there is considerable psychological vulnerability among some undergraduate and graduate students likely to show up in a dreams course. We base this on a range of anecdotal evidence, including autobiographical assignments in other courses in which students similar to those in our dream courses write about psychologically meaningful events, issues, and times in their lives. Often, themes emerge of family difficulties, abuse, trauma, and histories of clinical problems. Add this to the normal dilemmas of young adulthood regarding independence, autonomy, relationships, family, and career preparation, and there often is a fragility lying just beneath the surface. Although this doesn't mean that such students shouldn't work with their dreams, it is cautionary. Students in psychology, nursing, and the humanities may be somewhat more vulnerable than are students in general. The former are the very students most likely to take a dreams course.

Most students find the quasi-therapeutic quality of well-taught dreams courses to be beneficial. A few, however, may find working with their own dreams, and sharing them, to be disruptive. The course material will challenge defense mechanisms. The challenge is embodied in the subject matter, and is thus implicit, even if not intended by the instructor. If a student's coping strategy is to rely on and indeed to shore up defenses, then the course experience may be problematic.

One of us (King) has taught approximately 400 undergraduate students in dream psychology courses, in 24 classes over a 17-year period. Only a handful of students dropped the course because of what *may* have been discomfort with dream sharing. Sadly, early in these years one student committed suicide after the second week of a semester. Her problems had nothing to do with the course or dreams per se. No one in her life had any inkling of the seriousness of her issues and her emotional and mental state. But she was in the course, and had shared a dream in the very first dream group of the class. During her dream sharing she showed some affect—minor weeping, which is a bit unusual for a first session. Because of this and because the semester was new and the instructor did not know the student previously, he spoke with her afterward. She reassured the instructor that she was okay, and in fact seemed fine. Clearly, in retrospect, she was not.

The dream she shared involved dismemberment. Should that have been a red flag? The instructor wishes mightily that he had been a better diagnostician, as do all who knew the student.

What are we to make of this tragic event in terms of the question of dream sharing in college courses? Clearly, for almost all students dream sharing is positive, for some, it is a high point in their studies. For a small minority, dream sharing is negative and for a very few, may be harmful. We need procedures to protect the vulnerable without banishing dream sharing from courses on dreams. Instructors should provide full disclosure in the syllabus and at the first class meeting. Another safeguard would be to provide alternative activities for students who wish to take the course but who don't want to participate in the dream discussion groups. There could be two assignment "tracks" within the course. For example, one track would involve dream sharing, and the other would involve research on a topic appropriate to the course, such as studying in various ways, dream narratives from other dreamers not personally known. (Of course a "two-track" structure would be more demanding on the instructor. And we are hard pressed to recall students for whom this was needed.)

Alternatively, the instructor could incorporate dream sharing into the course in an attenuated manner as a one-time demonstration only, or by otherwise diluting its impact by reducing its emphasis. King has done this in his survey honors course in principles of psychology (although not in his dreams course), where one or two volunteer students share a dream in one class session. This has worked well. There have been no problems, and several students decided to major in psychology based on their experience.

Instructors can bring students' dreams into the course without discussing individual dreams in class. Students can reflect on their own dreams in a journal, as discussed earlier. Student dreams can be aggregated and distributed anonymously and analyzed in ways that don't involve interpretation.

Other mechanisms that can guard against psychological harm befalling students include screening before or at the start of the course, ongoing monitoring during the course, and follow-up "debriefing" after the course is over. Students flagged by this monitoring process could be directed to appropriate counseling and support. Protocols for these assessments have not been developed, but could be important for dream education. Taking Knudson's point about the psychological vulnerability of students who are war veterans, such screening and monitoring mechanisms may be needed broadly and routinely at universities in the coming years, beyond dream courses.

We do not wish to be overly timid on the matter of students relating their dreams. Deirdre Barrett found there *not* to be a problem resembling Knudson's teaching experience with dream sharing in her classes at Harvard. Occasionally, she'll get students who are disturbed and should really be dealing with their dreams in a clinical setting. Only occasionally has she had what she terms "extremely disturbed" students, and even then although this was bothersome to her and to the other students, the educational process was not unduly disrupted. She was able to teach around the pathology. The dream angle didn't enter in—it was the same as if it were another course—even a literature course—that involved sharing personal material.

It is possible to reduce automobile traffic accidents to zero by banning cars. Similarly higher education could reduce risk by avoiding or forbidding class activities and assignments that could conceivably be dangerous. We have to ask ourselves if we want higher education to be without chemistry lab, intramural sports, or dream sharing. Going to college should be an experience of opening new possibilities rather than foreclosing them. The process is by its very nature unpredictable, messy, and in rare instances, even unsafe—as is life in general. Learning about dreams is one activity among many in the academic and extra-academic journey, almost any of which can be difficult if experienced by the wrong person at the wrong time. This is not a reason to proscribe them, as the benefits for most can be important. Self-exploration during college, including learning about dreams, is deepening and strengthening—perhaps even necessary for some people—on the path to psychological and spiritual adulthood.

The upshot of this discussion is that we firmly believe that the educational and personal benefits of students working with their own dreams are great and that instructors should consider incorporating dream sharing as a core element of their courses. There is nothing in the field as valuable as immersion in one's dreams and subsequent reflection on them. At the same time, we take seriously the possible ill effects for a few students, and urge instructors to be mindful of these, and to take appropriate preventive and ameliorative actions in the course design.

In community settings, the audience and goals are different: In one-shot lectures the dreams teacher may want to consider carefully the advisability of doing a demonstration dream processing with an audience member. The self-selected nature of a volunteer from the audience usually will largely mitigate possible harm, but there is no guarantee. A bit of pretalk or "on-the-spot" screening and arrangements for follow-up may be advisable. Better that examples of dreams and their interpretations be given that open the audience to possible meanings of their own dreams, without treating individual dreams directly in that public, short-lived context. In community education or quasi-academic courses with ongoing dream discussion sessions, these cautions also apply, even though the learners may be older and somewhat more psychologically settled than are college students.

A central purpose of most conference-based or freestanding dream institute workshops is likely to be dream interpretation. Here, where students have come to explore the meanings of their dreams, the appropriate safety nets would be some form of screening before the fact, access to clinicians for any emergencies that may develop, and follow-up monitoring or clinical referrals as necessary. It is advisable to have clinical resources available, perhaps in the persons of the workshop leaders themselves.

Chapter 2

Dreaming as a Fundamental Academic Skill

Although some instructors of dream studies may not require students to keep dream journals, or to participate in in-class dream discussion groups, we have begun with some advice to those who do. Our experience has convinced us of the advantages of these practices as pedagogical tools in the study of dreaming. We also believe that dream studies can stimulate innovative teaching in all the curricular areas that examine the human mind, and the private and social worlds of imagination, expression, and the creation of meaning. In the chapters that follow we explore the potential for dream studies to incorporate knowledge from many established disciplines, and more significantly, to contribute to the revision of knowledge. Teachers in all contexts, at all levels, undertake this important work by proposing new courses, concentrations, and curricula, and by challenging students to keep raising critical questions in real classrooms.

Therefore, it makes sense to begin with a kind of course that nearly every undergraduate college student is required to take, one considered foundational at every level of education from first grade through graduate programs: the study of composition, or writing. By introducing dream studies and the dream journal into a course on writing, instructors may arouse wider interest in dreams, convince teaching colleagues and administrators of the value of dream studies, and provide models for organizing dream studies courses in other disciplines, for any general or special constituency.

Just as writing courses are adopted because they provide skills indispensable to further learning, the dream journal, dream discussion group, and study of the topic of dreaming can have an impact on students' whole orientation toward learning. These educational tools provide a number of benefits. They connect students' private experience of dreaming to academic pursuits. They demonstrate to students the advantages of mastering the skills and methods of varying disciplines in seeking to understand their own dreams. They introduce students to a community of other dreamers that reaches from their classroom discussions to the ancient world, the psychological theories of the past century, and the neurobiological breakthroughs of tomorrow. As these emphases provide models for study in all disciplines, they suggest the wisdom of "dreaming across the curriculum," for the same reasons that so many colleges have fostered writing across the curriculum: because this interdisciplinary approach focuses on essential capacities and skills that serve students well in all fields. Teachers of writing can use dream studies to stimulate interest in expressive writing as well as techniques of research, and dream studies instructors may learn new approaches to integrated learning from teachers of writing. It is in this sense that we propose conceiving of dreaming radically as a fundamental academic skill, rather than merely a topic to plug into familiar curricular emphases; we hold that dream studies offers unique advantages to students in framing, integrating, and synthesizing different kinds of thinking and knowledge. Because the same reciprocal benefits apply to instruction in the visual arts, and especially to rapidly expanding academic requirements for visual literacy and mastery of new media, we address that field in this chapter as well.

The difficulties of communicating the substance of the dream are proverbial not only because of its transience or its often bizarre features, but because in the dream one seems, to paraphrase Heraclitus, to be in one's own unique world. Philosophers (as we see in Chapter 5) have asked whether dreams can even be said to be experiences if they are not products of consciousness and cannot be objectively verified. Therefore, starting from the experience of their own dreams, students must confront the problem of finding the way between one's own world of sensations, ideas, and values, and the private worlds of others, as communicated in every form from poems and artwork to psychological theories to classroom discussions with their peers. Students who keep a dream journal and share dreams quickly develop an experiential knowledge of the continuity between their own excitement and challenges in doing so, and the experience of everyone who has written about dreams—in poetry, in psychology, in literature, in history. Encouraging students to examine their own inner worlds within an academic context increases their feeling of connection to the theories and thinkers they study.

This was the position notably advocated by Richard M. Jones in his consideration of dream studies courses, *The Dream Poet*. Having argued in *Fantasy and Feeling in Education* for the integration of psychoanalytic insights into educational practice, in *The Dream Poet* Jones detailed his experiences with "dream reflection seminars" during the 1970s at The Evergreen State College in Olympia, Washington, an environment avowedly dedicated to experimental interdisciplinary coursework. A psychologist by training, he crossed over into the traditional territory of English classes by leading students in the discussion of classic works by Chaucer, Shakespeare, Hawthorne, and Melville, and requiring students to keep a dream journal, and to write about their own dreams as a valid mode of response to their ongoing studies. In *The Dream Poet*, he argues, from a Freudian perspective, that the overcoming of repression is a key factor in preparing students to learn from their encounters with texts and new ideas—an insight that must be familiar to many instructors who have helped students struggle with challenges to their cherished beliefs. In particular, he encourages instructors to acknowledge the reality of deeply felt and unconscious responses to the challenges of learning, and to teach students that these experiences are valuable, accessible, and capable of articulation, and that they are relevant to understanding ourselves and the world better. For Jones, tracking dreams can be both a discipline and a technique for thinkers in their discovery of new ideas.

This proposition must be both welcome and familiar to many teachers of dream studies, as well as anyone who has kept a dream journal for any length of time. It also offers a particularly valuable, simple insight to instructors in all fields: it is crucial for teachers to find ways to convince students that their own minds are constantly generating valuable ideas, if only they can develop the means to catch and nurture them before they fly away. In this respect, Jones' emphasis on recovering the thoughts that arise in dreams is consonant with the pedagogical theory of writing in Peter Elbow's *Writing Without Teachers* and *Writing with Power*. Elbow's key ideas, which have been further elaborated by a generation of teachers of composition, are first, that students learn effectively by observing and articulating their own processes of learning (now widely referred to as *metacognition*); and second, that writing should be approached as a process, not a product. Students improve their work by recognizing what attitudes and skills are appropriate to each part of the process (i.e., separating your "editor" from your "idea generator"). The exercise of "free writing"—putting pen to paper with absolutely no boundaries or censorship—overcomes inhibitions and demonstrates to students that they always have something to say, so that they don't succumb to the terror of the blank piece of paper, and get stuck at the very beginning of writing——as so many student writers do. A corollary perception is that students unknowingly censor themselves when they suspect that what they have to say will be perceived as inadequate or unacceptable. Free writing has helped countless students to break conceptual blocks by reacquainting them with their own developing ideas. The relation to Freud's technique of free association is obvious. In a sense, Elbow extended the idea very naturally from the dream to the writing classroom. In each case, unconscious processes are redeemed from oblivion in the service of growth.[1]

Experienced teachers of writing at all levels of instruction will already be aware of how central Elbow's ideas and practices, and the debates around them, have been in the development of the pedagogy of composition since the 1980s. One may even discern a parallel between the wide influence of his "writing without teachers" approach—empowering students to take charge of their own mastery of writing—and the growing consensus in the same period that, through dream journals and dream discussion groups, individuals can learn deeply from their own dreams without the intercession of specialists. In actuality, of course, teachers often develop their approaches out of their own temperament, inclinations, and special gifts, rather than in response to even the most detailed arguments or the best-documented research. But to develop further arguments for the introduction of dream journals and dream discussion into writing classes—especially in presenting the method to students, teaching colleagues, and program heads—it may be helpful to state directly the dimensions it can bring to students' educational experience.

First, this approach initiates and identifies a method of *inductive learning*—that is, of going right to the investigation of the stated object of study as experienced through direct observation of examples, to which students have easy access through tracking their own dreams. This can be a powerful motivator to close and careful examination of their own dreams that may in turn encourage the formation of research questions and working theses about the fundamental issues in dreaming—especially because, as cannot be stated often enough, students are inclined to find their dreams really, really interesting! Students may then move from the inductive method to the evidence of expert testimony and tested hypotheses.

Second, as has been implied, students' dream introspection facilitates *active learning* methods. Student dream journalers do not passively accept the word of authorities but seek any means available to work with dreams (their own, their peers, or those they encounter in course materials). This results also in their spontaneously seeking expressive form for the content of their dreams—in poems, short scripts, drawings and photographs, and most recently, in YouTube videos—and in contemplating the similarities and differences between creative response and critical analysis. Active learning of this type works because it incorporates different styles and modes of comprehension, engages students powerfully and not passively with the object of study; and because it takes advantage of impulses that are often missing in the assignment to report on reading or to do a research paper. It works, not least of all, because it arouses enthusiasm.

Third, as many instructors can testify, dream sharing in any form fosters a mutually supportive *seminar model* of learning—an atmosphere in which students grasp experientially that they are all engaged in the same processes to make sense of their object of study, all able to understand things better when they listen carefully to others and answer responsively. The learning community is established even when in-class sharing of participants' dreams is not a regular feature of the course, because students respond to the introspective activity of keeping the dream journal as a shared adventure and want to discuss its ups and downs.

Barbara Bishop, of Marymount College in Palos Verdes, California, offers a particularly eloquent argument for dream study in the freshman writing course:

Teaching students to pay attention to their dreams holds numerous benefits: they have the opportunity to develop more than just their intellectual capacities, as universities have done traditionally; dream study holds the promise of developing their emotional, spiritual and social selves as well. Paying attention to their dreams can help students become independent and self-aware as they make important life decisions. Finally, group dream work brings students together in a playful, fun way at a time when they are feeling most alone, frightened and vulnerable.[2]

Every instructor hopes that students will contribute fully to critical discourse and group learning according to their diverse backgrounds, gifts, and obsessions. However, we all have seen students get stuck trying to figure out exactly what the instructor wants rather than starting from their own critical insights, and we all have seen—or been—instructors unwittingly constructing a course of study so tight that it leaves no room for students who want to make a real, active contribution to the approach taken to the object of study. With the unusual advantage of experience as a psychological counselor as well as an instructor of English, Bishop presents to students a model for emphasizing the cultivation of personal values and social responsibility while slacking in no way on skills training or mastery of content. Bishop finds that the topic of dreams forces the issue by allowing the students' real concerns into the classroom; it also naturally invites them to contribute perspectives according to their diverse cultural inheritances. As students' dreams reveal concern about local, national, and world events, they learn something of the deep engagement between the private and social spheres in the mind of any citizen. Bishop reminds us that:

> When students discover that their dreams provide useful information, to make them laugh and cry, to stop them from heading down a self-destructive path, to confirm something they intuitively sense or to help them appreciate the uncanny, spiritual aspect to their lives, they feel a greater confidence about attempting the difficult task of maturing and becoming independent, contributing adults.[3]

The dream journal and dream discussion group, then, allow students to share ideas and concerns in the writing classroom that address but go beyond personal experience—to make the connection between subjectivity and the social world that is called for in all writing modes. They also present constant opportunities for practicing both critical thinking and the intuitive grasp of key concepts. Logically, we can separate analysis and synthesis, mastery of concepts, and their recombination into original ideas. In real learning situations, the two modes are mutually dependent. Training in both provides relevant preparation for comprehension and interpretation in all disciplines, extending ultimately beyond academic settings to professional and social encounters. In a dream-centered composition course that builds academic skills by requiring critical study of readings in the social sciences and humanities, students may experience the benefits of drawing on different modes of investigation without straying beyond the limits of validity in assessing and comparing theories.

The first responsibility of college writing courses is to enhance students' command of academic writing, including critical analysis and research methods. Building on students' interest in understanding their own dreams, instructors may pursue this goal by challenging students to synthesize their growing understanding of psychological theories with a wide range of testimony on dreams from literature, philosophy, music, film, and art. In doing so, they distinguish between analytic and expressive modes of thought and writing, demonstrate to themselves that the characteristic methods of various disciplines serve different, well-defined purposes, and come to appreciate that academic study is not removed from the most urgent and personal issues. What we learn in school can help us understand even our dreams, as well as our most practical goals in life.

Jason Tougaw, the director of Writing Across the Curriculum at Queens College of the City University of New York, states his reasons for focusing on dreaming in an Honors English Seminar in a way that should overcome the customary skepticism of peers about the topic:

1. To get them excited about a topic that will require a lot of inqui-ry—writing, research, discussion, more writing, revision, etc.—to begin to understand it thoroughly.

2. To help them see that when it comes to dreams and dreaming, the experts are always hypothesizing—speculating intelligently, based on research and other kinds of evidence. Then, to get them to follow suit and do this themselves.

3. To help them develop a certain amount of expertise, so that they feel they can talk and write intelligently about the history of dream theory and representations of dreaming as well as contemporary debates, etc.

4. To get them thinking about the particular contributions made by neuroscience, psychology, religion, visual art, literature, etc. For example, as a psychiatrist/neurobiologist, [J. Allan] Hobson wants to explain the neural mechanisms that give rise to dreams, so that we might understand how this special kind of consciousness relates to ordinary, waking consciousness. But a novelist like Kazuo Ishiguro [in the dream-themed novel *The Unconsoled*] is interested in getting

readers to notice how everyday life—or consciousness—sometimes feels like the cognition of dreaming. Both thinkers are interested in a continuum of conscious states, but one wants to explain and the other wants to create an aesthetic experience.

5. To get them writing clearly and gracefully about a subject that can lead to fuzzy and unclear writing.

When it comes to dreams, students see pretty quickly that they have a lot of experience with dreams but very little understanding of them. They appreciate the fact that there are researchers who can help them understand. And, hopefully, they will follow in the footsteps of those researchers, at least to a certain degree.[4]

Teachers of composition often follow a method valued at least since the schools of rhetoric in ancient Rome. *Imitatio* means not only explicitly imitating the style of esteemed writers, but also identifying and trying to emulate some of their characteristic strengths. This is one of the key reasons offered for the emphasis on literary works in composition classes: All of the tools and techniques embraced by the concept of *style* merit study because they constitute ways of discovering and communicating meaning. And when we encounter in the writings of a psychologist or art historian a style as penetrating and engaging as that of any poet or dramatist, we praise it by saying that they have raised writing in their field to the level of art, or literature. The dream-centered writing course may choose from an extremely wide variety of memoirs, fiction, poetry, and other writings to provide models for students, for well-defined purposes that meet the established goals of composition classes.

At the California College of the Arts, Betsy Davids offers "Writing and Reading the Dream," a course that offers literary examples of writing about dreams to communicate a unique vision. In particular, she emphasizes two topics that bridge the distance between student writers and published writers. First is the study of the actual dream journals of writers. For example, William Burroughs' *My Education: A Book of Dreams* and Jack Kerouac's *Book of Dreams* present the recovery of dreams as a lesson in existential confrontation with the flux of one's own thoughts and identity. Michel Leiris' *Nights as Day, Days as Night* exemplifies the surrealist aesthetic as an invitation to bring irrational material into the realm of consciousness. Marguerite Yourcenar's *Dreams and Destinies* and Naguib Mahfouz' *The Dreams* exemplify how great writers of global scope have returned to dream life as a journaling technique to stay in touch with their sources of inspiration.

Second, Davids presents numerous examples of writers drawing on their dreams for inspiration, actually transforming the dream into a poem, story, or other text, and often telling the story of how they came to do so. There is a vast wealth of instances of dreams as creative inspiration that may be cited to students. Probably the three best-known examples come from English literature of the Romantic period. These are Samuel Taylor Coleridge's "Kubla Khan," written in a dream or reverie, famously interrupted by "a man from Porlock"; Mary Shelley's extraordinary vision of the monster that inspired her to write *Frankenstein* at the prodigious age of 19; and Robert Louis Stevenson's tribute to the "Brownies" who brought him the key image of *The Strange Case of Dr. Jekyll and Mr. Hyde*, among other tales, in his dreams.[5] It is worth noting that these stories of creative inspiration from dreams testify to a conception of an unconscious mental world that is an important part of the link between the culture of Romanticism and modern depth psychology. Furthermore, as the dream lore around these texts has unquestionably become a significant part of the occasion of reading the texts themselves, cited whenever they are studied, they testify eloquently to a dynamic relation between dreams and literary texts—ultimately realized in students' comprehension of the interplay of their own unconscious ideas with those of the writers they study. (We leave further discussion of dream themes in literature, and of the use of literary works in dream studies courses to Chapter 6, where these topics are treated in the context of general humanities study.)

Along with deepening students' understanding of literary forms, creative writing exercises may be used in traditional composition classes to increase students' awareness of their capacities for generating ideas. It is obvious that dreams can serve as a fertile source of plots and images for student writers of poems, stories, and plays. In creative writing courses in particular (or components of composition classes), the dream journal may also serve the larger function of exploring the involuntary, highly productive functions of mind at the root of artistic creation—and encouraging students to cultivate them along with the goal-directed functions generally emphasized in academic study. The most frequently noted characteristics of the phenomenology of the dream might form the basis of exercises to train student writers in the art of invention, and in finding the sources of their personal voice. For example, when students consider the surprising appearance in dreams of vivid memories of persons, settings, and objects from childhood, they may find a "royal road" to autobiographical writing, just as Freud found in dreams his "royal road to knowledge of the workings of the unconscious mind." Contemplation of recurring images from their dreams has inspired many students to create dream glossaries of personal symbolism. The fragmentary character of many dreams, and their apparently bizarre jux-tapositions, may lead naturally to the experiments in collage, chance processes, and random word games that the Surrealists used to subvert the tendency to fall into established pathways of language and thought. Even the tendency of dreams to plunge us into a representation of our deepest fears—"our worst nightmares"—may be motivation for introspective writing that explores anxieties productively. In the same way, classes may apply the methods of various kinds of dreamwork to writing exercises. As already mentioned, Freud's free-association technique is a model for free-writing. Jung's active-imagination method may be used to continue a dream. A writing exercise based on the Gestalt technique of dialogue with dream images can deepen understanding of the compelling autonomy of the products of imagination.

We have begun with a consideration of instruction in writing because it represents a universal and fundamental skills-building emphasis at all levels in American education, and because it offers practical examples of the value of dream awareness, the dream journal, and dream discussion among peers—the means by which students may learn to appreciate dreaming itself as a skill that can promote intellectual growth. Because we have proposed that the integration of dream studies can advance the goals of writing classes just as the exploration of writing methods can enhance and extend dream studies, instruction in writing also exemplifies the basic issues in interdisciplinary study that we raise throughout this book

However, contemporary teachers are well aware that academic preparation is not just about writing anymore. In the 21st-century classroom, research may mean the curating of images as much as the study of texts, and students may be as likely to present PowerPoints or digital-video documentaries as conventional research papers. At the same time, the emphasis on innovation in business and management programs has inspired a new enthusiasm for the methods of artists and creative writers. The recent and increasing dependence on images as well as text to convey ideas—in academic contexts and throughout the culture—may motivate a return to the traditional expectation that the well-educated person will master the production of images—according to the technology of the time. Given the well-established fascination of dreams for artists in a variety of creative fields, it seems natural to extend the same exercises as may be used by writing classes into the visual and performing arts. Memories recovered from dreams may be the subject of drawings and photography as well as of writing. Through tracking their dreams artists may cultivate an awareness of their personal vocabulary of symbols and engage in dialogue with recurring images or characters. The importance of editing practices in film may be conveyed by beginning with the fragmentary stuff of dreams. Dream studies courses may introduce exercises commensurate with the skills and training of participants, whereas studio art instruction can turn to dream studies for new sources of inspiration.

Digital video in particular has enormous potential both for allowing students to explore the dimensions of dreams, and for bringing developing artists to the topic of dreams—to a large extent because of the uncanny capacity of moving pictures in any format to imitate the dream as a totality (as discussed in detail in Chapter 7). In the Department of Visual and Environmental Studies at Harvard University, animated-film artist Ruth Lingford asks students to research dreams and hypnagogic states as sources of inspiration, and to consider how the bizarre elements in both content and structure of dreams might enliven animated films. Notably, both awareness of dream material and the mastery of visual-art skills are developmental processes that build from accessible early stages to refined skills.[6] In the experimental ACTLab program at the University of Texas, dedicated to exploring the possibilities of new electronic media in education, artist Allucquere Rosanne Stone offers a course called "Dream/Delirium." Instead of setting up dreaming and waking as a dichotomy, Stone encourages students to investigate "the continuum between waking and dreaming as a source of creativity, a resource for narrative, a space of exploration, and a frontier of research." This course of study motivates students to draw on intuition to imitate the mode of the dream, connecting widely disparate ideas to form unexpected and compelling meaning in a variety of traditional and new media. "Dream/Delirium" avowedly enacts the aesthetic of Surrealism as a practicum in enhancing creativity and offers students tools for navigating the journey from private and subjective experience to shared expression. As Stone says, "Dreams are engines of creation. How could we not use them?"[7]

Students may be particularly drawn to creating video artworks based on dreams—their own, or the real or fictional ones they have researched, or dreams they have imagined as original narrative fictions—because the technology is accessible and, for them, not especially daunting. (Phil King offers a model for using video editing as a creative means of teaching dream-content analysis in Appendix F.) Despite the fact that, as with any other medium or form of expression, it can take years to master motion-picture art, students can distribute their work immediately to a diverse audience on the Internet, and so get practice and receive feedback relatively easily. By the same token, instructors must be aware that contemporary students may expect to use blogs and other styles of Web sites to share information and ideas outside of the classroom—in part because the new media environment encourages the maintenance of contact, and in part because they lend themselves to the integration of words and images. Instructors of writing in particular, but ultimately any academic field, should consider how a blog can give structure to a pedagogical emphasis on process.

The same features that make blogs useful for extending contact among students outside the classroom and throughout the week also may inspire some trepidation, just as the in-class dream discussion group may do. First, blogs allow students to share dreams in whatever format they wish, without any even implicit understanding that they must be analyzed. Although this is a stimulating approach, it may raise concerns over the loss of both privacy of communication and the social support that is possible only in face-to-face interactions. Second, blogs promote a "wiki" approach to learning: A rapid and inclusive means of extending discussion also may invite bold assertion of untested assumptions, false claims, digressions, and irrelevancies. Therefore, instructors who introduce blogs in any course involving dreams should consider these ground rules:

- Test and select a reliable Web host. Whether your institution provides Web space, or you use a popular host like blogspot.com or wordpress.com, create your own test blog to familiarize yourself with procedures and possible problems before initiating class use.

- Choose settings carefully. You can set your class blog so that it is available only to class members; or so that it is readable by others but does not appear on public blog lists, and nonmembers cannot post comments. You can allow students to post comments anonymously, or using blog IDs that only you, or you and other class members, know. You can—and many instructors do—require all new posts or comments to be approved by you before they appear on the blog. All these choices reflect the balance of open communication and sensible limits that is most comfortable for the particular instructor and class.

- Take advantage of the blog's format to invite visual responses. When they have the opportunity to do so, students may start scouring the Internet for images and short video that can be shared much more easily than in class. Class sessions may start or end with a review of the blog through a classroom computer projection system, inviting questions and comments that reflect what is really on students' minds. (A review of a class blog at semester's end may provide an instructor with a quick, intuitive picture of how students' views developed over time.)

- Use the blog as you see fit. It can be a valuable tool for simply calling for informal responses to the week's readings, or for posting short drafts for comment by peers. Just as in dream discussion groups, blogs may invite dream sharing under clearly stated restrictions, such as sticking strictly to responses that begin with the "If this were my dream" formula. If students agree to take up the challenge, blogs can be a creative format for presenting research projects in an interactive format.

Jason Tougaw at Queens College and Welt at the Corcoran College of Art and Design regularly use blogs to allow students to write informally about their changing ideas about dreaming, in response to readings and their own dream lives. This practice also allows them to separate idea generation from the organization and presentation of ideas, and the expressive mode of communicating experience from the analytical mode of focusing on critical questions.[8] Class members also post any dreams that they feel moved to share, along with images from films and art, and their final research papers. The transaction of learning is no longer confined to student and teacher, as is so often the case with the standard research paper; the shared space of the blog functions as an ongoing seminar.

In an extended consideration of the pedagogy of blogging, Tougaw argues that the method used in this course "requires students to 'invent the university' in the sense that they must find ways to bridge the public and private, or the theoretical and the personal," and that "blogs have the potential to help students develop strong and distinctive voices in the pursuit of intellectual inquiry."[9] The Internet, often characterized by pundits as a kind of collective eruption of unconscious material, much of which might be better off suppressed, may be developing into a collective dream space that will increasingly serve the needs of education.

In this chapter, we emphasized that the study of dreams and dreaming may both bring students closer to the sources of their own creativity and original thought, and empower students to read, analyze, think, create, synthesize, produce, and revise, within and across disciplinary boundaries. The tools of study and communication that facilitate deeper and broader learning can reach from scrawling the details of a dream on a bedside pad to the most sophisticated techniques for multimedia presentation. Although dreaming certainly is not the only subject with the potential to engage such a wide variety of developing skills and capacities among undergraduate students, it has distinct features that make it an especially productive object of study: It is a universal human endowment, a significant factor in cultural and intellectual innovation, a celebrated source of artistic inspiration, and perennially a fascinating topic to young people as they explore the mysteries of the cosmos and of their own minds. As legions of writing instructors have long since discovered, dreams offer the shortest route to overcoming the common complaint among students that they cannot think of anything compelling to write about. Moreover, the advantages of a focus on dreams and dreaming in composition and creative writing classes extend logically to other fundamental academic skills involving observation, analysis, and hypothesis; to other expressive media; and to mastery of new educational technologies.

A dream studies course in the early phase of a curriculum can introduce students to theories of mind, culture, and art; to philosophical speculation on the nature of being and the limits of knowledge; to the variety of the world's religious traditions, their myths and scriptures, their rituals and sacred spaces; to scientific accounts of the brain and its functions, how humans resemble other animals, and how we may differ from them. Composition courses making use of dream studies can offer significant contexts for further coursework by requiring students to synthesize what they have learned from the findings of these various disciplines. Through exercises in keeping dream journals and participating in dream-sharing groups, students develop their capacities for introspection and self-examination, active listening, critical analysis and interpretation, comprehension of symbols and other rhetorical figures, collaborative learning, and supportive participation in discussion. Students who have the opportunity to apply what they learn from readings, lectures, and other course materials to their own experience in recording and sharing dreams have a model for integrating academic study with personal growth that will serve them all their lives.

Because all these benefits are widely acknowledged among experienced instructors of dream studies courses, we often have heard teachers express the wish that formal education welcomed the dream into its lecture halls and course catalogs more eagerly. Rare indeed is the department chair or curriculum committee that agrees with us that to stay in touch with one's dreams instead of ignoring them might in itself constitute an important preparation for scholarship, innovative thought, and contributing to one's community. Reconceiving the study of dreaming as training in a fundamental academic skill would mean not only making use of dreams in formative courses like composition, and recognizing the many paths to diverse areas of knowledge to which our dreams may lead us, but understanding that an awareness of dreams can meaningfully affect a student's whole academic career, offering motivation, inspiration, and perspective.

One might quibble at this point and ask whether *dreaming* can actually constitute a "skill"—or are we simply arguing that the whole battery of methods and topics covered in dream studies courses make it a good subject for courses intended to foster students' academic development? It makes sense to answer this with another question—a simple and profound one that has been asked by countless dreamers and theorists, and that still serves well as a starting point for our courses: *What is a dream?* Is it the hallucinatory experience during sleep that we think we have upon waking? Or the memory we think we have of that experience in our waking state? If we "know" the dream had elements we can't recall, are *those* part of the dream—or are they part of some mental limbo, ourselves and not ourselves? Is a dream a kind of story we tell ourselves or others, or the meanings we find in the story? If, as the Talmud says, a dream uninterpreted is like a letter unopened, is a dream that is not shared—well, to coin a phrase, like a tree that falls in the forest when there's no one to hear it? Does the *failure* to pay attention to our dreams—indeed, to consider them in any real sense a part of lives—inhibit our ability to rethink our cherished ideas, look at things from new perspectives, challenge ourselves to stay intellectually curious, open-minded, and creative in our academic work?

These questions are not merely rhetorical. They indicate only some of the ways that we would do well to keep our minds open about dreaming as we hope to encourage students to do. Thus, to promote wider interest in dreams in the contemporary world, and to encourage recognition of dreaming as a skill that conveys many academic advantages, we should not be too hasty in deciding that the dream is most significantly a private and mental experience, an occasion for enhancing social cohesion, a rough draft for a poem or film, or a revelation from the gods. Each field of knowledge may argue its own vision with legitimacy, and students can learn from each, developing their own views that may yet synthesize their learning in ways their proud teachers never could have imagined. In the chapters that follow, we draw on the experience of many dream educators in a variety of disciplines to illustrate how dream studies may enhance training, provide focus for the study of significant issues, and inspire students to originate, develop, refine, and communicate their own ideas.

Chapter 3

Psychology

Dreams, and dreaming, are complex and multifaceted. Because of this, the study and the teaching of dreams inevitably and properly call on a number of academic disciplines. We three authors reflect this in our own scholarly areas of psychology, political science, research methods, statistics and epistemology, philosophy, religious studies, literature, creative writing, and film studies.

If dream study is fundamentally multidisciplinary, why have we chosen to present separate chapters on the teaching of dreams from various individual disciplinary perspectives? There are a couple of reasons. First, we need some organizing principle that readers can use to gain entry to this book. A discipline with which the reader is conversant provides this portal. The second reason has to do largely with the institutional structures that mediate course offerings in higher education. The psychology department presents psychology courses, the English department literature courses, and so on. With the exception of John F. Kennedy University, there have been no stand-alone university programs in dream studies. Because the academy has organized institutional realities, socialized its students, and trained its practitioners in disciplinary rubrics, we configure this volume accordingly. We start with psychology.

Many fields have much to say about dreams, and writing is basic, as argued in the previous chapter. Psychology (i.e., the scientific study of the human mind, and of human and animal behavior), is perhaps the discipline that has spoken most centrally to dream phenomena, and not surprisingly we have run across more dream courses in psychology than in any other field. Our comments in this chapter apply to dedicated dream psychology courses and where relevant to smaller dreams modules within broader psychology courses, such as survey courses or offerings in personality theory, the psychology of consciousness, psychotherapy, existential psychology, or neuropsychology.

Psychology is broad in scope. It concerns behavior, motivation, development, learning, intelligence, perception and cognition, personality, emotion, consciousness, self-awareness and choice, meaning and identity—and their biological underpinnings. It has as a unifying focus the individual human being. Our ongoing life experiences, including our dreams, are constant referents and testing grounds for what we learn in psychology.

Different theoretical orientations—paradigms—have characterized psychology over the past 100 years and more. One of these, the cultural–psychosocial paradigm, belongs as well to anthropology, and we defer a discussion of it to the chapter on anthropology. This, and the remaining paradigms within psychology, briefly noted here, illuminate aspects of dreams and dreaming and approaches to their study and teaching.

Psychoanalysis

Sigmund Freud, the founder of psychoanalysis, and his one-time disciple Carl Jung, have profoundly influenced modern views of human nature, society, religion, and the arts. Although Freud and Jung were at odds on the structure and contents of mind, on the nature of instinctive drives and the functions of dreams, they both believed that human beings are strongly influenced by a powerful part of our minds that is outside our conscious awareness, and that dreams are an important conduit to the contents of the unconscious and its workings. Freud and Jung are the pioneers of modern dream theory. Their insights live on today in many tacit assumptions about dreams, and are still fruitful in research and in clinical practice. Freud and Jung are historically foundational and intellectually indispensable; we would expect that all psychology courses on dreams would include substantial treatments of their theories and practices.

Behaviorism

Dominating academic psychology during the middle third of the 20th century was behaviorism—an attempt to make psychology a science, by focusing on observable actions and the conditions and events in the person's environment that influence behavior. Although dreams are subjective experiences, dream reports are observable events, with their contents subject to recording and measurement. This paradigm's core axioms—that behavior is elicited by the environment and maintained by its consequences for the behaving person, and that emotional experiences can be associated with inherently neutral events through conditioning—are useful in assessing dream-related actions, including recalling, writing down, discussing, and valuing dreams. The positive legacy of behaviorism is a respect for carefully collected data and the testing of hypotheses. Any teaching referring to overt behavior, including behavior in dreams, draws on this paradigm, as do quantitative content analyses where reliability and validity of measurement are important.

Phenomenological and Existential Psychology

Phenomenology is the study of all possible appearances in human experience, during which considerations of objective reality and subjective responses are excluded. Existentialism emphasizes among other things the uniqueness of individual experience, freedom (and necessity) of choice, and the responsibility for one's choices and their consequences. Although distinct, phenomenology and existentialism both stem from European philosophical trends of the 19th and 20th centuries, and often are considered together. These philosophic systems have affected how many see psychological phenomena. Phenomenology focuses on moment-to-moment experience, including dream experience, unburdened by the overlay of critical analysis. The apperception of a dream involves a full phenomenological awareness of dream events as they occur, and is the starting point for further understanding. Existentialism ponders the limits—the finiteness—of human existence in waking life, and in dreams. Dreams, although experienced idiosyncratically, pose existential questions of purpose and meaning that are fundamental to all humans. Dream instructors can include phenomenology theory, phenomenologically based awareness exercises and discussions of existential values and meanings as course topics and activities.

Neuroscience

Neuroscience has evolved rapidly in recent decades and along with cognition is one of the two dominant paradigms of early 21st-century psychology. Its central focus is the brain structures and processes that underlie, mediate and indeed make possible human action, experience and emotion, including dreaming. Advances in technology have made possible a study of brain activity in real time—we can see what the brain is doing when it is doing it. Brain functioning enables sleeping and dreaming and imposes constraints on how we dream. Although brain activity produces dreams, a question for dream educators is what this activity has to say, if anything, about their meanings. Instructors can choose course topic readings, lectures, and discussion, of biological underpinnings of dream experience, and can, if resources permit, involve students directly in physiological and even neurological research.

Cognition

Cognitive psychology contributes to dream studies in its comparison of dream thinking to waking thinking, and differences in dream thinking patterns of different groups—in particular different age and gender groups. The groundbreaking work of David Foulkes on children's dreams and many dream-content analyses using coding systems (most notably the Hall–Van de Castle system) illustrate this paradigm. Cognition is not simply a function—that is, an effect—of underlying brain processes, our unconscious mind, or environmental contingencies. Rather we have a self-directing capacity to change our ways of thinking in waking, in dreams, and about dreams in waking. We can choose how to think about things and with practice can improve our abilities to think, and act, in the ways we have chosen. For example, we can learn more optimistic cognitive habits. Thus, the autonomy of cognitive processes dovetails with existential principles of freedom and responsibility. The dream teacher can develop this existential–cognitive connection, and can cover developmental differences in cognition, by comparing children's dreams at different ages with adult dreams.

Transpersonal Psychology

This paradigm is less prominent within mainstream psychology than those previously outlined but merits inclusion because of its evident relevance to dreams. Transpersonal psychology studies the self-transcendent, mystical, or spiritual aspects of human experience within psychological theory. Types of experience examined include religious conversion, altered states of consciousness, trance, and spiritual practices. Although the transpersonal perspective has many overlapping interests with theories and thinkers associated with the term *New Age*, the former is an academic discipline, the latter a religious or spiritual movement. The transpersonal perspective includes the contributions of the spiritual to psychiatry and psychotherapy, aging and adult spiritual development, meditation research and clinical aspects of meditation, and consciousness studies; also parapsychology, diagnosis of religious and spiritual problems, dying and near-death experience, and ecological survival. The defining concerns and topics of transpersonal psychology overlap with material in Chapters 5 (Philosophy and Religious Studies) and 8 (Psychotherapy and Counseling), illustrating the impossibility of confining dream studies into any one distinct category.

Psychology's Dual Nature

Whichever paradigms we employ, when we look at dreams through the spectacles of psychology we find that we are wearing bifocals, and initially have to crane our necks and shift our focus back and forth so that we can see both near and far. This is because of psychology's dual nature—it seeks understanding of individual uniqueness as well as attempting to establish lawful regularities that transcend the individual. It is interested in the person, the self, but as a science strives to establish empirical generalizations. The methods appropriate to these two tasks are different.

Foulkes posed the situation nicely in an early issue of the scholarly journal *Dreaming* as he pondered the directions dream studies might take:

> Is dreaming something we can study abstractly and ahistorically? Are causal explanations at all possible? Or is the most we can hope for some sort of interpretative understanding within the framework of an individual's particular life history? Is there some way in which both goals may be pursued, side by side? Is there some third alternative?[1]

In teaching the psychology of dreams we face this gap between scientific analyses of dreams and understanding dreams as experiences. The former builds knowledge but can relegate the experienced dream to a secondary position or obliterate it altogether. The latter embodies meanings but does not create knowledge. In teaching about dreams in psychology, we attempt to do justice to both sides, and to straddle the chasm between them. We seek Foulkes' "third alternative," one that combines the strengths of science with the humanities' strengths of creative and evocative engagement.

When elements of an individual dream are aggregated with those of other dreams, the dream itself is lost to the dreamer and to the observer. It is both decontextualized and obscured. Yet if we only stay at the level of the individual dreamer or dream, we are not building an edifice of knowledge. Martin Seligman has noted (correctly in our view) that we cannot construct a scientific psychology on case studies.[2]

In seeking to understand the individual dream and dreamer, psychology attempts to illuminate experience. In this, its goals overlap with those of the humanities. This tack is idiographic and can even be clinical in a way, but is not "scientific," as we generally conceive science to be.

It is arguable whether psychology should be the major discipline used in conveying individual meaning and deepening experience. This may primarily be the job of philosophy and the humanities (see Chapters 2 and 5-7), although psychology can make a significant contribution. Correspondingly, however, we note that the humanities do not build bodies of tested and verified knowledge about the empirical world—that is the purview of science (represented in this book by Chapter 4 on anthropology, and in some respects Chapter 8 on psychotherapy and counseling, as well as this one).

In teaching the psychology of dreams, we must not lose individuals' dream experiences and the dream narratives that result. Within psychology, as well as the humanities, we value and suggest a fidelity to the dream story and the dreamer. This is in contrast to the standard scientific view in which one would consider the individual person or dream merely to be vehicles that "carry" the variables that are the real focus. We further believe that one need not choose between the individual and the aggregate, although linking the two is challenging. Instead, we can push science in the direction of the dream story and push the dream story toward science, by developing modes of inquiry and teaching that retain dream stories while setting them in larger contexts—narrowing if not entirely bridging the epistemological gulf between the particular and the general.

Irvin Yalom, author of definitive textbooks on existential psychotherapy and group psychotherapy, illustrates in the progression of his career the impulse toward story telling as a mode of discourse within psychology. There is a change in Yalom's writings over time, from theory, data, and generalization to case study narratives to memoir and even to historical psychological fiction. The narrative mode becomes increasingly present as his quest for knowledge abstracted from human experience expands to make room for that very experience as a vessel for holding and carrying meaning.[3]

We think that viewing the dream narrative as central is compatible with scientific approaches to studying and teaching about dreams, and would affirm Foulkes' implicit suggestion, or hope, that scientific and interpretive understandings can not only co-exist but also combine. We would make this combination a goal of teaching dream psychology, which should be, among other things, a psychology of narrative.

The hallmarks of conventional science are intersubjectively replicable methods, the search for empirical regularities and the testing of falsifiable hypotheses derived from theory. These estimable strengths of science are qualities stemming from the Enlightenment and are fundamental to dream scholarship. To understand the contents of a dream, however, our scientific conceptions must expand to include more humanly interactive ways of discovering dream meanings, in which an engagement and dialogue with the dream text takes center stage.[4] In this sense we recognize that the Enlightenment, valued so much for its transcendence of medieval scholasticism, has its own built-in limits of understanding.

A scientific approach to dreams in principle can retain a focus on the individual while still making meaningful multiple dream and cross-person analyses. In this regard, a teaching tool of great potential is the individual dream series. G. William Domhoff has suggested and demonstrated this approach in the comparison of an individual's dream content to established norms.[5] Dream series (multiple dreams from a single dreamer) or sets (one or more dreams from multiple dreamers) can provide the "raw data" for dream analyses in class research projects.

Students' own dreams will be more meaningful to them than will dreams of others. This is a good and almost irresistible reason for using them as the material for thematic or other analyses of dream content. Where the student is analyzing his or her own dreams, or when the dream "authors" are anonymous, student concerns about their dreams not remaining private are mitigated. (The instructor will have some access to the dream content to the extent that the student's research product reflects it.)

Using class members' dreams is not necessary if ethical concerns, as discussed in Chapter 1, weigh against it. Other existing sets or series of dreams, or significant individual dreams of persons outside the class, also can work well. One person's dream often will resonate with others, if it is tapping a shared existential concern. This is the principle, after all, behind the aforementioned Ullman–Taylor projective dreamwork approach ("if it were my dream, it would mean . . .") in dream-sharing groups.[6] This same principle can be effectively employed in teaching by having students contemplate and respond in some fashion to the meanings for them in others' dreams.

Course Activities

The suggestions for course activities and content themes to follow take into account psychology's several paradigms, its dual nature as both a knowledge and meaning-seeking enterprise, all in our attempts to do justice to both general patterns and associations, and to the individual dream.

Laboratory Studies

If the professor and students have access to a sleep laboratory, hands-on research on the dreaming process is possible. The late Ray Rainville taught for many years a course on sleep and dreams that was entirely laboratory-based.[7] We like laboratory involvement, especially in its ability to illuminate the connections and the disjunctions among sleeping and dreaming processes, and dream qualities and contents. Most courses, however, are not likely to have access to a sleep lab for student projects. If instructors in these courses want to teach about brain processes that underlie dreaming, they will need to use standard texts, laboratory visits, videos, and any computer-based virtual interactive programs that may become available.

The connection between dreaming processes and dream content is fascinating to many but problematic in nature. Dream researchers are considerably less certain now than they were 30 or 40 years ago that there are clear correspondences between the two. Recent work has begun to identify those aspects of dreams that seem to be determined by brain structure and process prior to and apart from particular life experiences of the dreamer. Some notable scholars argue that there may be an unbridgeable ontological gap between biological processes essential to dreaming, on the one hand, and the experienced dream and its meanings, on the other. We'll say more about the brain and dreaming process versus the mind and dream content conundrum later in this chapter—all of which is grist for the mill of dream instruction.

It is certainly true that one can profitably study and teach about dreaming processes and dream contents separately. Dream courses in psychology would be enhanced by (but need not include) substantial material on dreaming processes. Instructors who wish to focus on dream content analysis or using dreams in psychotherapy, for example, may want to spend less class time on underlying dreaming processes.

Content Analyses

Adam Schneider, G. William Domhoff's former student and later research colleague at University of California-Santa Cruz, has developed computer procedures for quantitatively analyzing and comparing dream content. Domhoff and Schneider have incorporated these methods into the DreamBank, which connects word search and methods for statistical analyses with a computerized repository of some 20,000 dreams from different individuals, groups, times, and cultures. Based on the classification systems of Calvin Hall and Robert Van de Castle, this quantitative analysis technique and the dream collection are readily available via the Internet to students and scholars at www.dreambank. net.[8] Domhoff's system provides a useful tool and focus for dream psychology courses that complements an attention to individual dream meanings. Analyses can connect aggregate dream patterns and themes in some instances to the life experience and personality of the dreamer, and in other instances to the historical periods and cultures within which the dreams were dreamt.

The dream repository and Hall–Van de Castle system are separate and distinct; one can use the dream archive for any analytical purpose with any categorization system. See Appendix E for a more thorough discussion of content analysis and the DreamBank, and suggestions about how one can incorporate and modify it for psychology courses.

Interpretive Analyses

Teachers can introduce interpretive analyses as class exercises and student projects, on individual dreams or on series of dreams for one person. These analyses can involve the student's own dreams, dreams of other students in the class, or dreams from persons both accessible and inaccessible who are not in the class. Interpretive analyses can partake of a large array of schemes and theories. (See Gayle Delaney's *All About Dreams* for a helpful discussion of interpretive models.[9]) We believe that the value of any particular interpretive template lies in the degree to which it illuminates the understanding of dream content—its subjective power in revealing hitherto concealed meanings. This epistemological stance is unabashedly subjective. Intersubjective agreement between dreamers and interpreters ("dream appreciators," in Ullman and Zimmerman's phrase)[10] can strengthen confidence in the meanings discovered from application of any interpretive perspective.

Individual "big" dreams can be deeply meaningful and even life-changing. They tend to be rare events, however. We have found, following Jung's suggestion, that stable and sound interpretations, especially in a course context, are best derived from a series of a person's dreams over time than from any one dream. Even a short series of dreams can reveal recurrent themes not as evident in the "snapshot" of one dream. In our teaching experience, as few as three dreams often are adequate to produce a surprisingly comprehensive, nuanced, and subtle picture of the dreamer's existential concerns, when the student is analyzing his or her own dreams—because the dreams the student chooses to analyze will contain themes that are important to him or her both consciously and unconsciously.

As with dream discussion groups, the use of students' dreams in interpretive analysis projects is a double-edged sword. What one gains in relevance and interest to the student one may lose in concerns about intrusiveness and unlikely but possible disruptive effects on the more psychologically vulnerable. There can be no hard-and-fast rule about this matter that does not compromise in some way either the spirit of free inquiry or, on the other side, the privacy and psychological status quo of the student. The self-selected nature of dreams to analyze is an important and usually effective buffer against too much emotional vulnerability.

It certainly is safer to do interpretive analyses on dreams of persons neither known nor present who will not be affected by the process or results of the analysis. However, this approach misses the opportunity to corroborate interpretations with the dreamer, which is the key factor in determining their validity and usefulness. The most ingenious and sophisticated interpretation of dream meanings will fall flat if the dreamer doesn't concur, assuming the dreamer is available for comment and willing to consider the interpretations. (Of course, the dreamer him or herself can contribute to the interpretive dialogue and have the final say about the dream meanings, depending on how the dream-sharing and interpretive procedures are structured.)

Perhaps the best compromise is for students to analyze their own dreams, or series of dreams from accessible volunteers who can comment on the analysis. Domhoff has done the latter in his work and its teaching applications by soliciting cooperation of volunteers who (anonymously) have given dreams (sometimes thousands from a single dreamer) to the public domain. Several of these dreamers have responded to students by giving feedback as to whether their inferences about the dreamers' waking lives derived from the (quantitative) dream analyses did, in fact, hit the mark.

Student Research

We strongly advocate that psychology courses include an original research component. By "original research" we don't mean library research in which existing facts or views are collected and reshuffled, but rather research on raw (ideally student-generated) data, from which new knowledge of some kind is generated. We want students to experience themselves as creators of new findings and insights that no one else before them has ever produced. It is empowering for students to realize that they have the ability to test theory and create knowledge as well as passively absorbing existing knowledge. We want psychology students to become familiar and comfortable with doing empirical research on a routine basis.

One student in Phil King's course analyzed the emotions in a DreamBank sample of an English woman's dreams spanning many years before, during, and after World Wear II. The dreamer had resided in London and lived through the Blitz. The student found that the levels of emotionality in the Londoner's dreams were higher in the years before and after the war and considerably lower during the war. Why was this? Did the dreamer experience emotions more fully and vividly in waking during the war, such that her dreams were not needed to bring them forth? Does this support the hypothesis that dreams compensate for incomplete emotional experience in waking? One can see how this research project produced surprising (and counterintuitive) findings that spoke to all sorts of questions about the functions of dreams. In this way student research stimulates curiosity and propels the educational experience.

This process of student involvement in research is enhanced when the students study their own dreams, and we approach a newer form of participatory research which has been termed *organic, naturalistic,* and *cooperative* inquiry. These differ from the conventional approaches in their emphasis on experience and on potentially transformative participation in the research process by both researchers and subjects (subjects being the student-dreamers in the present context). These modes of research are distinguished from both quantitative and qualitative research. Michael Hewett, in his thoughtful review, notes John Heron's definition of quantitative research as research *on* people, qualitative research as research *about* people, and cooperative inquiry as research *with* people.[11]

One fruitful approach in course-based dream research of this type is to focus on dream motifs and, or, themes. We define a dream motif as a setting and initial situation recurring across dreams. "*Motif*" has connotations of template, form, domain, context, realm, and arena. Examples of motifs include a family at home, people at work, players on a stage, or people playing sports or painting pictures. We understand themes as likely representations of the dreamer's existential concerns. They may be symbolic, or direct and undisguised. Themes can be *both* selected *a priori, and* identified inductively from the dreams. Existential themes are valuable in a course because of their universality. They connect to but also transcend cultural, gender, age, and other demographic factors. Examples of themes include purpose, failure, success, isolation, connection, grace, awkwardness, and so on.

Besides conventional research papers, products from student projects of this kind can include collaborative constructions of composite dream vignettes—short stories or screenplays designed to faithfully portray and evoke the content themes previously identified. Classes can even produce these as live or video plays. In Hewett's words, "this kind of dramatic reenactment . . . is intended to possibly facilitate a deeper appreciation and understanding of the (dream themes) discovered than can be conveyed in the academic linear prose that is normally mandated for research or journal reports. . . . (This) model . . . (is) from a new genre of research outcomes known as *evocative representations*" (italics added).[12]

The educational goal is that participation in class research projects affects students both intellectually and personally. If the process goes as planned, it will produce new objective knowledge, a deepened understanding of the dreamer and the dreams, and enhanced ability in encountering dreams. When organic inquiry has quantitative components the focus becomes, in the words of one of our students: "to personify statistics; to substantiate the dream narrative; to retain the person behind the numbers." The interested reader will find in Appendix F a summary report on a project conducted by King's dream psychology students using this approach.

Lurking just beneath the surface of advocating the incorporation of students' dreams into courses, and the importance of subjective dream experiences, are questions of what we *mean* by "dream meanings" beyond the distinction between scientific regularities versus individual subjective significances. We take up the important question of "the meaning of meaning," in Roger Knudson's apt phrase, in the concluding chapter to this volume, when we look at dream interpretation and its teaching.

Course Topics

This section suggests a series of topics to cover in psychology dreams courses. We encourage a wide range of course contents depending on instructor and student interests. The list here should be viewed as a template that one can adapt. Many specific topics are sufficiently interesting and possess enough material to take up an entire course. Instructors should select carefully from the available resources, which are large and continually expanding. Topics in a dream psychology course might reasonably include the following, in the order given:

1. An introduction to dreams, demonstrating their ubiquitous quality and presence in daily life, and common beliefs about dreams and the dreaming process. This should include a treatment of factors in contemporary culture that encourage and discourage an attention to dreams.

2. A historical review of how people viewed and used dreams in various cultures and times. This material is voluminous and must be severely winnowed lest it take time better used (in a psychology course) on other matters. One way of doing this is to focus on the history of psychological approaches to explaining and using dreams (see Kelly Bulkeley's *An Introduction to the Psychology of Dreaming*). Another editing principle is that psychology courses taught in a Western cultural context may want to emphasize Western themes, the value of non-Western approaches not withstanding.

3. The biology of dreaming, including sleep cycles and neurological and other physiological activities associated with dream production. Contemporary evidence about the degree of dependency of dream form and content on specific neural mechanisms should be addressed, as should the epistemological matter of reductionism (see the discussion later) and the usefulness of addressing dream content and meaning separate from underlying dream generation mechanisms.

4. Psychological theories that attempt to explain the sources and functions of dreams, and guide the interpretation of dreams. This topic provides the theoretical underpinnings for the topic of clinical and personal growth applications (Topic 6).

5. Psychological research on dreams, to include historical and contemporary investigations. The first emphasis here will be on concomitants of dreaming and dream content in the traits, cultural and social circumstances, and waking experiences of the dreamer. The second emphasis is on dream content per se, including that of individual dreams, content patterns aggregated and compared over many dreams and many dreamers, interpretive processes, the relation of dreaming process and content to cognition and memory, and changes in dream content from psychotherapy and other waking experiences.

6. Applications of dreams in psychotherapy, counseling, and personal growth. More is published on this topic than on any other within the field. This is especially the case if we subsume lucid, paranormal, and spiritual dreams within this umbrella category. We note that for psychology courses, treatment of lucid, paranormal, and spiritual dreams, as well as dreams in the humanities and arts, should be grounded in replicable empirical research and interactive models of engagement as the operative modes of validating claims. For example, assertions about spiritual qualities of dreams should both be connected to psychological theory (e.g., their relation to concepts in humanistic, existential, and transpersonal psychology), and tested, in so far as possible, regarding their intersubjective validity. That is, if one encounters one's dreams in a particular way in particular circumstances, what kinds of spiritual experience follow?

An important component of this topic—and a central focus of many courses—consists of skills and experience in dream discussion groups. Most students take to this like ducks to water, and develop impressive abilities relatively quickly. It is not unusual by the end of the course for some students to be capable of leading dream discussion groups on their own, and on several occasions our former students have gone on to organize and run informal dream groups on an extracurricular basis.

Course activities inside and outside class will include lectures, demonstrations, discussions, films, and individual and group work with dreams (subject to the ethical and practical considerations previously discussed), and students' original research. We believe that there should be an explicitly open-minded but skeptical "hard-headed" stance in dream psychology courses. This is important in order to balance the otherwise credulous attitude that easily can dominate one's approach to a subject matter that resonates so powerfully on a personal level. Our intent is not to rob the dream experience of its wonder, but to study it rationally and systematically from a bit of a distance, before and after "diving in." In Henry Kariel's phrase, we don't want only to "wallow in experience," but also to come back from it and contain or explain it in clarifying ways.

Sleeping and Dreaming

We now turn to a consideration of teaching about the dreaming process—the physiology and neurology of the generation of dreams. This is a topic in biological psychology; we treat it here in the psychology chapter. We define dreams as experiences occurring during sleep. So where do sleeping and dreaming processes come in? Are there not profound connections between neurological activities that underlie dreaming, and dream content? How clearly can we map dream content onto sleeping? Can mind, and dreams, be well understood psychologically without resort to their putative material bases? Should courses on dreams include substantial material on sleep, sleep disturbances, and the biological mechanisms of sleeping and dreaming?

Opposing arguments pull at us, as grappling with these questions thrusts us into some fundamental philosophical uncertainties about the nature of mind and its relation to body. A number of scholars have pondered these questions in ways valuable to decisions of what to include in teaching about dreams. Domhoff, Mark Solms, James Pagel, Van de Castle, and Milton Kramer offer views of the connection of sleeping to dreaming, and brain structure and function to dream content. Jeffrey Schwartz and Sharon Begley have written more generally on the relations of brain to mind in ways that have implications for courses on dreams.

Domhoff, in *The Scientific Study of Dreams*, advocates investigating the neurophysiological substrate underlying dreaming as one of three prongs of a scientific approach to dreams (the others being conceptual systems of schema and scripts in a developmental perspective, and aggregate dream content analysis). He rejects past emphases on anecdotal dream reports, clinical theory unsupported by evidence, and speculations about the effects of the brain stem activity on dream content.[13] He clearly sees brain processes as a fundamental component of understanding dreams as a topic (if not understanding individual dream meanings).

However, on the question of including a module on sleep phenomena in dreams courses, Domhoff finds it difficult to do both sleep and dreams justice in a typical one-semester course. He treats sleep briefly in the context of the (1950s and 1960s) laboratory era of dream research. He does believe that sleep phenomena such as narcolepsy, sleep talking, and movement deserve mention in a survey course on dreams, but cautions against a physiological reductionism that would explain dreams in terms of underlying brain functions.

As Solms points out, persons with damage to certain areas of their brains do not dream, have dreams compromised in various sensory aspects, or dream with decreased frequency, which may bespeak deficits in dream memory.[14] The inference is that dreaming is inextricably connected to brain activity, and that some features of dream content are functions of neurological processes.

Pagel illuminates a core philosophical question when he contrasts the older Cartesian (dualist) view that mind and brain are separate entities, with the ascendant unitary (monist) view (brain and mind are inextricably connected, that mind is a function of brain).[16] He argues that there are important gaps in the mapping of dreaming mind onto dreaming brain. There are few clear correlates between brain behavior and dream experience. The monists attribute these misalignments to limits of theory, technology, and current knowledge, all surmountable in principle with more research. Pagel is not so sanguine; scientists have not even been able clearly and unambiguously to demonstrate correspondences of sleep stage to the presence or absence of dreaming.

Pagel is a sleep disorders physician and scientist as well as a researcher on the uses of dreams in creative processes. In his review of the neurology of dreaming, he concludes that there may be unbridgeable gaps between the biological brain and the experiential world of dreams. A reductive brain model does not explain aspects of cognition, emotion and creativity in some dreams, and their sheer sensory wonder and existential impact.[16]

Other dream scientists' views reinforce Pagel's. Van de Castle cites Foulkes' statement that:

> psychophysiological correlational research now appears to offer such a low rate of return as not to be a wise place for dream psychology to commit its limited resources. . . . Dreaming is a mental process and it must be studied as we now study other mental processes. Whatever brain events accompany dreaming, what the dream is a mental act.[17]

Van de Castle concurs:

> I have no doubt that considerable progress will be made in advancing our knowledge of the neurophysiological properties of the brain and that new information regarding the psychological principles underlying association, symbolism and memory will be forthcoming, but I think an irreconcilable Grand Canyon will always remain between these two competing explanatory constructs, regardless of what advances are made.[18]

Kramer is an eminent dreams authority who states quite bluntly that you cannot get there from here—you cannot follow a pattern of firing neurons to the experience of dream imagery and meaning.[19]

Schwartz and Begley do not treat dreams directly. Nor do they reject fundamental brain–mind connections. They do argue in *The Mind and the Brain* that the causal relations go both ways—mentation can affect brain. Focusing on the neuroplasticity of the brain even in adulthood, they show that the application of focused attention can change brain structure. Consciousness can exert mental force that affects neurological activity. Whereas brain manifests mind, the exertion of will and mental decisions modify brain.[20]

There are many positions regarding the brain–mind divide. Although a thorough discussion of these would take us far a field, we do direct the potential instructor to Schwartz and Begley's excellent short review of the philosophies of the relation of mind to matter. In order of descending materialism, these are *functionalism* (holding that mind is a mere byproduct of the brain's physical activity); *epiphenomenalism* (the mind is a real phenomenon but it cannot have any effect on the physical world); *emergent materialism* (mind arises from brain in a way that cannot be reduced to brain processes—and mind may have the power to effect both mental and physical change); *agnostic physicalism* (mind derives exclusively from brain matter, but nonmaterial forces may affect mental states, working through the brain); *process philosophy* (mind and brain are manifestations of a single reality, one that is in constant flux); and *dualistic interactionism* (consciousness and other aspects of mind can occur independently of brain).[21]

There is no way to prove that particular manifestations of mind transcend brain activity (even as they engage it). Our individual beliefs aside, as dream educators we are agnostic about questions of the brain–mind connection or divide, advocating only that instructors raise the topic. We think it is important that the instructor acknowledge the issue and expose students to the various viewpoints and their implications.

The dream teacher must be alert to both the relationships between mind and brain and the possibly insurmountable gaps between brain activity and dream content. The two may be from different ontological realities. When teaching them together one should clearly draw the limits of what we know and don't know about their connections. The instructor should articulate the monist–dualist divide in historical context, and should differentiate aspects of dreaming and dreams that are well explained from those that are not. Pagel's account, cited earlier, is a valuable resource for this purpose.

We believe, with Van de Castle, that sleeping and dreaming processes should be addressed in dream psychology courses. The question is to what extent and the answer will vary with the predilections of the instructor. Although time devoted to sleep topics is time taken away from dream topics, combining sleep and dreams in the same psychology course has advantages. If it is the only course on the sleep–dreams nexus, the combined topic will serve the student both in terms of sleep issues and dream awareness.

As noted previously, Rainville's dream course included a sleep laboratory where students got hands-on experience researching sleeping and dreaming processes.[22] Laboratory experience is valuable for students in actually doing science—design, measurement, and analysis—rather than only reading about it. Instructors with access to sleep labs will want to consider how to use them and their benefits and costs, including other possible uses of course time.

Tracey Kahan's current undergraduate course at Santa Clara University combines sleep and dreams in a thoughtful and adroit way. Her course syllabus is in Appendix B. Kahan took over a course lodged in a master's program in psychological counseling that emphasized working with dreams clinically.

She gradually modified this into an upper-division undergraduate psychology course with a scientific basis, with equal attention to sleep and dreams. Kahan's course goals cover a wide range, from students learning about sleep phenomena, including the effects of sleep deficits (an extremely important topic in our view), to learning how to work with their own dreams, and to getting experience as hands-on researchers.

The brain–mind relationship is an ongoing theme for reflection and discussion in Kahan's course. Kahan grounds the issue empirically whenever possible, for example by looking at "state constraints," that is, neurological limits, of dream versus waking emotion. She emphasizes the integration of theory, evidence, and students' direct sleeping and dreaming experience.

Kahan has students work with their own dreams, by recording them in a sleep–dreams journal (of at least 24 entries over an 8-week period), analyzing them outside class using various interpretive theories, then exchanging insights in two- (sometimes three-) person "paired sharing" discussions in class. She relates her own dreams, thereby legitimizing the disclosure and self-revelation that dream sharing embodies, and providing a model for students. Kahan participates in all the dreamwork exercises in class. She notes that there is much valuable material on both dreams and sleeping that she does not have time to cover. Such a sacrifice is inevitable in one course given the breadth of her subject matter.

We think Kahan's approach to a dreams psychology course is instructive for other teachers in that it embraces many aspects of sleeping and dreaming, including those often viewed as distinctly separate if not mutually antagonistic theoretically. Even separately, both sleeping and dreaming would lend themselves to several courses each. The two together could easily flesh out a robust master's degree. However, as a lone course in a liberal arts psychology program, her approach to dreams *and* sleep education serves as a model.

Most university-based psychology dream courses will include at least some attention to dreaming processes. For example, in her full dreams course (a seminar) at the University of Maryland, Clara Hill covers the physiology of sleeping and dreaming. In Allan Hobson's course, students came expecting dream interpretation but became very interested in his scientific approach.[23] Deirdre Barrett covers sleeping and dreaming processes in her courses on dreams.

An example of an excellent dream psychology course is Domhoff's at the University of California at Santa Cruz. (Domhoff's DreamBank was previously discussed.) Domhoff first became interested in dreams as a means and vehicle to test psychodynamic and early cognitive theory. Later he became interested in dreams per se. After many years, he became convinced of the stability, regularity, and meaningfulness of patterns in dream aggregates in contrast to the relative failure of classical clinically based dream theories to generate validated predictions.

Domhoff notes that there often is a tendency to assume the truth of interesting hypotheses and to uncritically project and generalize personally meaningful insights, rather than allow for the possibility of their disconfirmation through further scrutiny. For him and other scientifically minded educators, an important task is to rein in beliefs in propositions about dreams that are not supported by data. To manage unexamined enthusiasm about dreams, Domhoff organizes his course in dreams along somewhat more detached and neutral lines. His course is for everybody, not just for "gung-ho" students who easily recall and value their dreams. Domhoff encourages students to analyze their own dreams but does not require it; nor does he use dream groups in his class, feeling that it is wrong to force dream-sharing intimacy on students who do not necessarily want it. Instead, with him as the conduit, he has students anonymously share series of their own dreams with one another. Students analyze these dreams of other students according to one or more theories, write their analyses in a paper, which is then returned to the student dreamer via the professor. Students benefit from systematic reflection about their dreams by others, but the analyses are "blind" in that the analysts do not know the identity of the dreamer. The validity or at least usefulness of these blind analyses lies in the extent to which they illuminate the dreamer's personal experience and views of self.

Domhoff also covers dreams in their historical and cross-cultural contexts, with a focus on how people in the past and in non-Western societies have viewed and used their dreams. Additionally, every student must do some kind of original research—qualitative or quantitative—in which the focus is on dream patterns, recurrent themes, and regularities rather than on interpretation of the meaning of individual dreams. Students have the options of using several sources of dreams. These include:

1. fellow class members' dream series, as noted earlier;

2. the "most recent dream" of multiple dreamers;

3. their own dreams from a journal;

4. dreams gathered from their daily life connections, such as working with children; and

5. dreams garnered from the DreamBank's repository of thousands of collected dreams to research particular dream themes or demographic groups.

The themes researched through the DreamBank can be ones of personal interest to the student, such as pets, sports, relationships, spiritual experience, and the like, thus connecting students to their dreams but in an external pattern-seeking way rather than an internal interpretive way. The key for Domhoff is to find some interest the student has, and develop a dream research project around that interest, thereby being "personal" without undue intrusiveness or the necessity of public sharing of one's dreams.

Domhoff finds students to be quite variable in their dream proclivities, interests and skills. Some are, as one would expect, fascinated by their dreams and the meanings they may hold. Some become more interested in the other aspects, such as the research process, especially content analysis and the quantitative generalizations about patterns that they can extract from collections of dreams. All these students find a receptive home in the course. Domhoff encourages all students to give themselves some distance from their own dreams, to complement and balance the strong immersion experience of dreaming, and to avoid an undue focus on one's own dreams in the larger course context.

Domhoff's approaches that have met great success in his college course have not been successful in his work with younger students—high school or junior high school students working on dream projects. High school students have no background in nonexperimental research and thus cannot adequately negotiate the research process involved in content analysis. Junior high school students do not get the concept of metaphor and therefore have trouble seeing possible meanings in dreams. Systematic work on dreams with precollege-age students "falls on deaf ears," and becomes clinical rather quickly. Domhoff suggests that dreams be taught for these age groups as a module within some other course, for example, writing courses or courses on imagination. (For approaches to educating younger students about dreams, see Chapter 10.)

We emphasize throughout this text that dreams are inherently multidisciplinary. Course offerings based in psychology can bring in information and perspectives from other disciplines, as long as the instructor takes care to be cautious when venturing outside his or her area of expertise. This is possible. King, for example, discusses film excerpts in terms of psychological theory, not film theory.

As noted at the start of this chapter, psychology is the field most often associated with dreams, and there are more psychology courses on dreams than there are in any other academic discipline. So psychology was a good starting point for our exploration of the academic fields of dream education, and it continues to provide a useful standpoint as we move on to other disciplines, student groups, and settings. But there is more to see; many more perspectives and ways of studying dreams. In the next chapter, we discuss another discipline with much to say about dreams in their cultural contexts—anthropology.

Chapter 4

Anthropology

We now shift the focus from psychology to anthropology, the discipline that runs a very close second to psychology in the length and sophistication of its research tradition on dreaming. The primary audience for this chapter is teachers of undergraduate and graduate courses in anthropology who are looking for new strategies to help their students better understand the interaction of cultural and psychological forces in human life. We also address the chapter to the wider audience of teachers from other disciplines whose students can benefit from learning about the many fascinating discoveries in anthropological dream research over the past 100 years. Dream-related courses in virtually any field can effectively broaden their students' range of knowledge by including an anthropological perspective among the readings and class discussions. Indeed, for many teachers today there is no way to avoid cross-cultural issues, thanks to shifting trends in the demographics of higher education. College and university students are becoming increasingly multicultural in their backgrounds, interests, and life experiences. The best educational practices of the 21st century will acknowledge this reality and provide these students with the conceptual tools they need to feel confident stepping into a world of growing pluralism and diversity. As this chapter shows, dreaming is an ideal subject for cross-cultural exploration, and anthropologists have led the way in developing useful methods to study these dimensions of dreaming.

Anthropology arose in European and North American universities in the late 19th and early 20th centuries as a scientific discipline aimed at understanding the premodern ways of non-Western "primitives" and "savages." The earliest research was morally ambiguous, to say the least, insofar as it was usually funded by the same colonizing forces (military, economic, religious) whose encroachment was destroying the native cultures the anthropologists were trying to study. Although originating independently from psychoanalysis, anthropology was strongly influenced in its early years by Freudian ideas about dreams and their symbolism. Several pioneering anthropological studies of dreams used psycho-analysis as their chief interpretive lens, and a number of later anthropologists combined their field research with professional training in psychoanalytic theory and practice, leading them to develop novel ways of analyzing the relationship between Western researchers and non-Western informants. We start this chapter with a discussion of these psychoanalytic approaches to cross-cultural dream study, looking at their useful insights as well as their theoretical limitations.

After that we describe three other milestones in the anthropology of dream-ing that bear special significance for present-day teachers and students. The first is the work of Dorothy Eggan, whose interest in the "manifest content" of dreams showed how anthropologists could learn valuable information about people and their cultures without relying on the questionable interpretations of the "latent content" by Freudians. Eggan's approach opened the way to a new appreciation of dream reports as valuable windows into a culture's impact on people's thoughts and feelings, particularly around issues of change to people's traditional ways of life.

Next is a section on the controversy surrounding the dream beliefs and practices of the Senoi, an indigenous community from the Malaysian rainfor-ests. Reports published in the mid-20th century by Kilton Stewart described an idyllic "dream people" who practiced a powerful method of consciously controlling their experiences while dreaming. These reports were tremendously influential on popular dreamwork in the United States and Europe from the 1960s through the 1980s. Subsequently, serious questions arose regarding the reliability of Stewart's anthropological work, and a sharp debate ensued over the possibility of ever knowing what the Senoi thought about dreams prior to their first encounter with Western civilization. The Senoi debate offers a good case study of the difficulties of cross-cultural analysis, including the complex legacy of colonial history, the danger of unreflective projection, and the romantic yearning to reconnect with premodern spiritual wisdom.

A third post-psychoanalytic development has pushed the field in the direc-tion of greater self-reflexivity and critical awareness. Barbara Tedlock has made a particularly big impact in this area, beginning with the anthology she edited in 1987 titled *Dreaming: Anthropological and Psychological Interpretations*. Ted-lock's fieldwork with the Quiché Maya of Guatemala involved a deep personal exploration of her own dreams, prompting her to become trained and initi-ated by the Quiché as a dream interpreter. In her writings, Tedlock points to other anthropologists who have been consciously or unconsciously influenced by their own dreams while studying non-Western cultures, and she argues that such dreams reveal the mutual influences at work when two different cultural perspectives come into contact. This same dynamic can be observed in the classroom when students learn about the dream beliefs of non-Western others—their own experiences of dreaming are inevitably brought into play, a fact that savvy teachers can put to good pedagogical use.

The remainder of this chapter surveys the teaching practices of several contemporary educators who have developed innovative methods of teaching undergraduate and graduate students about the cross-cultural dynamics of dreaming. The students in their classes learn that dreams do not simply reflect the internal psychology of the individual, but also express the dreamer's thoughts and feelings about various aspects of the cultural environment, including its moral codes, gender identities, childrearing practices, and religious symbol systems. More than that, the dreams reveal how deeply the cultural categories of a particular time and place reach into the unconscious imaginations of each person in that community. Many of the classroom exercises used by these teachers are aimed at eliciting an experiential insight into precisely these kinds of psychocultural processes. Such insights can become precious "aha!" moments for the students in which the abstract themes of the course are crystallized in a highly vivid and personally relevant form.

Anthropology and Psychoanalysis

The 20th-century partnership between anthropology and psychoanalysis produced many important collections of dream material from a wide variety of cultural traditions. The most lasting result of this research has been to validate the idea that dreaming is a panhuman phenomenon. Freud, Jung, and other psychologists proposed this idea early in the 20th century, but they drew their evidence primarily from the limited selection of people they saw in their clinical practices. When anthropologists began the serious study of the indigenous cultures of Africa, Asia, Australia, and the Americas, one of the first things they discovered was the universal prevalence of dreaming. People everywhere sleep, dream, talk about their dreams with others, and try to interpret the meanings of their dreams. Anthropologists proved that Freud and Jung, although wrong about many other things, were right on this basic point: Dreaming reflects some of the most deeply rooted psychological processes in human nature.

However, much of the early anthropological material is difficult to use in the contemporary classroom because scholars applied the mostly Freudian psychological categories with such a heavy hand that the dreams themselves become obscured and hard to understand in their own terms, apart from the author's interpretations. The major work from this era is Jackson Stewart Lincoln's *The Dream in Primitive Cultures*, which uses Freudian theory as a scientifically objective tool to "find out how far it is possible to determine accurately through the dreams of primitive peoples, a few of the motive forces of human culture in some of its more primitive phases."[1] To his credit, Lincoln offers a wide-ranging collection of dream information from various cultural and historical sources, and his work shows how psychological questions about dreams become more interesting when framed in a cross-cultural context. Unfortunately, his Western rationalist biases are so domineering that readers today cannot trust that they are receiving an accurate portrayal of the "primitive" people's dream lives (for more on problems with the psychoanalytic view of non-Westerners, see Celia Brickman's *Aboriginal Populations in the Mind: Race and Primitivity in Psychoanalysis*). In fact, Lincoln's work is so egregious in its crude Freudian reductionism that it could serve as a good case study for upper-division or graduate classroom discussions about the dangers of misapplying psychological methods to anthropological data. This would represent a kind of "against-the-grain" analysis that encourages students to think critically about the texts they are reading, questioning the author's choices and interrogating his or her motives, assumptions, and biases.

Fortunately, recent years have seen the publication of several neo-psychoanalytic studies of cross-cultural dreaming. Although the influence of Freud remains important, these approaches go further than classic psychoanalysis in describing the cultural systems of meaning in which different people experience and understand their dreams. Good representatives include Waud Kracke's studies with the Kagwahiv people of the Amazonian rainforests, Gilbert Herdt's research on the Sambia of New Guinea, and Douglas Hollan's work among the Toraja of Indonesia.[2] Each of these anthropologists has been trained in psychoanalytic theories that set aside the quest for objective truth and focus instead on the interpersonal dynamics between the analyst and patient (or between the anthropologist and native informant). In their view, much can be learned by paying close empathetic attention to the social, cultural, and linguistic circumstances in which people talk about dreams. The ways in which a dream is expressed—what does or doesn't get said, who does or doesn't get to hear it, why it's interpreted, which methods are used to elucidate its meaning, what actions are or are not taken in response to it—are inevitably shaped by the dreamer's cultural environment. All of this varies from person to person and situation to situation, and people's actual practices sometimes deviate from the mainstream standards of their culture. Kracke states the methodological point: "If the investigator is willing to make the additional effort of understanding the cultural world of the person being interviewed and to be receptive to the subtle, implicit, not always culture-syntonic messages that the person conveys about his or her emotional state, psychological understanding can be both possible and beneficial."[3]

He put this principle into practice in his conversations with a Kagwahiv man, Jovenil, whose two sons had just died and whose dreams revealed the presence of deep emotional conflicts generated by his culture's restrictions on public mourning. Kracke describes how these conversations gave him unusually vivid insights into Kagwahiv culture, insights he could only gain once he had overcome "my own reluctance to abandon the relatively protected, semi-detached role of anthropologist and to enter the deeper emotional involvement entailed in depth interviewing."[4]

The work of Kracke, Herdt, Hollan and others like them reflects the recent turn to a relational version of psychoanalysis, one that pushes into the foreground the mutual interplay of people's thoughts and feelings about each other in the analytic encounter. In Freudian terms, this can be described as an interactive process of transference and counter-transference (discussed in more detail in Chapter 8); in Jungian terms, it's the back-and-forth of conscious and unconscious projections. The big advantage of this development in the anthropology of dreams is that it does not fall into the trap of claiming an unwarranted degree of objectivity. It concentrates instead on the interactive meanings that people create in their dream communications with others. One can observe this in many different circumstances—between the members of the native culture, between a native informant and an anthropologist, and even between teachers and students in the classroom. As is seen later in this chapter, some educators have turned that insight into a basic premise of their teaching about the cross-cultural dimensions of dreaming.

Eggan and the Manifest Content of Dreams

The main drawback to any approach derived from psychoanalysis is that it depends on a close interpersonal encounter with the dreamer and a highly technical method of interpretation that was developed for treating mental illness. This can easily give teachers the impression that anything involving dreams is beyond the reach of undergraduate students and perhaps inappropriate for the classroom. To counter that impression, we believe it's important to highlight the work of other anthropologists who have pointed to the wealth of information that can be gleaned from nonpsychoanalytic methods. Eggan made creative headway in this direction in the mid-20th century with two articles in *American Anthropologist*, "The Significance of Dreams for Anthropological Research" and "The Manifest Content of Dreams: A Challenge to Social Science." She argued that the manifest content (i.e., the surface elements of the verbal or written report, the "dream as dreamt," in contrast to the hidden underlying "latent content" proposed by psychoanalysis) provides an accurate reflection of the individual's emotional response to important social realities in his or her waking life. Eggan tried to wrest dreaming away from the exclusive control of psychoanalysis by shifting from an inward focus on early childhood conflicts to an outward view of the individual's current experiences in his or her cultural environment.

A few years later, Eggan wrote another journal article, "The Personal Use of Myth in Dreams" to provide a case study of this kind of anthropological dream analysis. She described the dreams of a Hopi man she called Sam, whom she had known for 16 years. She gathered 292 dream reports from him, which she analyzed in terms of their manifest content's connections to Hopi myth and folklore. She found that 73 of Sam's dreams included a highly personalized guardian spirit, sometimes appearing as a man and sometimes as an animal, who helped him during difficult times in his private life. Various mythic characters, including the powerful Water Serpent and Tuwapongwuhti, "Mother of All Living Things," appeared in other dreams of Sam's, which Eggan interpreted as his unconscious psychological effort to make meaning out of his life by weaving personal concerns around traditional spiritual teachings: "he not only uses folklore in dreams but his dreams in turn modify the way in which he interprets folklore situations."[5] His shame about being a poor hunter, his distress at the death of a child, his worries about being an outsider in a community that values group cohesion—all of these fears are merged in his dreams with the fears of the legendary heroes of Hopi myth. Through his dreams, the stories of those heroes become part of Sam's understanding of his own life. Eggan shows how his dreams reflect not only the formative influence of culture on the individual, but also suggest a reciprocal process by which individual dreams generate novel bursts of cultural creativity. In Sam's village, for example, several people who heard about his dreams became more interested in traditional teachings about guardian spirits as a result of his experiences.

The pedagogical relevance of Eggan's work lies in its support of anthropologists approaching dreams not as pseudo-psychoanalysts *but as anthropologists*, using their own discipline's unique set of conceptual tools to study dreaming as an important and evidently universal form of cultural expression. Her basic method with Sam's dreams can be used by teachers today as a topic for a research essay or classroom exercise: Take a dream or series of dreams and interpret it in light of the myths, legends, and sacred stories from the individual's waking cultural environment. (A more advanced version would start with the students themselves gathering the dreams from other people; this can be an excellent introduction to fieldwork practice, but to do it appropriately the teacher needs to make sure the students follow the ethical principles we discuss in this book, along with any relevant guidelines from their school's human subjects committee.)

As with psychological approaches, an anthropological approach can be pushed too far, and the issue of over-interpreting dreams needs to be part of an initial classroom discussion. Eggan's work suggests at least four practical means of guarding against over interpretation and promoting accurate, empirically grounded insights.

1. Gather a large number of dreams, so that the underlying patterns will show up more clearly.

2. Learn as much as possible about the language, history, and spiritual teachings of the dreamer's social world.

3. Learn as much as possible about the personal life of the dreamer, particularly regarding any conflicts she or he feels toward the culture at large.

4. Apply a systematic method of content analysis to the dreams, premised on the idea that the frequency of an item's appearance in dreams indicates its relative importance in waking life.

Eggan did not use Hall and Van de Castle's system, but she clearly shared their insight regarding the fruitfulness of studying dreams using social scientific methods *other* than psychoanalysis.[6] Her work has paved the way for anthropologists to develop their own methods of systematically exploring the multifaceted significance of dreaming.

Stewart and the Senoi

For much of the latter half of the 20th century, the attention of many was drawn to an exciting anthropological report of a primitive group who had developed an unusually powerful method of controlling their dreams. The people were the Temiar and Semai (collectively referred to as the Senoi), a small community of hunters and farmers living in the remote mountainous jungles and river valleys of Malaysia. The report came from Kilton Stewart, who visited the Senoi in the 1930s and wrote his PhD dissertation on their dream and healing practices in 1948. A few years later, he wrote the first of several articles about the Senoi and began teaching a version of their methods to therapy patients and experiential workshops. His 1951 article "Dream Theory in Malaya" was reprinted in Charles Tart's widely read *Altered States of Consciousness*, and from there the Senoi became the most popular icons of modern dream anthropology, referenced in countless books, media reports, and classroom discussions of dreaming ever since.

The essence of Senoi dream teachings, according to Stewart, was their dedicated, community-wide effort to become lucid in their dreams and take control of their contents: "every person should and can become the supreme ruler and master of his own dream and spiritual universe, and can demand and receive the help and cooperation of all the forces there."[7] He describes the Senoi as a remarkably free and happy people, untroubled by aggression, competition, or mental illness, and he attributed these utopian qualities to the central role of dreaming in their collective existence. Sharing dreams with other people was a regular part of Senoi daily life—"breakfast in the Senoi house is like a dream clinic."[8] When children had nightmares, their parents taught them to use the experiences as valuable opportunities to learn about the world of dreaming, so that next time a bad dream came the child could fight back against the negative

forces: "the Senoi believe and teach that the dreamer—the 'I' of the dream—
should always advance and attack in the teeth of danger, calling on the dream
images of his fellows if necessary, but fighting by himself until they arrive."[9]
Stewart says the Senoi are able, following these methods, to relieve their inner
psychological tensions and enjoy a happy, peaceful life.

This idyllic vision of the Senoi and their dream teachings has not been
well supported by other anthropological sources, according to *The Mystique of
Dreams: A Search for Utopia through Senoi Dream Theory* by G. William Domhoff
(whose work was mentioned in Chapter 3). The evidence gathered by Domhoff suggests the Senoi society did in fact suffer from some degree of conflict,
aggression, and psychopathology, and the people did *not* collectively practice an
elaborate method of cultivating lucid dreams. They certainly valued their dreams
and sought wisdom and guidance from them, as do most indigenous cultures
all around the world. But no other anthropologist has been able to validate the
idea that the Senoi's primary collective goal was to gain control and mastery
within the dreamworld. Stewart's romanticized version of the Senoi apparently
reflected more of his own spiritual ideals than their actual beliefs and practices.

The virtue of this mini history of the Senoi is the way it highlights the challenges facing all anthropological studies of dreaming. We encourage teachers to
discuss these challenges openly with their students, starting with the ever-present
temptation to romanticize the purity and simplicity of non-Western cultures
(which is the conceptual antithesis of summarily dismissing them as inferior,
irrational primitives). Stewart clearly fell into that trap, and so did many people
who read his articles and liked what they were hearing because it helped them
make better sense of what they felt was lacking in modern, secularized Western
society.[10] The myth of the noble savage has long been a haunting presence in
anthropological studies, and the dream teachings of the Senoi offer an object
lesson in the difference between social science and creative storytelling.

The story does not end there, however. As Domhoff acknowledges, many
people were inspired by Stewart's writings to try Senoi methods of influencing
their own dreams—*and the methods worked*. Even though the Senoi themselves
did not follow these methods, they were nevertheless effective for many Westerners who wanted to enjoy the psychological and spiritual benefits described
by Stewart (benefits that can be attributed in part to the feelings of intimacy
and trust generated by sharing personal experiences like dreams and the innate
flexibility of the dreaming imagination, which is indeed capable of an expanded
range of conscious awareness and volition). This raises some interesting questions:
Can an anthropological insight be pragmatically valuable even if it is factually
exaggerated? Why do certain ideas sound better or seem more appealing if they
are presented as originating with a far-away indigenous culture rather than a
contemporary Western individual? How can we ever be sure anthropological
reports are free of romantic embellishment? For that matter, how can we be sure

Stewart wasn't right? Perhaps he was able to learn the Senoi's deeper teachings that other researchers were not allowed to hear. How can we know if *any* of the information provided by the Senoi to Stewart or any of the other researchers reflects their actual ideas about dreams? They might be misleading all Western anthropologists in an effort to preserve their most precious cultural teachings from the prying eyes of outsiders.

In this book we are less interested in proving Stewart right or wrong than we are in prompting students to ask these kinds of questions, which go to the heart of the cross-cultural study of dreaming.

Tedlock, Dreams, and Shamans

As a counterpoint to Stewart, Tedlock's approach to the anthropology of dreaming depends on a carefully documented, critically self-reflexive, long-term immersion in the cultural life of people she was studying. In 1982 she organized a seminar entitled "Dreams in Cross-Cultural Perspective," the contents of which she gathered in her 1987 book *Dreaming: Anthropological and Psychological Interpretations.* All of the researchers included in the book (Kracke and Herdt among them) brought extensive fieldwork experience and linguistic competence to their analyses of the dream teachings of various non-Western cultures. They had lived for long periods of time among the people they were studying and participated in their daily life activities, including their ritual practices and spiritual ceremonies. Tedlock's chapter focuses on the Zuni and Quiché peoples of the Guatemalan highlands, whose different beliefs about dreams (the Zuni are very scared of death-related dreams, whereas the Quiché find them nonthreatening) derive, she says, from their different cultural, religious, and philosophical structures regarding the nature of the soul and the afterlife. In this way, Tedlock argues for an integration of Eggan's systematic analysis of dream content with the neo-psychoanalysts' heightened awareness of communicative context. She says all the seminar participants "agreed that the concept of manifest content should be expanded to include more than the dream report. Ideally, it should include dream theory or theories and ways of sharing, including the relevant discourse frames, and the cultural code for dream interpretation."[11] (25)

More than any other contemporary anthropologist, Tedlock has promoted dreaming as a phenomenon worthy of the best, most sophisticated methods of cross-cultural study. However, she does not hold much hope for social scientific approaches that apply abstract statistical models to decontextualized dream reports:

> The problems with comparing the phenomenology of dreaming between cultures begin even before the telling and interpretation of the dream, at the level of dream sorting, or classification, which is

linguistically coded and symbolically rooted in local epistemology and metapsychology. And the problems do not end when the dream comes to be talked about or performed; the outward dimensions of the performance may take nonverbal forms, and the meaning may be questioned all over again at a later time. From the perspective of possibilities like these, any attempt at counting and comparing the manifest content of verbal dream reports that have been deprived of their social and symbolic contexts appears groundless. . . . We need to find a way to move not from surface to surface, but from depth to depth.[12]

Taken in its strongest sense, this statement would seem to preclude any engagement with Eggan's quantitative efforts, let alone Hall and Van de Castle's system. We believe, however, that Tedlock's major point is that cross-cultural dream research requires more sophisticated methods than early 20th-century psychologists assumed. She reminds psychologists that dreaming, wherever it is found, is always intricately woven into the symbolic fabric of communal history, so much so that a researcher cannot justifiably claim to understand a particular group's dreams without taking their cultural environment fully into account. In our view, it is an empirical question whether or not a better form of content analysis may be developed that is compatible with Tedlock's methodological perspective, one that combines the broad frequency patterns of content analysis with the deep cultural insights of anthropology.

In recent years, Tedlock expanded the range of her interests to include the study of shamanic practices. In her 2005 book *The Woman in the Shaman's Body: Reclaiming the Feminine in Religion and Medicine,* she tells of her childhood education in dream divination from her grandmother, an Ojibwa midwife and herbalist. She only realized the full power of those teachings while she was doing her fieldwork with the Quiché people in Guatemala, when her own dream life suddenly came to life and began guiding her anthropological investigations. This led her to undergo training and initiation as a full-fledged Quiché shaman, a path she felt ready to follow because of her lifelong openness to dreaming. *The Woman in the Shaman's Body* takes her personal story as a point of departure for a critical review of the anthropological study of shamanism, which has long recognized the importance of dreams in shamanic rituals and healing but has focused almost exclusively on male shamans, ignoring the prominence of women as powerful shamans in cultures all over the world. Once the patriarchal overlay is removed, Tedlock is able to show that practicing shamans are in fact continuously engaged in ritualized gender shifting, partnerships of masculine and feminine energies, and careful attention to biological cycles and reproductive powers of women's bodies.

The differences and similarities between men's and women's dreams is a fascinating cross-cultural topic in its own right, and Tedlock's book provides a good framework for studying the gender dynamics of dreaming among different cultural groups. Whether they are highly trained ritual specialists like shamans or ordinary members of the community, people's dreams inevitably reflect the emotionally complex interactions of masculinity and femininity in their cultural environment.[13] Many students in our classrooms today are specifically interested in gender issues, and Tedlock's work shows how cross-cultural dream research offers exciting opportunities for new discovery in this long-neglected area of investigation.

Teaching the Anthropology of Dreams

In the preceding chapters we described a number of practical classroom techniques used by teachers in psychology to guide their students in exploring actual dreams. Teachers in anthropology have developed comparable methods of studying dreams in the classroom context, and in the remainder of this chapter we highlight a few of the most successful efforts in this direction.

Roger Lohmann teaches anthropology at Trent University in Toronto, Canada. He edited *Dream Travelers: Sleep Experiences and Culture in the South Pacific*, a collection of anthropological studies of the dream beliefs and practices of various indigenous cultures in Australia, New Guinea, and other parts of Oceania, and authored the chapter "Dreams and Ethnography" in Deirdre Barrett and Patrick McNamara's *The New Science of Dreaming*. His fieldwork has focused on the Asabano people of New Guinea, with special attention to the ways their dreams reflect the dramatic cultural changes and religious upheavals in their waking lives (the Asabano have nominally converted to Christianity in recent years, but they still struggle with the appeal of their traditional spiritual beliefs). When Lohmann teaches courses on psychological anthropology to undergraduates he includes a unit on dreams that starts with an introductory lecture on the subject, in which he describes several different cultural approaches (Western and non-Western) to understanding the meanings of dreams. He then organizes a "dream interpretation practicum," dividing the class into small groups of four or five students and asking for a volunteer in each group to share a dream (if no volunteers are forthcoming, he offers an anonymous dream report for the students to use). Each group is given the task of developing two interpretations of the dream's significance. The first is supposed to rely on the teachings of the Mekeo people as described in Michele Stephen's *A'aisa's Gifts: A Study of Magic and the Self*, a book the students are reading at this point in the class. The other method can come from either the Asabano, or psychoanalysis, or any other tradition mentioned in the introductory lecture or known to the students. Lohmann's goal with this assignment is to give his students a tangible experience of how the significance given to a particular dream is shaped by cultural assumptions and the social process of dream sharing.

After the group discussion is finished Lohmann asks the students to write an essay in which they give a precise description of the dream and the group's two interpretations, explaining the exact reasoning behind the interpretations and how they derive from the two dream theories. The students are encouraged to reflect on how dream experiences and narratives are influenced by the cultural theories used to interpret them. Once the students have finished their essays, they are ready for a follow-up classroom discussion about their findings and observations. Lohmann says these conversations usually lead into several interesting areas. For example, a deep philosophical question over free will versus determinism arises when students encounter the Iroquois belief[14] that dreams are inescapable prophecies that do come true, but whose consequences can be slightly diverted by a kind of sympathetic magic (e.g., if you dream of getting hurt, a friend will hurt you a little in waking life to prevent the dream from coming true in a bigger way). The different cultural views of sexuality and dreaming also lead to lively discussions. The Asabano believe that sexual dreams can symbolize good luck in hunting, whereas Freud claimed that sexual desires are hidden under nonsexual dream symbols—when students explore the cultural roots of these different beliefs, they discover new ways in which each individual psyche is influenced by the deep philosophical structures of his or her social world.

An additional benefit of Lohmann's interpretive exercise is that it gives the students an opportunity to reflect on the secular features of modern Western society, where dreams often are dismissed as the nonsensical firings of neurons in the brain with no special meaning or purpose. He encourages his students to think about the dream teachings of their own cultural environment, questioning why such a view has arisen and what happens when it encounters other perspectives.

Jeannette Marie Mageo of Washington State University also teaches courses in psychological anthropology, and like Lohmann she uses dream experience as an opening to broader questions in anthropology as a whole. In her edited book *Dreaming and the Self: New Perspectives on Subjectivity, Identity, and Emotion* she builds on Eggan, the neo-psychoanalysts, and Tedlock to develop an approach toward the "psychological problematics" afflicting people in various cultural settings. Mageo wants to make sure anthropologists do not succumb to a timid reluctance to sound disrespectful in saying anything critical about other cultures: "all cultures . . . have psychological problematics; to suggest that these problematics exist is not to presume inferiority, but rather a dynamic and vital element in culture, which must be considered in person-centered ethnography."[15]

Mageo has done fieldwork in Samoa with native people struggling to adjust their personal and collective lives to the presence of American colonization. For many of her informants, their psychological problematics revolve around the disturbing split between their public behavior and private feelings about the Americans who have taken control of their land. Their dreams accurately reflect the emotional distress and cognitive dissonance caused by this split, particularly in themes of technology, religion, and black and white color symbolism. In "Race, Postcoloniality, and Identity in Samoan Dreams," her chapter in *Dreaming and the Self*, she describes teaching a class to Samoan college students in which she invited them to practice various forms of projective dreamwork, drawing on the Western theories of Freud and Jung in addition to her own ideas and their cultural teachings.[16] The results showed that dreams are indeed a powerful means of studying "the slippage of public symbols in private fantasy life and its consequences for the self."[17] For example, in the case of a young woman she names "Penina," her dreams show the emotional strain of trying to find some kind of balance between her family's traditions and the modern world: "this instability . . . leaves Penina in an identity crisis: before others, she must hide and ignore feelings that are as precious to her as glittering gems [a prominent symbol in one of her dreams]. This is Penina's *experience* of being a person in a postcolonial transnational world. Her dream is a 'royal road' to this experience."[18]

Mageo continues to include dream interpretation exercises in her classes at Washington State University. In "The Self in Culture," an upper-level undergraduate course in psychological anthropology, she makes one of the learning objectives "to discover relations between self and culture through dreams." At the beginning of the class she asks the students to keep a dream journal for the duration of the class, making sure to include a date for each entry. She talks with them about various means for increasing dream recall. She reassures them that they are not required to write down dreams they don't want to share, but she does encourage them to record as many as they can since the dreams will provide a resource for their written assignments and final paper. Students turn in their journals with the final paper, to be checked for completeness and returned to the students at the end of the semester.

Using their own dreams as an experiential touchstone, the students in Mageo's class read about the various systems of dream interpretation outlined in *Dreaming and the Self*, including Freudian and Jungian approaches and her own method of "dream play." The students learn a great deal about Samoan culture (Mageo's specialty), and also about American culture as seen in anthropological perspective. She uses several films to supplement the readings, including *Citizen Kane, Trance and Dance in Bali*, and *Spellbound*. Three written assignments are given during the semester in which the students are asked to take a dream (ideally one of their own, but a friend's dream is acceptable) and interpret it in one of two or three different theoretical/cultural modalities. Their analyses are then presented and discussed in class. These assignments prepare the students for the 7- to 10-page final paper, in which they analyze two different dreams using the following five-part format:

1. the dream report,

2. why the student chose this particular dream,

3. which interpretive methods were being used and why,

4. the analysis of the dream, and

5. a conclusion discussing the relationship between the dream, the dreamer, and his or her culture.

Mageo's classes are usually in the 50- to 60-student range, considerably larger than most other courses where dreams are shared and discussed, but she reports having consistent success with her methods. She manages the process by starting with an introduction to dream interpretation in which she offers the analysis of one of her own dreams to show the students how it's done. In talking openly and comfortably about her dreams and their different levels of meaning, Mageo models the kind of process she then encourages the students to try for themselves. As the semester proceeds she regularly reminds them to be respectful and attentive to each other, particularly when a powerful dream leads to surprising and unsettling emotions. Mageo's maxim is "go gently," allowing the dreamer to set the bounds of what feels safe and appropriate. She finds dream sharing in the classroom to be a valuable educational tool, empowering students to write critically and gain new knowledge about the cultural dynamics of forming and maintaining a sense of self. The subject of dreams quickly engages their interest, giving them a strong sense of personal relevance to what goes on in the classroom. Mageo attributes her positive teaching evaluations for the class to the intrinsic curiosity the students bring to their own dream lives. Her teaching methods seek to develop that curiosity into a guiding force in anthropological education.

However, Mageo does offer a note of caution. She says the dream-sharing process can be an intense experience not only for the students but for the instructor, too. As indicated in Chapter 1, we agree with her when she recommends that teachers should recognize this challenge at the outset. Dreams are unpredictable, and so are students' reactions to them; a teacher who brings dream sharing into the classroom needs to pay close, careful attention to dynamics of the discussion as it unfolds, alert to sudden shifts and unexpected turns in the emotional tenor of the discussion. Experience helps, of course, and so does a general conceptual flexibility—most problems arise when someone tries to impose an overly rigid interpretation on the dream. The most important factor is the ultimate respect the teacher gives to the dreams shared in the class, because that's the best way of nurturing the same respectful attitude in the students and thereby enhancing the positive educational effects of the course as a whole.

A surprising discovery in cross-cultural dream education has been made by Jayne Gackenbach, a psychologist and former IASD president and author of several books and articles on lucid dreaming. Gackenbach is personally familiar with the difficulties of bringing dream research into the academic mainstream: "When I was put up for full professor, the colleague who was nominating me said that although I deserved to become a full professor he 'wished I hadn't done the research I had done. That is, dream research."[19] She has written of her experiences in teaching psychology classes in community colleges in Alberta, Canada, where most of the students are members of the Cree indigenous culture. Although not trained as an anthropologist, Gackenbach found that her classes became powerful learning experiences for students and teacher alike on the subject of cross-cultural conflict and understanding. Reflecting on this dream-mediated classroom dialogue, she realized it held unexpected possibilities for the significance of her work as a teacher:

> I am aware that I am in a position to reenergize the value of the dream and indeed the value of many of the traditional spiritual teachings for the Natives I come into contact with. In my role as teacher, with a doctorate in psychology, they listen to me about the science of dreams and states of consciousness which I integrate with standard psychological concepts. In some ways my teaching serves as a stamp of approval from white society, encouraging them to appreciate some of the truly beautiful traditional teachings. I do not presume to tell them anything about the specifics of their traditions, rather I speak simply of the science and clinical work with these states of being and emphasize my belief that my culture was and is simply wrong in dismissing or minimizing them.[20]

What Gackenbach finds in her classes with Cree students, teachers in anthropology and other disciplines may also find: Their knowledge and intellectual trustworthiness can give students the encouragement necessary to overcome negative stereotypes so they can reconnect with their own cultural traditions, whatever those traditions may be.

Mary Dombeck teaches at the University of Rochester School of Nursing in New York, applying her anthropological perspective to the practical training of future health care professionals (Dombeck's work is also mentioned in Chapter 8). Her dissertation and first book, *Dreams and Professional Personhood: The Contexts of Dream Telling and Dream Interpretation among American Psychotherapists*, applied an ethnographic method of analysis to the practices of dream telling and interpretation in the contemporary American health care context. Her findings illuminated a significant bias against talking about dreams in such settings because of the cultural belief that "dreams are crazy" and not worthy of serious attention. In her teaching Dombeck challenges that bias by encouraging her nursing students to familiarize themselves with the empirical findings of current dream research and to explore their own dreams through group dream sharing and personal reflection. Strongly influenced by the hermeneutic philosophy of Paul Ricoeur and the depth psychology of Montague Ullman, Dombeck uses a dream-sharing process in her classroom that focuses on elucidating the metaphorical, symbolic, and mythological qualities of meaning. For example, she will bring a myth to class and ask the students to interpret as if it were someone's dream, and then choose someone's dream and ask the students to interpret it as if it were a culture's myth. As she has gained experience in facilitating such groups Dombeck finds she trusts the class members and their insights more and more, and she primarily aims her efforts toward creating a safe classroom space in which the students can explore dreams, their own and others.

Iain Edgar teaches anthropology at Durham University in Durham, England. Much like Dombeck, his dream interests began with his dissertation/first book on the cultural dimensions of group dream sharing in contemporary British caregiving practices. *Dreamwork, Anthropology and the Caring Professions: A Cultural Approach to Dreamwork* examined the psychosocial dynamics of experiential group dreamwork methods, with a focus on how the group members made sense of their dreams by using "the language of metaphor and a political, often feminist, analysis of life events."[21] Edgar provides a valuable examination of the present status and future potential of dreamwork methods in professional therapeutic practices with the terminally ill, refugees, and children. Although it is a work aimed primarily at anthropologists, Edgar's book provides important insights for psychologists, psychotherapists, and medical professionals as well.[22]

An anthropologist at the University of New Hampshire, Robin Sheriff teaches a course on "The Anthropology of Dreams and Dreaming" for upper-level undergraduates. The syllabus covers Western and non-Western cultural approaches to dreaming, from Freud and the sleep lab to Eggan, Tedlock, and Lohmann. Sheriff assigns three written exercises for the students: a self-study of the students' own dreams, an ethnographic observation paper about the language people use in talking about dreams, and a final paper summing up the course. The ethnography assignment gives the students the opportunity to do some "fieldwork" of their own to test their ideas. Here are the instructions she gives to her class:

> This assignment is timed to coincide with our discussion of how
> dreams are shared in different cultures. Your task is to observe how

dreams are shared in your own culture. This will require that you spend time in those places that you think dream sharing is most likely to occur. Keep your ears open for dream conversations that occur naturally and in which you are at least implicitly accepted as a participant. When you "catch" one, listen and observe very carefully so that you can reconstruct the event and the dialogue in the greatest detail possible. Who were the participants? (Please don't use names; only approximate age and gender.) What was the context? What was the conversational exchange? What emotions and interactional dynamics characterized the exchange? If you don't manage to overhear any dream conversations, an alternative is to initiate them—but do it in a way that you believe fits in with how people in your culture tend to initiate such conversations. You might, for example, tell your own dream to a dorm roommate during breakfast. Bed partners might share dreams on awakening. If you live at home and have a younger sibling who is still a child, he or she might report dreams in a way that is different from the adults in the family. Another possibility is to interview several people about the last time they told someone their dream. You can invent variations of this assignment, provided your goal is to learn and communicate something about dream sharing (or the lack thereof) in our own culture.

Aim for two or three separate observations or interviews and in two or three full pages, describe what you observed. Direct quotation is impossible unless you choose to ask permission to record the conversations before they occur. Nonetheless, try very hard to remember interesting phrases and quote them in your essay. Then discuss what you learned from the assignment, especially in terms of cross-cultural comparisons. How would characterize dream sharing in your culture given what you observed?

Sheriff uses this exercise to teach her students several basic principles of ethnographic research, using dreams as a kind of test subject. She says her administrative superiors have never raised any concerns about the course, which is as academically structured as any other. One colleague from another department wondered if her teaching the course might unleash wild, potentially problematic sexual material in the classroom. In practice, however, that did not happen: "But it worked well. In fact, I now wonder if I was more cautious with the dreaming assignments than I needed to be."

At University College London, Charles Stewart teaches a course called "Dreams and Society" in the Department of Anthropology. He describes the aim of the class as developing an ability to recognize dreams as "important data for historians and anthropologists interested in understanding societies and cultures 'from the native's point of view.' Dreams have been little exploited by historians even though they offer unusual access to a society's values and preoccupations." The main text he asks students to read is Gananath Obeyesekere's *Medusa's Hair*, with each week's lectures accompanied by an extensive list of additional required and suggested readings. Early in the course the students read selections from Artemidorus, the second century CE Roman dream interpreter, in tandem with Michel Foucault's postmodern analysis of what the dreams gathered and interpreted by Artemidorus reveal as historical documents about ancient Roman experiences and feelings around the topics of family life, illness, and sexuality. Stewart guides his students in learning how to do with other cultures and traditions what Foucault does with Artemidorus, namely examine the dream narratives in relation to their cultural and historical context.

Beyond anthropology, we must admit that we do not have much to report about other social scientific disciplines. A few historians have written high-quality studies of dreams (e.g., Carlo Ginzburg's *The Night Battles: Witchcraft and Agrarian Cults in the Sixteenth and Seventeenth Centuries*, Mechal Sobel's *Teach Me Dreams: The Search for Self in the Revolutionary Era*, Carla Gerona's *Night Journeys: The Power of Dreams in Quaker Transatlantic Culture*, Carole Levin's *Dreaming the English Renaissance: Politics and Desire in Court and Culture*), but we do not know of any history class devoted specifically to dreams. Nor do we have any empirical insight into dream education in sociology, economics, or political science. However, the success of dream-related courses in psychology and anthropology might inspire educators in other social science disciplines to think creatively about possible points of contact between their teaching goals and current knowledge about the basic patterns of human dreaming.

For example, the subject of dreams might seem far removed from the central concerns of political science, but Bulkeley's recent work on dreams and American electoral politics suggests more potential to dream research than has been generally acknowledged.[23] He found strong correlations between people's sleep and dream patterns and their economic circumstances, political views, and religious beliefs. Briefly, people at the lower end of the economic scale slept considerably worse than people with high incomes; political conservatives slept better and had less bizarre dreams than political liberals, whose dreams involved a wider range of imagined possibility; people who consider themselves "spiritual but not religious" take great interest in dreams, in contrast to people who are very regular (more than once a week) church-goers. The methods and resources Bulkeley used in generating these data (dream journals, survey data, DreamBank analysis) are well within the reach of undergraduate students, enabling classes in sociology, economics, and political science to do research projects testing his findings and exploring other sociocultural variables that might be meaningfully reflected in people's dreams.

Olaf Hansen's International Perspective

We close with reflections on the work of Olaf Hansen and the practical dimensions of promoting the study of dreams across cultural and national boundaries. His efforts show how the anthropology of dreaming can have direct and valuable relevance for real-world initiatives to alleviate human suffering and foster better global cooperation.

Hansen, a recent president of the IASD, serves as the director of the Danish Center for Culture and Development, working in coordination with the UN on various projects promoting international cooperation in Africa, Asia, and Latin America. He has been particularly active in providing resources to those in Africa suffering from the "colonization of the mind" stemming from historical and contemporary conflict with Western imperialism. He sees the shared human experience of dreaming as a powerful means of fostering greater cross-cultural communication. For many African people, dreams represent an immediate, living source of connection with ancestral spirits. Hansen has long argued that Westerners need to understand and respect those cultural beliefs if they want to make a real contribution to African development. At the same time, he sees potential in Western dream research for educating Africans about the multiple dimensions of dreaming, which he believes can help counter the problem in many parts of Africa of people using simplistic, naïve, and/ or deceitful interpretations to accuse other people of being witches, thereby justifying their oppression and the violation of their human rights. According to Hansen, more education about the metaphorical and symbolic qualities of dream imagery can help victims of this kind of attack defend themselves and fight against the aggressive efforts of those who claim an absolute authority over the interpretation of dreams or anything else.

For Hansen, as for all the educators mentioned in this chapter, dreaming provides a powerful language of shared human experience that is best appreciated by pushing past literalist certainties and exploring the complex, multifaceted meanings that emerge in the dynamic interaction of psyche and culture.

Chapter 5

Philosophy and Religious Studies

Philosophical and religious issues often emerge of their own accord in classroom discussions of dreaming. Dreaming has been a topic of philosophical debate throughout the ages, and religious traditions all over the world have venerated dreams as important means of human–divine communication. No matter where a dream discussion starts, it frequently leads students to confront the great existential questions of human life, such as:

- How do we know the difference between reality and illusion?

- How do we know what we believe is true?

- What is the ultimate nature of the human mind?

- Do we have a soul that survives after death?

- Why is there evil?

- Does God exist?

- What is love, and how does it relate to sexual desire?

- What's the best way to lead a good, fulfilling life?

The disciplines of philosophy and religious studies are devoted to expanding our knowledge of the various ways people have answered such questions through history. For that reason, these two fields of study are necessary resources in virtually any educational effort involving dreams. We address this chapter to teachers whose primary specialization is philosophy and religious studies and also to dream educators in all fields who may find it useful to deepen their understanding of the philosophical and religious aspects of their classroom work. To our knowledge, relatively few teachers in philosophy or religious studies offer courses specifically focused on dreams. Nevertheless, dreaming often comes up in their classroom discussions on other topics, offering "teachable moments" of heightened student interest and engagement, particularly in schools where the students come from different religious and cultural backgrounds. We orient the chapter around three of these dream-relevant topics, highlighting pedagogically useful ideas and suggesting specific lines of student research and classroom conversation.

We start with questions about the complex relationship among reality, perception and dreaming. Philosophers and religious leaders through the ages have debated the exact nature of dreaming as a kind of reality and argued over its reliability as a source of knowledge. This is an excellent topic to introduce philosophy students to basic issues in ontology and epistemology. Second, we consider the ethical issues related to dream experience. Included here are questions of whether people are morally responsible for what they do in their dreams and how to interpret emotionally disturbing dreams of taboo behavior. The third topic revolves around "lucid dreaming," or experiences of self-awareness within the dream state. Lucid dreams have played a significant role in Hindu and Buddhist traditions, and they appear in some form or other in virtually every religious tradition. The recurrent themes in these experiences of consciousness-within-sleep provide an opportunity for philosophy and religious studies teachers who want to stimulate deeper comparative inquiry and discussion among their students, especially because many of the students likely will have experienced lucid dreams themselves and will be curious about their significance.

Along the way, we share the pedagogical insights of several colleagues who told us of their teaching practices in these disciplines. They include Christopher Dreisbach, who taught a history of dreams course in the philosophy department of St. Mary's College of Maryland; Fariba Bogzaran, whose teaching at John F. Kennedy University (JFKU) specializes in lucid dreaming, integral philosophy, and artistic creativity; Eleanor Rosch, whose dream class at University of California, Berkeley is officially a psychology course, but delves deeply into religious and philosophical issues; Kimberley Patton, who teaches a graduate course on dreams and world religions at Harvard Divinity School (HDS); and Patricia M. Davis, lead instructor in a course at the Graduate Theological Union (GTU) on dreams as a source of comparative religious inquiry and practical caregiving insight.

Reality, Perception, and Dreaming

In the first pages of *What Does It All Mean?: A Very Short Introduction to Philosophy*, Thomas Nagel introduces his readers to philosophical reflection by asking them how they know whether or not anything exists outside their own minds. The crux of the problem, according to Nagel, is how to distinguish their waking perceptions from their dreams:

But couldn't all your experiences be like a giant dream with *no* external world outside it? How can you know that isn't what's going on? If all your experience were a dream with *nothing* outside, then any evidence you tried to use to prove to yourself that there was an outside world would just be part of the dream. If you knocked on the table or pinched yourself, you would hear the knock and feel the pinch, but that would be just one more thing going on inside your mind like everything else. It's no use: If you want to find out whether what's inside your mind is any guide to what's outside your mind, you can't depend on how things *seem*—from inside your mind—to give you the answer.[1]

In this view, which reaches back to the earliest periods of both Western and Eastern traditions, the "problem" of dreams is the beginning of philosophy. Before we can claim to know *anything*, we must find a way to distinguish the experiences of dreaming from the reality of the actual world. The verisimilitude of dreaming, its capacity to mimic waking life in perfectly convincing detail, raises doubts about what we *think* we know about reality outside our own minds.

Depending on the nature of the class, the instructor can pursue several paths. For courses on ancient Greek philosophy, Plato's *Theaetetus* provides a classic expression of the "dream problem." Socrates asks the young student Theaetetus, "[W]hat evidence could be appealed to, supposing we were asked at this very moment whether we are asleep or awake, dreaming all that passes through our minds or talking to one another in the waking state?"[2] Socrates poses this question as a way of initiating Theaetetus into the fundamental processes of philosophical thought, which involve shedding all previous assumptions, questioning conventional ideas, and seeking reliable evidence to justify our beliefs and actions. Even though Theaetetus finds himself confused and disoriented by such strange questions, Socrates says these feelings are the sign of an opening mind: "This sense of wonder is the mark of the philosopher. Philosophy indeed has no other origin."[3] In general, the goal of Socratic dialogue is to extend this kind of wondrous, self-critical questioning as far and wide as possible. Socrates' pedagogical practice in *Theaetetus* makes use of personal dream experience to further this goal for students who are new to philosophy.

Much later in the Western tradition, René Descartes (1596–1650) introduces readers to his philosophical system by raising the same basic question. Although Descartes does not explicitly credit Socrates, he turns the phenomenon of dreaming to similar philosophical ends:

I must remember that I am a man, and that consequently I am accustomed to sleep and in my dreams to imagine the same things that lunatics imagine when awake, or sometimes things which are even less plausible. How many times has it occurred that the quiet of the night made me dream of my usual habits: that I was here, clothed in a dressing gown, and sitting by the fire, although I was in fact lying undressed in bed! It seems apparent to me now, that I am not looking at this paper with my eyes closed, that this head that I shake is not drugged with sleep, that it is with design and deliberate intent that I stretch out this hand and perceive it. What happens in sleep seems not at all as clear and as distinct as all this. But I am speaking as though I never recall having been misled, while asleep, by similar illusions! When I consider these matters carefully, I realize so clearly that there are no conclusive indications by which waking life can be distinguished from sleep that I am quite astonished, and my bewilderment is such that it is almost able to convince me that I am sleeping.[4]

For Descartes, the wonder he feels in contemplating the relationship of dreaming and waking inspires him to ask similar questions about his life as a whole, and the rest of his system flows from this starting point. Thus, it can truly be said that dreaming is the experiential genesis of Cartesian philosophy.[5] Thanks to the scholarly detective work of John R. Cole, author of *The Olympian Dreams and Youthful Rebellion of René Descartes*, we now know the extent to which Descartes' own dreams influenced his philosophical ideas, more than might be expected given his theory's strong emphasis on abstract rationality and logical reasoning. Apparently, Descartes did not want to acknowledge the impact of irrational phenomena like dreams on the development of his system. In this regard, Descartes represents a cautionary tale about the relationship between personal experiences in dreaming and philosophical theories in waking. We suggest teachers discuss the complex ambiguities of this relationship with their students so they can understand better the deep intertwining of life and work in the great thinkers of history.

Courses on Asian cultures also can draw on classic historical texts from Hinduism, Buddhism, and Daoism to study and discuss the philosophical puzzle of dreaming versus waking reality. The Upanishads of Hindu tradition first appeared around 700 BCE, and several Upanishadic writings discuss the nature of dreaming and its relation to the waking world. Lest anyone assume that early religious traditions were naïve or unsophisticated in their dream theories, here is a clear rational analysis found in a text known as the *Brihadaranyaka Upanishad:*

This is how [a person] dreams. He takes materials from the entire world and, taking them apart on his own and then on his own putting them back together, he dreams with his own radiance, with his own light. In that place this person becomes his own light. In that place there are no carriages, tandems, or roads; but he creates for himself carriages, tandems, and roads. In that place there are no joys, pleasures, or delights; but he creates for himself joys, pleasures, and delights. In that place there are no pools, ponds, or rivers; but he creates for himself pools, ponds, and rivers—for he is a creator.[6]

There is no one definitive Hindu position on dreams, but this passage from the *Brihadaranyaka Upanishad* indicates that at least some ancient Indian sages were well aware of the philosophical questions surrounding the highly realistic qualities of dream experience. In a similar vein, many Buddhist teachers also encouraged their followers to look at dreams not just as unreal, but as unreal in the same way that waking reality is unreal (i.e., as a creation of the mind). Several excellent books are available for pursuing Buddhist dream theory in the contemporary classroom, including Serinity Young's *Dreaming in the Lotus: Buddhist Dream Imagery, Narrative, and Practice*, Angela Sumegi's *Dreamworlds of Shamanism and Tibetan Buddhism: The Third Place*, and the Dalai Lama's conversation with a group of Western researchers published as *Sleeping, Dreaming, and Dying*.

Similar philosophical and religious themes may be found in the Daoist tradition of China, where an especially famous dream text comes from Zhuangzi (369-286 BCE) in his work *The Inner Chapters*:

Long ago, a certain Zhuangzi dreamt he was a butterfly—a butterfly fluttering here and there on a whim, happy and carefree, knowing nothing of Zhuangzi. Then all of a sudden he woke up to find that he was, beyond all doubt, Zhuangzi. Who knows if it was Zhuangzi dreaming a butterfly, or a butterfly dreaming Zhuangzi? Zhuangzi and butterfly: clearly there's a difference. This is called *the transformation of things*.[7]

Socrates would heartily approve of Zhuangzi's line of questioning. The "butterfly dream" expresses what seems to be a pan-human curiosity about dreaming and its relationship with our waking perceptions of reality. Most students have probably heard Zhuangzi's story in one version or another. Much like the *Matrix* films, the "butterfly dream" can prompt the kind of intellectually daring self-reflection that both Western and Eastern traditions consider essential to a philosophical approach to life.

A Course on Dreams and Philosophy

A good model of a Western philosophy course centering on dreams is the one taught for several years by Christopher Dreisbach at the College of Notre Dame of Maryland. An advanced-level class available to the school's undergraduates,

"Topics in Philosophy: Dreams" examined the significance of dreaming through-out the history of Western philosophy and its division into five major branches (metaphysics, epistemology, ethics, aesthetics, and logic). When we asked him to describe the academic skills and perspectives he was trying to communicate to his students in this class, he answered in clear, administrator-friendly language:

General skills include the appreciation for and application of the history of ideas; critical thinking; and epistemological humility. Specific objectives in the Dream Course include:

1. To explore views concerning the source, content, location, and value of dreams;

2. To identify several metaphysical, epistemological, ethical, aesthetic, and logical problems presented in these views;

3. To identify and to evaluate critically several proposed solutions to these problems;

4. To develop a sense of the historical development of the philosophy of dreams;

5. To articulate and evaluate our own positions about all of this.[8]

We asked Dreisbach about the course's significance in the broader context of undergraduate education, and he replied:

As Socrates said, philosophy begins in wonder and dreams and dream narratives are wonderful. As I explained in my essay for *Dreaming* in 2000[9] dreams are a significant subject in the history of philosophy and in each of the major branches of philosophy. So a course on the philosophy of dreams is a great opportunity to study philosophy. To the extent that philosophy enhances, and arguably provides the founda-tion for, general education, any course that adds value to philosophy offerings will contribute to general education. The enthusiastic response to the dreams course is strong evidence for its value to the offerings of the philosophy department.

The initial motivation for the course was Dreisbach's personal fascination with dreams, dating back to his early childhood. When he came to the College of Notre Dame of Maryland he found an opportunity to combine his dream interests with his philosophy teaching. Perhaps due to his position as chair of his department, he encountered no resistance when he proposed the course, and it was approved by the school's curriculum committee as both a general education and major requirement. Dreisbach encouraged his students to use their own dreams in thought experiments introducing them to the basic issues of philosophy, although he was careful to prevent the class from turning into a group therapy session. "Our focus was always on the philosophical relevance of the dream and I discouraged attempts to interpret other people's dreams. If someone wished to weigh in on another's dream story, she would begin with 'If this were my dream . . .' or 'I notice that you refer to X several times in your narrative, what might that mean to you?' "[10] Sometimes Dreisbach felt it worthwhile to ask the students how the dreams being discussed would be interpreted by different theorists, with special attention to the recurrent symbols and themes that sparked student interest. Even then, he always tried to bring the conversation back to the philosophical issues at hand.

Ethical Issues

Dreisbach's course touched on the ethical issues that arise in human dream experience, issues that relate not only to philosophy but to theology and religious studies as well. The urgency of these moral questions arises because of the simple, vexing fact that we occasionally dream of acting in "taboo" ways. We indulge in forbidden forms of sexual activity, cheat on school exams, treat other people with violent cruelty, and commit countless other violations of our waking-world moral code. In virtually every culture through history, people have pondered the questions engendered by such dreams: Where do they come from? What do they reveal about our "true" nature? Is the individual ethically responsible for them? What should the individual do, or not do, in response to them? Teachers in philosophy and religious studies can use these experientially based questions as an effective way of introducing students to different systems of ethical reasoning and moral psychology. Undergraduate students in particular are likely to be involved in emotionally complex social relationships outside the classroom, frequently giving rise to vivid dreams of romantically ambiguous and possibly taboo interactions with other people. By inviting serious, careful reflection on the general nature of dreaming, teachers can indirectly support these students as they struggle to make ethical sense of their personal lives.

Looking again to the classical origins of the Western philosophical tradition, Plato devotes several passages in the *Republic* to the moral import of dreaming. His skeptical analysis laid the basis for the next two and a half millennia of Western philosophy's ethical condemnation of dreams:

> [I]n sleep, when the rest of the soul, the rational, gentle, and dominant part, slumbers, but the beastly and savage part, replete with food and wine, gambols and, repelling sleep, endeavors to sally forth and satisfy

its own instincts. You are aware that in such case there is nothing it will
not venture to undertake as being released from all sense of shame and
all reason. It does not shrink from attempting to lie with a mother in
fancy or with anyone else, man, god, or brute. It is ready for any foul
deed of blood; it abstains from no food, and, in a word, falls short
of no extreme of folly and shamelessness. . . . . There exists in every
one of us, even in some reputed most respectable, a terrible, fierce,
and lawless brood of desires, which it seems are revealed in sleep.[11]

In this view, dreaming represents the antithesis of moral goodness. It
reveals uncivilized, animalistic desires within each person that must be strictly
controlled by the rational waking self and the laws of society. According to
Plato, the worst thing a person could do is act out in waking life the contents
of his or her dreams. Such a person would be like a political tyrant, driven by
brute instinct alone, lacking all reason and ethical self-restraint. At the same
time, Plato acknowledged that dreams *could* be a source of true knowledge and
philosophical insight if the individual lived a temperate life of controlling the
instincts and cultivating reason. Plato made it clear that he felt such individuals were rare.

Several centuries later the Christian bishop Augustine (354–430 CE) gave
Plato's idea a decisive theological twist by dismissing sexually improper dream
experiences as separate and distinct from the activity of his true eternal soul.
As he recounts in his autobiography *Confessions*, Augustine converted to Christianity at the age of 32, following many years of enthusiastic sexual activity,
including a long relationship with a mistress who bore him a child. After his
conversion Augustine pledged himself to chastity, but to his dismay he found
himself still experiencing in vivid dreams what he had pledged to deny in
waking life. Like Plato, Augustine interpreted the dreams as the expression of
something alien to his soul, outside the core of his being: "we did not actively
do what, to our regret, has somehow been done in us." Following this line of
reasoning, Augustine was able to conclude he was not morally responsible for
the contents of his dreams (although he could still be held accountable if he
dwelt on their images). Humbled by this revelation of the unruly passions that
seize control over his dreaming mind, Augustine prayed to God to help him
"extinguish the lascivious impulses of my sleep."[12] Even so, Augustine could
not completely dismiss the value of dreaming, since his mother Monica was
an avid dream visionary with an innate talent for interpretation and spiritual
discernment. Like Plato, Augustine left open in his system a tiny possibility
for meaningful, morally virtuous dreams to occur, although he did little else
to develop or encourage the idea.

Plato and Augustine are two of the mainstays of introductory courses on
Western philosophy and religious studies, making it relatively easy to bring

dream themes into those classroom discussions. These two voices are not the only ones that count, however, and we encourage teachers to present Plato's and Augustine's ideas about dreaming in a broader historical context. E. R. Dodds' *The Greeks and the Irrational* provides a good philosophical background for Plato's arguments, while Morton Kelsey's *God, Dreams, and Revelation* includes translations of several other early Christian treatises on dreaming. Neither Plato nor Augustine developed his view in a vacuum; both of them were responding to cultural dream beliefs reaching all the way back to the dawn of recorded time.

Islam has a long and rich history of dreaming, and medieval philosopher-theologians like Ibn Arabi (1164–1240) and Ibn Khaldun (1332–1402) developed the earlier teachings of Ibn Sirin (d. 728) to address the ethical concerns about improper dreams by distinguishing different types of dreams.[13] The best dreams, in this view, are those coming directly from God, clearly and without symbolic ambiguity. Such dreams appear in the *Qur'an*, the holiest and most authoritative text in Islam, and also in the *hadiths*, the sayings of the Prophet Muhammad recorded by his earliest followers. Dreams with bizarre, emotionally upsetting, and/or morally improper contents are classified as demonic by the Muslim authorities, and the individual who has such dreams is encouraged to ignore them. According to Ibn Khaldun, "confused dreams" are from Satan, because they are futile, as Satan is the source of futility. Many Muslims in the contemporary world still pay close attention to their dreams, hoping for signs of divine favor and guarding against demonic temptations. Any college or university course on Islam, or any course wanting to introduce students to important aspects of Muslim culture, can easily make use of dreams as a key topic of historical continuity from the religion's founding through its "golden age" all the way to its present-day practice.

Historically speaking, the ethical dangers of dreaming seem to be less frightening to Muslims than to Christians, with less persecution of dream-inspired heretics and more interest in the visionary insights gained through dreaming. This is a debatable point, however, and one that we encourage students to examine for themselves. Teachers may find it a useful classroom exercise to compare the dream teachings of Islam and Christianity, as a way of highlighting both their theological differences and shared historical origins. A recently published text edited by Bulkeley, Adams, and Davis, *Dreaming in Christianity and Islam: Culture, Conflict, and Creativity* provides the basic resources necessary to conduct such a comparative exercise.

Let us add a final note about the ethical questions that students may raise about their own dreams. By now we hope readers have learned to appreciate the general method we have been advocating for the safe and responsible discussion of student dreams in the classroom. When those dreams include morally troubling contents, the same basic method still applies. It encourages looking at multiple possible dimensions of meaning, and balances critical self-reflection with openness to symbols of growth and creativity. Our approach always puts the dreamer in charge of how much or how little is shared. If a student comes to a teacher feeling guilty about an immoral dream, we recommend the teacher remind the student about the wide range of possibilities disclosed in dreams, both positive and negative. Many dream theories, ancient and modern, regard nightmares as potential harbingers of insight and wisdom, so the superficial negativity of a dream does not automatically justify shunning it. On the contrary, a dream evoking such strong emotions probably has some significance to it and merits further reflection. At this point the teacher will have to make a judgment whether to continue such reflection in more detail with the student, or suggest the student talk to a friend or family member about the dream, or, if the situation seems more problematic than that, recommend the services of a therapist at the campus health center (ideally a therapist who knows something about dreams). In our experience, students rarely need professional counseling just because of a troubling dream. Much more often, the students simply want the opportunity the share the dream with someone they trust who can help them safely explore its possible meanings.

Lucid Dreaming

Lucid dreaming is the phenomenon of becoming aware during sleep that one is dreaming. It may additionally include the ability to influence and control what happens within the dream. Not everybody experiences such dreams, but many people do, particularly in childhood and adolescence. A majority of students in our dream courses have experienced lucid dreams at one time or another. The subject almost always comes up in classes on dreams, and some teachers have taught successful courses devoted specifically to lucid dreams.

The great religious traditions of Asia already mentioned—Hinduism, Buddhism, and Daoism—have reported lucid dream experiences for many centuries. In their analyses of lucid dreaming, these traditions tend to emphasize two points (which we are drastically simplifying given the space limitations of this chapter). First, lucid dreams help people realize that the creative illusion of dreaming is directly analogous to the creative illusion we call waking reality; to achieve this realization is to take one step further down the path toward greater spiritual understanding. Second, the ideal approach to dreaming is to cultivate the ability to continue one's meditation practice into the sleep state, with the result that ordinary dreams are eliminated and only pure consciousness remains. Tibetan Buddhists have preserved a strong lineage of interest in lucid dreams reaching at least as far back as the 11th-century C.E. sage Naropa. The contemporary leader of that tradition, the Dalai Lama, had this to say in *Sleeping, Dreaming, Dying*:

There is said to be a relationship between dreaming, on the one hand, and the gross and subtle levels of the body on the other. But it's also said there is such a thing as a "special dream state." In that state, the "special dream body" is created from the mind and from vital energy (known in Sanskrit as *prana*) within the body. This special dream body is able to dissociate entirely from the gross physical body and travel elsewhere. One way of developing this special dream body is first of all to recognize the dream as a dream when it occurs. Then, you find that the dream is malleable, and you make efforts to gain control over it. Gradually you become very skilled in this, increasing your ability to control the contents of the dream so that it accords to your own desires. Eventually it is possible to dissociate your dream body from your gross physical body. In contrast, in the normal dream state, dreaming occurs within the body. But as a result of specific training, the dream body can go elsewhere.[14]

The Dalai Lama's metaphysical claims may go farther than some Westerners are willing to follow, but this passage accurately expresses his tradition's views about the nature and significance of dreaming. Furthermore, the Dalai Lama is suggesting something that Western philosophers and theologians also acknowledge: The form and content of dreams can be influenced by intentions set in waking life. The technical term for such practices, *dream incubation*, refers to presleep rituals performed in special locations (e.g., a cave, shrine, mountain, forest, graveyard) with the goal of eliciting a certain kind of dream experience.[15] In theistic traditions, the sought-after dreams usually involve a beneficial appearance by a god, spirit, or ancestor. In Buddhism, incubation rituals tend to focus on enabling the individual to develop a state of consciousness beyond normal dreaming. This is the goal, at any rate. Buddhists still experience "ordinary" dreams, and they even grant such dreams a degree of value as useful diagnostic signs of the individual's current spiritual condition. But most Buddhist teachers encourage their followers to transcend regular dreaming and find a higher consciousness within the realm of dreamless sleep.

Surprisingly little interest can be found through the course of Western intellectual history in lucid dreaming and the variability of consciousness in sleep. Aristotle mentions it briefly in an obscure treatise, and Augustine once wrote a letter describing a lucid dream report he heard from someone else. One of Descartes' secret dreams involved a lucid moment in which he began interpreting what was happening while he was still dreaming. Neither Freud nor Jung talked about lucid dreaming in any depth or detail, which made it easier for the analytic philosopher Norman Malcolm to claim in the mid-20th century that lucid dreaming is impossible by definition:

If a man could assert that he is asleep, his assertion would involve a kind of self-contradiction, since from the fact that he made the assertion it would follow that it was false. If such an assertion were possible then it could sometimes be *true*. While actually asleep a man could assert that he was asleep. There is where the absurdity is located. "While asleep, he asserted that he was asleep" is as senseless as "While unconscious, he asserted that he was unconscious," or "While dead, he asserted that he was dead."[16]

Despite the seemingly contradictory logic of claiming to be conscious and self-aware while asleep, psychological research in the last few decades by Stephen LaBerge, Jayne Gackenbach, and Tracey Kahan has persuasively demonstrated that many of the cognitive faculties common in waking life can also be present and active in dreaming, including memory, volition, decision making, and self-reflection.[17] The mental qualities of dreaming turn out to much closer to the mental qualities of waking than assumed by philosophers like Malcolm. In fact, the empirical evidence from modern Western science confirms the general insight of Hinduism, Daoism, and Buddhism that the sleeping mind is capable of a variety of complex cognitive activities.

Two Courses on Lucid Dreams

Here we outline two courses that focus on lucid dreaming. The first is Fariba Bogzaran's "Lucid Dreaming" class in the Dream Studies Program at JFKU in Pleasant Hill, California. (We discuss this program in Chapter 9.) The master's level students in Bogzaran's class are provided with an interdisciplinary overview of current knowledge of lucid dreaming, ranging from world religions to neuroscience to the history of art. Bogzaran is well qualified to guide students in this kind of overview, as she has experience as a sleep laboratory technician and as a professional artist and curator of the works of the surrealist painter Gordon Onslow Ford (1912–2003). Her students often come to the class with prior knowledge of contemporary dream research (thanks to the various dream-related offerings at JFKU), enabling her to focus her pedagogical efforts on developing a dynamic classroom interaction of theoretical and experiential learning. She teaches the students several different methods of stimulating greater consciousness in sleeping and in waking, and she encourages them to study the empirical results of their self-experimentation. The students at JFKU tend to be working adults seeking greater professional development through graduate education, so Bogzaran's course includes a great deal of attention to the practical applications of lucid dreaming in nightmare treatment, problem solving, artistic inspiration, and spiritual discovery (much of which is discussed in her co-authored book *Extraordinary Dreams and How to Work with Them*). She encourages her students to experiment with various techniques of cultivating greater lucidity and self-awareness within dreaming, combining the practice of creative stimulants like dance, music, drumming, and painting with scientifically based observation and analysis of the dreaming experience results.

The second course to mention is officially a psychology course, but it freely touches on topics of philosophy and religion, with special attention to lucid dream experiences. Eleanor Rosch's "The Psychology of Dreams" is an introductory level class for undergraduates at the University of California, Berkeley. Like Bogzaran, Rosch provides her students with a multidisciplinary perspective on dreaming, ranging across the sciences and humanities. With her background in cognitive psychology and her personal experiences with meditation Rosch is able to frame the course in high-level academic terms while taking the next step of encouraging the students to reflect carefully on their own dreams in light of the different theories and interpretive methods. Rosch's particular interest in lucidity stems from her investigations of mindfulness practices in religious and secular settings. Her class finishes with a unit on dream incubation and lucidity, using teachings from Buddhist and Hindu contemplative traditions to explore the potential insights to be learned from lucid dreaming experiences. In a follow-up Psychology Department seminar Rosch teaches for a smaller number of advanced undergraduates and graduate students, she adds a dream discussion process to each class meeting as a way of illustrating the approach being studied that day. Besides helping the students learn how to apply the given approach, Rosch says she also "felt I needed to be on guard against the students encroaching on the dreamer's personal space more than (s)he was offering, though that paranoia proved largely unnecessary as the students soon appeared to meld themselves into a gently interested and sympathetic group that understood this to be a class not a therapy session and was naturally respectful of boundaries."[18]

Whether or not a class focuses on lucid dreaming, the topic is likely to come up at some point, so teachers are well advised to be prepared to make the most of the discussion. Perhaps the most important point to make, beyond simply acknowledging the reality of lucid dreaming, is that dream awareness does not necessarily require dream control. A person can be aware and conscious within a dream state without trying to manipulate what's happening in the dream. Buddhist and Hindu teachers, along with many contemporary psychologists, emphasize the value of heightened awareness in dreams and caution against the intrusion of ego-oriented desires from the waking world, which ironically can reduce the dream's potential meaningfulness. The temptation to use lucid dreaming as nothing more than a private video game will be strong for many students from contemporary Western society, and thus the challenge for teachers is to enable the students to appreciate the greater discoveries to be made once ego control is suspended and the dreaming imagination is allowed to unfold of its own accord.

Two Courses on Dreams and World Religions

We close with a discussion of two classes that take dreaming as a topic in the comparative study of the world's religious and spiritual traditions. Whereas other courses described in this chapter and elsewhere in the book have referred to particular religious texts or teachings, these two courses aim to evaluate dreaming within the broad scope of human religious history, using the latest methods of comparative religious research to guide the process. Both are graduate level courses for academic and ministerial students. Here is the catalog description of Kimberley Patton's "Dreams and the Dreaming" course at HDS:

> The course will consider the religious role of the dream as initiatory experience, metaphor for aboriginal time, gateway to the other world, venue for the divine guide, healing event, "royal road" to the unconscious, occasion for quest or journey, epistemological paradox, and prophetic harbinger of the personal or collective future. Theories of dreams, the history of dream interpretation, and the relationship of dreams to both myth and ritual will be examined cross-culturally. The course will also evaluate current research in the psychology and neurobiology of dreams with respect to relevance for the theological and spiritual dimensions of human dreaming.

Next is this description of Patricia M. Davis' "Dreaming in the World's Religions," which she taught at the GTU in Berkeley, California:

> Dreams have served the world's religions as a powerful source of revelation, guidance, and healing. We will explore the dream teachings of many religious traditions including Christianity, Islam, Judaism and Buddhism. Topics will include the types of dreams people experience, interpretation strategies, and incubation practices. We will cover research on dreams from history, theology, psychology and neuroscience and discuss the practical implications for pastoral care, spiritual direction and other forms of care giving.

Davis' GTU class had a somewhat higher proportion of students preparing for ministerial and chaplaincy work, and thus her class included more emphasis on connections with pastoral psychology and counselling. Patton's HDS course focused in greater depth on particular themes in comparative religion (e.g., healing, ritual, visions, exegesis), which was appropriate given her expertise in this field[19] and the higher proportion of students from other academic (non-ministerial) programs.

Davis, a doctoral student with a Newhall Award teaching fellowship, taught her course with two faculty mentors, Kelly Bulkeley and pastoral psychologist Lewis Rambo. The class met once a week for 3 hours, which Davis divided into a two sections, the first devoted to discussion of the readings (led by Davis) and the second to practical work with group dream sharing (led by Bulkeley). This team-teaching approach worked well, giving students the chance to hear more than one perspective and allowing the teachers to pace themselves better during the long class. Patton's students gathered once a week for a 2-hour lecture, and then met in small groups with a teaching assistant for 1 hour per week.

Both courses covered the major religions of the world (e.g., Christianity, Islam, Hinduism, Buddhism) as well as indigenous traditions (e.g., Australian Aborigines, Native Americans); both emphasized Jungian psychological ideas (Patton through a classroom visit from Jungian analyst Robert Bosnak, Davis and Bulkeley by using Jung's *Children's Dreams* to frame the classroom dream sharing); and both included references to current scientific research on sleep and dreaming.

Of course it is impossible to give adequate attention to all the world's religions in the space of a single course, so teachers have to make choices about what they can and cannot cover in the time available. Even though the HDS and GTU courses made effective use of Jungian psychology, this is not the only theory to use in bridging dream research and religious studies (nor should Jung's ideas be used in a simplistic or doctrinaire fashion). We encourage teachers in religious studies to examine a wide range of psychological perspectives and develop new ways of testing their adequacy in accounting for the cross-cultural patterns of religiously significant dreams.

A Final Word about Dreams and the Paranormal

Precognition. Telepathy. Clairvoyance. Ghostly visitations. Synchronicity. Déjà vu. For ages these topics have prompted controversy over the nature and legitimacy of dreams. Throughout history and into the present day people have reported dreams that seemed to predict something that later happened, or that perceived something happening in a distant location, or that brought a visit from the "spirit" of someone who is dead in waking life. In modern times, such phenomena are the main flashpoints in a debate over the scientific legitimacy of dream research—or, phrased differently, over the limits of what conventional science can tell us about dreams. Our experience is that any classroom discussion of dreaming, on whatever topic, has the potential to lead into the area of paranormal occurrences. Students clearly have a lively interest in considering possible explanations for these kinds of dreams. A discussion of different points of view can stay within the bounds of valid academic discourse as long as the teacher helps the students concentrate on issues of evidence, analysis, and theory building.

Philosophy and religious studies are appropriate disciplines to guide the study of these phenomena for at least two reasons. First, they bring a historical awareness to the analysis and evaluation of paranormal dream experiences. Without that wider lens, the recurrent patterns in those experiences cannot be identified as easily, making a general analysis more problematic. Second, philosophy and religious studies are centrally concerned with precisely the kinds of questions about reality, the soul, and the power of the human mind that are raised by paranormal dreaming. Religious studies scholars like William G. Barnard, Jeffrey K. Kripal, and William Parsons have written extensively about paranormal phenomena and their relations to classic religious experiences on the one hand and intensified psychological functioning on the other.[20] These scholars share the general thesis that paranormal experiences are more widespread and more influential in shaping people's religious/spiritual/philosophical worldviews than is generally recognized by mainstream academics. We recommend their works as a resource for educators who want to explore in greater depth the significance of paranormal phenomena for the study of dreams.

Even if a teacher does not want to delve into such topics, the students may spontaneously raise them anyway. At a minimum, then, educators should prepare themselves for likelihood that these kinds of questions will arise at some point. It might seem easiest and most academically respectable to tell the students, "We simply will not discuss such matters in this course," or something to that effect. However, considerable risks come with the "Just say no" response, including the danger of shutting down student interest, imposing unexplained boundaries on class discussion, and modelling an uncritical acceptance of the intellectual status quo.

We believe a better approach takes advantage of questions about paranormal dreaming to open up a broader conversation about philosophical and religious views of human nature in relation to current psychological research. Ideally, this conversation will allow the consideration of several points of view, including hard-nosed scepticism and creative speculation.[21] As long as the teacher reminds the students to back up their assertions with sound evidence and thoughtful analysis, an unexpected classroom digression into questions about paranormal dreaming actually can strengthen the overall mission of the course.

Chapter 6

General Humanities

Any instructor in the humanities who develops an interest in teaching a course on dreams and dreaming has the same initial conceptual hurdle to leap: Aren't dreams by their nature within the province of the psychology department? If we have questions about the origin and functions of dreams, aren't they addressed by empirical observation and by psychological theory? Aren't our quandaries about dreams really about matters that can be decided not by examining poems or theorizing about imagination, but only by scientific inquiry? If we want to know what dreams really are, why not just ask a psychologist? (And even at that, as the psychology department itself may chime in at this point: Isn't this topic, starting from radically subjective, insubstantial experience, just a little *flaky*, anyway?)

For potential instructors, these questions may come from administrators, academic advisors, students, and most importantly (and we hope productively) from within. In truth, there aren't at present a lot of humanities courses devoted to the topic of dreaming, or even making much use of it. By far the majority of dream studies courses are offered in psychology departments (including many multidisciplinary surveys of the topic, providing cultural context as well as psychological theory, as noted in Chapter 3). But the larger question is: Do the humanities offer distinctive resources and methods of study that can make a genuine contribution to our understanding of dreaming?

From this question proceed two others, which will occupy our attention in this chapter. First, can the study of dreams and dreaming offer new perspectives and ideas in the study of the humanities? Second, beyond the vast array of questions about dreaming that can be legitimately investigated through humanities scholarship, what can the study of dreaming bring to our actual pedagogy? What can we *do* with a course on dreams?

The humanities are defined according to the objects and methods of the natural study, in contrast to those of the natural and social sciences and practical arts. The subject of the disciplines of the humanities comprises all aspects of what it means to be human, or what we consider fundamental to the human condition. Thus one of the humanities' key concerns must always be to inquire what is given to humans as their natural and universal endowment, and what is particular to a specific culture, period, or socioeconomic system. What we really study in humanities courses is not just texts and objects, but the dynamic response of humans and their institutions to circumstances and historical change. These cultural institutions include: literature and the fine and performing arts (i.e., all visual art, music, dance, theater, film and the new electronic and digital media); languages; philosophy and religious beliefs; law; and politics. In practice, study may be either specific to one culture area or cross-cultural

For example, in most humanities fields, acquaintance with the range of human culture is usually undertaken in area- or society-specific courses (such as American Literature, or Roots of The French Revolution), whereas wider perspectives are the basis for comparative study and theory courses of a defined field such as poetry, or the nature of the State. A relatively recent development is the introduction of "area studies," which allows cross-disciplinary concentration on in-depth knowledge of a world region or cultural tradition. Equally significant is cultural studies, which constitutes more an approach than a field of study. Cultural studies began in Great Britain as a movement to integrate progressive politics into academic scholarship and pedagogy, and thus investigate all manifestations of ideology—the cultural system that supports or critiques existing power relations, especially along lines of class, race, and gender. An area-studies approach to dreaming, then, examines cultural patterns of dreaming and interpretation in relation to social structures, beliefs, and the arts, within one culture area; while cultural studies considers how dream practices reflect power relations in a society. Together, these curricular paths suggest the direction of many robust programs and departments that have promoted interdisciplinary humanities study by consolidating diverse constituencies and interests. In contemporary Women's and Gender Studies, departments of African-American, Native-American, and Asian-American studies, and programs in Peace Studies, Environmental Studies, and Disability Studies, we see a turn to the preparation of students to use all resources of the university, to understand and ultimately affect the world according to their own affinities, commitment, and passion. In practical terms, much depends on how a particular institution of learning aligns its departments to make best use of its resources, and on decisions about the place of the humanities in distribution requirements or in a core curriculum.

For all the urgent issues that genuinely interdisciplinary education seeks to address, it also inevitably lessens curricular emphasis on the second traditional goal of program in the humanities: extended and rigorous training in the methodologies specific to a particular discipline such as philosophy or art history. Defining a field according to its object of study opens up opportunities for thinking outside of traditional boundaries, especially in areas such as ethnic or gender identity that can benefit from constantly refreshing ideas to suit—and shape—new realities. But educators owe it to students, and to their fields of study, to maintain the intellectual integrity of their methods even as they rethink and revise them to apply in new contexts. It is for this very reason that humanities study has traditionally occupied so prominent a position in undergraduate core curricula and requirements. We propose that it is in this area that interdisciplinary humanities study of dreaming can serve general education with extraordinary effectiveness—by guiding students' personal enthusiasm for an absorbing topic into examination of central issues in critical inquiry across the fields of the humanities.

The institutionalized requirement that future doctors, civil engineers, and digital-media designers devote a certain part of their study to considering the human condition proceeds from a long-established belief that formal education can help all our students achieve the fullest realization of their individual potential. With this goal, an educational emphasis on career preparation is perfectly reasonable—but so are the development of personal values, and commitment to forming a community of informed citizens. The means to these ends (as we often find ourselves arguing to students at the beginning of a semester) are the defining methods of study in the humanities.

Humanities disciplines do not offer training in the empirical research or statistical methods of the physical and social sciences, or in the skills and techniques of the fine and practical arts. They acquaint students more deeply and richly with the culture in which they live, so that they may better contribute to it; and with other times, places, and conditions, so that they may develop new perspectives. The humanities receive curricular emphasis particularly because so much of the getting of knowledge of any kind derives from mastery by students of basic skills in critical analysis of texts and other cultural products, and in presentation of their own responses in coherent, developed writing. Critical thinking means asking questions that take arguments apart, uncover hidden assumptions and pursue implications, and further define key terms. It also means developing creative but valid interpretations, in discussion with peers, or alone in a dorm room late at night. It means engaging fully with texts and their writers and with other cultural artifacts and their producers, with a commitment to intellectual honesty, across distances of time and worldview.

The study of dreams and dreaming seems ideally suited to these aims. A humanities course on dreaming will require students to consider how knowledge lives and breathes, and what it feeds on, by virtue of the dream's traditional status as an impossible object. "What is harder to capture than a dream?" nearly every culture, and practically every poet, has asked. To the extent that the dream has always called the very possibility of knowledge into question, it demonstrates the urgent value of defining what we can and cannot validly conclude about life, culture and the cosmos. As we have heard from Jason Tougaw in Chapter 2, dream study can demonstrate to students how different disciplines theorize their valid range of inquiry and form theses about humanity and its arts and history. For example, students must consider carefully what inferences they may draw from their reading on sleep and dreaming without serious training in the sciences. They can critically examine relevant texts and other evidence of all kinds, including works of psychological theory. Even without firsthand experience of sleep-lab study, or quantitative data analyses, they can develop a respect for scientific method, and learn from scientific findings about a biologically based, universal human phenomenon that, although it is marginalized in almost every field of academic study, occupies us for a good part of every night of our lives.

As has been emphasized in previous chapters, we also advocate directing students' attention to their own experience as dreamers because it adds an experiential dimension to their awareness of the subject, and against some prevailing prejudices, validates dreaming as an object of study. In the humanities course, the methodological justification for this approach is that it can enhance crucial skills in understanding the cultural dimensions of dreaming (including the growth of dream studies and theories of dreaming themselves). This model is proposed as "oneirocriticism" by Carol Schreier Rupprecht and Kelly Bulkeley in "Reading Yourself to Sleep: Dreams in/and/as Texts," their introduction to Rupprecht's *The Dream and the Text*, a key collection of essays on the dream in literature and literary theory.[1] Rupprecht and Bulkeley identify oneirocriticism as a practice of study, interpretation, and hypothesis continuous with traditions of dream study predating modern psychology, combining established means of exploring dreams with critical insights from dreams themselves. Examining their own dreams simultaneously with cultural traditions, students develop standards for validity in interpretation, while forming original views that bear the traces of their own original dreaming. Dreaming is thus both the subject/object of inquiry itself and significantly part of the process by which inquiry proceeds. A general humanities course on dreaming can balance emphases on the experience of the individual student and that of humanity in all times and places, as context for study of the variations introduced by different cultural patterns, social interests, media of transmission of ideas, and disciplinary perspectives.

Humanities scholars will be well aware of the potential for dream-related seminar courses with specialized topics that can enrich the advanced student's experience and provide the instructor with collaborators in new research. For example, Marjorie Garber has demonstrated that analysis of Shakespeare's use of dreams and ideas about dreaming in *Romeo and Juliet*, *A Midsummer Night's Dream*, and *Richard III* not only reinforces an understanding of the playwright's tremendous debt to Ovid, but also invites us to question modern dream theories' relative lack of interest in metamorphosis in dreams.[2] In *Dreaming the English Renaissance*, Carole Levin has offered insight into the world of James

I through consideration of dream interpretation, dream therapies, and dream diaries, in a study that might serve as a model of dream historiography.[3] A classics course on dreams and divination in the ancient world can transform a student's understanding of daily life and fundamental beliefs in Mesopotamia or Julius Caesar's Rome.

The dream is a particular focus of interest in Romantic thought and 19th-century European and American literature, providing a huge wealth of possible topics and objects of study. The celebrated dream visions of E.T.A. Hoffmann and Gérard de Nerval, culturally distinct as they are, contribute to the Romantic idea of the capacity of imagination to transform the world, and are thus key progenitors, just as much as the aesthetic theory of Kant or Hegel, of the modern cultural prestige of art. The narrative of Jan Potocki's astounding *Manuscript Found at Saragossa* prefigures much of contemporary fantasy literature by presenting the dream as a space where not only the personal past and present, but also the modern and historical cultural influences of Europe meet. Beyond Romanticism, the mutual influence of Surrealism and psychoanalytic theory of the dream—particularly as they reciprocally enhance each other's position in the history of both academic discourse and popular culture in the 20th century—provides an exemplary topic for specialized study in art history, literature, social history, or philosophy.

These instances suggest that although dream-related topics courses in many specialized fields of study need not lie beyond the reach of the nonspecialist student, the pedagogical foundation for dream studies is in the interdisciplinary general humanities course, which can present a variety of topics as units of extended study. Properly conceived, the general course invites students to consider study in the humanities as a model for integrating knowledge drawn from a variety of different fields with lifelong introspective inquiry—to study the human condition without neglecting to look within.

Such a course does well to direct students' attention to their own experience of dreaming by asking them to identify the questions—about dreaming as such as well as their own dreams—which they would like to have answered. Their first questions are likely to raise just the issues that have defined the field for decades, if not centuries. The class can grasp easily that these questions cannot be answered by the methods of the physical or social sciences, and quickly brainstorm how humanities study can set them on a path of investigation and contemplation.

1. What is dream experience? Is it a mental event? Is it meaningful? Is it a message, something like a thought, or a random collection of images and sensations?

2. How can dream experiences be comprehended and communicated? Is the dream account "the dream"? Can we understand another

person's dream? Our own? What does "understanding a dream" mean? What constitutes an interpretation?

3. What is the relation of dreaming to the capacity of imagination in the broadest sense—that is, the ability to form symbolic images and projected scenarios of events? Are dreams the primal form of creativity? What does it mean to call part of the mind "unconscious" and "irrational"?

4. How does the culture we live in determine what we make of our dreams?

These four topics define the parameters of an oneirocriticism that pursues the path we have suggested for dream studies in the humanities: from (a) the dream experience to (b) the sharing of dreams in whatever form to (c) the universal capacity to dream to (d) cultural influences, significance, and values relevant to dreams and dreaming.

It is then not hard to demonstrate for students that each of these questions invites exploration through the traditional humanities methods of serious reading, critical analysis, and persuasive writing based on relevant evidence. Instructors may proceed to point out that scholarship in the humanities is often grounded in research derived from other fields, citing instances such as the value of psycholinguistics or cognitive studies in understanding literature, or economics as a factor in interpreting history. Topics raised by studies in dreaming may help the class to comprehend some key issues raised by a variety of disciplines, and to learn more about their characteristic methods of identifying and investigating problems. For example, in Chapter 3, we have alluded to the importance of distinguishing between a theory of dream interpretation and a theory of the origin and function of dreams, as psychology defines these issues. Students in a humanities course on dreams should master contemporary accounts of the activity of the brain during dreaming well enough to consider the pros and cons of the argument that rapid eye movement (REM) sleep equals dreaming, and to appreciate the significance of the distinction between brain and mind. In Chapters 4 and 5, we proposed the value of cross-cultural study of the relation of dreaming to fundamental conceptions of the spirit, spiritual beings, and other planes of existence, and revisited the historical importance of dreaming in philosophical study of epistemology and ontology.

This survey approach not only defines major areas of inquiry in dream studies generally, it also invites students to scrutinize how they learn what they learn: What are the foundations and limitations for the growth of knowledge? It presents the basis for validity in interdisciplinary study as a matter of balance between exploration of the common aims and objects of different disciplines and an indispensable awareness of their respective limits. The great variety of perspectives and approaches in the study of the phenomenon of dreaming drives home the point that every branch of knowledge has its own history that should be critically examined. Although this may seem a commonplace in the teaching of the history of ideas, it's a position associated especially with the French theorist and cultural historian Michel Foucault, particularly as discussed in his *The Order of Things*.[3] An especially trenchant example has already been cited in Chapter 4. The reception in the United States of Kilton Stewart's essay, "Dream Theory in Malaya," serves not only as a lesson in anthropology but also a means of raising serious questions about Western images of indigenous peoples, as well as the assumptions built into our frequent pedagogical separation of Western from non-Western traditions.

A general humanities course may benefit students by exemplifying the characteristic methods and respective reach of varied disciplines of study. However, it need not make this its consistent, self-conscious pedagogical focus. Equally important is the oneirocritical approach advocated by Rupprecht and Bulkeley, framing students' experience with the dream journal and dream sharing as a dialogue with others who have also explored dreams and dreaming.[4] (This is what Richard M. Jones, as cited in Chapter 2, called a "dialectical dream seminar" emphasizing continuity between students' own writing and their assigned readings.) When students feel engaged in conversation with other dreamers from a broad range of cultures, periods, and traditions of thought, they can better understand themselves, their society, and humanity, in the best traditions of thinkers through the ages.

In a general humanities course in which all participants are investigating their own dream lives, literary works can set the terms for the understanding of dream experience as seriously as any theory, as well as suggesting how students may themselves respond thoughtfully and creatively to dreams. The instructor need not have an advanced background in literary study to guide students through exemplary readings of texts that invoke, contemplate, or derive from dreams. Samuel Taylor Coleridge's 1816 poem "The Pains of Sleep" may provide one good example, out of dozens that might be chosen, of the value of analyzing literary texts as both evidence of the nature of dream experience, and the imaginative equivalent of inquiry, hypothesis, and the formation of theory. The poet famously describes his experience of nightmares:

> Desire with loathing strangely mixed
> On wild or hateful objects fixed . . .
> Deeds to be hid which were not hid,
> Which all confused I could not know
> Whether I suffered or I did . . .

as well as his response on waking:

Such punishments, I said, were due
To natures deepliest stained with sin,—
For aye entempesting anew
The unfathomable hell within,
The horror of their deeds to view,
To know and loathe, yet wish and do!
Such griefs with such men well agree,
But wherefore, wherefore fall on me?[5]

Every class will find different points to emphasize in this text. The general value, however, derives from Coleridge's articulation of genuine or feigned puzzlement in the presence of his own terrifying dreams: even the repetitions and rhythms express frustration while hinting at a disturbing subliminal awareness that dream images are, after all, always a product of one's own mind. When we consider that Coleridge was a prolific and influential commentator on the human mind as well as a poet, his personal testimony to his confusion, his attempt to sort out the situation through measured writing, and the problems of interpretation posed by his poem demonstrate how complex the lessons of a literary text may be. They can also motivate us in the attempt to understand our own dream experience through intensive study of the topic of dreaming.[6]

Through literary study, students may appreciate how the conventions of rhetoric and figurative language can transform the profoundly subjective and personal experience of a dream into a contribution to an understanding of ourselves, our social relations, and our systems of belief. For example, Shakespeare and Milton both exploit the paradox of seeing truly only in the darkness of dreams in celebrated sonnets. Shakespeare's love sonnet is playful, practically seductive. It makes of sleep a refuge and a harbinger of greater pleasures to come in the waking world:

William Shakespeare: Sonnet 43

When most I wink, then do mine eyes best see,
For all the day they view things unrespected;
But when I sleep, in dreams they look on thee,
And darkly bright, are bright in dark directed.
Then thou, whose shadow shadows doth make bright,
How would thy shadow's form, form happy show
To the clear day with thy much clearer light,
When to unseeing eyes thy shade shines so!
How would, I say, mine eyes be blessèd made,
By looking on thee in the living day,
When in dead night thy fair imperfect shade

Through heavy sleep on sightless eyes doth stay!
    All days are nights to see till I see thee,
    And nights bright days when dreams do show thee me.[7]

By contrast, Milton makes the sonnet into an elegiac form. His own blindness to outward forms, of course, is not a mere contingency of sleep, but the permanent and emblematic condition of his being in the waking world as well. The pleasures of dreaming are a bittersweet illusion. The inversion of night and day, sleeping and waking, blindness and sight, serves as a reminder that human existence is founded on a loss that can only be restored through salvation and grace:

John Milton: Sonnet 23

Methought I saw my late espoused saint
    Brought to me, like Alcestis, from the grave,
    Whom Jove's great son to her glad husband gave,
    Rescu'd from death by force, though pale and faint.
Mine, as whom wash'd from spot of child-bed taint
    Purification in the old Law did save,
    And such as yet once more I trust to have
    Full sight of her in Heaven without restraint,
Came vested all in white, pure as her mind;
    Her face was veil'd, yet to my fancied sight
    Love, sweetness, goodness, in her person shin'd
So clear as in no face with more delight.
    But Oh! as to embrace me she inclin'd,
    I wak'd, she fled, and day brought back my night.[8]

As different as they may be, Shakespeare's and Milton's poems share something significant with Coleridge's that may ultimately help students appreciate the importance of understanding dreaming in a social and cultural context: the theme of the dreamer seeing a world at odds with waking life, and struggling to reconcile the two through relation to beloved others. The sharing of the dream, with all its paradoxes, may be presented as a means toward unifying a split existence. We present classic and often studied poems in this example to emphasize the point that considering their evident relation to dreaming may refresh their meaning for both teacher and student. The individual instructor may think of many other examples in historical and modern poetry.

Just to affirm the value of occasionally proceeding from the sublime to the ridiculous in the classroom, let us suggest that the same fundamental theme may be introduced to students through some examples in a comic and ironic mode.

These may provide models for the serious analysis of popular culture, and of paraliterary forms such as the comic strip. A particularly fascinating example of the sustained exploration of the phenomenological quandary of the dream is Winsor McCay's justly celebrated graphic series, *Dreams of the Rarebit Fiend*, originally published from 1904 to 1913.[9] In each sequence, a fantasy we would now identify as "surreal" plays out in the metamorphosis of common objects, images of transformed or threatened identity, the terrible consequences of wishes that come true, and other familiar dream themes. Just as in Shakespeare's and Milton's dream sonnets, the dreamer awakes, seeking to find a meaning for the visions of the night in the shared waking world—in this case by blaming it all on eating toasted cheese before bedtime! The most significant result of presenting McCay's cartoons for classroom discussion is that, even before invoking theories that attribute dream content to infantile wishes or divine inspiration, students' careful observation of these dream scenes may inspire them to identify common themes and symbolic forms from their own analysis.

Another very helpful as well as entertaining document is the Warner Bros. Studio 1946 cartoon *The Big Snooze*.[10] As Bugs Bunny follows Elmer Fudd into his at-first sweet dream *("West and wewaxation at wast!")*, he torments him as in all their adventures, but this time with all the resources of the nightmare: Elmer is paralyzed, pursued, denuded, and cross-dressed, finally falling from a great height back into the waking world, which he now accepts as preferable to the immersion in private but uncontrollable fantasy. *The Big Snooze* offers students a compendium of common dream features, which leads them to consider possible universals in the phenomenology of the dream, inviting a search for a theory: Why do so many dreamers find themselves in similar situations—especially ones we rarely encounter in waking life? In a cartoon, we might take these as symbolically expressing the character's situation of crisis. Is it possible that this applies to our own dreams as well? The purpose of the focus on the nightmare in both these comic examples could as well be served by other instances from any of the arts, depicting compelling dream visions that seem to insist on some response to aid in the dreamer's return to the waking world. This response—nothing other than the fundamental impulse to ask, "What did my dream *mean*?"—can serve as a model for how we come to ask our own questions about dreaming and the interpretation of dreams. (The study of cinema offers so many outstanding examples and theoretical issues relevant to dream studies that we devote Chapter 7 to a separate discussion of the topic.)

Our examples here have come from literary texts, but the same themes and principles apply in art-historical study. For example, dreaming is at least as relevant a topic in studies of the visual art of Romanticism or Surrealism art as of their poetry and prose. Aside from celebrated examples such as Albrecht Dürer and William Blake, we have no way of knowing how many artworks through the ages were directly inspired by dreams. Among modern artists, Jean Arp, Salvador Dalí, Frida Kahlo, Marc Chagall, Wassily Kandinsky, Odilon Redon, Jasper Johns, and Paul Klee are especially well known for work that draws on their dreams or aims to replicate the feel of a dream, as are the contemporary artists Jonathan Borofsky, Laurie Anderson, Francesco Clemente, Marcel Dzama, and Bill Viola, among others. Lynn Gamwell presents a large archive of instances along with essays useful for introducing students to the topic of dream art in *Dreams 1900–2000: Science, Art, and the Unconscious Mind.*[11] Dreams have certainly inspired works in other arts, such as the performing arts of dance and music, and there dream visions appear as a theme in music and dance, but it is difficult to see just how they might be used pedagogically in teaching the theory and history of those forms. We acknowledge that it must fall to someone deeply experienced in music or dance, as practitioner or theorist, to explain how dreaming can be introduced into instruction in those fields. So far we have encountered no syllabi or articles that provide models. We may note that conspicuous instances, such as the dream ballets of American musical theater, or the *Symphonie Fantastique* of Hector Berlioz, suggest that in dance and music, the dream is primarily a device for shifting the audience's expectations from narrative realism to fantasy, which allows for variation of style, mood, and focus. For example, Berlioz' *Symphonie* uses the fiction of a reverie to justify an expressionistic wildness into a definitively Romantic musical piece. The celebrated dream ballets of *Oklahoma!* and *West Side Story* both allow the central characters to express through stylized, lyrical movement emotions that are repressed in their ordinary lives. One also hears anecdotal evidence of musicians and dancers who attempt to incubate lucid dreams that will allow them to practice their technique at an unconscious level.

In fact, given the traditional interest in dreams among artists in all media, it is not surprising if the most relevant models for dream studies straddle the line between theoretical study and artistic practice. In Chapter 2 we discussed approaches to writing instruction that integrate training in research, the expository essay, and expressive writing with a dream group, and considered how such an approach can be extended to the new media of education such as digital video, blogging, and Web site construction. The outstanding example on record of a similar approach in instruction in the visual arts has been Bogzaran's course "Dreams, Art and the Inner Worlds" in the Dream Studies Program at JFKU (discussed in Chapter 9). Like many classes in American studio art programs, Bogzaran's course emphasized concepts over instruction in technique; like many innovative art-history courses, it also required students to undertake practical exercises in art-making to explore their own sources of creativity. Course units on dream incubation and lucidity challenged students to extend the range of what is generally considered artistic practice, and introduction to the Surrealists' theory of psychic automatism and to contemporary performance pieces required then to rethink their own notions of the limits of art. Ideally, the contemporary classroom can accommodate a very broad range of interdisciplinary practices as long as they serve the course goals set by the instructor. Here we have briefly argued only that developing an appreciation for what poets and artists do is as important to dream studies as understanding what psychologists and philosophers do. However, in addition to drawing on dream accounts from historical sources and participants' own experience as well as dream scenes from literature and the other arts, the general humanities course on dreams may significantly address fundamental theoretical issues in the study of mind, the arts, and culture. Freud's view of dreams, for example, may be presented through textual analysis of *The Interpretation of Dreams*, on the one hand as one of the germinal texts of modern thought, and on the other, an autobiography achieved through the disguised confession of one writer's dreams as a key to his own crucial life themes. (The length and complexity of the book will almost certainly dictate presentation of selected passages.) A critical understanding of Freud may begin with a consideration of the validity of his pronouncements on dreams in the light of later discoveries and theories, and proceed to the development of a broad cultural perspective on the enormous influence of psychoanalytic culture upon the modern era. Freud inspired artists from Bloomsbury to the Surrealists, modern ideas about family, women, religion, and sexuality, and 20th-century movements to make a political goal of liberation from psychological repression.[12] To emphasize that all this began with one person's experiment in keeping a dream journal provides a dramatic point of departure for students engaged in the same humble activity. Instructors may apply similar textual and biographical approaches equally to Jung and other theorists, without diminishing students' responsibility to consider the arguments of important psychologists on their own merits.

Indeed, one of the great benefits of introducing dreaming into humanities courses is the opportunity to explore dream psychology as a source for the general theories of mind and culture so influential in humanities study. Freud's theory of dreams is acknowledged by contemporary psychologists for its historical importance but rendered somewhat marginal, if not actually invalidated, by a century of research since its first appearance. In humanities scholarship, however, *The Interpretation of Dreams* initiated a thorough transformation of ideas about culture through placing concepts such as repression, the personal unconscious, and the sexual etiology of neuroses, at the very center of modern thought. To study the psychoanalytic view of dreaming is not only to master a key theory, but also to gain entry to a perspective on mind, signification, and culture that remains influential in the humanities to this day. Similarly, when Jung is introduced through dreams—looking for evidence of the thesis of archetypes and the collective unconscious—his reinterpretation of myth and religious ideas and its influence on 20th-century culture are rendered accessible to students through direct contact with examples.

In humanities courses on dreaming, we can further broaden students' perspectives by looking not only to the historical influence of the classic theorists,
but also to the potential of the contemporary psychology of dreaming to help
us better understand culture and society. Ernest Hartmann's view that dreaming represents the spontaneous figuration of emotional responses in the form
of metaphors invites comparison to the emphasis on metaphorical thought in
the linguistic philosophy of George Lakoff and the deconstructive criticism of
Jacques Derrida, both of which have had far-reaching influence in humanities
study.[13] A basic acquaintance with the neurobiology of dreaming, or with content
analysis (as discussed in Chapter 3) may fundamentally shift students' view of
the study of culture in relation to universal biological endowment or statistical
models. Students with little previous background in the sciences may be inspired
to apply perspectives from cognitive psychology to the study of literature and
the arts.[14] Even J. Allan Hobson's activation-synthesis model, which may appear
to suggest that dream content is random and to render dreams meaningless
as an object of study, may provoke new ideas. In *The Dream Frontier*, Mark
Blechner has suggested that Hobson's model does not necessitate such an extreme
conclusion. Meaning in dreams may be construed as a process, flowing from
the generation of dream imagery (whether random or not) to introspection,
to transactions with others.[15] This conception fits in nicely with a prominent
view in contemporary criticism of literature and the arts that locates meaning
in the realization of artworks in acts of communication involving both artist
and audience. Like Hartmann, Blechner also maintains that it is the very hyperassociativity of images in dreaming—resulting in bizarre content—that gives them
unique value. This insight may serve as a context for understanding Surrealism's
aesthetic of the dream. Although it's true that Surrealist artists like Salvador
Dalí are known for painting dream imagery, the Surrealists' experimentation
with generating poetry and visual art through random processes as a means
of breaking conceptual bonds in order to reveal new possibilities of meaning,
seems remarkably relevant to Blechner's response to Hobson.

Because dream interpretation is historically important (and culturally
celebrated) as a turning point in the development of modern psychology, it
is not surprising that scholars in the humanities have turned to psychological
approaches to dream interpretation for guidance in understanding culture and
the arts. In fact, countless critical essays on literature and the arts have applied
the dream-interpretation practices of either Freud or Jung directly to artworks
without pausing to justify doing so by explaining how art is like dreaming.
This leap cannot be justified, but it springs from an important modern insight:
However much the reception of art depends on the perception of form, defining conventions, standards of taste, or cultural authority, some large part of the
value of art resides in its expression of themes and images from the unconscious
mind (personal or collective) and the resonance of these themes for the audience.

Students may thus appreciate that artworks that represent dreams are especially fitting subjects for the application of psychoanalytic theories of literature and art.

The scope of serious questions about the nature of the dream also has been enlarged by applying concepts from rhetoric and the modern discipline of semiotics. (Both seek to establish principles for the analysis of discourse, but since ancient times, rhetoric has traditionally focused on oratory and literary texts, while semiotics sets out to look at all forms of communication, in all media and social contexts, as signifying acts.) In *The Rhetoric of Dreams* and *Dreaming and Storytelling*, Bert O. States uses concepts from rhetoric such as metaphor, metonymy, synecdoche, and irony to cut through some common conceptual confusion about how dreams signify. States characterizes dreaming as a mode of thought that is the precondition for symbolism and figurative language.[16] In "The Dream as Text, The Dream as Narrative," Patricia Kilroe asks what it means to consider the dream as a text (explaining that in semiotics, the term "*text*" is used to denote any act of communication occurring within a code).[17] She extends States' theory by proposing that dreams may be considered not only a proto-rhetorical system but proto-narrative. Dreams are not a failed form of story, deficient compared with the well-shaped stories we tell of real events in the waking state, but a precondition for our structuring stories in our minds at all. Cyd C. Ropp, in "A Hermeneutic and a Rhetoric of Dreams," attempts to re-interpret the interpretation of dreams in the ancient world and modern psychology by applying States' ideas to them.[18] These discussions of the dream as text and proto-rhetoric decidedly are not geared toward the undergraduate generalist, but may be useful background for the instructor to emphasize the relevance of dream interpretation to all other sorts of textual interpretation. They can serve as the theoretical foundation for the relation of the inner world of dream experience to the outer world of dream discourses—in dream reports, dream literature and cultural practices, and dream theories.[19] By proposing more permeable borders around dream and story, they may provide the instructor with a fresh approach, for example, to literary works that turn on transformation between worlds of waking and dream, such as Shakespeare's *A Midsummer Night's Dream*, Calderón de la Barca's *La vida es sueño* (*Life is a Dream*), or Arthur Schnitzler's *Dream Story.*

Instructors may also borrow from rhetorical tradition in organizing course materials—which can be a challenge in a general dream studies course that presents students with ideas and instances drawn from such diverse sources as literature, visual art, film, psychology, anthropology, philosophy, and the history of ideas. In surveying the vast literature on dreaming while naturally gravitating toward their own strengths and interests, instructors may organize according to what rhetorical analysis would call topoi or motifs: recurring themes common to beliefs about dreams as well as to their depiction in literature and art. Identifying some conventions in the characterization of dreams may offer the advantage of facilitating cross-cultural study by setting aside some of the assumptions often made about Western versus non-Western—or indigenous versus industrialized, or ancient versus modern—societies. We offer here as examples six key themes that Welt uses in his classes to focus discussion on universals as well as cultural differences in the cultural expression of dreaming.

Theme 1: Dreams Constitute a "Place" One Goes to While Sleeping, or From Which Visitors May Come

Examples range from Lewis Carroll's *Through the Looking-Glass* and the 1939 film of *The Wizard of Oz* to the standard conventions of the dream vision in European, Indian, and Chinese literature. The anonymous medieval poem *The Pearl* and Chaucer's *Book of the Duchess* and *Parliament of Foules* are especially celebrated examples. (Contemporary teachers should not write off literary works in Old English as too esoteric for today's students; they survive contemporary translation as well as works in any other foreign language, and to miss out on them would be a real shame.) The dreamy worlds of Edmund White's *Forgetting Elena* and Kazuo Ishiguro's *The Unconsoled* are particularly brilliantly achieved examples of tendencies in contemporary postmodern fiction that appear decidedly oneiric, especially the counter-realist proposition that each work creates its own unique field according to its rules and inner logic.

Theme 2: Dreams Are Identified With the Ultimate Reality of Myth, the Afterlife, and/or Supernatural Beings

From anthropological literature (as cited in Chapter 4), students may be introduced to concepts of dreaming as a plane of reality among Australian or Amazonian indigenous peoples. *The Strange Tales from a Chinese Studio* by the 17th-centry Chinese writer Pu Songling and "The Expedition to Hell" by the 18th-century Scottish fabulist James Hogg, on the other hand, both represent literary traditions borrowing from folktale traditions around the dream. In practice, both the concept of the collective unconscious among Jungians and the aesthetic of the dream in surrealism exemplify a tendency to view the dream as a glimpse of the reality behind socially constructed illusions. In what is perhaps the most successfully realized of all contemporary works of dream literature (one likely to have a special appeal to many students), Neil Gaiman's *Sandman* series of graphic novels, the character Dream of the Endless rules the land from which all stories come, the meeting-place of personal and collective imagination.

Theme 3: There May be True and False Dreams

A key theme in the ancient world, exemplified by Homer's Gates of Horn and Ivory and Gilgamesh's concern for finding the true meaning of his dreams, this is also a concern of Coleridge's in "The Pains of Sleep," and in a sense the basis of Freud's theory of distortion in dreams. Along with *A Midsummer Night's Dream* and *Life is a Dream*, Clarence's dream in Act I, Scene iv of *Richard III* is an indispensable example in Shakespeare of a man finding the truth of his life in a dream, while Mercutio's "Queen Mab" speech in Shakespeare's *Romeo and Juliet* is an often cited disavowal of meaning in dreams—although voiced by a deeply cynical character.

We have already mentioned Carole Levin's study of dreams in the English Renaissance, a good source for a reading on James I's "providential" dream that is supposed to have led him to discover the Gunpowder Plot. Another accessible example is Robinson Crusoe's dreaming of Friday before he encounters him, which appears to prepare him to act quickly and resolutely upon their actual meeting. (Because the story is so well known, the passage can work very effectively even when the whole novel is not assigned.) Defoe may well have had the famous example of James I's dream in mind, as well as the well-known tradition that Adam dreamed of Eve as the Lord created her while Adam slept.

Theme 4.: Because of the Value of Authorized Dream Interpretation, Some Persons are Marked Out as Dream Specialists With Arcane Practices and Theories

The recognition of this theme establishes the significance of the links between Artemidorus and Sigmund Freud, and provides a context for the Biblical dream literature that highlights the complex rhetorical interplay between the stories of Joseph and Daniel in Biblical myth. Indeed, consideration of this theme enriches a view of Freud as a carrier of a Jewish tradition important in the Hebrew Bible and Talmud. If examples of Biblical narratives and criticism are familiar among students in a particular class—as they often are not these days—this can lead to a very fruitful comparison of dream interpretation and scriptural interpretation that can help students understand why humanities scholars invest so much in comprehending the works of Milton or James Joyce.

Theme 5: Dreams May be Sought for Guidance in Times of Crisis

As a cultural practice, dream incubation may be studied as part of sacred therapeutic traditions in Greece and Japan; or a feature of vision quests among traditional Plains Indians (and some Surrealist artists). Against this background, it may be noted that dreams come to many literary characters at moments of life change and initiation, from Cicero's *Dream of Scipio* to Dorothy in *The Wizard of Oz*. Children's literature is full of dreams that appear to come at moments of crisis, to serve as initiation into adulthood.

Theme 6: Dream Sharing May Have Important Cathartic and Socially Cohesive Functions

In this final motif is the foundation of much of both dream literature and the contemporary dreamwork movement. Modernist works such as August Strindberg's *A Dream Play* and Arthur Schnitzler's *Dream Story* proceed from a theory that in sharing dreams, artists provide an Aristotelian catharsis for the community, uniting its members by exposing the fears and fantasies they believe divide them. Of course, students may experience this theme for themselves as bonds develop in their own dream-sharing group.

Conclusion

In effect, the purpose of this chapter has been to offer reasons for encouraging recognition of dreaming as a vital issue in understanding cultural productions of all kinds. Our aim has been to offer a few selected examples, among countless possibilities, of how instructors may provide cultural context for the study of dreaming through instances from literature and the other arts, along with the examples from philosophy and the social sciences cited in earlier chapters. We have furthermore expanded on the argument in Chapter 2 by advocating the use of the dream journal and dream discussion group as pedagogical methods that confer unique advantages in the humanities, particularly by proposing to students frequent comparisons between their own creative, introspective, expressive, and interpretative activities and those of the thinkers, writers, and artists whose works they study. We believe, that is, that dream study can make humanities study more vivid, engaging, and accessible. Our examples in this chapter have come largely from literary study primarily for a very simple reason: because in encouraging students to compare their own experiences with those of dreamers in other times and places, it is helpful to remember that to share a dream is usually *to tell a story*—and then to think over that story, consider the various ways a story may generate meanings for various listeners, and perhaps ultimately to develop theories of how stories hold and convey meaning.

This simplified account may suggest why the methods of literary study have been so widely adopted in the modern humanities. The advent of semiotic

approaches in American universities, largely under the influence of French literary theory, trained scholars to treat all cultural productions as coded messages
whose rules may be analyzed in the same way as actual languages—as "texts,"
in the sense we discussed here. So far we have not specifically addressed the
one kind of text that seems to have most in common with the dream itself,
according to the testimony of innumerable critics, artists, and members of
the general public: the motion picture. In the following chapter, we propose
that the analogy between dream and cinema is not merely superficial, but has
distinct hermeneutic advantages for students as well as scholars in both fields.
Students of cinema have much to learn from studying dreams and dreaming,
and scholars of dream studies may benefit significantly from acquaintance with
the methods and theories of contemporary film studies.

Chapter 7

Film Studies

Although the analogy between dreaming and cinema has been a staple of popular culture and film theory almost since the first appearance of moving pictures, it is only rarely that serious dialogue between dream studies and film studies has been undertaken. Both dreaming and cinema consist of the detailed, elaborate, audiovisual presentation of imagined scenes, in states that induce in the subject a distance from the everyday world and an almost hallucinatory immersion in a fantasy. The differences are just as evident: Most importantly, the dream is considered the definitively private experience, whereas films are intensely collaborative products, experienced (at least until recently) in a collective space subject to its own specialized social conventions. This fact alone often has placed the dream in the realm of personal psychology, whereas cinema is studied as an aesthetic field and a social discourse.

The same is true of the relation between the dream and other cultural productions that are studied in the arts and humanities. As already suggested, one of the great advantages of encouraging dream studies in general humanities education may be its special potential for training students in bridging the gap between private experience and public expression through informed critical reflection. Because of its unique ability to present a sensorially detailed, shared public dream, film offers special possibilities for exploring with students new perspectives on dreaming—and dream studies may help students frame questions about the cinema in new and productive ways. As was the case with our discussion of general humanities, we attempt to raise issues that may be discussed in a range of courses, from specialized studies of the dream–film analogy to dream studies classes featuring a short unit on film.

Cinematic dream sequences, as well as the use of the dream as a narrative convention to frame a fantastic plot, are very familiar to popular audiences, and most instructors of dream studies are accustomed to choosing favorite examples to illustrate concepts. But for the discipline of film studies, the key issue has been and remains the characterization of cinema as "dream art" (or "oneiric art"). In addition to broadly describing the similarities and differences between dream and film as quasi-hallucinatory experiences, filmmakers, philosophers, and theorists have considered the implications of an actual derivation of the medium of film from the experience of dreams. Susanne Langer was one of the first to argue (in her influential survey of aesthetics, *Feeling and Form*) that basic conventions of narrative cinema reproduced key features of the dream experience, rather than perceptions of external reality as was often assumed. For example, the montage technique of cutting from scene to scene with minimal transition, or the symbolic use of spatial relations to convey emotions, are elements of cinema that appear to derive from our dreams, even when they are employed in the service of realism.[1] Parker Tyler, who explored psychoanalytic perspectives on Hollywood films in pioneering and influential essays, eloquently demonstrated that mainstream cinema actually thrives on lyrical use of symbolism and associative patterns of imagery—"the order of the dream"—just as much as experimental films. Countering the prevailing assumptions of cinematic realism, he argued that narrative films actually attempt to represent not what cameras can objectively record, but the world as humans experience it—not a world of appearances but of constant imaginative transformation, whose richest realization in ordinary experience is in our dreams.[2] The fullest exploration in print of the dream–film analogy to this date, is the philosopher Colin McGinn's *The Power of Movies: How Screen and Mind Interact*, which provides a highly discursive overview of the many questions raised by the intuition that movies are "like" dreams. McGinn essentially holds that cinema, like dreaming, allows for projection of the spectator into emotionally rich and evocative situations that constitute virtual experience of our central concerns in life.[3] An advantage of acquainting students with this approach is that it provides a model for paying close attention to their own experience of the basic perceptual features of both dreaming and viewing films. McGinn accordingly directs his readers to consider in careful detail the means that movies use to convey that a scene takes place in a dream—an indispensable focus for any classroom examination of oneiric cinema.

A radically different line of exploration of the dream–film analogy is found in French film theory of the 1960s, which attempted to ground semiotic analysis of cinema—the study of film as a system of signs—in the post-Freudian psychoanalytic theory of Jacques Lacan. Because this view has had considerable influence in American academic film theory, it is worth addressing, although the theory is notoriously abstruse and quite difficult for undergraduates who are not already familiar with post-structuralist thought. Briefly: In his very influential study *The Imaginary Signifier: Psychoanalysis and Cinema*, Christian Metz considers the dream–film analogy as a rationale for applying directly to films Freud's scheme of dream interpretation. But the usefulness of his discussion is vitiated by his uncritical allegiance to Freud's dream theory.[4] Jean-Louis Baudry also draws on Freud and Lacan to maintain that the development of cinema represents the inevitable realization of an age-old human drive to project the subjective world of our dreams visually into public space. (He reads Plato's parable of the cave, with its flickering shadows on the wall, as a first manifestation of this desire in Western thought.) The "apparatus" of the cinema, on his argument, is the whole social system that directs these projections of highly emotionally charged and persuasive material toward ideological ends.[5] To support this account, Baudry draws on the American psychoanalyst Bertram D. Lewin's notion that film-viewing mimics and recalls the regressive state of sleep first experienced by infants at the mother's breast. The same notion is advanced by Robert Eberwein in *Film and the Dream Screen,* which argues that the experience of watching films is "regressive" in Freud's sense, and that this explains the similarity of both content and form in films to dream experiences.[6] Noël Carroll, an important contemporary philosopher of aesthetics, provides some perspective on the claims of Metz, Baudry, and Eberwein, in *Mystifying Movies: Fads and Fallacies in Contemporary Film Theory,* by arguing that in actuality, cinema is less complex and easier to comprehend than the workings of the human mind—and that therefore using a speculative theory of the unconscious to explain the whole institution of cinema is a questionable enterprise. Not a bad point to keep in mind whenever we are tempted to get carried away with a theory!

The history of these academic controversies should not obscure the advantages of using the dream–film analogy as a practical and accessible starting point for exploring what we can actually learn about cinema from dreams and vice-versa. The instructor must determine how best to offer some essential background training in critical analysis and theory of cinema, highlighting the questions most clearly related to the dreamlike characteristics of cinema, and the cinematic representation of dreams. An oneirocritical approach (as described in Chapter 6) may include but also look beyond the perspectives of modern psychology on dreaming, drawing on the cultural history of dreaming, and on students' own experiences as dreamers. As they view selected films, students may be directed to consider them under three aspects. First, how each instance uses cinematic conventions to depict the dream experience, and how these depictions further the aesthetic or other goals of the film (such as the elaboration of character). Second, whether the film exemplifies an identifiable theme in beliefs about dreaming and their meaning. And third, whether it proves productive to undertake analysis of dreams depicted in the film, or to consider the film "as if it were a dream."

Instructors who wish to plan a course on dreams and film—or just to become better acquainted with the range of films that might be used in any course on dreaming—can make use of a few key resources. Using the Power Search feature at the online Internet Movie Database (www.imdb.com), selecting for the appearance of the term "dream" in "Plot" and "Keyword," will yield lists of hundreds of dream-themed movies from all film eras and national cinemas, with links to summaries and reviews. A helpful preselected list can be found at the IASD's Web site under http://www.asdreams.org/videofil.htm. New entries are added as they appear in dream psychologist and educator Deirdre Barrett's "Videophile" column in the IASD member publication, *Dream Time*. In *Dreams 1900–2000*, Lynn Gamwell provides an extensive list of significant dream-related films; and there is an excellent survey of the field in the volume *Film & Dreams: An Approach to Bergman*, although it reaches only to the publication date of 1981.[8] Instructors may select celebrated dream sequences, onscreen discussions of dreams, and other excerpts to illustrate specific points. But if the goal of the class is to explore the potential of dream theories to influence critical approaches to film and vice-versa, it makes sense to screen films in their entirety to emphasize their integrity as aesthetic objects, so that students may offer coherent, focused critical analyses in response. If projection facilities at the institution allow, special screenings (whether held during class time or as required lab sessions) of some or all scheduled films can be held; colleges generally allot extra hours to film studies courses to facilitate these sessions. Although students can stream many films directly to their computers now, screenings encourage students to consider why some commentators have maintained that being part of a film audience may feel like experiencing a collective dream. Welt often reminds students that the most important skill a film critic must master is taking notes in the dark (significantly, also helpful for anyone who wants to keep a dream journal). Instructors new to assignments in film analysis quickly learn to set intermediate light levels that can sustain cinematic illusion while also encouraging critical reflection. Requiring students to write papers on dream-related films of their own choice, or to offer seminar presentations based on their own selection of excerpts may extend the range of films analyzed.

Some of the topics and films that instructors might consider as defining major areas of inquiry are discussed next.

Conventions of the Dream Narrative

For the first and most ancient of conventions, that the dream is a journey, there may be no better object of study than *The Wizard of Oz* (Victor Fleming, 1939). But the less-known fantasy *The 5000 Fingers of Dr. T* (Roy Rowland, 1953), conceived, scripted, and designed by Dr. Seuss, uses the same device in an intriguing variation on the same purpose. In each case, the central child character learns from a dream to adjust to an unsatisfactory home and family structure, drawing on unique individual gifts of courage and imagination. A propensity to dream well is what saves them. *MirrorMask* (Dave McKean, 2005), written by Neil Gaiman, the author of the *Sandman* comics, is self-consciously another fantastic dream journey pursuing the same theme.

The metaphorical journey of dreams occurs within the context of an actual journey of initiation in one of the greatest of dream films, *Wild Strawberries* (Ingmar Bergman, 1957); Isak Borg's dreams both reveal layers of his character to the audience and revive his fading interest in humanity. *Wild Strawberries* also represents one of world cinema's most moving depictions of the power of dreams to revisit and recover the personal past, especially long-distant scenes of childhood.

In popular variations on an ancient theme, the protagonists in *Dreamscape* (Joseph Ruben, 1984) and the Japanese anime *Paprika* (Satoshi Kon, 2006) resolve mysteries by penetrating the dreams of others, in journeys that may be fruitfully compared to the plots of quest legends and myths. *The Science of Sleep* (Michel Gondry, 2006) offers an interesting example of the exposure of conventions of dreaming in film by focusing on a character who cannot distinguish between dreams and reality and retreats into a separate world of dreams.

Film and Psychoanalysis

The first film to depict psychoanalytic dream interpretation, *Secrets of a Soul* (G. W. Pabst, 1926), is an especially important document in the cultural history of Freudianism and psychotherapy.[9] (*Secrets of a Soul* was produced with the consultation of Freud's colleagues Karl Abraham and Hans Sachs, although Freud himself emphatically refused to participate in the project, disdaining both popularization of his ideas and the cinema itself as a vulgar medium.) Since this landmark production, still very much worth studying for its depiction of dream symbols and atmosphere, dreams have sometimes been introduced in films as part of the depiction of psychotherapeutic process. They also may appear on the understanding that they reveal a character's unconscious concerns—as with the crucial use of a dream sequence in *Vertigo* (Alfred Hitchcock, 1958) that memorably signals the protagonist's descent into psychosis. The most famous instance is the dream sequence designed for *Spellbound* (Alfred Hitchcock, 1945) by Salvador Dalí. But here as in *Secrets of a Soul*, the film as a whole, and not just the cinematically presented dream, may be used to ask students more searching questions about the relationship of cinematic art to psychoanalytic theory. First, since notably symbolic imagery is used throughout both films and not just in their dream sequences, we might ask if the dream sequences operate as "primers" in how to read film imagery generally—and as statements of the themes of the film in highly condensed, symbolic form. Second, in each case, the account of psychoanalysis in the film cannot be reconciled with the classic theory. Does the disparity represent the perils of popularization or something deeper—an Oedipal revolt against the tyranny of the theory? A covert critique, perhaps?

A prime example of Hollywood Freudianism is the classic science-fiction film *Forbidden Planet* (Fred M. Wilcox, 1956), in which a key character's unacknowledged aggressive desires emerge in monstrous form as he sleeps. ("Monsters from the Id!") Archetypal imagery may be found in any number of dream films—that all-purpose dream film, *The Wizard of Oz*, seems particularly to beg for a Jungian reading in which Dorothy Gale's helpers incarnate as-yet unintegrated aspects of self. (Anyone familiar with the classic film and with archetypal theory will immediately think of the Scarecrow, the Tin Man, and the Cowardly Lion as negative *animus* images for the female dreamer/hero, defined by their deficiencies in intellect, feeling, and courage—or brains, heart, and let us say, manhood.) Certainly Federico Fellini acknowledged that reading Jung changed his films from *8½* (Federico Fellini, 1963) onward, and Jung stands in the background of Bergman's *Wild Strawberries* as well. An obscure short film based on a W. Somerset Maugham story, "Lord Mountdrago," featured in an anthology film of supernatural tales, *Three Cases of Murder* (George More O'Ferrall, 1955) is a remarkable depiction of the Jungian Shadow emerging in dreams (although one might say the same of *Forbidden Planet*, even if it's explained in the film itself in terms of the Freudian id).

Avant-garde, Experimental, and Surrealist Film

There are a number of sound pedagogical reasons to emphasize experimental film and video in discussing oneiric cinema. Students may be drawn to the spirited free play with the formal features of film language in experimental films, while recognizing in them elements of the thoroughly familiar forms of the music video and the commercial. The availability of many short representative examples facilitates in-class screening and close analysis as compared with mainstream feature films. Furthermore, students can connect directly and instantaneously to an active contemporary experimental film culture via the Internet. Fundamentally, there is a deep connection between the avant-garde film tradition and the dream. Parker Tyler noted long ago that, while cinema is essentially an oneiric art form, experimental films are distinguished by refusal to rationalize the most dreamlike features of cinema. Instead of by finding excuses for bizarre or fantastic elements, emphatic symbolism, strange juxtapositions, and visual distortion, as conventional narrative films do, experimental films simply delight in exploring the distinctive features of dreams.[10]

Although students should certainly be encouraged to research up-to-the-moment experimental films, important cultural context may be provided by acquainting them with the tradition of Surrealism.[11] Salvador Dalí and Luis

Buñuel's *Un chien andalou* (*An Andalusian Dog*, 1929) is a short course in Surrealism and the aesthetics of the dream in itself, although Germaine Dulac's *La Coquille et le clergyman* (*The Seashell and the Clergyman*, 1928), from a text by the influential author Antonin Artaud, now often is deemed the first actual Surrealist film. Jean Cocteau called his *The Blood of a Poet* (1930) an "expressionist" rather than "surrealist" film, but it clearly represents an outstanding attempt to realize the private world of the dream in cinematic form. Among important American independent filmmakers, whose work has clearly exerted over time a huge stylistic influence on the cinematic mainstream, Maya Deren (especially in *Meshes of the Afternoon*, 1943), Kenneth Anger (especially in *Fireworks*, 1947), Jack Smith, and James Broughton are particularly associated with exploration of dreamlike features in cinema, and their work now is widely available online and through rental outlets. Kino Video's *The Brothers Quay Collection: The Astonishing Short Films, 1984–1993* collects several of the oneiric films of the contemporary filmmakers Stephen and Timothy Quay, professionally known as the Brothers Quay. Their work acknowledges the influence of Jan Svankmajer, the Czech filmmaker renowned especially for stop-motion animation, whose films famously follow the narrative logic of dreams, even when they do not explicitly refer to dreaming. It should be noted also that the whole animated film tradition, including the classic cartoons of Max Fleischer (especially the Betty Boop cartoons), Walt Disney Studios, and Looney Tunes (Warner Bros.) provides countless instances of the propensity of film to represent the dream state and dream elements. From the early days of Winsor McCay's hallucinatory series of *Dreams of the Rarebit Fiend* to current art-house favorites and YouTube sensations, animators have been fascinated by the unique capacity of their medium to represent the metamorphosis of forms that so often is a feature of dreams. At Harvard University, professor of the Practice of Animation Ruth Lingford, whose own short films offer outstanding contemporary instances of the oneiric animated film, has used Svankmajer's films extensively in introducing students to the idea that making animated films is inherently more like dreaming than is the production of other films, particularly because, as in dreams, each moment presents the artist with the possibility of a transformation that defies the rules of waking reality.

Dreams within dreams, or "nested" dreams, provide the complicated structure of Luis Buñuel's *The Discreet Charm of the Bourgeoisie* (1972), which demonstrated that the subversive program of Surrealism could survive in a feature-length film with commercial production values. Since then, many American independent filmmakers have gravitated toward oneiric cinema in feature films. None is more famous—or notorious—for doing so than David Lynch, who has repeatedly compared his films to dreams. Particularly challenging but rewarding examples of the representation of dream states in cinema are his *Mulholland Dr.* (2001) and *Inland Empire* (David Lynch, 2006). *3 Women* (Robert Altman, 1977) and

Akira Kurosawa's *Dreams* (1990) are particularly celebrated examples of films based on the writer-director's own dreams.

The Horror Film as Nightmare

In film genre criticism, there has long been an interest in exploring the evident relation between the horror film and the characteristics of nightmares. The connection is readily apparent to students, who probably will be much more conversant with the genre than most instructors, and thus can themselves volunteer many examples for analysis. A particularly rich instance is *A Nightmare on Elm Street* (Wes Craven, 1984), which is explicitly concerned with lucid dreaming and dream control as means of dealing with the threats to identity of adolescence, which erupt into nightmare images in the film. Other interesting examples of the derivation of horror films from terrifying dreams include *Paperhouse* (Bernard Rose, 1988) and *Dreamscape* (1984), both of which, like *A Nightmare on Elm Street*, build unusual plot structures upon the characteristic experience of being unable to wake from a nightmare. This feature is brilliantly conveyed in the underrecognized British anthology film *Dead of Night* (Alberto Cavalcanti, Basil Dearden and Robert Hamer, 1945), one of the cinema's most complex and successfully realized depictions of dreaming. *Dead of Night* not only raises the nightmare film to a high level of art but provocatively presents such questions as whether psychoanalysis can explain the dream experience, and whether the paranormal dream is a genuine revelation of something real but imperceptible in the waking state.

Some special understanding of the nightmare makes an enlightening background for the study of horror films. Freud's interpreter and colleague Ernest Jones, in *On the Nightmare*, was the first to raise the relation of literary horror stories and gruesome folklore to nightmares in psychoanalytic terms.[11] A more recent guide to the topic, likely to be of greater relevance to contemporary students, is John E. Mack's *Nightmares and Human Conflict*, which argues that the fantasies of persecution, annihilation, and incorporation common to nightmares and standard horror-film violence, derive largely from pre-Oedipal fears of dissolution of identity in the face of a hostile world. Patrick McNamara's *Nightmares* includes an extensive, up-to-date discussion of the appearance of nightmare themes in horror cinema, supernatural beliefs, and other popular cultural manifestations.[12]

The Dream–Film Parallel

For encouraging active critical analysis and original reflection on the nature of both dreams and cinema, instructors cannot do better than to screen films that represent screen artists' own exploration of the dream–film analogy. One of the greatest is Buster Keaton's *Sherlock, Jr.* (1924), which hits on the brilliant device of a projectionist who falls asleep and "projects" himself into a film in his dream. The audience has no trouble following the complexities of this situation and comprehending how the gags depend on appreciating that cinema constitutes a kind of collective dreaming, or sharing of our fantasies in a briefly realized virtual world. In Federico Fellini's *8 ½* (1963), the central character, clearly a surrogate for the director, finds in his dreams the imaginative power to break out of a creative block; Fellini returned to the dream–film parallel in *Juliet of the Spirits* (1965) and *City of Women* (1980). In what is clearly an homage to Fellini's great dream films, Tom DeCillo transferred the same issues and devices to the American independent film scene in the witty, underrated *Living in Oblivion* (1995), in which the similar dreams of several characters give them a chance to remake the film they are all working on, according to their own fantasies.

Metaphysics of Dream and Cinema

A prominent theme in any discussion of the dream–film analogy must be the problem of distinguishing between reality and illusion in the face of a sensorially detailed, highly convincing representation, whether originating in the dreamer's mind or in immersion in images projected on a screen. (In this respect, films might have offered Descartes an interesting case to consider in addition to dreams, as discussed in Chapter 5.) Indeed, this may be the defining issue for all other problems and categories encountered in exploring the relation of dreaming and cinema. It may be particularly instructive to demonstrate that different academic disciplines will approach the problem according to their own competencies, assumptions, and methods, borrowing freely from others. Thus, film theorists have welcomed the research of cognitive psychologists that explores the actual responses of film spectators, and have called for more. Rhetoricians and narratologists may describe the problem in terms of conventions and literary topoi familiar from everything from Lewis Carroll to the folklore of India to a once-famous season of the 1980s television series *Dallas*, which turned out to be nothing more than a character's dream. Filmmakers and critics schooled in surrealist and experimental cinema may argue that subverting the audience's capacity to distinguish between the products of imagination and a socially constructed, conceptually restricted "reality" is the most valuable function of both dreaming and cinema. Psychoanalytic critics may maintain that the prevailing mode of immersion in fantasy in dream and cinema represents a psychic regression that may be liberating when confronted and understood, but dangerous if the dreamer/spectator uncritically submits to the power of illusion.

In all this there is very fruitful ground for discussion. It also is valid, and perhaps important, to propose that dream films may be one of the means our culture has found of posing authentic philosophical questions in popular and accessible form. The nature of these questions has been suggested in Chapter 5. Is the dream *really* true or false? Is the movie merely a seductive set of appearances or a means to see through appearances to ideas? (Does art deliver an illusion or the truth, after all?) A recent spate of well-received films giving such concerns narrative and audiovisual form, including *Donnie Darko* (Richard Kelly, 2001), *Eternal Sunshine of the Spotless Mind* (Michel Gondry and Charlie Kaufman, 2004), and *The Matrix* (Andy Wachowski and Larry Wachowski, 1999), has certainly convinced many that the illusions of cinema may dispose viewers to a popular form of metaphysical speculation. (The emergence of this particular popular fantasy of living in an entirely illusory world is sometimes ascribed to a younger generation's awareness of an increasing immersion into a world of media-generated images, experienced as a kind of collective dreaming.) Of the films already cited, *The Discreet Charm of the Bourgeoisie*, *Dead of Night*, and *A Nightmare on Elm Street* are particularly well suited for consideration of the capacity of dream narrative and cinematic form to portray genuine existential crisis, as the plots of all these films trap characters within dreams from which they cannot escape. This is the case also with one of the richest and most provocative of recent dream films, Richard Linklater's *Waking Life* (2001). Its central character experiences a slowly unfolding set of nested dreams, drifting in and out of a lucid state, moving among other dreamers, increasingly concerned about the possibility that he will never return from the illusions of dreaming to the world of the waking. Linklater intensifies the dream atmosphere by using the dream-making capacities of animation (through a rotoscoping process that transforms live-action film sequences into drawings), and frequently trains the audience's attention on the dream–film parallel—encouraging them to experience an unusual lucid film spectatorship, as it were. In many ways, *Waking Life* recalls the most original features of Walt Whitman's extraordinary poem "The Sleepers" (1855), which defied the existing conventions of Western dream literature to depict a dreamer who not only passes among other dreamers but steps fluidly in and out of their identities, moving (as actual dreamers will do) back and forth from childhood to adulthood, male to female, through several eras in American history. In "The Sleepers," Whitman appears to foresee the montage techniques of cinematic form and the subversive tactics of Surrealism, resulting in a depiction of dreaming as a mode of being complementary to waking existence, rather than an aberration to be disclaimed, derided, or explained away. Comparing Whitman's poem and Linklater's film in class can promote the most vital goals of a course on dreaming, whether in film studies or elsewhere in a curriculum, by proposing truly radical ways of thinking about dream experience.

Chapter 8

Psychotherapy and Counseling

In this chapter we discuss uses of dreams in psychotherapy and counseling. We ask fundamental questions of whether and to what extent clinicians (psychiatrists, psychotherapists, counseling psychologists, clinical social workers, and others) employ dreams, and the effectiveness of therapy that uses dreams. We state what we believe to be the value of dreamwork in therapy, and discuss how clinical dreamwork is different from lay dreamwork. Turning to dream education for clinicians, we see that it is scanty and suggest some reasons why. We then note the work of several excellent clinical educators in university settings. Finally, we review the uses of dreams and dream education for nurses and for pastoral counselors, and discuss dreamwork with clients suffering from post-traumatic stress disorder (PTSD).

Unfortunately, dreams receive too little attention in the professional training of psychiatrists, psychotherapists, and psychological counselors. Of necessity, therefore, the discussion in this chapter is as much prescriptive as descriptive. We set forth our ideas about what clinical dream education should include and where it should take place, as well as learning about existing programs and curricula.

Research on the Clinical Use of Dreams

Dreams are indeed a tool in psychotherapy. A survey by Keller et al indicated that dreams were used at least occasionally by 83% of a sample of 228 therapists in private practice, and moderately to almost always by 31%.[1] In a study of 79 German psychotherapists, Schredl and colleagues found that dreamwork occurred in about 28% of the therapy sessions, that half of the clients had worked at least once with a dream, "and that of this group about two-thirds of the clients had initiated work on dreams, with one-third of the work on dreams stimulated by the therapist." The Schredl et al study also found that in the therapists' judgments 70% of the clients who had worked with dreams had benefited from doing so.[2]

Although these two studies are not definitive, they indicate that patients' dreams often are a topic in therapy and that dream discussions may occur perhaps more frequently at the instigation of the patient, rather than the therapist. Are therapists relatively disinclined to broach dreams, compared to their own clients?

A key issue in dream education is that of the evidence supporting various claims about dreams, including those that are axiomatic for dream enthusiasts, such as the value of dreams in both lay and clinical usage. We urge dream educators of all kinds to be mindful that all empirical assertions about dreams and dreamwork are subject in principle to testing and possible disconfirmation. It is important that educators distinguish between normative and empirical assertions. It also is important to note the distinction, "I believe that approach 'A' is valuable in dream psychotherapy" (normative) "because of these research findings that demonstrated effects X, Y, and Z" (empirical). It also is important to note the distinction between beliefs and practices supported by data and those supported by clinical experience and judgment.

Research on the effects of treating dreams in psychotherapy is part of a voluminous and complex literature on the measurement of therapeutic outcomes in general.[3] It would go well beyond the scope of this volume to discuss this material in detail. We note its crucial importance to dream educators, whose teaching gains credibility in proportion to the extent that suppositions and arguments are indeed supported by facts. In regard specifically to the effects of dreams in psychotherapy, an instructive treatment is a series of studies done by Clara Hill and her colleagues. Hill and Melissa K. Goates summarize this research in Chapter 12, "Research on the Hill Cognitive-Experiential Dream Model," in Hill's edited volume *Dream Work in Therapy*.[4]

Among the factors studied by Hill and her co-workers were the effects of the following:

1. dream work versus dream monitoring;

2. work on patient's own dream versus other's' dreams vs. troubling events;

3. Hill's model versus unstructured sessions;

4. traits associated with benefiting from dream work including volunteering, and level of dream recall;

5. therapist facilitation versus client self-guidance;

6. dream valence, dream arousal, waking stress, and attitudes toward dreams;

7. description of dream versus associations to dream;

8. focus on dreams versus loss;

9. dreamwork versus control (wait list); and

10. waking life versus spiritual interpretations.

Hill concludes from these studies that dreamwork in psychotherapy is effective, based on both session assessments and treatment outcomes; "Clients rated dream sessions high on depth, working alliance, and insight. Clients made consistent gains in understanding their dreams, with more modest changes in symptomatology and interpersonal functioning. There were four predictors of success in dreamwork:

1. Clients who have positive attitudes toward dreams volunteer more for and profit more from dream work.

2. Clients seem to prefer and benefit more from working with therapists than from working with dreams by themselves.

3. Clients need to be actively involved in dream work to profit from it.

4. All of the components of the Hill model (i.e., exploration, insight, action) seem to be helpful."[5]

These findings certainly support the proposition that dreams are clinically beneficial, although as Hill notes more research within and outside her team of researchers and her particular approach remains to be done.

Hill's studies all concern her model, and Schredl et al.'s survey (cited at the beginning of the chapter) was limited to psychotherapists practicing in two German cities. However, their research approaches are sound and widely applicable to a range of assessment questions about the effects of working with dreams in psychotherapy and other contexts.

The educator is left impressed with the complexities of research design, data collection, and analysis in establishing valid findings about the clinical efficacy of dreamwork, which can be measured by therapist and patient opinion, assessment instruments, and objective measures of client well-being, all based both on individual therapy sessions and on longer-term outcomes. Although not all dream teachers are scientific researchers, all should be familiar with the corpus of empirical findings that buttresses dream theory and supports the legitimacy and value of clinical dream education.

Dreamwork in Psychotherapy

In considering dream education for clinicians, our orientation expands from the personal into the therapeutic. There are important distinctions and demarcations that come with this shift. Although there is a continuum from deprivation through maintenance to enrichment along which personal growth occurs, in clinical contexts the starting point is somewhere in the deprivation range. Clients generally are troubled, or hurting, or dysfunctional in some significant ways. They are experiencing constrictions in their lives beyond which they want to move. Required are skillful and wise interventions especially sensitive to their needs. More directive approaches may be indicated in working with clients' dreams than in lay dream discussion groups among peers (which we discuss in Chapter 9).

In our view, there are two important reasons for education in dreams to be a basic, even foundational, part of clinical training in psychiatry and psychology. One has to do with the clients, the other with the clinicians. First, helping clients involves dealing with their inner and most often unshared experience—the very "stuff" of dreams. It can be difficult for clinicians to solicit clients' statements about their inner experience directly, and even more difficult to induce subjective re-experiencing with its benefits of cathartic insight. Such frontal approaches to clients' closely guarded private worlds often stimulate conscious resistance and activate unconscious defenses. Coming in the side door by inquiring after the client's dreams is likely to provoke less resistance and will provide a platform for conversational engagement of client issues.

Moreover, dreams can reveal pointedly and often with great clarity perceptual, emotional, and behavioral themes in clients' lives. Changes in dreams over time are one source of information about the effects of therapy. In short, dreams are an efficient way of identifying key issues and patterns and tracking progress, in addition to providing a relatively nonthreatening frame for discourse.

The second important reason for dream education to be a key aspect of clinical training has to do not with clients' dreams, but with therapists'. The context for this latter point is the personal therapy that prospective therapists *should* experience, but mostly do not, as part of learning how to help others. The ancient dictum "know thyself" should be de rigueur for persons claiming authoritatively to be able to know and help others.

We think that good dream education for clinical professionals would teach both theory and clinical skills. It would involve group work and dyadic work. It would include a practicum component, which could go hand in hand with supervised clinical experience. It would have students work actively with their own dreams as well as dreams of others. We cannot overemphasize that meaningful experience with one's dreams is a sine qua non for doing dreamwork with patients.

A core ethic in working with a person's dreams is that the dreamer is the final arbiter of what his or her dream means. Another person can suggest possibilities. In lay dream-sharing groups, this often takes the form "if it were my dream . . ." (the projective dreamwork approach discussed earlier).[6] This tack makes the projection of the "other's" sensibility onto the dreamer open, explicit, and conscious, defusing the potential for harm from off-the-mark interpretations. In the individual psychotherapy context, the "other," the interpreter, is the authoritative therapist. The egalitarian assumptions of lay dream groups do not hold. The dreamer/patient will be likely to yield to the therapist's authority. It is crucial that the therapist show sensitivity and forbearance. The therapist may not know what the dream means. If the therapist *does* know, the time might not be right to tell the patient. As with insights generally in therapy, for dream insights to be helpful the patient must be ready to hear them. A correct but premature insight will not take, even if understood intellectually.

Good therapists will have both valid and mistaken thoughts about the layered and often subtle meanings of their patients' dreams. The trick is to convey and discuss meaning *possibilities* in ways that allow the gems to emerge and the dross to fall by the wayside. The "if it were my dream" approach so useful in lay groups of equals may not work so well in the context where the patient (rightly) expects the therapist to have a degree of expertise. The approach should be somewhat more directive in the clinical setting, along the lines of asking the patient to re-engage the dream, perhaps reenacting it, asking what meanings he or she thinks the dream might have, and then nudging the conversation along by suggesting possibilities for the patient to consider. This preserves and respects the patient as final authority while guiding interpretive efforts down promising roads that the therapist sees but the patient may not. In discussing possible dream meanings, the therapist may want to explicate the theoretical basis of his or her approach and opinion. "From a Jungian (or existential, or Gestalt, or sociocultural) standpoint, the dream could be indicating that. . ." Such an open approach conveys respect for the patient's intelligence and agency, and is consistent with the potential for a dream having many meanings and different types of dreams having different meanings (see Harry Hunt's *The Multiplicity of Dreams*).[7]

Variations on the projective dreamwork approach may work well in group psychotherapy, with the dreamer and the group members responding to the dream both benefiting. We suggest to the reader Irvin Yalom's seminal text *The Theory and Practice of Group Psychotherapy*[8] to judge if the approaches and processes described therein can lend themselves, with suitable modifications, to dreamwork.

Excellent resources for clinical students, practicing therapists, and clinical instructors who wish to incorporate dream perspectives and skills into their repertoires are *The Clinical Use of Dreams* by Walter Bonime,[9] and Alvin Mahrer's *Dreamwork in Psychotherapy and Self-Change*.[10] Clara Hill's *Working with Dreams in Psychotherapy*[11] is very useful. Interested readers may also find valuable perspectives on dreams in therapy in *Trauma and Dreams*[12] (Deirdre Barrett, ed.), and *Existential Counselling and Psychotherapy in Practice*,[13] by Emmy van Deurzen, among others. Kelly Bulkeley's *An Introduction to the Psychology of Dreaming*[14] and *The Wilderness of Dreams*[15] provide synopses of different theoretical approaches to dream interpretation and examples of how different theories would view the same dream. There are dozens of reputable books on dreams providing by argument and illustration useful information for deepening therapists' understandings. Beyond receiving explicit training in theory and technique, extending one's overall knowledge of dreams contributes to wisdom and skill in working with them clinically.

Especially useful is Gayle Delaney's discussion in *All About Dreams*[16] of different theoretical assumptions and interpretive methods. Delaney asks these questions: What are the theoretical assumptions of the interpreter? How do the theoretical assumptions influence or even determine the methods used and the interpretations made? What exactly is the method or combination of methods actually employed? What are the roles played by the interpreter and the dreamer, and can the same person play both roles in any given method?

The Dearth of Dreams in Clinical Education

We make the case in this chapter that the state of clinical education for dreams in American universities is relatively underdeveloped overall, despite some notable exceptions. At the outset, however, we take notice of psychoanalytical training institutes. Institute programs are largely Freudian in orientation but include a number that are Jungian, including schools in New York, Philadelphia, Boston, Chicago, Los Angeles, and San Francisco. These—both Freudian and Jungian—are important not only historically but as a contemporary resource for dream students.

The American Psychoanalytic Association (APsaA) was founded in 1911. Its membership includes 29 accredited training institutes and 42 affiliate societies in the United States. APsaA is a component of the International Psychoanalytical Association, which has 70 constituent organizations in 33 countries with more than 12,000 members.

Judy Kantrowitz, in her investigation a decade ago of curricula at Freudian psychoanalytical institutes, observed that although the analysis of dreams was central in to Freud's theories of mind and the unconscious, dreams no longer seem to hold the same centrality they had for analysts who were trained prior to the 1980s. Kantrowitz compared theoretical and clinical courses on dreams in 1980–1981 and 1998–1999 and found that the number of hours devoted to teaching dreams had in fact decreased. However, there were indications that a renewal of interest in dreams was then occurring, at least in some institutes.[17]

Psycholoanalytical institutes, despite their somewhat diminished curricular focus on dreams, remain important for clinical dream education not only because of their central role in training psychoanalysts, but because of their offerings of shorter training courses and programs. Some examples: The Academy of Clinical and Applied Psychoanalysis in New Jersey offers a psychoanalytic certificate, a master's in psychoanalysis, and a master's in psychoanalytic counseling. A course in these programs is Symbolic Communications and Dreams, covering communication expressed in dreams, fantasies, and symbols.

The Western New England Psychoanalytic Society and Institute has a course on dreams in its core curriculum of 15 courses: Theory of Dream Interpretation, a seminar centered around a close reading of *The Interpretation of Dreams*, which also addresses technical issues in dream analysis.

The Dallas Psychoanalytical Institute requires first-year students to take a dream course using Freud's *Interpretation of Dreams* as the central work. There is an emphasis on the specimen dreams with particular relevance to their historical significance in both psychoanalysis and Freud's life. Dreams are studied again in years 3 and 4 in the program, when students are exposed to a clinically oriented course consisting of two intertwined parts: the literature dealing with the many facets of dreams as they emerge in the psychoanalytic situation; the other is a clinical conference format where each student presents dream material from one or more cases.

So our view that there is a relative paucity of clinical dream education is tempered by the substantial number of psychoanalytical training programs that pay at least some attention to Freudian (and Jungian) conceptions of dreams and dream analysis.

Ernest Hartmann reminds us of the irony in the fact that it was a psychoanalyst, Montague Ullman, who was most responsible in spreading dream analysis beyond psychoanalysts to other clinical professionals and lay persons, and beyond Freudian theory to other theories and procedures.

Dreams in University-Based Clinical Training

A long-standing entry point into the clinical treatment of dreams is through sleep disorders. Sleep physician James Pagel notes that sleep disorders used to be the domain of psychiatrists, who had a psychoanalytic perspective and were interested in dreams. Now pulmonologists treat sleep disorders, and they do it from a medical approach—a 180-degree shift. They have little or no psychoanalytical training and minimal psychiatric training, and therefore are neither educated nor interested in dream theories or their evidentiary bases. They may be pulled into dreams by treating parasomnias—disorders that interfere with sleep, including sleepwalking, night terrors, and bed-wetting. Dreams then would be considered symptomatic of these ailments. In PTSDs, dreams are a main symptom complex. Drugs to suppress dreaming, rather than psychological interventions, are the treatment of choice. (We have more to say about dreams in treatment of PTSD later in this chapter.)

Pagel suggests that medical education should include an exposure to dream theory, and that students' own dreams might be the hook or attraction that could underlie an increased attention to dreams in medical education. However, within medicine even psychiatry is now so brain-based that it is difficult to get physicians interested in dreams qua dreams. An attention to mind as well as brain is still valuable, despite its neglect.

Expanding now our attention beyond psychiatry to encompass psychologists and other professional working with clients' psychological issues: The idea that a person could be capable of providing good therapy without having wrestled with his or her own psychological issues is dubious in the extreme, yet the requirement for personal therapy as part of clinical education has shrunk to a pro forma level in most programs. Unfortunately, the clinical student getting significant personal therapy in training has become far more the exception than the rule.

Wayne Myers decried this trend years ago,[18] and it appears to be worse now than it was then, although we have not systematically investigated the matter. Myers documented the dangers of countertransference stemming from therapists' inadequate self-knowledge. Therapists all too easily can unconsciously shift feelings properly associated with persons in their own lives onto the client, to the great detriment of the therapeutic process and client well-being. ("Transference" is the term used when this dynamic is patient-to-therapist in direction, "counter-transference" when it is the other way around.) University psychologist and therapist Johanna King agrees with Myers' view, noting that in clinical training there is little attention to counter-transference or even knowledge of the construct.

Therapist education as generally done can be likened to training swim instructors without having them ever swim in the deep end or touch the bottom of the pool. How can therapists take their clients to places they have not been themselves, including places illuminated by dreams? Therapists can learn about themselves from their dreams, but if clinical training fails to include significant personal therapy and dream instruction then an attention to dreams will not occur, and trainees will not learn to work with clients' dreams. '

We believe that dream education should be a core component in the preparation of new clinical professionals, and a regular topic in continuing education for established professionals. The latter is particularly important as a "catch-up" activity for those who were not educated about dreams (i.e., most) and their use during their initial training. If you are a clinical professional, clinical educator, or student in the helping professions then the fact that you are reading this book (and other books on dreams) is encouraging.

The resurgence in popular interest in dreams connected with self-exploration, and the persistence of dreamwork in therapy contrast with dreams' diminished emphasis in conventional clinical and professional training. Dream education in mainstream university undergraduate and graduate programs has actually decreased over the past 20 years or so. Leading clinical teachers such as Alan Siegel and Roger Knudson find that almost none of their graduate students have ever had a course on dreams. At most, dreams were talked about for an hour (i.e., part or all of one class period).

There are notable, if few, exceptions to the general rule that dreams are not taught in universities as complete courses, either in the undergraduate curriculum or in graduate clinical training. One can find them mainly in postgraduate, continuing education units, and in freestanding institute programs (which we discuss in the following chapter). This is not ideal; it would be better if more courses were available in university degree programs. Siegel notes that 40 years ago dream courses in the academy were just as rare, but at least dream theory was taught as part of psychodynamic courses, which have now fallen out of favor.

There is not necessarily an active dislike of dream courses in clinical programs. Harvard's Deirdre Barrett observes that psychology departments and university faculties in general don't particularly *want* dream courses, but they will tolerate them if taught as electives. In clinical training—(i.e., social work and psychology) there are so many required courses that there is little room for electives. Students in university undergraduate and graduate programs have little say. In contrast, courses are demand-driven in postgraduate continuing education.

Faculties and deans may believe that there is little desire for dream courses. However in Barrett's experience students are very interested and enrollment is high. She suggests a tactic of polling students regarding their interest level relative to other courses, to make the case that dream courses would attract students.

There are several reasons why dreams topics are scarce in university-based clinical training. First, many view dreams as an aspect of Freudian theory, and as Freudian influence in psychology declined, the profession discarded the dreams baby with the Freudian bathwater. As Kantrowitz' survey pointed out, dreams have diminished in importance somewhat even within psychoanalytical training, where in the mid- to late 20th century the importance given to dreams declined compared with other associative techniques—dreams were not considered special. The idea grew that simply asking for dreams "leads" the patient and is manipulative. (We note that by this criterion, one could construe *any* statement of the therapist as leading or manipulating the patient.)

Dream theory and practice has moved well beyond Freud into Jungian, existential, Gestalt, and other theories, and spiritual, holistic health, and other realms—all fertile areas for clinical training and practice, and all likely nurturing homes for dreams. It is a mistake to cast out dreams with Freud, as it also is a mistake to dismiss Freudian dream theory itself.

Second, clinical psychology's emphasis on short-term, behavioral and cognitive-behavioral therapy (in our opinion driven as much by health insurance economics as intrinsic merit) has further contributed to the retreat of depth approaches to therapy and the neglect of the client's (and the therapist's) inner worlds. With the advent of managed care has come the belief that there is no time to deal with dreams, or that dream therapy wouldn't be approved for payment. The belief that dream therapy would be an inefficient use of therapy time is mistaken, as we see it. (Some cognitive-behavioral approaches are more receptive to dreams, e.g., the work of Clara Hill, discussed later.)

A third factor in the neglect of dreams in clinical work has been psychiatry's shift away from a psychodynamic orientation (previously noted) to one emphasizing psycho-pharmacological intervention. Psychiatrists relegate dreams to the role of symptoms only, for example nightmares as indicators of sleep disturbance. Little wonder that the psychiatric and psychotherapeutic establishments largely ignore dreams in training practitioners.

Fourth, many in universities where there is a scientific emphasis do not see dreams as a sufficiently "scientific" field. Psychology faculties above all else want to be seen as scientific. Unfortunately this can manifest itself in a preoccupation with the trappings of science, especially the production of quantitative data seemingly for their own sake, without due attention to the merit or meaningfulness of what is being researched and measured, and how it should best be addressed. We believe with others including Siegel, Barrett, Knudson, and Pagel that this attitude smacks of scientism. We decry scientism while agreeing with these scholars and others who value truly scientific approaches in creating new knowledge. In fact, there is an increasingly broad, rich, and sophisticated scientific literature—theory and data—on dreams.

Fifth, even in the academy there is some residual, irrational prejudice against dreams based on lingering religiously based prejudices and their emotional concomitants—dreams as the devil's work and sinister. These attitudes may interact with and mask for some a fear of encountering their own dreams—which is understandable in that dreams can be troublesome and disturbing.

Flowing from the convergence of these factors is the neglect of dreams in clinical training. In consequence, most clinicians are not skilled in their therapeutic use. Lack of knowledge, interest and use, confidence and skill mutually reinforce one another. It is a chicken and egg problem. Clinical dream education is needed to support clinical dreamwork; the latter is needed to provide the demand for the former.

Some Good Examples of Clinical Dream Education

Despite the general lack of clinical dream education in university programs, there are a few places where people do it. We profile a few of the best examples here.

Roger Knudson, Clara Hill, and Laurel McCabe are three leading educators of doctoral students in clinical, counseling, and depth psychology, respectively.

They are exceptional in mainstream university departments in that they both value and use dreams in their teaching. Tellingly, they came to work professionally with dreams *after* receiving their own doctorates and establishing themselves. They are tenured, which serves as a buffer against criticisms of their involvements with dreams, and provides a relative immunity from challenge by their university and professional colleagues.

Knudson is a psychology professor at Miami University of Ohio, where he directed the PhD program in clinical psychology from 1994 to 2007. He was a member of the Council of University Directors of Clinical Programs (CUDCP). This is a group within the American Psychological Association (APA), which surveys clinical programs every other year about their dominant theoretical orientations. Around 1992, approximately half were behavioral or cognitive-behavioral; roughly 10% each psychodynamic humanistic, and family systems; and about 5% clinical-community. Fifteen years later the pattern has shifted radically to more than 90% behavioral or cognitive-behavioral. Knudson sees this as an "incredible homogeneity." In Knudson's view, the cognitive-behaviorists have taken over APA and driven other orientations out. He agrees that this stems from the economics of health care insurance, which pays only for short-term therapy. This is a big reason why dream education is scarce in clinical training programs.

Knudson notes Duquesne University's phenomenology-oriented clinical psychology PhD program as an interesting case. In 2002–2003 the APA granted it accreditation; however, it was turned down for full membership in the CUDCP, on the grounds that it wasn't "scientific" enough. In Knudson's view, this is an example of the scientism, mentioned previously, that pervades clinical training programs.

Students in graduate clinical programs are, in Knudson's phrase "disinclined to deal with their own process." Entering students have rarely studied dreams. Of the 24 top applicants to Miami University's clinical program in 2008 (those invited to campus as "finalists" in the selection process) none had ever had a course in the topic.

Knudson characterizes himself as a "maverick outsider" in his field in that he values dreams and all sorts of experiential approaches to them. He notes that although dreams are scarce in psychology clinical education, they are showing up more in the humanities, anthropology, and religious studies. (See the chapters on these topics.) Knudson would like to see as many different approaches as possible to get students involved experientially, including some kind of dream work, and involving disciplines beyond psychology, such as theater and literature.

We introduced Hill above in discussing research on dream therapy's effects. She teaches at the University of Maryland in the doctoral counseling psychology program and in undergraduate programs. Her courses on therapy and counseling include units on dreams, and she teaches as well freestanding dreams courses, both graduate and undergraduate. Hill's research is a breakthrough regarding empirical measurement of outcomes of clinical dream interventions.

Hill agrees with Knudson in characterizing the dream movement outside academia's clinical training programs as in part a backlash against the dominance of quantitatively oriented cognitive-behavioral short-term therapy. Hill started to incorporate dreams into her teaching only after she had attained full professor status. She notes that her scientific (empirical) work and publications have given her cover to teach about dreams.

Hill teaches a graduate proseminar in counseling with a helping skills emphasis, which is similar to teaching basic skills in responding to dreams. In this class, she brings in dreams at the end of the semester. She does a group dream interpretation and analyzes a dream of a volunteer client. Students discuss their dreams but no student is required to submit one. Hill "strongly encourages but do[es] not mandate" students to get therapy. The therapy that some do get is extrinsic to the academic program. It is the students' private business.

Hill notes that there is a danger of inadequately trained people doing dreamwork: Although some people are intuitive and can do good work, others will do damage. The best model for training clinicians in working with dreams involves a "back-and-forth" movement between intellectual and intuitive sensibilities. (It is important to get trainees to think critically, and involved in experiences that change them.)

Hill emphasizes that student clinicians really need to experience and practice dreamwork; it is not something that can be meaningfully learned at a remove, entirely on a conceptual and intellectual basis. This is why Hill deals with dreams near the end of her basic skills proseminar course. She exposes students to different theories and methods of dream interpretation. She guides students in trying each approach, and in gradually incorporating various approaches into their personal styles.

In explicating her dream-processing model, she wrote the steps down in a systematic way. To teach others, she had to impose a structure on what for her personally was a fluid process. She notes that grounding intuitive leaps and intuition in a well-learned rational, linear procedure and technique may in fact be what the best therapists do—the techniques and steps are there; one can summon them as needed.

Are dreamers, and dream therapists, "born" or "made"? To what extent can they be trained versus simply found with a natural affinity? Hill believes there are important biological and early family experience components. She cites Ernest Hartmann's "thick vs. thin boundaries" account of personality constructs. Persons with thinner boundaries between components of their mind—(e.g., thinking and feeling)—may have easier access to their own dreams and be more effective in dealing with dreams of their clients. Hill observes that the students in her courses love dreams. In contrast to our overall impression, Hill sees dreaming as becoming more respectable in the academy. Having a sound empirical basis is very important to the legitimacy of the subject matter. Especially important is research on the clinical effectiveness of dreamwork as part of a therapy/counseling regimen. In working with dreams (in education, clinical/counseling, or research) one should resist the temptation to tie oneself too closely to any particular theory, avoid scientism, and intertwine theory, practice, and assessment.

Hill conducts dream workshops with professionals. A structure that she has found to be effective is first to talk for 90 minutes about her dream model; then she divides the large group up into small dream discussion groups with her graduate students as group leaders, allowing each attendee to hear something personal about his or her own dreams. Something that has not worked well for Hill is demonstrating dream group process in front of a larger audience. The audience did not get involved.

In her dream groups, Hill "coaches" participants to lead the process by running through the steps; rather than Hill being the leader, she gets the group members to practice being leaders, enabling them to learn by applying the procedures, not by watching.

Laurel McCabe's graduate program in depth psychology at Sonoma State is interesting in that it teaches an unconventional subject matter in academic psychology in a conventional university setting. In the past, Sonoma State's Psychology Department was home to a master's degree program in humanistic psychology, and as the popularity of humanistic approaches waned and that of depth psychology grew, the current program replaced the old one. The existence of the Sonoma State program shows that one can teach dreams as a central enterprise in graduate university settings. McCabe said she has never run into any obstacles there in incorporating dreams into her teaching. Depth psychology, after all, includes dreams as a core topic.

McCabe teaches both graduate and undergraduate courses in which dreams are a component. She also has taught dedicated dreams courses that include theories and points of view other than Jungian. She does dreamwork in the classroom, finding that the advantages outweigh the disadvantages. Ground rules include provisions for confidentiality and safety. She helps students find a "safe internal place, a place of serenity," via meditation and breathing exercises. Experiencing how dreams resonate in the body is her preferred approach. (See Chapter 11 for a discussion of "embodied" approaches to dream meaning-seeking.) This works for some students, not for others. She attempts to keep the dream alive and to work with the energetic experience of it, staying away from the "danger of theory." Students can go in and out of working with a dream image; they can "retreat to their inner state"—moving inward rather than outward. This reduces students' fear of frightening dreams—they don't have to go all the way in.

McCabe also uses poetry and haiku—again some students like it and some don't. Her educational mission is to provide information, to facilitate engaged and transformative learning (i.e., a new place of inner consciousness). She finds that almost any dream can be transformative.

Her graduate students are eager to work with their dreams. She takes a gentle approach and won't hesitate to back off the dreamwork if the student is getting distressed. However, she notes Jeremy Taylor's observation that persons generally are equal to the task of working with the dreams they dreamt and remembered. Then again, students *can* be overwhelmed. A certain level of ego strength is required to be a dreams student.

Hill, Knudson, McCabe, and others in mainstream university psychology departments are relatively unassailable. Tenure and their records of achievement protect them. Others who may want to incorporate dreams in graduate studies or pretenure research and teaching are more vulnerable to negative sanctions.

In contrast, and perhaps as a response to its scarcity in conventional university settings, dream education is happening more frequently outside formal university degree programs: Once people have earned advanced degrees, some in clinical and faculty positions reach out and broaden their perspectives, through extra-university programs that deal with dreams. As an example, Knudson went to Jungian analyst Robert Bosnak's workshop, and to the Pacifica Institute for Stephen Aizenstat's advanced course on his model of "dream tending." (In the next chapter we discuss innovative programs in freestanding institutes, as well as one at a university.)

For aspiring clinical students, there is another consideration, which pits the practical against the ideal. The APA may not approve even accredited graduate programs in freestanding institutes. Students receiving doctorates in non-APA-approved programs find it impossible or difficult to land an APA-approved postdoctoral clinical internship, the demand for which recently has exceeded the supply by some 700 per year, according to Knudson. Moreover, some organizations, including Veterans Affairs (VA) clinics, require APA certification as a condition of employment as a clinical psychologist. And it is difficult if not impossible to get tenure-track faculty appointments at conventional universities if one's graduate degree is from a freestanding institute. Students considering investing time and money in doctoral programs should weigh the costs of forgoing APA certification against the benefits provided by the better fit with their interests they might find in an "off-brand" program. On practical grounds, we recommend against seeking degrees from programs that are not academically accredited. The key questions to ask are whether the program is accredited, whether it is APA-approved, and whether its graduates can obtain clinical internships, sit for state licensure examinations, and qualify for university faculty appointments. We have sympathy for students who must choose between conventional graduate programs that are short on dream education, and programs not in the academic mainstream which do a better job with dreams but whose graduates are handicapped in seeking both clinical and teaching positions. We would like to see this distinction narrow, by dreams becoming more accepted and widely taught in universities, and by degrees from freestanding institute programs becoming more acceptable in clinical and academic hiring. This can happen if freestanding institutes hire more faculty members with doctorates from mainstream programs, and if curricula in freestanding programs become more rigorous, especially methodologically so.

That there are a few clinical training programs incorporating dreams is encouraging to a point, but does not contradict the atypical status of these programs and teachers. The relative absence of dreams as a topic in graduate psychology education, especially clinical psychology, leads to its lack of salience and status, reinforcing its neglect. Clinicians not knowledgeable and comfortable in using dreams for self-understanding and as a therapeutic tool will be disinclined to embrace their potential. (Perhaps this explains Schredl's finding that patients are more likely to initiate discussions of dreams than are their therapists.) Only a minority of clinicians will happen upon dreams as a topic and focus independent of graduate training.

In the absence of well-established dream education in most clinical training programs, teachers and learners need to be pragmatic in connecting with dream education where they can find it. Siegel's strategy is not to spend his energies battering the ramparts of universities, but simply to do clinical dream education wherever he can. Clinical students and working professionals would do well to take a similar approach in searching widely for existing venues, courses and continuing education, subject to our cautions about the trade-offs involved in investing time and money in degree programs that are not accredited and APA certified.

Dreams in Medicine and Nursing

Having dreams knowledge and skills in one's clinical repertoire can be useful for other human enterprises where there are clients and a psychosocial dynamic. Medical patients' dreams can be a supplementary source of information about their conditions. Physicians and other medical personnel can tap "prodromal" dreams—those that reveal impending or incipient conditions, and that signal healing processes and outcomes—if they are aware of their potential. Robert Van de Castle has written persuasively on this topic in *Our Dreaming Mind*.[19] The holistic health movement can incorporate dreams into its perspectives and topics. Intriguing work in this area of dreams and healing is underway by Wendy Pannier and Tallulah Lyons.[20] Pannier and Lyons note that an increase in dream recall, in particular of frightening dreams, often accompanies the onset of a serious illness such as cancer. Many cancer patients have dreams about their illness before diagnosis. Pannier and Lyons believe it is important for cancer patients to be tuned into health issues—particularly ways for improving health—that may appear in their dreams.

The primary goal of their "Healing Power of Dreams" project is to use dreaming to help balance the mind–body–spirit connection for cancer patients. They teach basic dreamwork techniques and help participants integrate the healing imagery that evolves through ongoing dreamwork—particularly relaxation/ guided imagery approaches. Pannier and Lyons track the effects of ongoing group participation using an adaptation of quality-of-life assessment tools used at The Wellness Community and other cancer centers. Through 2006, they found that 80% of participants used positive dream imagery in meditative activities, and that all participants reported decreased stress and anxiety, increased senses of connection with others and to their inner resources, increased understanding of healing at multiple levels, and an increased quality of life—particularly emotional, social, and spiritual. 100% reported increased feelings of control over life and health issues, increased feelings of hope, and an increased understanding of how to live fully. Pannier and Lyons' work melds dream processing with cancer patient support groups. Their work exemplifies the potential of dreams in helping medical patients, and leads us naturally to a consideration of the professionals most connected with patients interpersonally—nurses.

Nurses can benefit from their own dreams in terms of self-knowledge and nurturance, as well as in communicating with patients about the latter's dreams. An unpublished study by King identified five themes in nurses' dreams of their professional experience: correcting physician errors, treatment failures where the patient gets worse or dies, treatment successes where the patient improves or gets well, deficits in hospital staffing and other resources, and psychological and spiritual self-healing. King labeled this last function of nurses' dreams "healing the healer," indicating the value of an attention to dreams as a counter to the emotionally stressful and draining aspects of nursing, particularly hospital acute care.[21]

We introduced Mary Dombeck in Chapter 3 as an anthropologist. In her doctoral dissertation, published as *Dreams and Professional Personhood*,[22] Dombeck dealt with the use of dreams in clinical social work and psychiatry. At the University of Rochester nursing school she teaches epistemology, also family therapy, group therapy, and psychopathology.

Psychiatric nurses understand dreams both as a clinical phenomenon and as material for their own personal growth. Dombeck's focus has been on the nurses' dreams rather than patients' dreams. However, familiarity and comfortableness with their own dreams allow nurses to address patients' dreams in an easy and unselfconscious way. Ongoing dream groups with medical patients may work especially well with those with chronic illnesses who would be patients over an extended time.

In Dombeck's dream groups with nurses there are six or seven sessions, six members, with one participant relating a dream in each session. Students learn how to listen and respond to dreams of their colleagues. This translates well into working with patients' dreams. Increased self-knowledge and clinical skills develop hand in hand.

We include nursing here because of nurses' close contact with patients and patients' psychosocial problems, and the significant levels of stress experienced in the nursing profession. It is likely that the dreams of physicians and persons in healing professions across the board can have similar communicative, self-healing, and restorative potential. Healing professionals of all stripes could benefit by discussing their dreams with their colleagues. This is what happens in lay dream-sharing groups, and there is every reason to expect it to happen among professionals as well, in properly supportive contexts.

Dreams in Posttraumatic Stress Disorder Therapy

Another important clinical application of dreams knowledge, and potential area of clinical instruction, involves a target group of dreamer-clients, the clinicians who work with them, and two promising settings. The group is military combat veterans suffering from PTSD and other psychological problems that reduce their ability to function well in daily living. The settings are the many VA clinics scattered around the United States, and (increasingly) colleges and universities where returned veterans are getting their educations.

PTSD has been recognized by different names in different wars: shell shock (World War I) and combat fatigue (World War II). The first group of veterans for which PTSD was clearly understood were Vietnam War veterans. The VA (not part of the U.S. military) recognizes the high incidence of PTSD among veterans. However, there remains reluctance in military culture, particularly in combat commands, to acknowledge the reality of this disorder. Lest we wander too far a field, we confine our observations here to the use of dreams in psychotherapy and counseling for veterans, and within that realm narrow our focus still further to the education in dream therapy for the clinicians who deal with veterans.

VA clinics have paid increasing attention to PTSD therapy in the treatment over the past 20 years. The major vehicle through which veterans are treated is through the VA's mental health clinic combat trauma processing groups. Both dynamic and cognitive–behavioral group therapies are used. The common features of all group treatments of combat PTSD involve the development of trust and the communalization of trauma within a cohesive group.[23]

One example of employing dreams comes from the Combat Stress Program Department of Psychiatry in the Phoenix, Arizona VA Medical Center. Stephen S. Brockway described the intervention as "a method for detoxifying combat nightmares in a group treatment setting" and illustrates the method in a three-dream sequence:

When viewed as a direct road back to the trauma, the nightmare can be transformed into a powerful therapeutic tool if deciphered empathically in the company of combat veterans who, like the dreamer, have survived similar catastrophic events. Successful depotentiation of nightmares gives PTSD patients increased control and confidence in working through the aftereffects of trauma.[24]

It is noteworthy that this article is from 1987. It is not that people haven't recognized the potential of dreams in combat trauma therapy; it is that such therapy has been implemented only sporadically. VA clinicians bring their education, skill and clinical experience to their work. Sometimes this includes knowledge of dreams and an inclination to address veterans' dreams in the therapy group context. But as with dream education in general, it is a fortuitous matter whether the therapists have the background. Dream education for clinicians is not routine but is "catch as catch can."

Bob Coalson's experience confirms the inconsistent use of dreams in therapy for PTSD sufferers. Coalson is a twice-wounded Vietnam War veteran who worked for many years as a VA counselor, and currently teaches a course in dreams at Pacific Lutheran University. Coalson worked with veterans' dreams to good effect in the VA.[25] He trained many interns—often second-year graduate students in clinical psychology. Only one of these over the years had any previous education in dreams (having studied under Clara Hill at the University of Maryland). Coalson sees a big void in the dream education of clinicians, which he attributes to the same cognitive-behavioral bias in graduate education identified by Roger Knudson. Coalson notes wryly that cognitive-behaviorists "don't necessarily have a great appreciation for the unconscious." When Coalson retired from the VA, the clinical psychologist supervisor queried Coalson's successor—his former intern—about the very existence of the unconscious.

Coalson had much creative freedom in his VA work to seek the most effective way of doing therapy and helping his clients, including working with their dreams. However, he retired 10 years ago, and has the impression (although we have not documented this) that the VA has since moved to a more "centralized template" for treating therapy, involving a "here-and-now" approach that does not delve into the past or into dreams.

Coalson agrees with us that colleges and universities increasingly are important settings for using dreams in the treatment of PTSD, as more veterans are returning from combat duty and enrolling in higher education. He forewarns veterans in his dream course that dreamwork can act as a trigger for trauma-induced nightmares, and urges them to arrange for appropriate therapeutic help outside the course if this happens.

Carl C. Smith is a combat veteran of the Vietnam War, who experienced PTSD and has participated with commitment and energy in VA combat trauma-processing groups, and in individual VA therapy that has included working with dreams. Smith sees dreams as movies of the trauma, and found value in an almost " 'frame-by-frame" re-viewing and analysis of the dream-movie. He likens the process to the painstaking analysis made of the Zapruder home movie of the John F. Kennedy assassination: Where is the picture that reveals the trauma and helps the veteran to begin to react to it less severely and integrate it into his current life in helpful ways?

Ernest Hartmann has discovered through his research important distinctions between what are commonly termed PTSD nightmares and ordinary nightmares, distinctions crucial for clinical education. The former should not be termed a nightmare at all but instead "an encapsulated memory that can intrude suddenly into the consciousness either during sleep (non-REM as well as REM) or waking. It is not a REM sleep dream, although it may intrude upon a dream."[26] Hartmann notes that veterans suffering from PTSD nightmares differ from veterans with ordinary lifelong nightmares on a number of factors. These include the age at which they experienced the trauma (the PTSD nightmare group is younger); their personalities (the PTSD nightmare group having thicker boundaries between thinking and emotion, thus more likely to "wall off" the trauma); and the helpfulness of different psychoactive drugs in reducing symptoms (with the PTSD nightmare group helped by various anti-depressants).[27] PTSD nightmares may be less responsive to "talk therapy" than ordinary nightmares. PTSD nightmares may not be able to develop over time into more benign versions of themselves, as ordinary nightmares can do. The distinction, which may blur at the margins and which awaits further empirical confirmation, is between PTSD nightmares that replay the trauma repetitively versus regular nightmares that symbolize the trauma and can more easily change.

Changes in recurrent nightmares can signal healing and when attended to consciously can enhance the healing process. An example: One of our university teaching colleagues was a Vietnam War veteran who had participated in an airborne raid deep in enemy territory. Enemy soldiers had chased his group through jungles and rugged terrain; they finally just barely escaped with their lives back over the border into safer territory in Vietnam. He was troubled by his war experience, and had not received therapy. For years afterward he had a recurring nightmare in which he was once again fleeing through rough territory, through jungles, up and down gullies and up steep hills, pursued by the enemy. Interestingly, over a 15- to 20-year period, the dream gradually changed, in simple yet telling ways that marked psychological healing: The terrain became less difficult—the jungle was less dense, the land flatter, his fleeing easier, and the feelings less frightening.

Distinctions in susceptibility, etiology (including relationships between childhood experience and later combat trauma), and recommended psychopharmacological and psychotherapeutic treatments would be among the important components of dream education for those working with combat veterans and other PTSD clients. We refer interested readers to the *Journal of Traumatic Stress* for research on factors related to PTSD etiology, prevention, and treatment, with possible implications for clinical dream education.

Combat veterans are not the only PTSD sufferers. Others include victims of natural disasters, accidents, refuges from wars and the attendant social chaos, rape, other crimes and domestic abuse or neglect. They too have nightmares that are windows to their trauma, and there is hope that they too can find their dreams transforming over time, reflecting the healing they experience through therapy—or even on their own in some instances. Therapists of all stripes who work with these groups could benefit by systematic clinical education in working with trauma-induced dreams.

Dreams in Pastoral Counseling

Pastoral counseling is another potentially fruitful arena for the quasi-clinical use of dreams. Persons commonly experience powerful and often frightening dreams when going through a time of major life change, crisis, or conflict—situations that lead many people to seek help from a religious counselor (most of our information comes from Christian pastoral caregivers, although our basic ideas apply to caregiving practices in other religious traditions as well). By paying close attention to dreams during such times, a religious counselor can help the individual gain important insights. Some dreams are spiritually transformative experiences in and of themselves, and many religious counselors know from personal experience how significant such dreams can be. Most people have had one or two special dreams during their lives that have served as spiritual touchstones, deepening their faith and expanding their sense of sacred presence in their lives. In a pastoral context, such dreams can be a valuable resource for prayer, reflection, and spiritual exploration.

Secular counselors and psychotherapists also should take into account their clients' religious and spiritual beliefs, practices, and sensibilities and use them as vehicles for bringing about desired change. Every therapist and counselor has to discern, disentangle, and engage the various spiritual, emotional, cognitive, and behavioral strands in their clients' situations, dealing with each appropriately. Some client concerns are spiritual in the sense of relating to fundamental existential questions. Others are more conventionally religious in being concerned with doctrine and doctrine's implications for how to see the world and how to deal with one's emotional and interpersonal life. Ritual and community, both arguably deficient in modern Western society, are resources for spiritual counseling in that both can contribute to psychological nurturing and healing. Clients can be encouraged to embrace and increase their involvements in community religious life with its associated rituals. Rigid doctrines that ignore or deny the reality of psychological matters that are troubling the client can be problematic. More flexible, sophisticated, and thoughtful doctrine can be used to good effect as systems for framing meaning and addressing clients' psychological and spiritual difficulties. Clients' religious and spiritual worldviews are potential allies for all counselors, whether or not they themselves are of a particular faith or affiliated with a religious institution.

Here's where dreams come in, because there is no limit to the symbolic dimensions of dreaming, meaning they are always open to new potentials. Our belief systems, including religious ones, produce dream content and can be used to interpret dreams' meanings. Religiously imbued dreams may have meanings for the dreamer and for the larger community. Pastoral counselors educated in dreamwork will be able to help clients make sense of their dreams at their various levels of meaning, including the transcendent. As indicated in Chapter 5, there is a rich history of dreams in sacred texts, showing that dreamwork is not the exclusive province of psychology—religious people through the ages have been discussing and analyzing their dreams. We believe the most successful pastoral work with dreams will combine the historical richness of religious teachings with modern insights of empirical psychology.

Several pastoral counselors and therapists who use a merging of Christian theology and Jungian psychology have written influential books on the spiritual practice of dream interpretation, including Morton Kelsey's *God, Dreams and Revelation*,[28] John Sanford's *Dreams: God's Forgotten Language*,[29] and Jeremy Taylor's *Dream Work*.[30] Although neither a theologian nor a pastor, Kelly Bulkeley has taught and written in this area, including the article "Dream Interpretation: Practical Methods for Pastoral Care and Counseling" (2000),[31] which lays out a step-by-step process for pastoral caregivers with no previous experience in working with dreams; and *Dreams of Healing: Turning Nightmares into Visions of Hope* (2002),[32] which explores the religious and cultural dimensions of traumatic dreams, focusing on PTSD nightmares following the terrorist attack of Sept. 11, 2001. *Dreaming Beyond Death: A Guide to Pre-Death Dreams and Visions* (2005),[33] co-authored by Bulkeley and Patricia M. Bulkley, a former Presbyterian minister and hospice chaplain, explores the spiritual and psychological dimensions of dreams experienced by terminally ill people just before they die; and *Dreaming in Christianity and Islam: Culture, Conflict, Creativity* (2009),[34] co-edited by Bulkeley with Kate Adams and Patricia M. Davis, includes chapters on the healing power of dreams in both Christian and Muslim traditions.

These works offer resources for caregivers in a variety of religious contexts who find themselves confronted by dreams they intuitively recognize as meaningful but who have not received any training or information about dreaming, either from scientific psychological or theological perspectives. As with secular psychotherapists, pastoral counselors have been poorly served by their seminary and divinity schoolteachers in regard to the diagnostic and therapeutic potentials of dreams. The problem is not lack of resources, nor lack of student interest; it's rather the familiar contemporary bias against the "unscientific" nature of dream interpretation, combined with a dubious theological belief that attention to dreams leads to demonic temptation.

Summary

We can summarize this review of clinical training in dreams: Dream knowledge is valuable for clinician self-understanding and as a tool for working with clients. It is a key subject matter, which for various historical, economic, political and psychological reasons is largely missing from conventional graduate curricula.

Knowledge and skills in working with dreams are valuable beyond psychiatry and clinical and counseling psychology, in fields including nursing and clinical social work, and pastoral counseling. Any profession involving interaction with clients' about their psychological functioning (including teaching!) can benefit from discussing dreams.

There are perspectives, skills, sensitivities, knowledge, and wisdom important to good clinical dream therapy beyond those needed for dreamwork in nonclinical situations such as lay dream groups. Therapist–client interactions differ from peer interactions in purpose, process, power relations, and assumed expertise. An especially important arena with potential for dreamwork is therapy with combat veterans in VA mental health clinic trauma-processing groups, and with other trauma sufferers.

Because there is an unfortunate and regrettable dearth of dream education in mainstream, university-based graduate degree programs and pastoral training programs, the availability of clinical training in dreams is spotty at best—interested learners will have to continue to reach beyond university degree and licensure programs to free standing institutes and continuing education programs.

Some nonuniversity graduate programs receptive to dreams may not be APA accredited. Graduates of these programs may not be eligible for university faculty hiring, for postdoctoral APA-approved internships, nor for hire at jobs requiring APA-accredited internships, such as VA clinical positions. This is the price currently paid for seeking a more expansive clinical education beyond the constraints of conventional academic psychology. Clinical psychology students may want to get degrees from fully APA-accredited programs, picking up their dream education on the side, or in continuing education post degree, internship, and clinical licensure.

Dream education may make steady inroads into clinical training. These inroads are likely to be modest, however. In the near- and mid-term, students will need to take initiative in seeking out their dream education in creative ways. Clinical faculty members (and undergraduate professors) will need to swim against prevailing tides in efforts to include dream education in their curricula.

Chapter 9

Alternative and Community Education

Dream education pops up anywhere interested learners encounter willing teachers. If the formal gardens of higher education have grown dream flowers only sparingly, dream wildflowers have taken root and bloomed elsewhere where the soil is more fertile. Excellent, innovative dream education is taking place outside the hallowed halls of traditional universities and colleges. In this chapter we discuss community dream education. We take *community* to be both a locus and an attitude—the locus being outside conventional schools and university degree programs, the attitude one of seeking new approaches to dreams and new kinds of learners. Community dream education can be for lay dreamers or for graduate students, clinicians, and others who work with dreams professionally. It takes place in alternative institutes of higher learning, churches, community centers, public libraries, private homes, over the Internet, in freestanding institutes, at conferences—or even on occasion back on college campuses as noncredit continuing education courses.

Alternative and community dream education may lack the imprimatur of a college or university, but also can be far less constrained by standard academic bureaucracies and entrenched paradigms. Teachers are freer to find an audience and teach about dreams in their unique ways. Dream teachers and learners with compatible perspectives can come together. What one loses in academic cachet one gains in creativity, access, and enthusiasm all around.

We describe organizations, persons and activities in community dream education. This review is far from exhaustive; we focus on what we know, and on the persons who gave us information. There are many worthy examples that we will not cover or will mention only in passing. This does not mean that they lack merit. Our hope is that the reader will be motivated to seek out and explore a wide array of existing teachers and programs.

In researching this book, we have come to the rather surprising conclusion that dream education very well may be more robust currently outside colleges than inside. People do not want a "church of dreams" (in Richard Wilkerson's phrase) but still desire an experience of connection and community from their dreams involvements. They go outside conventional formal higher education to find it.

In the preceding chapters we have focused for the most part on classes, programs, and schools catering to undergraduate students, and on graduate clinical education in conventional institutional settings. We have structured our book according to traditional disciplinary divisions, even as we have emphasized that effective dream education draws on the methods and findings of multidisciplinary approaches to both research and teaching. In this chapter we expand the discussion to consider ways of teaching dreams outside the bounds of traditional academic frameworks.

First we look at dream study programs at private graduate institutes, then at dream teachers who work in a variety of community-based settings, including ongoing dream discussion groups. We also discuss dream education through life, and give some attention to the special case of what we term "charismatic gurus."

The reader will discern that in general we are well impressed with these innovative approaches and their practitioners. However, our main purpose in this chapter is not to trumpet or praise these efforts and achievements, but rather to describe them dispassionately and note how they fit in the larger arena of dream education.

Private Graduate Institutes

Some psychotherapy training schools operate apart from traditional colleges and universities. Institutes of Freudian and Jungian psychology also have developed their own educational practices in ways that would not have been possible in a conventional academic context. In addition to dream clinical education in psychoanalytic training institutes (discussed in the previous chapter), the study of dreams has an important place in the curricula of many of these alternative schools, whose classes offer creative incubators of new methods in dream education. The graduates of these programs often have a better understanding of the diversity of dream theory, research, and practice than do most mainstream psychologists. However, the pragmatic concern over issues of academic training and accreditation (also raised in Chapter 8) should be kept in mind in evaluating which students are best served by private graduate institutes, and in preparing students in their choices of graduate education and career paths.

The advantage of these programs is that they each offer more than one course on dreams, allowing for creative cross-fertilization from class to class. They provide training in experiential dream study and its relation to academic research. They create a student community of people interested in dreams, sharing resources, and supporting each other's works; and they educate students in the kinds of interdisciplinary approaches we have been advocating throughout this book.

A number of alternative educational institutes offer classes and programs on dreams. Here we focus on the basic approaches used at three schools with dream courses as standard parts of their curricula. All three of these schools are located in California, and all share many of their core values and teaching practices. But their differing histories and emphases should give readers an inkling of the various ways dreaming appears broadly in nontraditional school settings.

The Saybrook Graduate School and Research Center in San Francisco was founded in 1971 as the Humanistic Psychology Institute, affiliated with Sonoma State University. It later became an independent school with masters and doctor of philosophy programs in psychology, and a clinically focused doctor of psychology program, all aimed at mid-career adults looking for ways to develop new skills and deepen their understanding of their chosen personal and professional paths. Saybrook's philosophical origins lie in the humanistic psychology of Carl Rogers, Abraham Maslow, and others in the mid-20th century who rejected the impersonal approach of behaviorism and the determinism of psychoanalysis, instead calling for a new psychology focusing directly on human experience. This new psychology would not only provide a better way of helping people who are suffering, it would show the importance of vibrant psychological health and spiritual development.

Today Saybrook has a dream certificate program administered by Stanley Krippner and Jacquie Lewis, which consists of three required courses (Personal Mythology and Dream Psychology; Neuropsychology of Dreams and Dreaming; Art Based Inquiry) plus a practicum course in which the student chooses a topic to pursue. An integrative paper completes the requirements for the certificate. As one of the foremost scholars of cross-cultural and psychological dream research, Krippner provides a wealth of experience for his students to draw on. Saybrook's education uses a method of "community-based distance learning." Professors conduct online group courses and read papers sent in via e-mail. Students share dreams when Krippner teaches online. Krippner reminds us that word *education* stems from the Latin *educare*, to lead out. He finds that dreamwork "leads out" students' potentials, and this needs to be the mission of education today.[2]

Pacifica Graduate Institute is situated in the foothills of Santa Barbara. It offers master's and doctoral programs drawing on depth psychology. Its history reaches back more than 30 years into a cluster of local programs that taught methods of clinical psychotherapy with attention to the tradition of depth psychology, described by the school on its Web site as "in-depth studies of Freud, Jung, alchemy, Hippocratic medicine, dream interpretation, mythology, and classical literature." Clinical psychologist Steven Aizenstadt organized and led these programs into its current incarnation. Pacifica offers wide-ranging courses for a student population similar to Saybrook's and other alternative programs as well, serving adults at least several years out of college looking for training to pursue a new and/or enhanced professional career, with some students pursuing the degree for primarily personal education and enrichment. In 1992, Pacifica became the home of the library of Joseph Campbell, the famous comparative mythologist, boosting the school's programs on mythological studies.

All the programs at Pacifica draw in some form or other on Aizenstadt's method of "DreamTending," which involves treating dream images as living entities, making their presence available to the dreamer in the waking state. Following in the line of Jungian thinkers and clinicians (especially James Hillman) who have focused on the power of the archetypes and the depths of the soul, Aizenstadt teaches his students how to listen to dreams, not analyze them. He takes a "psyche-centered" rather than "person-centered" approach that his students learn to use in therapy with individuals and in cultural reflection on collective realities.

The Dream Studies Program at JFKU in Pleasant Hill originated in a single class given by Fariba Bogzaran and Daniel Deslauriers in 1989. They co-taught an 11-week, three-unit elective course in the Consciousness Studies master's program. Founded in 1964, JFKU offers evening and weekend programs for working adults in business, law, psychology, and holistic studies. Within the latter, several masters programs offered courses on alternative forms of medicine, philosophy, spirituality, and mind–body practices. The master's in Consciousness Studies gave Bogzaran and Deslauriers a platform to design a course that covered a wide range of perspectives. Bogzaran, whose work was mentioned in Chapter 6 with her course in lucid dreaming, has a background in sleep laboratory science, East–West psychology, phenomenology, and art. Deslauriers also has a background in cognitive psychology, along with training in narrative research. By combining their resources, they put together an interdisciplinary course. Bogzaran continued teaching at JFKU for a number of years while Deslauriers went on to teach the course at the California Institute of Integral Studies (CIIS) in San Francisco.

Out of that original course Bogzaran eventually developed and directed a broad program of interdisciplinary dream studies program at JFKU. It took many years of administrative struggle and academic political maneuvering for her to succeed in creating a high-quality educational program devoted to the study of dreams. Over time, the program has moved from a concentration within Consciousness Studies to a stand-alone 36-unit certificate program, and now to a specialization available to the master's students in the Consciousness and Transformative Studies programs.

Bogzaran's teaching focuses on integrative dream methodology, art, lucid dreaming, and the science of sleep. Several other teachers have contributed to the interdisciplinary nature of the program. Marilyn Fowler, the current director of the program, is one of its earliest graduates and an expert in comparative methods of dream interpretation. She teaches courses on dream group facilitation and ethics. Jeremy Taylor, whose teaching is discussed later in this chapter, has taught classes on dreams and archetypes for many years at JFKU. Kimmy Johnson teaches courses on "Dreams and Indigenous Ways of Knowing," which look at dreaming in relation to ancestry and families of origins. Kelly Bulkeley has taught several courses at JFKU on the psychology and the cross-cultural history of dreams.

Deslauriers has been a professor at CIIS where he teaches in the East–West Psychology program. The core philosophy of CIIS comes from Haridas Chaudhuri and his "Integral Philosophy." Bogzaran and Deslauriers are currently co-authoring a book titled *Integral Dreaming,* which addresses the integral perspective, theory, and methodology in the field of dream studies.

Other Community Dream Programs

Many educators are teaching about dreams in smaller venues and contexts in community environments. Following is a sampling. We look at one freelancer who teaches in a variety of settings, and two who work individually through their own dream institutes—nondegree-granting organizations whose sole purpose is dreams education. We also note two teachers who embody dream education in their professional lives and civic involvements.

Jeremy Taylor has been teaching about dreams for 40 years. His work illustrates the wide variety of settings in which one can teach about dreams. Taylor started using dreams as part of a Unitarian Universalist Service Committee-sponsored community organizing exercise aimed at overcoming (unconscious) racism. Over the years, he has taught a number of formal classes at different colleges, universities, and institutes. These include Sonoma State University, Saint Mary's University, the Haden institute, the Institute for Transpersonal Psychology, John F. Kennedy University, the Chaplaincy Institute for Interfaith & Arts Ministries, and (for more than 35 years) at the Starr King School for the Ministry in Berkeley, California. He also teaches in various conference and summer institute settings, among which are the IASD, the International Association for Transpersonal Psychology, the International Association for Psychosynthesis, and the Spiritual Director's International. His community dream teaching extends to prisons, hospitals, residential treatment programs, hospices, churches, community development organizations, and private dream groups. He also works with individual clients.

Taylor uses a Jungian framework in his teaching. He teaches basic Jungian concepts, and encourages students to pursue whatever aspects of that large body of knowledge and theory to which they are most drawn. Taylor believes that all dreams have multiple meanings, and that all the major theories of dream meaning are correct, at the levels that they address. They all are valuable, in his view, and all worth teaching and studying. He finds Jung's work on archetypes of the collective unconscious more consistently useful than many of the others.

Taylor asks students to keep a dream journal, and to get into the habit of giving their dreams titles when they record, and sketching them. He gives students an extensive list of suggested readings, and encourages them to participate in class discussions of the various dream theories and schools of thought, and in sharing and exploring dreams of their own to "unpack" with projective analysis, the "If it were my dream . . ." technique. He encourages students to share their own dreams in class, stressing that sharing is voluntary at all levels of participation. "The name of the game is dreamer's choice." He always begins with a review of the "rules" of anonymity, and emphasizes that any participant can shift the whole group into strict confidentiality any time he or she desires to do so. Taylor believes there are many advantages of using students' actual dreams as the focus of the class; their learning is anchored in their own interior experience and is more likely to be integrated into their lives.

In classes with academic credit Taylor gives all students either a "pass" in "pass–fail" systems or "A" in letter grade systems, at the start of the course. Student interest, effort, and performance in Taylor's classes is generally at a high level, exceeding academic norms and justifying in his view the up-front "Pass' or "A" grade (which removes grade concerns from the interpersonal dynamic between teacher and student). In his experience, dream learning is a matter of participation, experience, and mastery. Like swimming, either you learn or you don't. Evaluation is based on students doing the projective dreamwork, on group discussions and one-to-one meetings. Taylor finds that the dreams themselves are the best teachers. He sees an increasing acceptance of "dream studies" as a legitimate discipline in all settings, community, and academic.

Other community dreams teachers are identified more with a single organization. One of these is Nicole Gratton, who created in 1992 and has since run a dream institute in Montréal, Québec, the École Internationale de Rêves, and the associated Académie du Sommeil. There she teaches people about dreams, trains fledgling dream instructors and writes books (in French) about the nature and uses of dreams. Gratton combines in her teaching psychological and spiritual approaches, with due attention to scientific research on sleeping and dreaming. She believes that dream teachers should ground themselves well in their knowledge of multiple cultures' differing beliefs about and approaches to working with dreams. In Gratton's course, students read 20 books about dreams, and attend class in 3-hour sessions, half on learning theories, half on their own dreams. Her certification for dreams teachers requires 200 class hours (the equivalent of about five semester-long college courses), and summary presentations of the contents of the assigned books.

Gratton also provides ongoing monthly dream discussion sessions of 3 hours, open to former students and new people.

Gratton's focus in teaching is on the strengthening of student autonomy. Dreams and students are diverse; each is different and somewhat unpredictable. An attitude of openness to the unexpected and respect for the unknown is called for. Students are happy to regain their own power to work with their dreams. Gratton avoids transference from her students by supporting their known interpretations, never saying, "No, you are wrong." She does not set herself above her students as an authority, but shares her own dreams and life as examples of teaching points, and remains open to different approaches to dreams besides her favorites. She regularly keeps her dream journal and shares it with students. Her greatest success in teaching is seeing students develop confidence in their abilities in dreams as a useful tool.

Gratton's wish is that the average person would incorporate dreams more routinely into waking consciousness and daily life. She views her work as a contribution toward the development of increasing societal awareness of the value of dreams, a "collective consciousness"—in the sense of broadly valuing and nurturing one another's dreams and the insights and wisdom they provide. Gratton finds that people tend to avoid their dreams because they don't want to have and recall "bad"—that is, unpleasant—ones. They want to avoid the dark side of their experiences and themselves. However, all experiences can be ultimately life affirming and therefore positive; this is part of the educational message.

The business of establishing and running a dream institute requires a blend of creativity and structured business acumen, in Gratton's experience. She took 5 years to develop her institute, gradually making the transition from working full time in another field and doing dream-related activities on the side, to quitting her former occupation and devoting herself full time to dreams. In this process, she met for 2 years with a group of businesspersons, to learn how to be one. She learned that one must be at ease with the inevitable uncertainty surrounding an entrepreneurial enterprise. Too much stress on making money can sabotage integrity, and one must guard against this. There must be a higher purpose, with helping people as the focus.

A second freestanding dreams education enterprise is Justina Lasley's Institute for Dream Studies in Charleston, South Carolina. Lasley offers a certification course for work with dreams in private and clinical settings. She designed it for therapists, counselors, spiritual directors, ministers, health care workers, and teachers, as well as others interested in personal development. The program of study consists of four weekend sessions and at-home studies during the first year and a year of internship during the second year. Attendance at the IASD annual conference is encouraged in order to broaden the participants' exposure to various experts and areas of dreamwork.

Lasley believes that students' dreams, not the instructor, are the best teacher. Lasley sees dreamwork as different from therapy and the teacher to be a facilitator. As a teacher, she does not feel that she needs to take charge of the process—the dream is in charge. She does not need to know or provide any answers. Dream teachers are re-educators, helping people relearn what they already knew but lost—that is intuitive knowledge. Her goal is to help people to open up and listen to each other's viewpoints. Lasley sees dream education as moving ahead of the general culture. The dream's integrating potential is strong.

It is exhausting and not easy to combine the role of dreams educator and dream business entrepreneur. Both Lasley and Nicole Gratton are sensitive to the potential problem of monetary considerations diluting the quality of the dream education and dreamwork process. Maximizing income is not necessarily compatible with maintaining high program quality. It is possible to spread oneself too thinly, with the quality of the work suffering. Both these dream institute heads are committed to the integrity of the dream and their students' needs.

A third freestanding organization dedicated to dreams is The Dream Institute of Northern California, in Berkeley, founded and directed by Meredith Sabini, with Richard Russo as associate director. The Dream Institute is, in the words of its Web site, "an experimental cultural center that offers public lectures and workshops, dream study groups, dream-based cultural events, professional dream consultation, and the innovative method "Culture Dreaming."[2]

There have been many other dream education programs, including the online Electric Dreams Community, European Association for the Study of Dreams (an IASD Affiliate), Stephen LaBerge's Lucidity Institute, Craig Webb's D.R.E.A.M.S. Foundation,—the Bay Area Dreamworking Group, Richard Wilkerson's DreamGates History of Dreaming online course, the Haden Institute, Jeremy Taylor's Marin Institute for Projective Dreamwork, Delaney and Flowers' Dream and Consultation Center, and the New England Dreamwork Institute. The enormous potential of programs encouraging the use of dreams as a way to greater artistic creativity has been tapped by Victoria Rabinowe's "Art of the Dream" workshops in Santa Fe, New Mexico, and Sheila Asato's Monkey Bridge Arts Center for Art, Dreaming & Creative Spirituality in Minneapolis.[3]

Henry Reed, a transpersonal psychologist at Atlantic University, has been promoting innovative dream education practices for more than 30 years, combining his training as an academic psychologist with his spiritual and artistic interests. In conjunction with Robert Van de Castle, Reed developed the "Dream Helper Ceremony," to stimulate greater dream recall and appreciation for the power of dreams. As the founder in the 1970s of *Sundance: The Community Dream Journal*, Reed helped cultivate a broader public interest in dreams that opened the door for many dream educators who followed.[4]

As a group, these and other teachers and programs represent tremendous educational innovation. We suggest that interested readers contact one or more of them to see if what they offer is appealing, to learn more about dreams, or as sources of ideas, materials, and approaches for your own teaching. Of necessity, and in the absence of significant assessment studies (see Appendix I for a discussion of assessment and evaluation in dream studies) you will need to make your own judgments about the value of what you discover. We have found gems of insight, wisdom, and innovation in many sources. The task is to discern these gems, learn about them and incorporate them into your repertoires.

Short Community Programs

Other forms of community education include discreet talks to community groups, such as Rotary and Lions Club meetings, churches and workplace gatherings, and other time-limited teachings such as weekend workshops. Such events are particularly important because they bring an awareness of dreams to the public who may have little prior dream knowledge and only a latent interest in the subject. In this way, teachers can bring dreams to the general population. Adults past their formal schooling may have no other exposure to information about the value of their dreams. This is unfortunate because in adulthood, the search for self-understanding, psychological, and spiritual growth can begin in earnest, and dreams can contribute significantly. The opportune contact with dreams through a Jaycee breakfast speaker, for example, can initiate a valuable journey.

One-time talks about dreams can also take place with younger people outside their regular school settings. As an example, Phil King and Johanna King (no relation) gave a presentation to a group of Mexican immigrant high school students in conjunction with a summer educational enrichment program they were attending at the University of California at Santa Cruz. This was a somewhat fortuitous occurrence, as King and King happened to be on campus for the annual IASD conference at a time that coincided with the high school program. The enrichment program organizers requested a speaker from the dreams conference and the Kings volunteered. Accidental though it was, the presentation was well received and it seeded an awareness of dreams in the minds of students who had no previous exposure to dreams as a subject of study.

Johanna King notes that what works well in one-time presentations is to ground the inherently esoteric parts in the meat and potatoes of sleep cycles and dreaming processes. This takes little time. Phil King characterizes this as "first getting in the shallow end of the pool." Johanna King suggests having a list of common questions about dreams to ask the audience. This gives them the experience of talking, in general terms, about their dreams. (For an early but still useful list of common questions, see Montague Ullman and Nan Zimmerman's *Working with Dreams*.[5])

Note the distinction between the public presentation or one-shot workshop versus therapy group or ongoing dream group contexts. One should perhaps not work with—or at the very least be careful working with—individual dreams in a public lecture setting, where the dreamer is too exposed. One way of responsibly working with an audience member's dream in such public settings is to solicit a volunteer ahead of time, and discuss the process with that person, to assess his or her vulnerability and suitability.

The basis of Johanna King's caution about workshops is that there is no follow-up, as there is with therapy or even with lay dream groups. Some workshop leaders tend to go too deep given this lack of tracking the effects on participants. To put it somewhat dramatically, there is a danger that the surgeon opens up the patient and then walks away. Another metaphor is to liken the process to flying a kite in a strong wind; if the string breaks, the kite is unmoored and flies away eventually to crash land. The distinction here is between programs consisting of multiple sessions over time, where the teacher can ascertain and deal with effects of preceding sessions, and one-time events where the nonimmediate impacts on the participants are unknown. There is an inherent tension between the dramatic and evocative nature of workshops (which is a large part of their appeal and economic viability) and their lack of ability per se to monitor participants' well-being. Responsible workshop leaders will include mechanisms for follow up—ways by which participants who are unsettled by the experience can contact them, and receive support.

Training, experience, and ethical sensitivity strengthen the kite string and provide safeguards. These qualities are not necessarily always present if the leader lacks experience; Johanna King notes that in the State of Washington, for example, persons with a bachelor's degree can be counselors, promote themselves as such, and run dream workshops.

Community-based dream workshops differ from one-time presentations in that the participants are more self-selected on the basis of a prior interest in dreams and, or, self-exploration. Activities also tend to last longer, at least several hours, extending in some instances over a day, a weekend, or beyond. They are, shorter, however, then ongoing dream discussion groups that may extend indefinitely.

Dream education need not be a matter of discrete events. It works well when integrated into the sensibilities, activities, and skills of individuals who have multiple professional roles and other involvements in the community. Two good examples of such people are Jody Grundy and Iris Maria Heller.

Grundy, a therapist, life coach, community organizer, and political activist, echoes Gratton, Lasley, and Taylor in her view that "dreams really are teachers within." Grundy notes that much important teaching and learning is outside schools. Her dreamwork is with her clients, but she brings a dreams sensibility to all her encounters. She finds it helpful in working with dreams to listen more deeply, not so much to interpret. Grundy sees dreams as giving us a direction and then challenging us to bring the dream insight into the world. We go beyond ourselves. "It's not about ego, even though ego is needed to implement the insight."

Grundy leads dream groups using Montague Ullman's method over a 6-week process, 6 or fewer people with sessions running from 2 to 3 hours. There is self-revelation in a slow and safe way. Each week the group deals with one dream from one person. The final session is a collective ritual featuring the making of a collage, based on a typed and duplicated dream report. Grundy draws the analogy of dream groups to theater (especially Greek theater): Both bring participants to some kind of catharsis.

Heller represents in her work several of the themes running throughout this book, including community education, interdisciplinary approaches, and juxtapositions of dreams, film, and writing. A native of Germany, Heller holds master's degrees in rhetoric and American studies, and in media arts and production.

Inspired by German author Uwe Kolbe's dream class, where she molded dreams into scripts, myths, storyboards, or comics, Heller combined this practice with her film analytical studies at the Eberhard Karls University Tübingen. In her thesis, "The Discourse of Dream in American Film," Heller dealt with the connections between dream and film. At the University of Technology in Sydney, Australia, Heller created a series of short, dreamlike sequences that invite the viewer to be freed from a narrative thread and instead follow a flow of images through different spaces and moods. The cinematography employs a subjective observing, a dreamer's point of view.

Heller teaches dream classes on a community level, always with the filmic affinity in the background. A 2009 class with seven students met weekly in a coffee shop. There, little dream stories come into existence as narratives on paper, but also in visual ways like drawings, storyboards—or film. The focus was not on dream interpretation but on using dreams as springboard to creative projects, which included stories, scripts, comic books, essays and paintings.

Dream Education in Adulthood

In Chapter 10 we take an extended look at dream education for children and adolescents. Here we discuss community dream education for adults. For younger adults we adopt a Jungian conception of the first half of life as being a time primarily for establishing competencies and achievements in the external (waking) world. Reflections about self and internal development occur, but take a back seat to outward effort and attainment in education, establishing relationships and families, and careers. To this Jungian foundation, we add an existential framework. Young and middle-aged adults make fundamental choices, which they exercise with more or less skill and care. Wisdom and self-understanding come mostly in hindsight. In Soren Kierkegaard's phrase, we live life forward, but understand it backward. Dreams are a way of self-discovery in their linking of the external with the internal. Areas of restriction and potential are experienced, and new directions contemplated and tried out. One can make new choices in waking life and affirm old choices. During these years, interpretation of dreams is an appropriate activity, guided by the evolving realities of one's waking life.

Young adults in college or graduate school may be able to study dreams in academic courses. Adults in the future work force may come across dreams as part of employee development programs, although we know of no such programs currently in America. Freestanding dream institutes' programs are available to those who seek them, as is the array of useful books on the subject. One may find dream discussion groups here and there in conjunction with community centers or churches and other places of worship. The resources of IASD are available. A single interested dreamer can form a "dream group" based on community contacts and the Internet.

Jung's conception is that in contrast to one's earlier adult life, where the proper emphasis is on competencies, achievements and relationships, there is in later life the possibility of individuation—the resolution of psychological conflicts and the melding and integration of unconscious and conscious mental strengths. We add to Jung from humanistic psychology ideas of a self-actualization process—striving to come ever closer to attaining one's unique potentials.

From these perspectives we believe that there is a substantially conscious, willed quality to personal growth. The implication is that it is quite possible to stagnate and even to live one's entire life without affording oneself possibilities for psychological development. Being interested in dreams and other psychological and spiritual matters is a sign that a person is consciously growth-oriented.

A consideration of dreams can greatly aid self-development in later life, whether one conceives of dreams in Jungian or other terms. While the mechanics of dream education for older people are the same as for younger adults, the emphases can be quite different. Older people have completed most of their life journey, and personal development includes looking back on previous ports of call, acknowledging wise and foolish actions, appreciating successes and accepting failures. Switching metaphors, one needs to see the threads of fulfillment in the life tapestry one has already woven. Since people often focus on their failures, there is a need to reorient them toward the positive value that nearly all lives have in abundance. An appreciation of self and reconciliation with self are worthy emphases that permit life to continue forward in healing and progressively whole ways.

An 80-year-old man was in one of our dreams classes. At some level, he was searching for a sense of completion and ease. He had a rather low opinion of himself. His attitude was a kind of resigned pessimism. An exploration of his dreams led him to identify continuing currents of integrity in them and in his waking life. His existential stance changed from one essentially of regret to one of appreciation and gratitude. It was not *all* in how he viewed things, but viewing them in a new way allowed him to see elements that he had missed or forgotten. This was enough to turn his perspective around in his life's 11th hour.

So dreamwork with older persons can profitably include a "re-viewing" of the life lived. Such devices as collages of photos, written autobiographies, and other compilations and presentations of self can complement working with dreams and will stimulate new dreams.

Dream educators must seek out older adults. It is a rare older person, such as the man just described, who will show up in contexts where most students are substantially younger. Institute programs and public presentations will attract some, if they already have an interest. Additionally, venues such as university continuing education programs, workplace groups and gatherings, Lions clubs and other civic organizations, Elder hostels, churches, adult education programs, adult exercise and health groups, senior centers, and senior volunteer groups can all be fertile territory. Nursing homes are a special case, as often the reason for the person being a resident is a diminished mental capacity, which may make focusing on dreams problematic. Many senior care facilities now stratify themselves in terms of health status, with independent living and assisted-living programs incorporated under the same umbrella as more intensive nursing home care. Residents in independent and assisted-living environments would be good candidates for learning about dreams.

Consider a continuum encompassing society outside and inside care facilities, running roughly in terms of increasing age, with employment groups, civic and religious organizations at the younger end, active senior organizations in the middle, and care facilities at the older end. These are the possible environments for adult community dream education.

One dream course for older people is actually in a university setting. We bring it up in this chapter on community education, however, because the setting is beside the point—the purpose is life enrichment, not academic credits toward a degree. Patricia Garfield, a well-known author in the field, teaches the course. The classes she is teaching on dreams are for the Osher Lifelong Learning Program (OLLI), a program for people aged 50 years and older. Garfield's course is at the Dominican University of California, in San Rafael. The course title is "Lifelong Dreamers." Following an introductory session, participants examine common negative dream themes around the world, as well as their positive versions. They discover how their dreams portray these themes, especially in senior issues such as retirement, physical aging and the loss of a loved person and subsequent bereavement. Participants also learn methods—both modern and ancient—for preventing and banishing nightmares, practice methods for inducing dreams on specific topics, and explore how to use dreams for creative purposes. Garfield demonstrates the most common features in imagery that appear in dreams dealing with these important senior issues. She also presents several dream methods to support coping with the stressful aspects of seniors' lives, along with ways to use their personal dream material as a creative resource to enhance waking life.

Garfield taught in the same OLLI program a new course called "Movies of the Mind: How Metaphors of Emotion Reveal Meaning." Basically, this is a course on dreams in film.

Garfield's courses are useful models for seniors' dream education in university settings and elsewhere in the community. Seniors are rapidly growing in numbers; as a group, they promise to be especially receptive to learning about dreams.

The Quality of Community Dream Education

In dream education outside academia there are fewer guarantees that teaching will meet high standards. There also are fewer limits on what one teaches and how, except those stemming from the knowledge and integrity of the people involved and the checks of the marketplace. Responsibility for teaching quality falls almost solely on the teacher.

The great majority of community teachers of dreams in our experience are responsible, caring, and ethical. The IASD, under the guidance of Taylor and Carol Warner, has taken great pains over the years to promulgate a thoughtful ethics statement (see Appendix C). However, not all dreams teachers are members of IASD and follow its ethical precepts. Additionally, even the best-intentioned and skilled teachers can make unsupported truth claims or lead learners to places they are not ready to go. The potential danger and drawback of freestanding dreams education, especially in dreamwork, is the lack of outside expert quality assessment. (To be fair, the same problem faces dream psychotherapy and psychotherapy in general—i.e., the absence of external validation.) Ultimately, the learner must be his or her own learning assessor. This is difficult if not impossible to do well, especially for novices.

One quality control on dreamwork education is the IASD annual international conference and regional conferences, where many dream educators working in the community present papers, hold panel discussions, and conduct workshops. The conferences' program committees determine which presentations are likely to be good and within ethical bounds, and which not. The latter are not invited or if accepted once but not proving out, are not invited again. Although this screening process does not directly affect educators and programs outside the IASD sphere of influence, it does establish a standard and set a tone for the field.

In recent years, the IASD has expanded its efforts in community education by offering home study/distance learning courses to the public.[6] These courses, like presentations at IASD conferences, are APA approved for continuing education credits for clinicians, and are certified by the California Board of Behavioral Sciences. So they are useful both for dreams education for the lay public and for professional development and licensure for clinicians. Organizers based the first round of distance learning courses on reading books and taking multiple-choice exams—one book per course. Whether completion of the courses will be transferable to academic credits in universities, and if so what the credit equivalency calculus will be, remains to be seen.

Domhoff is a notable dream educator who is not entirely comfortable with trends in nonacademic dreams teaching that focus on the subjective experiences and particular approaches of personable and charismatic teachers. He notes that they have their set ways in which appeal often trumps corroboration, and that there is something of a "cultish feeling" about educational programs unconstrained by the norms of evidence and academic consensus building.

Domhoff notes an interesting distinction between people who research and teach about dreams along with other subjects in university settings, versus what we would term *dream entrepreneurs*, those who make their livings writing and teaching about dreams in the community. For the former group, dreams are simply one of their interests (if an important one). Their livelihoods are not dependent on their dream involvements. The latter group is more dependent not simply on dreams but on their success in selling, literally, their points of view and presentation style. The former are likely to be more dispassionate and detached in their work. The latter are likely to be more committed to particular views and modes that work for them commercially as well as personally. Although each could benefit from some of the perspectives and attitudes of the other, there is an inherent difference in principle between wanting to build knowledge and wanting to promulgate a point of view.

Johanna King sees the academic versus dream entrepreneur distinction as not as important as the teacher's level of education and training. Dream entrepreneurs may be very well educated and their teachings very sound. Even if one does not favor a particular approach, one can still recognize that it is legitimate and responsible. What is dangerous in King's view is the combination of some intuitive feel for dreams along with minimal training, for example, having gone to a workshop or two and then setting yourself up as a "dream worker."

We would add that dream education, particularly in extra-academic settings, is potentially susceptible to the same kinds of abuses that historically have punctuated new psychotherapies and spiritual, religious, and personal growth practices concentrated in a subculture of believers. These range from subtle group conformity pressure to violation of the autonomy and dignity of participating individuals. Abuse always is possible and dream educators of all stripes should guard against it.

We do not intend these cautions about potential pitfalls in community dreamwork education to discourage the reader from studying or teaching in community contexts. On the contrary, one can find excellent education and training in many programs and with many teachers. On balance, as we have noted, we think there is a richer array of dream education, particularly in working with one's own dreams, outside university settings than within them. University environments, to be sure, generate the research that underlies important advances in dream theory and understanding, and the mechanisms of accredited higher education generally serve at least their intended purpose of constraining loose or ill-founded claims and misrepresentations.

Many, perhaps even a majority, of the approaches to dreamwork in community education are Jungian in orientation. This is a two-edged sword. Jungian theory is meaningful and heuristically productive. However, its concepts are abstruse and difficult to verify. Its mystical qualities and mythological precepts make it more a template for creative narrative building, less a theory that one can test empirically. (The narrative-building ability of Jungian theory may be its strength; see the discussion in Chapter 11 on alternative assumptions in dream interpretation.) Although the best "neo-Jungian" dream teachers do fine, even profound, work, some may be inadequately educated to do good teaching and dreamwork from that perspective.

Charismatic Gurus

One important mode of dreams teaching is that provided by what we call, with only a bit of hyperbole, *charismatic gurus*. (We owe the term to Alan Siegel.) By "charismatic" we mean persons who impress by the appeal and force of their personalities and presentation as well as the contents of their teaching. By "gurus" we mean teachers who, explicitly or implicitly, claim to possess *or* are viewed as possessing special talents, abilities, or insights, which are available to others through practices and disciplines with the teacher as exemplar and conduit. Charismatic gurus, as leaders and teachers, require followers and believers—the students.

Perhaps most dream teachers have the potential to take on a "guru" persona. It's almost inevitable that when a teacher introduces the wonders of dreaming to students for the first time, some of them will treat the teacher *as if* he or she has special abilities and insights. This is old-fashioned transference from the students that can lure teachers into playing the role, rather than channeling the energy back into the study of dreams. We all feel it; we're all vulnerable. The point is to be aware so we can at least avoid the biggest problems.

We address the charismatic guru as a type, describing generic qualities and dynamics. It is difficult to know where to place charismatic gurus in the chapter structure of this book. They may teach in universities, freestanding institutions, or on their own. Their students include undergraduates, lay adults, and clinicians. We discuss them here because their entrepreneurial bent makes them ill suited to institutional constraints. They are most at home and most effective working solo in community settings.

We have mixed feelings about these practitioners and their teachings, admiring much about them. Yet we caution against uncritically embracing this mode of teaching or learning, as there are potential dangers. Charismatic gurus can be among the brightest, most dedicated, knowledgeable, and innovative dream teachers. They may be important as theorists and authors. Much of what they profess deserves consideration for incorporation into learners' dream knowledge and teachers' repertoires. They can be appropriately circumspect and cautious in their writings but at times less so in workshop and lecture settings. We respect the abilities of many of these teachers, but are not fans of the cults of personality that can evolve.

Charismatic gurus may have connections with IASD but do much on their own, including one-shot presentations, and courses of study, including online dream classes. They make their livelihoods substantially through the appeal of their talks, workshops, and books. Presentation and persuasion can become more important than reflective consideration or empirical support. There may be claims that are self-validating or otherwise incapable of disproval. Their language and rhetoric can be bold and brilliant; it also can go beyond supportive evidence. Creative storytelling can substitute for more mundane analysis. Assertions based on one person's dream experience and perspective can push into the background facts or arguments inconsistent with the promulgated view.

Charismatic gurus interpret some dream experience in depth psychological, esoteric cultural or mystical terms that are prone to fuzzy or exaggerated claims because of their lack of familiarity. Metaphoric modes of discourse can be carelessly reified (by the student if not by the teacher). Anecdote can become generalization.

There is a long history of charismatic showmen in America, from the elixir salesmen and rainmakers of the past, to spiritual leaders imported from Eastern cultures and their Western disciples, to modern proponents of new therapies and consciousness raising practices. Typically, there is a cycle where the "latest thing" is first touted as an all-encompassing worldview, and greeted with enthusiasm. Followers gather; insular and odd practices thrive. After a while, when the new thing fails to live up to the hype, it is shoved to the side to make room for even newer, or reworked systems. Residual cores of value in discarded systems are retained in commonly accepted practice and belief. Sometimes systems are recycled, with new generations unaware that essentially the same package had come around 30, 50, or 100 years before.

Not frequently but too often these consciousness practices, as we call them, form the basis of cults, with adherents cut off substantially from society's modulating norms and protections. In such instances, psychological, financial, and sexual exploitation of followers by charismatic leaders ensues with disturbing regularity.

This has not happened in the dreams field but it could. Dreams are about consciousness and deepening self-knowledge. There is an elusive quality to them and to attempts to understand them. They are in the same domain as other psychological, spiritual, and health regimens and susceptible to the same potential abuses.

The more immediate danger in our field may be subtler than the threat of cult formation. It is the substitution of persuasiveness and induced emotion for logic, proof, and reflections on experience. This delicate matter evokes our distinction between dream experience and dream science. Dream experience is credulous; in its touching and probing of deep feeling and meaning it may sweep aside considerations of consistency and generalizability. We advocate a stance that combines openness to experience with intellectual skepticism. Rita Dwyer has characterized this as striking a balance between being open and having *discernment*. We should allow ourselves to be moved by the power of the dream experience, but then assess it. Was there a guru or group persuasion effect that swept you up? Where there are empirical claims, what is the quality of supporting evidence? Do assertions that particular ways of dealing with dreams have certain consequences hold up in practice?

Community Dream Groups

Lay dream discussion groups are among the most meaningful and valuable forms of community dream education. There are many such groups scattered around the country; all of which we are aware respect their members and the integrity of members' dreams. These groups can vary considerably in their structure and operation. "Dream groups" may meet once or twice a month, once a week, or at other intervals. Meetings may last a couple of hours, or longer. Longer sessions may have built-in breaks, and may accommodate every member present sharing a dream. Shorter sessions may not. Groups may be long standing, or relatively new. They may meet at members' homes, or in churches, or community centers. They may be open to new members drifting in and out, or they may have a more fixed membership. If the former, members may be of quite different levels of knowledge about dreams and sophistication in working with them. If the latter, members will tend to a higher and more equal level of sophistication. Some groups may include as participants mental health professionals, some not. Groups may have one leader or leadership may rotate among the members. The ethos will tend to be egalitarian, but not necessarily, if there is a leader who is a professional trained in working with dreams, in which case participation fees may be charged. (This would be an exception to the more typical practice of lay participants and no fees.) Groups may employ one theoretical perspective in their engagement with dreams, or (more frequently) take an eclectic approach. Similarly, they may hew to a fixed procedure, such as the projective dreaming method, or they may be flexible in their procedures, depending on context.

We take no position on the relative merit of groups' orientations and practices on each of these dimensions, feeling that there is value in all, and that each group should structure itself according to its needs. There is no single configuration most suitable for everyone. (However, see Appendix C for a list of general considerations and ethical principles in establishing and running a community dream group.)

The ethical considerations involved in sharing dreams surface in somewhat different and substantially attenuated forms in community dream groups compared to dream groups lodged in academic courses. Not present, or present in much reduced degree, are issues of authority and power differentials, and matters of informed consent—people join dream groups, after all, precisely to discuss their dreams. There is still the core matter of respect for the autonomy and ultimate authority of the dreamer over the meaning and significance of his or her dreams, and others' deference to that authority.

There are many community dream groups currently active. Here, briefly, are two examples. One is the metro DC dream community in northern Virginia.[19] This group, led by Rita Dwyer, former IASD executive director and president, has met continually since 1983. They gather monthly, in a 4-hour weekend session. Meetings sometimes break up into subgroups if the group size warrants. Members make an effort to hear a dream from all present who wish to share one.

Meetings are held in a neutral site—not a member's home, but a public library, community center, or similar setting. The group is open to anyone; there are no fees, and no expectations other than that the members comport themselves according to ethical guidelines for dream sharing. Activities are structured to stick with dream content and not expand or drift out to the issues in the waking lives of the participants.

This group is oriented toward spiritual development. Meetings begin with a meditative, centering exercise, in which those present "name and claim themselves," and say how they feel.

A second example of dream groups is one in Yellow Springs, Ohio, ongoing for 20 years. It meets twice monthly at the home of one of its founding members, Maxine Skuba. In contrast to the northern Virginia group, it is not open to anyone but has a continuing membership of eight people, some of whom have been with the group since its inception. Several of the members, including Skuba, are professionals in psychotherapy or counseling, and although an interpretive sensibility informs their discussions, there is no agenda to move participants to a particular place (as may be the goal in counseling). Members know one another outside the group so discussion expands to include the life contexts of the dreams—members share what is going on in their lives. The theoretical orientation is eclectic.[20]

Although there are many points of difference between these two groups, they are not antithetical and we think members of one group would be comfortable in the other. Both these community dream groups are successful, as evidenced by their longevity and by their members' enthusiasm for the value they gain from participating. The differences between the two groups illustrate the many permutations of dream group that exist, and the choices members can make in their design and operation. There is no one best mode for all, just as there is no one best way to interpret dreams.

Chapter Summary

This chapter has focused on the wide variety of settings, audiences, teachers, and programs in community dream education. Is it possible to generalize about this rich, yeasty mix of energies and activities in comparison with, and in contrast to, dream courses in conventional college and university environments (noting their overlap in that many dream educators are active in both realms, and that independent dream institutes straddle the two camps)? Let's give it a shot: The *strength* of community dream education is that it is relatively unconstrained by academic processes and norms. And the *weakness* of community dream education is that it is relatively unconstrained by academic processes and norms!

Dream education outside academia and within its hallowed halls complement one another. The former encourages and promotes explorations at the fringes of accepted theory, procedure and practice that may find a tougher time being accepted in universities. As examples, one could cite explorations in lucid dreaming or attempts to contact via dreams spirits of the deceased. Investigators and teachers outside academia are employing mainly what Fred Kerlinger termed the *logic of discovery*, in which new ideas, theories and practices are developed through experience, reflection, and intuition—really through any and all means of human invention—without being subject to the limits and disciplines of scientific standards of conventionally accepted testing and proof.[7]

Scholars and teachers in academia do, of course, generate new theory and practice but then rely on the *logic of verification* (again in Kerlinger's phrase). How we know becomes a criterion for assessing the validity of what we think we know. Here intersubjectivity is the watchword, in which findings are replicable by objective procedures, and truths not limited to individual experience and belief. Carefully collected data are posed against theoretical claims, with theory then modified in response to the findings from the data. The modified theory is then set against newly collected data, and corroborated or changed accordingly in a continual process. All this is done openly, subject to collegial critique. (Although this is the general procedure and process of the sciences and social sciences, it also generally characterizes humanities scholarship within academia, allowing for the intrinsic differences in methodology.)

The logic of discovery is the dominant operative theme in community dream education, as the logic of verification is dominant within academia. As the two logics complement one another and form a whole, so does dream education form a whole in its characteristic intra- and extra-academic modes. The strength of dream education lies in a potentially increasing and robust dialogue between the two realms, and a taking on more of the other's strengths—bolder theorizing and exploration within academia, and more careful and rigorous logic and evidence gathering in extra-academic settings.

Chapter 10

Primary and Secondary Education

The developmental trajectory of dreaming across the life span is a vital topic for all teachers, with implications for pedagogical strategies and classroom practices at every age. Although we are only reaching the subject of dream education for primary and secondary school students now, toward the end of the book, we believe the information presented in this chapter provides a valuable and necessary foundation for teaching students of all ages and at all levels of schooling.

The process of talking about dreams with younger students brings extra educational challenges that should be highlighted at the outset. Children and teenagers are still developing their basic physical and cognitive abilities, and their skills at self-reflection and emotional communication have not yet matured. As a result, certain qualities of their dream experiences are different from those of mature adults, and they often struggle to express these qualities in words. This is not to demean the psychological integrity of children and teenagers (many people who are chronologically adults still have underdeveloped aspects of their personalities). Rather, we want to emphasize the importance of teachers knowing as much as they can about their students' developmental situations so they can calibrate their lesson plans accordingly.

An additional challenge stems from the privacy concerns of the parents of minor children, which must be respected at all times. To be sure, we believe the benefits vastly outweigh the risks in talking with children and teenagers about dreams, but we do take seriously the ethical issues raised by such discussions. As always, feelings of safety, trust, and mutual respect are key to effective learning, and our approach depends first and foremost on that kind of confidence being shared by everyone involved.

The Family Context

No one knows for sure when exactly dreaming begins in human life. We only know when children are old enough to tell us about their experiences during sleep. Granted, we have some evidence suggesting that actual dreams occur prior to the development of verbal language abilities. Fetuses and very young children spend more than twice as much of their total sleep time in REM than do adults, a fact that seems significant given the close connection (but not identity) between REM sleep and dreaming. Many parents will swear their infants have awakened from a deep sleep crying out because of a disturbing dream. But such evidence regards only the external aspects of arousal in sleep, not necessarily the subjective experience of a dream. In a way, the question is identical to the one about animals dreaming—if a creature does not have the ability to provide a verbal communication of its dreams, how do we know if it can really dream at all? Teachers may find their students spontaneously raising this question once the general topic of dreaming has been broached. It is an obvious point of curiosity for anyone who has observed an animal or a human baby asleep and seen its jittering eyes and twitching limbs. We encourage giving students the opportunity to debate the arguments for and against the idea that dreaming occurs in animals and human babies, as it will sensitize the students to many other interesting psychological and philosophical questions that arise in the study of dreams.

We derive a pragmatic insight from this unresolved (and perhaps irresolvable) debate. The high percentage of REM sleep among fetuses and infants corresponds to the massively complex process of neural development in the growing human brain. To the extent that much of our dreaming in later life occurs during REM sleep, it can truly be said that dreams are "regressive" in bringing us back to a mode of existence that was especially prominent in the earliest phase of life. This recalls the poetic romanticism of Wordsworth and his view that we enter into this world "trailing clouds of glory. . . . Our birth is but a sleep and a forgetting."

Whether or not humans actually dream before the ages of 2 or 3, they definitely do dream from that point forward for the rest of their lives, and their oneiric experiences remain a living bridge to the dynamic creativity of their growing minds. Seen in this light, the goal of cultivating an educated awareness of dreaming becomes a matter of strengthening and widening that bridge as a way of promoting general mental health. The natural place to begin that process is within the family.

At some point, most parents face the middle-of-the-night challenge of soothing a child who has awakened from a nightmare. The well-intentioned but dismissive formula, "It was just a dream," rarely succeeds in dispelling the vivid realism of the child's emotional reaction. A better approach, according to Alan Siegel and Kelly Bulkeley in their 1998 book on children's dreams, *Dreamcatching*, is to provide comfort and reassurance while taking the nightmare seriously as an expression of the child's imagination and emotional concerns. This not only reassures the child that his or her parent understands the feelings of the bad dream, it also opens up the possibility (when it seems safe to do so) of joining together to look at the dream's possible meanings through conversation, drawing, role-playing, or the use of dolls and action figures. The frightening nightmare can thus become a source of shared insight:

> Dreams frequently express feelings that are too overwhelming for children to put into words. Relating a dream, therefore, opens a crucial channel of communication between parents and their children. Describing the characters and activities of a dream allows a child to express worries and even joys in a safer format than through direct verbal expression.[1]

Most cultural traditions include beliefs about dreams and practices of dream interpretation that families share and pass down through the generations. Our concern in this book is not to provide parenting advice, but simply to highlight the fact that these family teachings represent the original context of dream education. Parents, siblings, and family elders provide most people with their initial guidance into the world of dreaming.

Preschool

In *Dreamcatching* and several of his other writings, Bulkeley has likened dreaming to a kind of play, the play of a mind temporarily detached from the sensory demands of the waking world, free to imagine, create, and explore.[2] As developmental psychologists have long known, play is a powerful tool of learning for young children. Dreaming shares a number of similarities with play behaviors, including these:

- Dreaming and playing both involve the creation of a quasi-real space, a special environment set apart from non-play reality.

- Both are safe, in that dreaming and playing actions do not have the same consequences that similar actions would have outside the imagined space.

- Strong emotions often emerge in dreaming and playing, both positive ones (affection, happiness) and negative ones (aggression, frustration, anger, sadness).

- Dreaming and playing both take their raw material from the major survival concerns of daily life.

- Both have a tendency toward extravagance, exaggeration, and rich variation.

- The rules, boundaries, and structures that govern ordinary life are suspended in play and dreams, providing the opportunity to experiment and explore.[3]

In summary, dreaming and play seem to be kindred biopsychological phenomena associated with survival and growth. The implication for preschool teachers is that children's dreams should be treated as another form of playful self-expression. In practical terms, this means adult-level analysis and interpretation should be avoided in favor of age-appropriate appreciation, support, and guidance. A good teacher would probably not say to children playing a spirited game of house, "Ah, I can see that you are practicing adult roles for future life." In the same way, we hope that a good teacher would not say to a child sharing a dream about flying, "Hmm, you must be fantasizing about power and freedom."

We encourage preschool teachers to prepare for those times when the subject of dreams spontaneously comes up in their students' conversations. Simply acknowledging that virtually everyone dreams can provide young children with an instructive lesson in itself. Beyond that, preschool teachers can stimulate further reflection with open-ended questions ("Can you say more about what the dog looked like?" "What kind of a car was it?" "How did you feel while you were flying?") and follow-up practices ("Can you draw a picture of your dream?" "Can you show me the dream with the toys in the sandbox?"). If these comments and suggestions are made in a playful, nonjudgmental way, they can help the students discover new aspects of their own creative imaginations. The children may respond to the teacher's comments briefly and move on to something else, or may become energized by the opportunity to bring more of their dreaming experiences into the waking world. Either way, the goal from a pedagogical perspective is to create a safe and nurturing space in which children's dreams, like any other form of playful activity, can be cultivated and developed.

Another source of spontaneous dream discussion in preschool comes from children's storybooks, many of which include dreams directly in their plots. Classics like Maurice Sendak's *Where the Wild Things Are* and Lewis Carroll's *Alice's Adventures in Wonderland* involve elaborate adventures that build on common dreaming phenomena, eliciting sympathetic responses from the children listening to the story. Preschool teachers interested in prompting more dream awareness among their students can use such stories as an indirect route into the general features and qualities of dreams. In addition to the works by Sendak and Carroll, we recommend Dav Pilkey's *When Cats Dream*, Leigh Casler's *The Boy Who Dreamed of an Acorn*, and Chris Van Allsburg's *Just a Dream*. Reading and talking about stories like these with young children further strengthens the basic message that dreaming is a natural part of life with interesting lessons to teach us.

The best empirical research on the form and content of young children's dreams remains Foulkes' 1982 *Children's Dreams: A Longitudinal Study*, although Foulkes gathered dream reports exclusively from sleep laboratory experiments, which may or may not accurately represent children's dreaming experiences when they are sleeping at home. According to Foulkes, the dreams of children between the ages of 3 and 5 tend to be very brief, with animals, family members, and friends being the most common characters. The dreams are usually set at home or in a homelike location. There generally is not much of a plot, nor much emotion or physical activity. The children frequently observe the images from a passive perspective rather than being actively involved with the other characters and elements of the dream.

Foulkes' profile leaves out the infrequent but very upsetting nightmares that many children experience in their first years of conscious life. Such dreams usually involve some combination of heightened emotion, bizarre characters, extended narrative, and vivid physical sensations. Nor does Foulkes' account make room for the "big dreams" that Jung claims occur for many people in early childhood, rare but uniquely memorable dreams with extraordinary symbolic energy and lifelong existential significance. Preschool teachers will likely hear all of it—the ordinary dreams about nothing in particular, the scary recurrent nightmares, and the breathtaking dream visions. We appreciate Foulkes' research on the general aspects of ordinary dreaming, but we encourage teachers to look beyond his ideas and be especially attentive to their students' extraordinary dreams as well. If Jung is correct that such dreams often occur in early childhood, then preschool teachers have a wonderful opportunity to play a positive role when their students suddenly find themselves struck by a big dream.

Before going further, we want to highlight two common challenges that can arise when children are encouraged to share their dreams in a school setting. First is the occurrence of dreams, and sometimes nightmares, about school itself. Many young children struggle mightily with the transition from home to school and back to home, and this struggle regularly plays itself out in their dreams. If teachers and parents are not prepared for this, they may be startled by dreams that feature themselves in a very unflattering light! For the most part, anxiety dreams about school reflect a normal, healthy expression of psychological growth as new life challenges are met and overcome. Talking about dreams can be a useful means of indirectly accessing and exploring the conflicted feelings some children feel when leaving home for school. However, should the dreams become so recurrent and disturbing they affect the child's sleep, we recommend seeking the advice of a mental health professional just in case a more serious problem is involved.

The second challenge appears when a child shares a dream that could be interpreted as indicating an experience of emotional or physical abuse. This is obviously very sensitive ethical territory, and we assume that every school has a well-defined policy regarding the proper response when such issues arise. In this regard, dreams should be treated no differently from any other potential source of evidence of improper behavior: they should be taken seriously as possible signals, but not accepted as definitive proof of any particular waking world event. Dreams of being abused do not necessarily mean actual abuse has occurred. We recommend teachers combine an appropriate attention to potential problems with a reflective awareness of the nonliteral aspects of dream imagery.

The best touchstone for dream education with young children is their own innate interest in the subject. From a very early age, children are drawn to their dreams and enjoy sharing them with others. If children's natural enthusiasm is kept at the center of educational practice, we believe the simplest and safest of efforts by preschool teachers can yield valuable gains in the development of their students' imaginations. We have already mentioned two specific practices: responding to a spontaneous dream report with encouraging, open-ended questions, and discussing dream themes in storybooks. In addition to these, a more proactive method is to invite the children to make their own dream journals as an arts-and-crafts project. Bulkeley did this with the students at his children's preschool (Kensington Nursery School in Kensington, California) for several years, with encouraging results. The students chose a colored piece of 8.5 by 11-inch construction paper and folded it in half, with four additional sheets of plain white paper folded inside. Three staples along the fold created an 8.5 by 5.5-inch booklet, the cover of which the children decorated with a drawing of themselves, colored designs, sparkles, and stickers. Every step of the way the children put their personal stamp on the journals, choosing the materials and doing all the work on it themselves. The process gave them a chance not only to talk about the dreams they had already experienced, but also to anticipate having more dreams in coming nights.

From there, preschool teachers can build on the interest generated by the journals to organize additional art projects around the portrayal of particular dreams (the students' own, or perhaps from famous historical people), acting out dreams with costumes and props as a form of dramatic play, creating an American Indian-style "dreamcatcher," or recreating a dream in a sand tray setting. As long as the process remains playful and respectful and no one worries too much when the dreaming shades into other kinds of imaginative play, these activities can be applied in virtually any preschool setting.

Michael Schredl, a leading researcher from Germany, has shown that dream recall in adults varies depending on their attitudes toward dreaming—the more interest people have in dreaming, the more dreams they remember. Schredl has further found that people's attitudes toward dreaming can be improved simply by having someone else encourage them to do so. Preschool, from this perspective, can be seen as a crucial developmental arena for a young person's emerging relationship with dreaming. Teachers in early childhood education should be aware of, and take pride in, the fact that their efforts can benefit the students' lives many years in the future, when they will have a healthier and more open connection to their dreaming selves.

Elementary and Middle School

For most children, school becomes increasingly structured and formalized as they get older, which is appropriate given the growing power and complexity of their minds. Play, art, and stories tend to recede in importance as the educational emphasis shifts to skill development and knowledge acquisition. If this shift is poorly planned or badly managed, the danger arises of the students shutting off their own creative imaginations in an effort to behave more "grown-up" and less like babyish preschoolers. The challenge for teachers of elementary and middle school students is to make sure this expansion of educational focus doesn't produce a sudden break from past modes of learning, with problematic implications for their future development.

As long as children have art as a regular component of their school curriculum, there will always be an easy and natural way of bringing dreams into their awareness. Any art project, from drawings and paintings to collages and sculptures, can be adapted to encourage the students to express an image, feeling, or theme from a dream. In so doing, the students learn how to find creative inspirations and aesthetic insights within their own personal imaginations. Additionally, students at these ages are often beginning to take an interest in the life stories of great artists, some of whom (like William Blake, Salvador Dalí, Jasper Johns, Maya Angelou, and Akira Kurosawa) had powerful dreams that inspired their creative work. Teaching art history with an eye toward examples like these can reinforce the discoveries students make in reflecting on their personal dreams.

The greater range of mental and physical skill among elementary and middle school children allows them to recognize and appreciate the deeper, more complex dimensions of dreaming. Even though children at this age tend to be "concrete" and "conventional" in their thinking (to borrow terms from Jean Piaget and Lawrence Kohlberg), the emergence of their cognitive abilities for abstract, postconventional thought is not so far in the future, and may even have begun appearing in various ways. For teachers seeking to prepare their students for that next vital stage of cognitive growth, the symbol-laden, metaphor-rich world of dreaming can serve as a gentle and easily accessible means of stimulating those "higher" modes of reflection on the world.

Learning to read and to write are two of the primary objectives at this general stage of school education, with the ultimate goal of stimulating a lifelong love of language and literature. The dream journal process we described in the preschool context can be adapted for older students as a classroom exercise in descriptive prose and personal narrative. Some students who find it difficult to come up with writing ideas may have an easier time if they start by simply writing out some of their dreams.

Jeff Grether at Windrush School in El Cerrito, California included a dream episode as one element in a long-term fiction-writing project for his fourth-grade class. To help develop the skills that fiction writers use in their creative work, Grether gave his students a series of prompts over the course of several months to guide them in writing a more detailed and elaborate story than they had ever written before. For example, one night's homework assignment was to write 8 sentences of description of a character; other nights it was 10 sentences of a sequence of actions, or 6 sentences of a character's inner thoughts. The students were encouraged to write more than that, in any direction they chose. But the exercises aimed at cultivating particular narrative abilities that enhance creativity in storytelling. Among these was the ability to describe and explore a dream. Here is the homework assignment Grether gave his class about 2 months into the writing process:

CHARACTER STORY HOMEWORK—The Dream

From where you are in your story have your character find somewhere to sleep, or have some reason for him or her to fall asleep. Once asleep your character begins to dream. Writing Goal: In four (4) or more sentences, describe the dream in your story. In the dream a clue or mystery should be revealed that somehow helps your character in the "real story." Yes, you may write more on your story after the dream! Examples of dream clue or mystery:

1. The dream foreshadows (tells before it happens) what will happen in your story.

2. When awake your character sees something from the dream and decides to find out more.

3. The dream reveals information your character needs.

The students found this one of the easiest assignments in the overall writing process, easy in the sense of requiring little effort to imagine and describe a dream for one of the characters in their story. They also found it a helpful way of adding depth to their fiction. Instead of writing out the plot in a linear series of activities, the dream assignment encouraged the students to enlarge the narrative scope of their stories by exploring the nonlinear fantasy elements of dreaming.

Sara Lev, a teacher at the Wildwood School in Los Angeles, developed another innovative approach to language arts in early education. Wildwood's unusual program has the kindergarten students stay with the same teacher through the first grade, meaning one teacher has the same "pod" of students for 2 continuous years. The goal is to enable the teacher to observe a broad developmental trajectory of each student's acquisition of academic, emotional, and social skills. In Lev's K–1 pod she lets the students know that each day's morning meeting is a space where they can share a dream if they want. She does not push anyone to do so, but she makes sure they know it's available. She also invites the students during the "writing workshop" portion of the day to describe their dreams as a way of prompting the children to write from their own personal lives.

All of this flows into the class dream journal, which is a collective book made out of an artist's unlined spiral sketchbook. Lev gave each child a 3 by 3-inch piece of poster board to draw images and/or characters from their dreams, which were then arranged on the front and back of the journal and covered with contact paper. She told her students that each time they remembered a dream in the morning or any other time of day they could go to the journal and write it or draw a picture of it. Lev had them date each entry and give the dream a title, and over time the children made multiple uses of the journal. They referred to earlier dreams for writing ideas, added new drawings, and pointed out connections between the dreams and other kinds of stories. Sometimes if the children couldn't remember one of their own dreams, they could "borrow" one of the other dreams in the journal. Lev told us in an interview:

> Now the journal is about 4 years old, and kids still look at it, read over other children's dreams, even those dreams that came from kids who have since left our classroom and gone on to third, fourth, or fifth grade. The children also will look back on their own dreams and reflect on how much they have grown as writers.

Once a girl in Lev's class had a nightmare in which she was attacked by a teddy bear. She was too scared to write it down, but when Lev asked if she could change the dream in some way to make it less scary, the girl drew a picture of the teddy bear inside a jail. This gave her a tangible sense of her power to change her response to the dream.

Other students in Lev's class write and draw their dreams in more figurative terms, as hopes for the future and visions of what they want to do when they get older. Lev does not correct the children when they stray from actual night dreams into other aspects of fiction and creative imagination. On the contrary, she encourages them to explore the ways dreaming connects to various forms of storytelling. For example, she introduces her students to the cartoons of Jesse Reklaw, whose *Slow Wave* comic strip was based on creative animated portrayals of people's actual dreams. Reklaw's book *Dreamtoons* is filled with four-panel cartoons that revel in the playful diversity of the dreaming mind, and Lev inspires her students to try expressing their own dreams in this familiar artistic medium.[4]

Lev's ability to apply these methods of dream education successfully depends on both her knowledge of current dream research and Wildwood's progressive emphasis on nurturing the authentic self of each student. These factors may seem to limit the possible use of these ideas in other schools with other teachers, but we believe that is a mistaken assumption. Lev's approach requires no special technical training, just a familiarity with the kind of research presented in this book. The essential elements of what she does at Wildwood can be fruitfully applied in many other schools, whether in public, parochial, or independent settings. Lev is simply extending good elementary school teaching practices in a promising new direction.

Science projects relating to dreams can begin in elementary and middle school with simple experiments based on studying a collection of dream reports. The dreams can come from any of a number of different sources: the students' own journals, simple survey responses from friends and family members, or research databases like the DreamBank (discussed in Chapter 2). The students choose a question to explore (e.g., Do girls dream more than boys? Do children dream more than adults? How often do animals appear in dreams? How often do television or movie images appear in dreams? How often do students dream about school?) and analyze the dream reports with that question in mind. The results then can be compared with the findings of other scientists who have studied the same questions using more precise analytic methods and larger, more demographically diverse populations. These possibilities have special relevance for middle schools that sponsor science fairs, offering ideas for student projects aiming to combine innovative science with personal interest.

Teachers need to monitor the content of the dreams used in such projects to make sure no inappropriate material is included. Although most dreams tend to be quite tame and noncontroversial, there are a few reports on the Dream-Bank that would earn an R or even NC-17 rating at the movie theater. The same caution that teachers use with other Internet sources should be applied here as well.

Everything teachers do to discuss the nature of sleep and healthy sleeping habits also contributes to dream education. In elementary and middle school science classes, animals are often a topic of study because children have so much innate curiosity about nonhuman creatures. (Not surprisingly, animals appear on average much more often in children's dreams than in adults' dreams.[5]) Comparing the sleep patterns of various kinds of animals with human sleep can offer students a new perspective on their shared experiences with other members of the natural world. Nearly all mammals go through the same basic cycle of REM and non-REM sleep, and birds, reptiles, and even insects have their own distinct resting behaviors. The discovery that sleep is as biologically important to these creatures as breathing, eating, or drinking leads to a more sophisticated and informed awareness of the role of sleep in human life.

Many elementary and middle schools have a health-and-wellness component to their curricula with instruction on diet, exercise, drugs, and hygiene. We believe the more attention given in these classes to healthy sleep habits, the better. Children today are growing into a world increasingly filled with electronic distractions and around-the-clock stress that negatively affect people's capacity to get a sound night's sleep. It is never too early to begin encouraging the students to appreciate the importance and value of sleep for their personal health in childhood and all through their lives.

The dreams of children in the 6- to 12-year-old range frequently dwell on their friendships and social relationships. This makes sense in light of the continuity principle discussed earlier (i.e., that people's most important waking life concerns are reflected in the content patterns of their dreams). The joys and sorrows of friendship consume the emotional lives of most children, all of which is mirrored with surprising accuracy in their dreams. If we think of elementary and middle school as a time when new, more complex interpersonal skills are being tested and refined, then children's dreams become a potential source of very useful personal insight. Teachers and parents may never hear about these dreams, and perhaps that's not a bad thing. What matters is that the students themselves have been encouraged to develop the emotional intelligence and maturity of judgment to make sense of their own dreaming experiences as resources in navigating through the turbulent social world.

High School

The onset of adolescence brings so many radical changes in physical size, intellectual capacity, interpersonal dynamics, and social expectations that it's a wonder anyone ever survives the experience. Based on recent findings in neuroscience, we now know that the brains of teenagers undergo a burst of new growth particularly in those areas associated with advanced reasoning and self-control. We also know the sleep cycle tends to shift in the teen years, with later times of natural sleep onset. The National Sleep Foundation recommends 9 or more hours of sleep for teenagers, but survey results suggest that few high school students actually sleep that long on weeknights.[6] This teen sleep deficit seems to be a contributing factor in broader problems with academic performance, social behavior, car accidents, and immunological health. The diminished opportunity for dreaming ranks low on this alarming list, but it is another consequence of inadequate sleep among many contemporary teenagers. Ironically, adolescence is a time of life filled with emotionally intense, intellectually stimulating, life-altering experiences that often provide the raw material for highly memorable dreams. Dream education with teens should start with sleep education about the importance of developing greater self-awareness of what does and does not foster a good night's rest for each individual.

High school curricula offer many of the same dream-teaching opportunities already mentioned with younger children. English classes in particular can easily raise issues of sleep and dreaming without any major changes to the standard pedagogical focus. High school literature courses regularly feature works that include prominent references to dreams, whether in Shakespeare's plays (e.g., *Romeo and Juliet, Macbeth, A Midsummer Night's Dream*), American classics (*Moby-Dick, Leaves of Grass*), or even contemporary fantasy (e.g., the Harry Potter series of J.K. Rowling, the *Twilight* series of Stephanie Meyer). High school students reading these books are more capable than ever of appreciating the ways dreaming can be deeply woven into the emerging narratives of their lives. English teachers can help illuminate for them the different perspectives that great writers express in their portrayals of dreaming experience and its possible meaningfulness. Several good books have been written on the connection between dreaming and literature, and we recommend high school English teachers consult these ones especially: Carol Schreier Rupprecht's *The Dream and the Text: Essays on Language and Literature*, Naomi Epel's *Writers Dreaming: 25 Writers Talk about their Dreams and the Creative Process*, and Bert States' *The Rhetoric of Dreams* and *Dreams and Storytelling*.

Several years ago Jane White-Lewis, a Jungian analyst, taught an elective course on "Dreams and the Imaginal World" at the High School in the Community in New Haven, Connecticut. This magnet public school was designed to provide a more creative interdisciplinary curriculum for students from all areas of the crime-ridden, racially conflicted city. As she describes it in her essay "Dreams and Social Responsibility," White-Lewis prepared herself by focusing on four teaching objectives to demonstrate the educational, creative, psychological, and social value of studying dreams:

1. By considering the images of their dreams as metaphors and imaginal expressions of their feelings and concerns, the students could move from concrete to more abstract, symbolic ways of thinking, thereby increasing their capacity to think symbolically.

2. By studying and reflecting on their dreams and by tapping into their imaginal worlds, the students could get a sense of their own cast of characters and inner literature, both as a source for their own creative expression and as a bridge to literature, to the imaginal worlds of others.

3. By considering dream figures as aspects of themselves and the dream as an expression of their inner conflicts, the students would begin to know themselves better. In dreams we find missing parts of ourselves that point the way to our psychological development; we also find the rejected parts, the inner enemies, the seeds of prejudice.

4. Increased self-awareness fosters self-empowerment, self-esteem, a fuller sense of agency and more responsible life choices—all of which have social implications.[7]

She taught the class twice, once with juniors and seniors and once with freshmen and sophomores, meeting four times a week for 1 hour over the course of 9 weeks. She had the students start with collage work from magazine clippings as a way of initiating a reflection on the power of images, and then moved into discussions about images in dreams. Each student kept a dream journal and participated in a variety of dream-sharing exercises during class, which White-Lewis moderated to ensure the emotional safety of the process. As the course went on, she found the students themselves settled on a tacit level of understanding about where the boundaries of proper interaction lay. During class, White-Lewis suggested parallels between the students' dreams and the portrayal of dreams in literature and mythology, although she learned the hard way that her favorite cultural references did not always resonate with the students (they preferred the TV soap *All My Children* to the 19th-century novel *Wuthering Heights*). She gave them creative writing projects in which they elaborated on their associations to certain dream images and feelings, a process that helped the students develop a more personal voice in their writing generally.

White-Lewis designed her course to be flexible and open to student initiative, which was consistent with the school's overall philosophy. When she opened up the classroom to a free discussion of the students' dream experiences, they quickly zeroed in on some of the most emotionally charged issues in their lives—with the boys, dangerous encounters with the police and drug dealers; with the girls, anxious discoveries of unwanted pregnancy. These were in fact highly relevant threats in their current waking lives, and White-Lewis says the students appreciated the chance to talk about their feelings in response to the dream images, which she encouraged them to view not just in literal terms but also in metaphorical terms as well. By asking questions like, "If the dream is a reflection on an inner state or conflict, who is the cop?" or "What if the baby in the dream is understood as some young part of the dreamer, some potential that needs to be mothered?" she prompted the students to see more clearly the multiple dimensions of meaning that emerge in dreams and culture, with direct relevance to real issues in their lives. Although her time with the students and the school was short, White-Lewis saw evidence that the class had prompted many other students and faculty members to share their dreams and collectively reflect on their meanings.

Once again, we find a dream-focused teaching approach being tested in a school that does not follow traditional methods in American public education. In this case, the teacher had specialized training that allowed her to manage the classroom interactions successfully. These are not easily replicated conditions, but the basic principles of White-Lewis' approach can be adapted and applied to other high school settings. These principles include the establishment of mutual respect and safety in the classroom, a willingness to include students as co-creators of the class, a self-reflective awareness of unconscious biases and projections, attention to literal and metaphorical dimensions of meaning, and a playful, open-ended exploration of connections between dreaming and cultural creativity.

Jean Campbell, another educator with extensive familiarity with dreams, taught creative writing classes at a large public high school in Virginia Beach, Virginia. Her pedagogical practices illustrate many of the key themes mentioned in relation to all ages discussed in this chapter:

> One of the first exercises I used with these writing classes was to ask students to write down a dream and then write a short story from the dream. Inevitably this exercise led to a discussion of dreams: What does my dream mean? Aren't dreams just garbage being processed by the mind? What does it mean if I dream of a particular thing or person? But in the context of this exercise, the dream discussion could be brought into practical focus: What are the elements of my dream that create a story?
>
> From an academic perspective, I have found that this type of work with personal symbols develops an understanding of the meaning of symbols in general—and most particularly is helpful to students who are asked to grasp the complex symbolism of poetry and prose they are given to study in language and literature classes. During the time I taught at this particular high school, students went from not feeling qualified to enter State writing competitions to entering and winning prizes with poetry and fiction at the State and National levels.[8]

Campbell recommends an appropriate degree of caution and readiness to deal with unexpected personal situations. She maintains, as do we, that the benefits of dream education for children far outweigh the potential problems, but she urges all appropriate measures be taken when such problems arise, as they occasionally do in any educational setting:

Once I was invited by the Youth Director at a local synagogue to speak to the Youth Group, a collection of around thirty high school students. The discussion proceeded along the lines of how interesting dreams can be, and how their messages might be applied, until one clean-cut looking kid stood up in the back of the room: "What does it mean," he asked, "if you wake up standing in your parents' bedroom with a knife in your hand?" He wasn't kidding. When some of the girls in the group questioned him, he said no, it really happened. He had a history of sleep walking. One of the cardinal rules of dream work with young people is that it is necessary to know good boundaries, and keep them clearly in mind. Teachers are not psychotherapists, and even in the case where that might be true, troubled children, all children, are the legal wards of their parents, who must decide on any sort of treatment. In this case, a phone conversation with the parents (who assured me that everything was fine with their son) was all that seemed appropriate.[9]

We do not know of any high school science teachers who have included dreams in their curriculum, but both King and Bulkeley have received dozens of requests over the years from high school students who have chosen to do a science project on some aspect of dreaming. The same exercises mentioned in the psychology and anthropology chapters can in most cases be adapted from an undergraduate to a high school setting.

Education for the Future

Our focus in this chapter has been on American educational practices, but we suspect a similar pattern may be found in many other school systems in Europe, Asia, and elsewhere: a general lack of attention to sleep and dreaming, with a few enterprising teachers developing effective methods of responding to children's natural curiosity about dream experience. Beyond the ones profiled here, we know that other teachers are also involved in this kind of work, and we hope to hear from them in the future.

We end here with the work of Kate Adams, a dedicated advocate of educational efforts to expand children's awareness of dreams. Adams teaches at Bishop Grosseteste University College in Lincoln, England, as part of a program for undergraduate students training to be primary and secondary school teachers. The school system in Great Britain has a government mandate to teach students about comparative religions, and for that reason Adams has developed an expertise in religion, children's spirituality, and dreams. Her primary interest as a researcher is trying to understand better how children make meaning from their dreams, particularly highly memorable "big dreams."[10] Adams' courses and lectures at Bishop Grosseteste combine perspectives from religious traditions (Christianity, Islam) with scientific studies of human health and development. In her research on 9- to 12-year-old children in Britain, she found that a considerable number of them already have experienced what they consider to be an encounter with the "Divine," however their tradition defines that term. She says:

> Divine dreams are thus not confined to scripture and adult experience, but are also encountered and valued by some children living in contemporary western societies. By acknowledging this often hidden realm of children's experience, adults can draw other children's attention to the similarities between these Christian and Muslim children's dreams. In so doing, such action can only lead to enhanced understanding and acceptance that dreams can transcend religious boundaries.[11]

Educators in Europe, North America, and virtually everywhere in the contemporary world must find effective ways of preparing their students to survive and thrive in an increasingly pluralistic, multicultural world. Adams' research and teaching on the spiritual dimensions of children's dreams shows one way of accomplishing that goal. By learning more about their own dreams and the dreams of other children, students develop a stronger sense of empathetic understanding for how the world looks and feels through other people's eyes.

Adams' professional work as a teacher-of-teachers offers a concrete example of what it would look like for basic knowledge about sleep and dreaming to be integrated into the broader educational training system. It might not take many more teachers like Adams to effect a kind of "tipping-point" change in fundamental social and educational attitudes toward the role of dreaming in healthy child development.

Chapter 11

The Future of Dream Education

In considering what the future holds for dream education, we first restate our fundamental perspective: Above all, dreams are multifaceted and complicated. Their study and teaching transcend disciplinary boundaries and evoke the parable of the blind men and the elephant. Which parts of the dream elephant best describe and represent its essence? Can we perhaps hope in the totality of our views to understand the entire beast and convey that understanding in our teachings?

Dreams have sources in the life of the dreamer and perhaps beyond in a consciousness that transcends the individual. Our engagement with dreams in cultural context forms the meanings they hold for us. Recorded dream narratives are empirical phenomena subject to study and understanding via the procedures and rules of the sciences and humanities. Dreams influence and reflect religious doctrine, the history of civilizations, and our philosophies. Dreams inspire literature and artistic creation. Dreams affect us, as do the ways we choose to understand them. Our conscious thoughts and ways of being in the world return to penetrate and inhabit dreams. Waking and dreaming life dance together.

Artistic sensibilities and creations reflect dream contents and processes. Dreams in turn reflect conscious human creativity. Slow motion, for example, may be an inherent quality of dreams, but once brought to films and experienced by filmgoers it may be more frequent in their dreaming. In addition to being the fundamental proto-narrative, dreams are the starting point for communicating internal realities to one's waking world.

Dream information piles up as study builds on study. However, researches that answer old questions also pose new ones. The ratio of settled to unsettled questions never seems to increase. Indeed, it may shrink as our perspectives expand and knowledge horizons recede. Old theories and points of view stick around but get less attention as new ones come along.

Dreams are inside us as experiences and outside us as objects of study and reflection, for learner and teacher alike. Almost all individuals working in the dreams field have interests that are personal *and* social, experiential *and* scholarly. "New-age" seekers who approach dreams in the most esoteric ways are also interested in the latest scientific advances. Skeptical scientists and other scholars who research dreams objectively also become caught up in their own dreams. The balance of interest in an individual can vary greatly, but there is enough appreciation of the other world view that at least a wary mutual respect ensues. We are all phenomenologists and rationalists in some measure. The matter of dream phenomenology and dream science is not a battle to be won or lost, but a complementarity to be sustained and strengthened.

Let us look to the forms dream education may take in coming years. This is an exercise partly in prediction, partly in prescription, peering forward perhaps a decade or so; any longer would be overly speculative. We discuss three major topics:

1. Needed advances in dream interpretation;

2. The role of the Internet and related electronic educational possibilities; and

3. Future trends in interdisciplinary dream education and underlying epistemology.

Dream Interpretation

Virtually all dream educators are interested in understanding the meanings of dreams. Dream courses in higher education in all disciplines generally include activities and experiences in interpreting dreams. Dream education for clinicians and dream education outside universities for the lay public is concerned largely (although not exclusively) with dream interpretation. It is of the utmost importance that dream educators have a well-considered meta-level understanding of the nature of dream interpretation if they are going to teach it to others. Without this, there is increased danger of an overly narrow perspective. In fact, if there were just one thing we would wish the reader to take from this book, it is an appreciation for the intricacy of dream interpretation, and modesty about one's own ability, however developed it may be, to understand a dream. It is from these humble attitudes that the best dreamwork can be done.

We see some core questions that concern the basis of interpretation. On what grounds are we to assert that dreams have meaning, for an aggregated set or series of dreams as a group, and for individual dreams? Where are meanings located for individual dreams—when are they within the dream, waiting discovery, and when in ourselves, waiting to be placed on the dream after the fact? Stemming from this are questions of the value and use of various theories of dream meanings, and the choices of meaning for individual dream elements and the dream as a whole under the premises of a particular theory.

On the first question, we share Domhoff's perception of a bias among dream educators that dreams are wonderful and important, based on the impactful quality of their own dream experience. This colors dream education in general and interpretation in particular. The enthusiasm about and appreciation of dreams that teachers bring to their students, and the sometimes profundity of their insights, are all to the good. Not as good according to Domhoff is the tendency toward assuming value and meaning, and a credulous receptivity, rather than a more detached perspective that evaluates claims using some kind of empirical criteria outside the individual dream experience. For Domhoff, dreams are meaningful but reliable dream meanings are aggregate, inhering for example in how the accumulated contents of a series of one person's dreams differ from established norms.[1]

We agree with Domhoff's concerns about credulity and his position on the meaningfulness of aggregate dream contents, but part with him about his relative lack of focus on ascertaining particular meanings of individual dream narratives. It seems to us that subjective meanings *are* discoverable or at least creatable, and that they are *self-validating*. The claims that one should validate scientifically, as Domhoff rightly argues, are those of empirical regularity—the connections and influences among variables over a number of instances and measurements, and the degree to which they comport with theoretical predictions. But this has little if anything to do with felt (personal) dream meanings for the individual dreamer or with approaches to discovering such meanings. Domhoff comes the closest to wresting personal meanings from dreams when he compares levels and patterns in an individual dream series with normative data, as he did so ingeniously with Freud's and Jung's dreams.[2] In principle, (although not in the cases of the deceased Freud and Jung), the dreamer could ponder deviations of his patterns over many dreams from the norms, and note, for instance, that he has less anger, or more friendliness in his dreams than average, or that these levels have risen or fallen over time. Co-authors Bulkeley and King have each independently gained useful personal insights from aggregate quantitative analyses of their dreams.

Such endeavors, while producing interesting research findings as well as personal insights, may not be worth the effort for most dreamers, as contemplating individual dreams is a more direct avenue to determining their meanings than painstaking content analyses of multiple dreams. Also, there are easier ways to discern one's levels or trends of anger or friendliness that wouldn't require keeping a dream diary over a number of years. So although Domhoff's meanings really *are* dream meanings, and demonstrate connections between

dream content and waking life, they don't speak to the individual dream, and
his procedures don't lend themselves to the limited efforts at interpretation that
most dreamers are likely to muster.

The major question for us, both philosophically and pragmatically, is the
one concerning the sources of the meanings that we ascribe to our dreams
and the theories and methods we use to interpret them. How do, and should,
we arrive at the meanings that become subjectively true simply because they
are our meanings? Can there be criteria for validation of subjective meanings
comparable to scientific criteria for the meaningfulness of empirical regularities;
and if so what are they?

Bulkeley tackled this question head-on in a previous book by applying
hermeneutic principles to dream interpretation.[3] He argued, following the 20th-
century German philosopher Hans-Georg Gadamer,[4] that subjective bias in both
theoretical perspective and personal experience is inevitable, but is the *only* way
through which we can encounter a dream in search of its meanings. Biases can
be positive (i.e., useful) and can enable interpretation, if we are aware of them,
see what understandings they can bring and what possible understandings they
fail to touch. Encountering the dream with our biases, and a healthy dose of
skepticism, and then re-encountering them with other, different biases, gives
us the best chance to reap satisfying meanings. The watchword is the extent to
which biases open up possibilities as opposed to shutting them off. Bulkeley notes:

> These are very broad criteria, criteria that still do not allow for clear,
> certain judgments about an interpretation's being right or not. But
> again this is the nature of interpretation in the human sciences and
> the nature, in my view, of dream interpretation as well: we ultimately
> judge an interpretation not by how certain it is but by how much it
> opens up to us, by the new horizons it enables us to see.[5]

So to answer our own question: No, there can't be criteria for validation of
subjective dream meanings comparable to scientific criteria for the meaningfulness
of empirical regularities. The latter are objective, which is to say intersubjective: Different persons taking the same scientific approach with the same data
should arrive at essentially the same findings. The former is at best subjective,
which is to say intrasubjective: Different people interpreting the same dreams
may arrive at quite different meanings.

Interpretation, therefore, should be multifaceted, with different interpreters
bringing different life experience and perspectives well as different theories—in
short, different biases. Throughout the process there is the dreamer, who at its
end alone can affirm or reject any interpretation.

This brings up the question of the meanings in a dream to persons other
than the dreamer. We hold that a dream and its interpretation can have as
many meanings as there are persons who encounter it, just as a novel, play,

or movie can have as many meanings as there are readers or viewers. A dream once freed from only private contemplation of the dreamer-author into the "public" sphere can have meanings for others unintended by the dreamer—a messy state of affairs, to be sure, but one consistent with the nature of dreams as texts and with meaning-seeking human nature.

Instructors who teach dream interpretation (and, at one higher level of abstraction, teach about dream interpretation) should think through and clearly explicate their assumptions about the sources and nature of dream meanings. We attempt to provide an example of that here as we ponder directions dream education will take in the future.

Whatever the ultimate sources of (some) dreams, we hold, with Mark Johnson, that the meanings we impute to events, including our dreams, are deeply grounded in bodily endowments and processes.[6] (We thank Roger Knudson for introducing us to Johnson's work and pointing out its relevance for discussion of just what we mean by "meaning" when it comes to dreams.) This view has implications for theories and practices of dream interpretation. Johnson characterizes his book *The Meaning of the Body* as being about "the bodily depths of human meaning-making through our visceral connection to our world. . . . meaning is not just a matter of concepts and propositions, but also reaches down into the images, sensorimotor schemas, feelings, qualities and emotions that constitute our meaningful encounter with the world."[7]

Drawing on research and theory from scholars ranging from philosophers through neuroscientists. Johnson builds an impressive counterargument against the generally accepted dualistic view that body and mind are separate. (Note the contrast of his argument with the views of Pagel in Chapter 3.) In criticizing extant views, Johnson says about dualism, "We buy into the notion of thinking as a pure, conceptual, body-transcending activity, even if we realize that no thinking occurs without a brain."[8] Reducing Johnson's complex arguments to their essence, he proposes that "meaning runs deeper than concepts and propositions,"[9] lodged as it is in our biological inheritance, including (substantially unconscious) perceptual and motor activities, capacities and limits. Johnson characterizes the key implications of this views as follows:

1. There is no radical mind–body separation;

2. Meaning is grounded in our bodily experience;

3. Reason is an embodied process;

4. Imagination is tied to our bodily processes and can also be creative and transformative of experience;

5. There is no radical freedom (i.e., no transcendent self, no disembodied ego);

6. Reason and emotion are inextricably intertwined; and

7. Human spirituality is embodied——"grounded in our relations to the human and more-than-human world that we inhabit."[10]

To discuss the array of evidence that Johnson brings to bear in support of his thesis would take us well beyond the concerns of the present volume; the interested dream teacher will profit by an acquaintance with Johnson's book.

The Meaning of the Body is not about dreams but its perspective is valuable in attempting to understand dreams. One implication of meanings in general being grounded in the physiology, anatomy, neurology, sensory capacities, kinesics, and so on, of the body is that dream practitioners make use of these mechanisms in searches for the meaning of dreams, and frame teaching of dream interpretation accordingly. This is in contrast to a sole reliance on an abstracted cognitive process in which symbols are unpacked intellectually to reveal hidden significances, according to the precepts of various interpretive theories. We do not reject symbol analysis as one useful element in interpretation, but rather would add to this an engagement of the dream through various participatory, interactive, and otherwise experiential processes.

As all teachers of literature and art—among the other fields we have surveyed here—can testify, humans are meaning-ascribing as well as meaning-seeking. Are meanings placed onto the dream through a projective process in addition to being found within the dreams themselves? To the extent that meanings reside within the dream, we can view theories of dream meanings and interpretive procedures as variously correct or incorrect at ferreting out the inherent meanings. But to the extent that the latter is true—when we bring the meanings to the dreams—then theories and procedures serve not as spotlights illuminating the dream but as backpacks carrying to the dream the meanings that we need the dream to have. The theories then provide and legitimize the "positive biases" noted in Bulkeley's application of Gadamer's hermeneutics, and the contingent perspectives based on the interpreter's unique body–mind historical experience, along the lines proffered by Johnson.

Most dream workers would hold that dreams contain their meanings, although these meanings are often not transparent. One must tease them out of the dream narrative by various interpretive methods. In this view, the unconscious mind produces the dream *and its meanings*, often through clever symbolism. The unconscious intends meaning, and it intends specific meanings as well; if we can decode the symbols, the meanings are revealed. Sometimes the symbolic meanings are evident, sometimes more obscure. (A corollary of this perspective is that all parts of the dream are meaningful, i.e., contain some significance. Another corollary is that dreams have layers of meaning, with the dream images therefore over determined.)

The assumption that dreams contain their meanings is received wisdom, and we all have been mightily impressed at one time or another by the meanings our dreams seem to hold. Take the example of a man who in waking life was agonizing over whether he should get married to his girlfriend of many years. He had a dream in which he slipped a gold ring on her finger. The ring then broke into many pieces and fell off. The meaning is clear, and it seems to stem directly from the dream itself.

However, there is another way of looking at the interpretation of this dream and at dream interpretation in general. This is, we give at least some dreams the interpretations that we need them to have in order to make sense of our experiences and move our lives forward. We use the theories and other biases that serve our purposes. (Most dream interpreters whom we know, including those identifying strongly with a particular theory, are eclectic in practice—they use whatever theory seems to fit the dream at hand.) Reported dreams are stories about our lives. These stories are both mundane and profound. We look at these stories, and interpret them according to our needs, through our theories of meaning, mediated by the complexity of organic systems and processes adduced by Johnson. It is a projective process. The meanings may inhere partly in our unconscious minds and partly in conscious thought processes, but they don't necessarily come from the dream itself, at least not entirely. The dream can be the receptacle for the meanings later ascribed to it. *In this view, dreams and interpretive theories are vehicles that we use to give ourselves permission to think and talk about ourselves in helpful and clarifying ways.* Without the dream and its interpretation, it may be more difficult to develop the necessary life narrative.

From this perspective, the man contemplating getting married really did not want to, or he would not have been "agonizing" (his words) over it. He *wanted to* want to, but he did not want to. There were emotional and social prices to pay for deciding against marriage, or for it. He had trouble coming to terms with his conflicted feelings and motives. The dream's engagement ring falling apart was such a stark image that it nudged (better, elbowed) him into a clearer realization of his feelings. The dream played a role analogous to that of a good friend and confidant who might have said "Come on, Joe, do you really want to get married or not?"

It was up to this dreamer to ascribe meaning, which he did, and breaking the engagement was a waking consequence. Another dreamer having the *same* dream may have interpreted it in terms of financial difficulties or enforced separation or family disapproval threatening the prospects of a marriage he *did* want to happen. Again, in this view one brings meanings to the dream, and does not extract them from it. The specific meaning chosen is that which gives the greatest coherence to the larger life context.

This point of view—that meanings are brought to dreams as well as residing in them—finds empirical support in the relatively recent research of Carey K. Morewedge and Michael J. Norton.[11] In a series of inventive combinations of surveys and natural experiments, these social psychologists demonstrated

that people from both Eastern and Western cultures regard dreams as meaningful sources of information, more meaningful in fact than similar conscious
thoughts, and that their dream interpretations are motivated by their waking
and conscious concerns and needs:

> The meaningfulness attributed to specific dreams . . . was moderated by the
> extent to which the content of these dreams accorded with participants' preexist-
> ing beliefs—from the (dream) theories they endorsed to attitudes toward acquain-
> tances, relationships with friends, and faith in God.[12]

Morewedge and Norton's phrase, the "motivated interpretation of dreams"
is telling, and accords with our perspective. The basic idea that we interpret
dreams to align with our existing needs and beliefs (and bodily grounded meaning
systems) should frame the teaching of dream interpretation, and in conjunction
with particular theories inform the interpretation of individual dreams.

Jungian theory in its richness and fascination may be the prime current
example of bringing meanings to dreams in heuristically creative and useful
ways—this despite the reifying assumption of some (most?) Jungian practitioners that the theory's categories really exist in the unconscious, and bubble up,
as it were, in dreams. It does not detract from the pragmatic value of Jungian
approaches to consider that they may serve as creative fictions in addition to
(or instead of) identifying structural truths about the human mind—that is,
they may bring meanings to dreams as well as (or rather than) discovering
meanings within them.

The same possibility exists for other interpretive theories: Freudian, Gestalt,
and so forth. Their value may consist as much in the meanings they invoke
and permit as in the meanings they purport to discover. Even an existential
perspective, which is meta-theoretical in its assertion that existential limits,
opportunities, dilemmas and qualities *really exist*, and cannot be gainsaid, becomes
"just" another way of approaching a dream to see what nuggets of meaning
might be identified. So, although existentialists make a distinction between the
fundamental issues that they claim the dream addresses, and other theories that
purport to "get at" the dream's meanings, in practice any interpretive theory
could be akin to Dumbo's feather, with our *belief* in the theory allowing us to
see the theory's validation in the dream. Then again, perhaps the feather itself
is powerful, and perhaps the theory does illuminate reality and not create it
from whole cloth. We often have been impressed with how clearly a certain
theory resonates with a particular dream.

From a pedagogical standpoint, it is not important that we and other dream
educators resolve these matters, only that we identify and address them. We
advocate that dream teachers adopt an epistemological sensibility—that they
evaluate the bases for knowledge claims rather than taking them for granted.

The West Point football team of the mid-1940s had two great running
backs—Doc Blanchard and Glen Davis. They were dubbed "Mr. Inside" and

"Mr. Outside," from their penchant to run inside or outside the tackles, respectively. They come to mind metaphorically in pondering how dream meanings may come from inside or outside the dream. Which running back can gain more yards? Which interpretive perspective is correct, for particular dreams and in general? Can both be correct, for different dreams? How should one decide which model to adopt? Within a model, how then do we know whether a particular interpretation is the best one? Is the "a-ha" experience of an interpretation "clicking," with the dreamer sufficient, or is it unreliable? What other criteria for the correctness of an interpretation should one use? And how do theories and methods of dream interpretation mesh with the fundamental question of the loci of dream meanings?[11] These all are important questions for dream teachers. It is as important for instructors to think about, bring up, and discuss these unresolved matters as to pass on settled knowledge. It is especially important for teaching dream interpretation, a task that one should view as somewhat daunting, if faced responsibly. It's a tricky business. We share Johanna King's observation that it is easy to do bad dreamwork, difficult to do it skillfully and responsibly. Likewise for teaching the related skills and perspectives.

Whatever the degree to which dreams come imbedded with meanings or need us to bestow meanings on them, another important concern in dream interpretation is the effect of social norms and cues, and group influences. There is a large literature on social influence processes suggesting that perceptions, meanings and actions are not solely internally determined, but are strongly affected by social contexts, group pressures and authoritative demands. The Asch and Milgram experiments are prime examples.[13]

Another body of work on cults and other subcultural communities isolated from wider societal influences and norms shows the ease with which people can adopt almost any meaning system, including bizarre and harmful ones. Approval and acceptance needs can overwhelm critical faculties. Philip Zimbardo, for example, notes:

> A remarkable thing about cult mind control is that it's so ordinary in the tactics and strategies of social influence employed. They are variants of well-known social psychological principles of compliance, conformity, persuasion, dissonance, reactance, framing, emotional manipulation, and others that are used on all of us daily to entice us: to buy, to try, to donate, to vote, to join, to change, to believe, to love, to hate the enemy.[14]

These mundane and easily overlooked qualities of social influence concern us. There is a real danger that authoritative experts (therapists, teachers, dream group leaders) benignly intended though they are, will unduly influence the attribution of meaning. Influence processes routinely operate outside conscious awareness. One needs knowledge of influence processes and a resolution to be conscious about accepting or resisting them. Making them explicit with student or client dreamers would be most helpful in this regard. Dreamwork leaders must be self-aware social psychologists.

Yet increasing familiarity with the anthropological literature on dreaming and critical theory in the humanities should broaden even this perspective: In almost all societies, the interpretation of dreams is a complex social transaction, and when dreams are shared, dream meaning is created in and by the group, and for social purposes. It may serve us best to consider separately the sociology of dream sharing and the ethical questions raised by undue social influence, and to take both very seriously.

We believe that good and ethical dreamwork and dreamwork education must involve an ongoing thoughtful awareness of the issues discussed here. We hope and expect that dreamwork educators will become increasingly sophisticated on these meta-levels. It is not enough to combine cleverness and intuitive ability with competence in a particular interpretive calculus.

The Internet and Associated Electronic Technologies

The Internet is ubiquitous and lends itself to so many uses, that we couldn't place a discussion of it into only one of the preceding chapters. The Internet provides ready access to materials in any subject of interest, including dreams. It facilitates connection and communication, so that dream enthusiasts can exchange views and information. The general virtues, capabilities, and problems of Internet use apply to dream education as they do to political discourse, social networking, and other areas.

Internet-based course material and entire courses, some recent ones generated by the IASD, have come into being during the past 15 years. This strengthens dream education and attracts new members to IASD. Archived radio talks on the Internet are a related resource. These information sources promote "distance learning," in which students can take courses at home using their computer as conduit to teacher and other class members. They also can be integrated with conventional courses as resource materials and assignments. Lectures are available online, and class discussions are held in virtual chat rooms. The Internet is a most useful vehicle for conveying information and for discussing topics in an educational setting. Siegel notes that the Internet is a tool for "primary prevention" dreams education. Its potential uses include teaching parents about their children's nightmares, about dreams in pregnancy, teaching people how to keep a dream journal, and so on. Dream educators, authors, and researchers and organizations can link their printed books with interactive Internet Web sites.

The Internet is the wave of the future; it would seem futile to resist it. The Internet can do what books do, and more, because it is interactive. However, we need to be aware of its limitations. As a case in point, it is ironic that the virtual (some would say "pseudo") contact made possible by the Internet may increase the alienation that the sharing of dreams in face-to-face settings can reduce. Advances in video conferencing and Skype will inevitably improve the "personal" feel of Internet communications, although never entirely bridging the divide.

On the positive side, the Internet makes dream education accessible to persons who, for reasons of geographic isolation, time constraints, health, or monetary costs are not able to be present physically, where conventionally structured courses and other dream teaching take place. Additionally, students who may be too shy to participate in face-to-face class discussions may find it easier to do so if buffered by the relative anonymity the Internet provides. They may find their voices, especially in the sharing of personal material, if dream sharing is a part of the educational process, as it often is, and as we think it should be. Whether this contributes to or retards the development of face-to-face communication skill and ease is debatable.

On the other hand, virtual contact is not real face-to-face contact. It is different—further reaching but attenuated and blunted. Communication cues such as tone of voice, body posture and facial expressions are absent. The instructor cannot "read" moment-to-moment reactions of the students. It may difficult, if not impossible, to adequately process dream sharing. Being connected electronically may activate vulnerabilities, but the absence of subtle cues and feedback will hamper recognition that this is happening and subsequent emotional resolution.

The potential problems with dream sharing in class discussed earlier in this volume are heightened in distance learning. Instructors need to take special care, and should consider modifying dream analysis activities and assignments to protect the students, who are truly separate from the teacher and each other regardless of their virtual connections. The intimacy one thinks one has is often illusory.

For these reasons, we think that the Internet is not the best mechanism or venue for dream sharing and interpretation, although it may work very well for other kinds of learning. Siegel notes that for mental health professionals it may be problematic legally to work online with persons in other states where the practitioner is not licensed. From an ethical standpoint, lack of face-to-face contact reduces the information available to the practitioner. Also, the "client" can easily disappear with no follow-up possible. So caution is in order about Internet-based work beyond information sharing and interactive exercises. Those doing Internet-based dreamwork should take care to address and resolve potential problems stemming from the distanced nature of the interactions that are inherent in the medium.

The Internet remains a valuable resource for research, curriculum design, and information sharing, as shown in Chapter 6 by the examples of Tougaw's and Welt's humanities courses, which use Web sites and blogs to allow students to share resources and formal and informal responses, liberating group study from the classroom by maintaining community through the week. The constant contact among dreamers the world over that we now take for granted is unthinkable without advanced electronic communications now within the means of most educators. The authors of this volume, working from Hawaii, Ohio, California, and Washington, D.C., might never have discovered or interviewed their primary resources (or communicated adequately with one another) without online syllabi, listservs, professional Web sites, and e-mail and instant-message exchanges.

Even in the time between our writing these words and their publication there will be ongoing technological developments that may lessen our concerns about electronically mediated dreamwork as they refine the fidelity of dream re-creations. Other developments in electronic technologies are giving us glimpses of near futures in which dreamers may be able to record dreams not simply by writing the dream narrative or picturing it in static artistic renderings, but by recreating the visual and aural qualities of the dream, in essence reproducing the dream as a short film. Already there are large archives of computerized photos and film clips, searchable and accessible by topic.[15] For example, if one has a dream flying while holding an umbrella, a clip from *Mary Poppins* may match it fairly closely. Superimposing and thereby substituting an image of the dreamer's head and face over that of Julie Andrews, and then toying with the resultant image and sequence may reproduce the dream experience to a fair degree of accuracy. The dreamer would use her sense of the closeness of fit of the re-created dream film to the remembered dream experience as the criterion of its veracity. Computer programs that create integrated visual and aural action sequences based on the dreamer's telling of her own dream could supplement, or become an alternative to, the use of stock footage. The "soundtrack" could be a voice over by the dreamer, in a kind of narrative documentary form, or the recreated dream characters could speak for themselves.

Other persons—for example, dream discussion group members—could then experience the finished vignette in a visceral way, adding a dimension of connection and immersive understanding to the natural empathic and intellectual qualities that currently allow one to relate to others' dreams. We are on the cusp of achieving this kind of dream portrayal, and there are other electronic innovations not too far over the horizon about which we can only speculate. We believe that future technological advances will affect in fundamental ways how we deal with dreams, even though the specifics will remain somewhat obscure until the new technologies are upon us.

Recently, we watched *War Games*, a 1983 movie in which a high school student inadvertently hacked his way into a Pentagon computer system, almost setting off World War III. How quaint the "advanced" technology in the film seems 28 years later. There was no Internet, no cell phones, no chat rooms, no MySpace or Facebook. The changes in lifestyle and consciousness lodged in the substitution of abbreviated e-mail language for Standard English, the ability of anyone to create films and put them on the Internet for all to see, the withering away of reading books for some youth, were nonexistent or embryonic. No doubt these trends will continue and other developments hitherto unanticipated will emerge. We expect overall for there to be more use of associational logic, more breadth and less depth in thinking. Simulations of reality by electronics will become more sophisticated and will use more sensory modalities. There will be more blending of the real and the virtual. The opening ceremonies of the 2008 Beijing Olympics gave us a glimpse of a clever and seamless amalgam of the real and the idealized, as the program creators superimposed virtual fireworks onto live views of the actual city from above.

Richard Wilkerson notes that the Internet and associated technologies are evolving, and may come to embody sensory perceptions, even the ability to "see" another's dream as the dreamer narrates it on line. There have been some beginning attempts to re-create—or at least communicate the essence of—dreams with film. We noted the work of Iris Heller in Chapter 9. Phil King and his students created a composite dream based on 40 dreams from one dreamer with similar thematic content. They then used existing film footage with the composite dream narrative voiced over in an effort to communicate the dream themes. (See Appendix F for a longer description of this project.) At an IASD conference some years ago, Robert Bosnak connected himself to the Internet so others could read his bodily responses (Galvanic skin responses) to interactions regarding his dream. Since then, he has introduced "cyberdreamwork," a real-time, method of doing group dreamwork on the Internet. His Web site states that his "in-depth work has been effective both individually and in groups and easily adapts to the Web because of its simple rules and group emphasis."[16] There is a disclaimer stating that the cyberdreamwork is not therapy and that those needing therapy should seek a therapist. Bosnak is one of the most creative and well-respected persons in the field. He and others moving into Internet dream education constitute the spearhead of a significant innovation.

These early forays in harnessing electronic technologies to communicate about dreams point the way to more sophisticated future possibilities. Past efforts in harnessing the capabilities of the Internet for dreams education are instructive for future trends, decisions, and policies. Wilkerson, with John Herbert and Jeremy Taylor, has experimented with various ways of sharing dreams on the Internet, including public access systems and user access groups. One model was a "big village" with open participation, like an open chat room. Widely differing levels of dream knowledge and sophistication among participants were a problem.

Wilkerson notes that the future of dream sharing on Internet could be analogous to chat room evolution. One could go into the "big" room, find the people you want to interact with, then go with them into a private room (a secluded area), and choose which sensory modalities to share, including seeing the dream unfold on the computer as the person relates it.

Wilkerson developed modules on various dream topics. These were used to bring people in Internet dream-sharing groups up to speed, and eventually became the contents of an online course for which students paid. The online dream group would try out ideas for the modules. This was grassroots education, involving no affiliation with a college and no course credits toward college degrees, although participants received certificates of completion.

Wilkerson notes the importance of distinctions among spiritual, clinical, and personal growth domains in working with dreams. The demarcations among them become obscured in online dreamwork as dreamers and their dreams are largely decontextualized, free-floating as they are in cyberspace. It may not be possible easily to identify persons who should be in a supportive face-to-face environment to discuss their dreams. There are questions of identity, what it means to be "here" and to be oneself in an Internet environment.

Another concern for Wilkerson has to do with the change from Internet as community to Internet as marketplace. How faithful can one be to the integrity of the dream and the needs of the dreamer when there is a money-making element to the interchange? The very technologies that spur creativity also commodify relationships in our market economy. Values besides monetary profit are in danger of falling by the wayside. Fortunately, dreams resist commoditization by their very nature.

No one begrudges dream teachers earning money from their work, and making a living at it if they do it as their main occupation and vocation. However, dream education should be widely accessible. There should be free or minimally expensive ways to learn about dreams and develop dream-related abilities that complement expensive conferences and programs of study. Books come to mind! The dream community should keep an eye on this to make sure that collectively we do not price dream knowledge out of the reach of people with modest financial resources. There will be an increasing number of dream databases and electronic resources for creative dream reconstruction. It would be good to have user access to them minimally affected by monetary considerations. However, if information on the Internet is free or cheap, one cannot make significant money from it. How money could be made without the annoyance of subjecting users to sponsors' commercials is not clear and remains a challenge for the future.

Both dream education content and the process of communicating that content and associated information electronically are evolving steadily. We may reach a point soon, as Wilkerson notes and we argued earlier, that we will be able to create vivid and compelling multisensory renditions of a dream directly or over the Internet. This may become an aspect of a wider societal paradigm shift, with visual imagery increasingly complementing the printed word with its linear logic (as the printed word joined and eventually substantially displaced older traditions of oral communication). Already one can find hybrids of traditional printed books with video clips. We tell dreams, we write dreams, and we increasingly will be able to show dreams, even at a distance.

The Future of Interdisciplinary Dream Education

Interdisciplinary education is not new; it has been with us for decades. One finds its advocacy and practice at all levels from elementary school to university graduate courses. It vies for resources, sometimes successfully, sometimes not, with other institutional needs and instructional constituencies, including conventional academic disciplines and educational approaches.

There are differences between formal university courses and extra-university teachings with implications for interdisciplinary education. The latter are less constrained by academic and institutional norms. The former may enjoy more resources. Another difference that *makes* a difference for interdisciplinary approaches is the age and sophistication of the students. It is easier to take an interdisciplinary approach either with elementary students for whom the level of discourse is simpler, or with postgraduate students and scholars who would have the background to understand sophisticated arguments and complex combinations of theory and method. It is in the middle to high school and college courses where we segregate subjects from one another that interdisciplinary teaching may prove more challenging.

There is one general point we feel important to emphasize, which is that interdisciplinary work in higher-education courses should be built on the foundations of a mastery of the constituent disciplines. It is good to have some background in both philosophy and neurology if one is venturing into neurophilosophy. We should avoid substituting the interdisciplinary course for the contents of basic curricula in the distinct fields. One can avoid this problem either by having basic courses as prerequisites for the interdisciplinary course, or by incorporating the basic content and methods into the interdisciplinary offering, which may expand the course be to the point that it warrants more credits than a standard course. For example, if one is to learn psychological theory *and* role-playing *and* film creation in a course on dreams, then that course may require an amount of work deserving 6, 8, 9, or 12 credits rather than the standard 3 or 4.

The dictionary makes little distinction between "multi-" and "inter-" disciplinary; both refer in a general way to making use of several distinct fields.[17] We see some differences in what interdisciplinary education in dreams might involve, along a continuum of less to more integration of discipline content and method. With this in mind, we would like to see interdisciplinary dreams education advancing on the following three fronts.

1. Separate courses on the same subject through different disciplines.
    An example would be anthropology, psychology and literature
    course offerings on dreams. We have reviewed many examples in
    this book. They bring in disciplines other than their own at most
    in a minor, supportive way, by, for example citing religious views of
    dreams in a psychology class, Or the studio art professor drawing on
    Jungian theory for subject matter. This is largely the current state
    of affairs, which we reviewed most directly in Chapter 6. Teachers
    use a few ideas and materials from other fields in order to enrich
    the dream courses taught in their own discipline. They appreciate
    that an understanding of dreams draws on many perspectives, and
    while sticking closely to their home field try to have their course
    reflect that reality to a degree.

2. Individual courses in which students get exposed fairly evenhandedly
    to more than one disciplinary perspective. In an academic context,
    such courses would likely be team-taught (but not necessarily,
    if a single professor is well versed in more than one field). For
    example, there could be a course on dreams and dreaming taught
    by a biologist, a psychologist, and a humanities scholar. Or, there
    could be one professor running the course, with a series of guest
    lecturers providing the "other" disciplines.

One could structure such courses in terms of distinct modules, or, better,
integrate the modules to an extent. For example, an historian could cite the
religious and psychological models of man dominant in different historical
periods that led to certain understandings of dreams. The biologist could trace
neurological "state constraints" in dreaming as they manifest themselves as features
of dream experiences and consequent dream narratives. The process of dialogue
between different contents, methods and perspectives could involve open-ended
faculty–faculty and faculty–student discourse, and collaborative research projects.

There is no reason why we cannot extend interdisciplinary curricula to
encompass dreams. A number of colleges and universities are hard at work
developing interdisciplinary programs, and putting significant resources into them.
Among them, and as examples of many colleges doing particularly good work,
are Grinnell and Macalester colleges.[18] Grinnell has interdisciplinary classes both
in the form of first year topic-based seminars, and at the upper division level.

3. A true integration of content, theory and method in the form of
    new, transformed approaches. The use of hermeneutical methods
    to interpret dreams through viewing them as texts to analyze for
    meaning (discussed previously) is an example. Yet another example
    would be combining the re-enactment of dreams through the kinds of

role-playing or "kinetic-sculpting" techniques used in family therapy with hermeneutics, or other activities that bring together analytical and experiential activities into the same process. The possibilities are legion; it's a matter of experimentation. Teacher creativity and the encouragement of innovation by those who dole out educational permissions and resources are necessary. The free-flowing and student-centered qualities traditionally associated with Montessori and Waldorf schools and their analogues in higher education are ideal environments for future dream education crossing disciplinary boundaries.

Teaching possibilities will parallel to a significant extent advances in technologies that will permit more and more faithful renditions of the specific dreams, so that persons other than the dreamer can experience something ever closer to what the dreamer experienced. In this important way our discussions of the future of electronic technologies and the future of interdisciplinary approaches connect.

Conclusion

We cannot assert as of this writing that we are on the verge of a "dreams revolution," although recent trends in interest are up. Time will tell. There is a continuing stream of good books, a steady trickle of research reports, and occasional popular articles (some of which, however, make light of dreams.) There seems lately be an increase in media attention. However, there are few if any continuing *series* of articles and columns in popular magazines, or on television. Dreams still have relatively low visibility in the public eye in general. Moreover, dream teachings in universities and in the community are economically (and institutionally) fragile. Dream teaching across the board is not well institutionalized, but depends on the wherewithal of individual scholars and teachers, which are limited and subject to fatigue.

Some predict that interest in dreams and dreams education will increase due to various global trends—for example, planetary ecological problems, along with the Internet and other global connections. Van de Castle observes that we're moving toward one global culture and are looking for something that unifies us, and that dreams are the vehicle par excellence. Dream education could benefit from the unsettled quality of our times in ways analogous to, but healthier than, such times stimulating various outré religious doctrines and practices. Anticipating "growth" may be in part wishful thinking, although IASD membership, activities and financial health all have increased significantly during the past 6 years.

Dreams are vivid experiences and vital statements about our aesthetic and spiritual realities, our internal psychological integration, intimate relations with others, and the social worlds in which we live. Learning about dreams and their dazzling meanings is life affirming and especially important in our socially and ecologically perilous times. It is our hope that this volume contributes to advances in dream education in the classroom and beyond. We encourage you in your work and in your dream journeys. We wish all dreamers and dream teachers well.

Appendix A

A Dreams Reading List
(and Other Resources)

Where should the dreams student and aspiring teacher turn for a core education on dreams, and for possible texts for assignments? We mention here books that we have found to be particularly useful—to us. Other books have influenced other persons, so we don't tout our list as definitive.

The central section on dreams in Freud's *Introductory Lectures on Psychoanalysis* may be the most lucid and accessible introduction to Freud's controversial but path-breaking theory. The shorter text *On Dreams* still fulfills its original function as a quick but complete run down of Freud's theory. We would reserve the study of Freud's classic *The Interpretation of Dreams*, certainly one of the most important books of the 20th century, for courses undertaking extensive study of psychoanalytic approaches to dreams and the unconscious, or to cultural or historical studies. The collection *Essential Papers on Dreaming* offers many recent perspectives on the psychoanalytic theory of dreams which may be selectively presented to students, and Mark Blechner's *The Dream Frontier* represents a particularly illuminating attempt to revise psychoanalytic dream theory in the light of more recent discoveries. Another useful source is *Basic Freud*, by Michael Kahn. Richard Wollheim's *Sigmund Freud* remains the best introduction for the instructor who wishes to comprehend Freud's view of dreaming in the context of his theory of mind, as well as of philosophical and cultural issues.

Carl Jung is the other great modern historical writer on dreams, and his theories continue to carry much weight. Jung's essay "Approaching the Unconscious" in the volume *Man and His Symbols* is a particularly accessible explanation of the role of dreaming in the theory of analytical psychology. Other essential essays on the topic may be found in the volume *Dreams*, and in *Psychological Reflections*. Jung's discursive style can make it hard for students to grasp key points; we find Maria Mahoney's *The Meaning in Dreams and Dreaming*, Mary Ann Mattoon's *Understanding Dreams*, Robert Bosnak's *A Little Course on Dreams*, and *The Wisdom of the Dream*, by Stephen Segaller and Merrill Berger, to be particularly helpful guides. Barbara Hannah's *Jung: His Life and Work* is an interesting memoir. A bridge between Freud's and Jung's classic theories and more contemporary material is *The Forgotten Language*, by Erich Fromm.

Kelly Bulkeley's *An Introduction to the Psychology of Dreaming* offers a focused overview of the topic. Another short but fine introduction is Charles Rycroft's *The Innocence of Dreams*. *The Secret Language of Dreams* by David Fontana is a concise introduction that is especially good at conveying the visual quality of dreams. Robert Van de Castle's *Our Dreaming Mind* (soon to be out in a revised edition) may be the most complete comprehensive survey, well adapted to the undergraduate student's needs and interests; and Ole Vedfelt's *The Dimensions of Dreams* is similarly valuable. Another wide-ranging review, although pitched above the reach of nonspecialist undergraduates, is Anthony Shafton's *Dream Reader—Contemporary Approaches to the Understanding of Dreams*. Ernest Hartmann's *Dreams and Nightmares* integrates much material into a compelling and highly accessible view of the "origin and meaning of dreams"; his forthcoming work, *The Nature and Functions of Dreaming*, should be eagerly anticipated by all dream educators. *All About Dreams* by Gayle Delaney is particularly good in its treatment of how dreams have been viewed historically and in its discussion of ways to interpret dreams. *Dreamworking*, by Stanley Krippner and Joseph Dillard, is a thoughtful treatment with helpful guidance for using dreams in one's personal life.

Patricia Garfield's writings, especially *The Dream Messenger* and *The Healing Power of Dreams*, are fine examples of books focusing on the use of dreams in psychological and physical healing. In *Dreaming Beyond Death*, Kelly Bulkeley and Patricia Bulkley thoughtfully explore the role of dreams in terminal illness. Robert Moss sets forth provocative ideas about dreams' connections with spiritual dimensions in *Conscious Dreaming* and in *The Secret History of Dreaming*. Alvin Mahrer's *Dreamwork in Psychotherapy and Self-Change* is an excellent entry to the use of dreams in clinical work and training. *Trauma and Dreams*, edited by Deirdre Barrett, discusses trauma as instigators of troubling dreams and the role of dreams in healing from trauma. In *The Wilderness of Dreams*, Kelly Bulkeley explores religious meanings of dreams in the West and delves deeply into perplexing questions of dream interpretation. Sivananda Radha provides a useful look at Eastern spiritual approaches to dreams in *Realities of the Dreaming Mind*. Thirty years after its publication, Montague Ullman and Nan Zimmerman's *Working with Dreams* remains a useful guide to understanding one's dreams by sharing them with others.

G. William Domhoff's books *Finding Meaning in Dreams—A Quantitative Approach* and *The Scientific Study of Dreams* provide a thorough discussion of dream content analysis and empirical approaches to studying dreams and testing dream theories. Mark Solms' *Neuropsychology of Dreams* treats the underlying biology of the dreaming process and dream imagery. Jim Pagel's *The Limits of Dream* explores the achievements of neuroscience in understanding dreams, and the activities of mind that appear to go beyond observable neurological processes. Harry Hunt's *The Multiplicity of Dreams* discusses the many types of dreams and ways in which their study enriches our understanding of memory, creativity, and visual thinking. To introduce students to lucid dreaming, the essential guide remains Stephen LaBerge's *Lucid Dreaming,* and a useful new volume is *Lucid Dreaming—Gateway to the Inner Self* by Robert Waggoner. In *Nightmares,* Patrick McNamara has produced a definitive contemporary treatment of the topic that often first arouses students' interest in dreams; John E. Mack's *Nightmares and Human Conflict* proposes a fascinating theory of the relation between children's nightmares, play, and creativity. *Dreams 1900–2000: Science, Art and the Unconscious Mind,* edited by Lynn Gamwell, is a fascinating exposition of a century of dream-related art and its inspirations in psychoanalytical theory, with many illustrations that may be helpful in any dream studies course. Reading Bert O. States' *Seeing in the Dark,* the product of a lifetime's reflection on the unique features of the subjective experience of dreaming, is a richly rewarding literary and intellectual experience for student and teacher alike.

Dream Work in Therapy, edited by Clara Hill, is an excellent treatment of research on the effects of employing dreams in psychotherapy, and by extension a useful guide to issues of the general value and benefit of taking dreams seriously.

Advances in dreams knowledge appear first in conferences, only later in magazines, journals and books. A relatively new (and excellent) scholarly journal is the *International Journal of Dream Research,* based in Germany and edited by Michael Schredl and Daniel Erlacher, which has joined the longer established *Dreaming,* published in the United States by the International Association for the Study of Dreams (IASD). The IASD also publishes an important periodical magazine, *Dream Time,* holds a major conference and several regional conferences around the world each year, and provides distance continuing education on dreams, partially via the Internet. There is no better experience for the dreams student or teacher than to attend and participate in these IASD activities. A valuable side benefit of IASD conference going is the opportunity to meet and get to know a community of dreamers whose knowledge of dreams and welcoming friendliness is unmatched.

Appendix B

Course Syllabi

Here are three syllabi for undergraduate-level college dream courses: Phil King's psychology course, Tracey Kahan's psychology course on dreams and sleep, and Bernard Welt's general humanities course.

Syllabus: Psychology 4240: The Psychology of Dreams
Hawaii Pacific University
Dr. Philip King
(with professor's commentary in italics)

Course Description

The objectives of the course are to provide students with a broad theoretical understanding of dreams and dreaming, experience and skills in dream research, increased abilities to recall and use their own dreams in their lives in helpful ways, and an ability to understand other persons through the communication of dreams.

Topics to be covered include: (a) biological processes of dreaming; (b) theories of dream meaning, interpretation, and use; (c) recalling, understanding, and appreciating one's own and others' dreams; (d) dream content analysis; (e) dreams in relation to personal growth, physical illness and healing, and society; and (f) paranormal and lucid dreams.

This course is unusual, if not unique. It explicitly combines deep personal experience, conceptual and skill learning, and knowledge creation. You will experience your own dreams and explore their meanings. You will share your dreams with others to an extent that you will choose. You will contribute to dream knowledge through an original research project.

Our class meetings will be thought provoking; our dream-sharing groups will be welcome respites from the rigors of your week. Many students who have taken this course over the past 15 years have found it to be one of the high points in their college education. We hope this proves true for you.

(Dreams courses are special, out of the ordinary experiences for most students. Do not be afraid to tout this.)

Course Prerequisites and Requirements

This is an upper-division course. Students in the course should have completed introductory psychology, a research methods course, and at least two other psychology courses. A statistics course is recommended highly, although not required. Also needed is a willingness to communicate some of your remembered dreams to other class members.

(Undergraduate psychology dream courses can be at any level. Topics within it are so varied that it could even provide the framework for an introductory course in psychology, through which students learn the basics of neuropsychology, cognition, personality theory, research methods and statistics, etc. Introductory-level courses would not need prerequisites.)

Course Organization

Class will meet Tuesdays and Thursdays from 10:50 a.m. to 12:15 p.m. During most weeks, one class meeting will focus on theoretical material, with lecture and discussion based on the reading assignments. The other meeting will focus on the experiences of working with one's own dreams in a dream-sharing group. Depending on course enrollment, the class may split into two dream groups to provide adequate attention to each dreamer. If we do this, one of the dream groups may meet at a different time from the regular class time, to be determined.

(I have found that class meetings of 85 or 90 minutes are ideal, especially for dream-sharing groups. Usually you can cover two dreams reasonably thoroughly in that time. One hour or 55 minute meetings are too short. So if you have a choice, opt for two 90-minute classes per week. One 3-hour meeting works, but fatigue can set in, so schedule breaks. I find one longer break works better than two shorter ones. Experiment in 3-hour classes to see whether dream sharing works best in the first or second half of the class. If you have it in the first half, the mood may be broken in the second half. If you schedule it for the second half, the students may be tired and distracted. It is possible to use the students' fatigue or stress states as a feeling quality to connect them to the dream-sharing process, to good effect.)

ısly, students have gone on to organize their own dream-sharing groups
ıe course was over.

you wish to share a dream in the group, type it and make enough copies
members. It really helps if one can read the dream text while hearing
ramer narrate the dream aloud.

ıe basis for grading dream group participation will be attendance, atten-
s, thoughtfulness, responsiveness and support, not the profundity or
tness" of comments about the dreams.

*are many ways to incorporate dream sharing and dream analysis into a
See the text for an extensive discussion of options, their costs and benefits.)*

Dream Journal/Diary

eam journal will be a record of remembered dreams, dream fragments and
related thoughts, observations, drawings and exercises, kept in a bound
l or loose-leaf binder. Students will submit their journals at midterm and
ıt the end of the course. We will respect students' privacy in that no one
ıve to relate or submit material that he or she wishes to withhold. Nor
e professor read the dreams, unless the student requests that he do so.
e is material that you wish to keep private, either remove it from the
l (and indicate that you have done so, so that you can be given credit
or simply fold it over. The basis for grading the journals will be on the
ıt of content only.

see the text for discussion of ways to incorporate dream journals into a course.)

Exams and Quizzes

will be two examinations, one at midterm and one at the end of the
The final exam will not be cumulative; it will cover the second half of
urse only. There also will be between 5 and 10 quizzes, unannounced
ıand. Students may make up missed exams only if they inform the pro-
before the exam, and the reason for the absence is illness or a serious
ıncy. Students may not make up missed quizzes.

*less mature and less self-motivated students, you may need to use exams and
as ways to get them to do the work. The less you need to do this, the better
concerned. Some argue that the testing process itself is educative. I'm not so
out this, but it's worth considering.)*

Grades

will be based on class and dream group participation (10%), exams
research project (30%), quizzes (15%), and dream journal/diary (10%).
ts must complete all assignments in order to pass the course.

Texts

All About Dreams, by Gayle Delaney. HarperCollins,
Dreams and Nightmares, by Ernest Hartmann. Perseu
will be visiting the class during February 15–17.
The Complete Book of Dreams, by Julia and Derek Parke
Handouts from the DreamBank Web site (Universit)
Cruz), and other materials as appropriate.
(Consider bringing in at least some new books from teri
a continual flow of new information and perspective, and
discussions fresh. I have used 20 or more different texts o

Research Project

The project will be an empirical analysis of dream cont
by the student and approved by the professor, 15 page
font, 1-inch margins, not right justified, typed double-sp
will take one or more set or series of 100 or more dre
DreamBank or other sources, and systematically analyz
a statistical software package. The professor will serve a:
and will work with students one-on-one as needed.

It may be possible for one or two (excellent) studen
assistants on the professor's current project, which is a bool
This involvement would be in lieu of the dream content
(I believe that students benefit tremendously from assignmen
duce new findings, rather than only absorbing existing kno
empirical research empowers them as thinkers and scholars.)

Dream Group Participation

Activities will include bringing dreams to share, respondi
supportively to others' dream descriptions, and listening :
dreams and comments. Students may choose to relate or
on a particular day. Our experience in past courses is that
become comfortable with and enjoy sharing their dreams.

We will learn and use a modified Ullman-Taylor "if it v
dream-sharing model, in which decisions about the meanin
be up to the dreamer—not the group, not the professor.
students will learn how to lead the dream group process. (

(I don't grade students on the quality of products from experiential aspects of the course—only their diligence in producing requisite quantity.)

Class Attendance, Participation, and Other Matters

This course intertwines knowledge development, personal exploration. and interpersonal exchange. So as a courtesy to the professor and other class members, regular class attendance and promptness are especially important. Absences in excess of three classes for the semester may result in a reduction of your course grade. Two instances of tardiness constitute 1 hour of absence. Please read the assignments on time and be ready to discuss them in class.

(Courses where participants share dreams become little communities. Full participation keeps morale and energy high. Better that students drop the course early on than participate sporadically.)

Confidentiality

Class members should feel free to express themselves without concern about the confidentiality of what they say. Therefore, do not to share the dreams or other personal material communicated in class outside the course, without the dreamer's permission. (Do, however, share *your own* dreams outside the class!) *(Although it is impossible to ensure confidentiality, it should be an explicit policy.)*

Assignments

We may modify assignments depending on the pace at which we cover the material and how we choose to develop the research project.

(In a one-semester psychology dream course you will have to leave out or truncate treatment of some valuable topics. Select according to your interests.)

PSYC 135: Psychology of Sleep & Dreaming
Spring, 2009
Mon & Wed 2:15–4 p.m.
Daly Science 201

"Why does the mind see a thing more clearly in dreams than the mind while awake?"

—Leonardo da Vinci

Dr. Tracey L. Kahan
Associate Professor of Psychology, Santa Clara University
PRE-REQUISITES: Psyc 1, 2, 40, 43 (or permission of instructor)
(with professor's commentary in italics)

Overview

A theoretical, empirical, and experiential exploration of the psychology of sleep and dreaming. Topics include psychophysiology of sleep; circadian rhythms; sleep disorders; contemporary theories of sleep and dream functions; continuity in cognition, neurocognition, and affect over the sleep/wake cycle; memory for dreams; the role of sleep in memory processing; consciousness and dreaming; types of dreams (including lucid dreams); and consequences of sleep debt for professional and personal well-being.

(This course equally emphasizes the psychology of dreaming and sleep. As I am a cognitive-experimental psychologist, we emphasize the empirical approaches to dreaming [and sleep] within the general scientific framework of hypothesis testing and theory-evidence relationships. At the same time, there is a strong thread of personal/ phenomenological exploration. Students keep a sleep and dream journal through the quarter [guidelines are included after the syllabus] and we begin each class with a brief [5- to 10-minute] "sleep and dream-sharing" exercise. Students pair up and reflect on, variously, what they have recently noticed in their sleep and dreaming experiences, challenges they are facing with dream recall and/or sleep (generally, these center on the management of sleep restriction and regularizing sleep/wake times). Out of these conversations, students may (or may not) elect to offer a comment or raise a question with the entire class concerning (only) their own sleep or dreaming experience. Paired-sharing conversations are otherwise assumed to be more/less confidential. As the quarter progresses, students are introduced to various formal dreamwork techniques and invited to try each technique on their own. Although we discuss students' reactions to and questions about the dreamwork exercises in class, we do not analyze individual dreams as a class).

Intended Course Outcomes

Through their work in this course, students will:

1. develop comprehensive knowledge of the psychology and psychophysiology of sleep, sleep disorders, and dreaming;

2. hone their critical analysis skills through evaluating theories of sleep and dreaming in light of empirical research;

3. become attuned to the personal and public health consequence of chronic sleep restriction;

4. observe, and perhaps alter, their own sleep and dreaming practices;

5. apply various dream work techniques aimed at increasing self-understanding, creativity, spiritual awareness, or cultural sensitivity.

Required Reading

Books

Bulkeley, K. (1997). *An introduction to the psychology of dreaming*. Westport, CT: Praeger.

Moorcroft, W. H. (2003). *Understanding sleep and dreaming*. New York: Plenum.

Chapters and Research Articles

• Selected articles and chapters are available on ERES (password = sleep)

• Additional books and articles are available from Dr. Kahan's personal library.

• Other source materials may be identified and obtained by students for their

Final Paper

RECOMMENDED:
American Psychological Association. (2001). *Publication manual of the American Psychological Association* (5th ed).Washington, DC: Author.
(The fields of sleep and dreaming are dynamic and rich with emerging theories, research techniques, and discoveries. There is no one perfect book for this class; over the nearly 20 years I have offered this class, I have used a dozen different books; each has had its strengths and weaknesses. In my view, Bulkeley's book, although now more than 10 years old, remains the most balanced, accurate, and accessible introduction to the psychology of dreaming. Moorcroft's text is rather "encyclopedic" and so I offer considerable guidance to the students regarding what to emphasize within the reading. It does provide a comprehensive introduction to core topics in sleep. [Although it is now somewhat dated, I have also used with success Peretz Lavie's 1996 book, The Enchanted World of Sleep. New Haven, CT: Yale University Press.] Each year, I experiment with the combination of classic and contemporary source materials and I regularly add new resources to the course archives [which are accessible to the students as well]. Topically, the first half of the course emphasizes sleep, the second half dreaming. However, the discussions of sleep also include considerable discussion of dreaming).

Class Topics and Activities:
Introductions & Course Overview Why study sleep & dreaming?
    Guidelines for Sleep/Dream Journal
Psychophysiology of sleep & dreaming
    When do dreams occur?
Readings: Moorcroft, Chaps 1, 3; Bulkeley, Chap 1, pp. 51–58; Carlson: Chap 9 (pp. 291–296).

Psychophysiology of sleep (CONT'D)
  & Individual Differences
    How does sleep vary over the life span?
    How does sleep vary across individuals?
Readings: Keenan, S. (1999). Normal human sleep.
Sleep as a Circadian Process & Brain Mechanisms of Normal Sleep
  Sleep as a Circadian rhythm
  What brain structures and processes are involved in generating
  NREM sleep? REM sleep?
Readings: Moorcroft: Chap 2 (pp. 52–55), 4 & 5 [+ 1, 3 again]; Dement, W.
The sleepwatchers (Chap 3]; (Handout) Brain structures and processes of sleep.

Circadian rhythms cont'd
Consequences of sleep loss; sleep "debt"
Readings: Moorcroft: Chap 2 (all), Chap 9: pp. 205–221; Dement: The promise
of sleep, pp. 51–73.

Sleep disorders: Insomnia, Apnea & Narcolepsy

Readings: Moorcroft: Chap 10; Dement, W. The sleepwatchers [Chap 4]; Carlson
(Chap 9: Sleep, pp. 296–300)

Sleep disorders: Parasomnias (& Nightmares)
Readings: Moorcroft: Chap 9
Why do we sleep?
Why do we sleep?[& Midterm Review]

Readings: Carlson, N. R. (2007). Chap 9: Sleep, pp. 300–306); Moorcroft:
Chaps 12, 13
Re-visit: (handout). Brain mechanisms of sleep.

MIDTERM EXAM
(*An in-class Midterm Exam has proven effective in focusing students on mastering the
basic terms concepts, issues, theories, and findings related to the core topics in sleep*).

The Psychology of Dreaming: A variety of approaches
    Historically, what approaches were used to study dreams?

Readings: Bulkeley: Chap 1, pp. 51–58 again]; Moorcroft: Chaps 6, 7; (handout)
"Issues in function & meaning of dreams"

The Psychology of Dreaming:
Issues in the Function and Meaning of Dreams

Readings: Bulkeley: Chap 5 (all); (handout) "Issues in function & meaning of dreams"

Contemporary Approaches in Dream Psychology
What questions are at the forefront of contemporary dream research?
What methods are currently used in the scientific study of dreaming?

Readings: Foulkes, 1991. Why study dreaming? One researcher's perspective; Nielsen, T. A., & Stenstrom, P. (2005). What are the memory sources of dreaming? Nature, 437(27), 1286–1289.
(Because the field of dream psychology is so diverse, we spend considerable time in class discussing frameworks [theoretical and empirical] for approaching the study of contemporary issues in dream science. Class discussions are initiated through students' responses [based on their reading] to a set of initial questions included on the syllabus. I sometimes use "break-out groups" wherein I give small groups of students particular reading-related questions to discuss; each group then leads the larger class discussion of that question. This is an effective way of encouraging students to assess their understanding and mastery of the material and it gives them practice in representing their knowledge and teaching others.)

Cognitive approaches
What is the relationship between dreaming and waking cognition and emotion?

Readings: Bulkeley, Ch 5 (again)]; Schredl, M., & Hofmann, F. (2003). Continuity between waking activities and dream activities. Consciousness and Cognition, 12, 298–308.
LaBerge, S. (1998). Dreaming and Consciousness. In S. Hameroff, A. Kaszniak, & A. Scott (Eds.), Toward a Science of Consciousness II (pp. 495–504). Boston: MIT Press; Children's dreaming (Foulkes, 1993).

Neurocognitive approaches
How do neuroscientists explain dream generation?

Readings: Moorcroft pp. 188–199; Cavallero (2000). REM sleep = dreaming: The never-ending story.

MEMORIAL DAY HOLIDAY: no class
Applications of dream studies: Personal, interpersonal, and cross-cultural

Readings: Bulkeley Chs 2–4; Tedlock, B. (1994). Anthropology. (anthropological approaches to the study of dreams and dreaming); Cartwright, R. (1991).
Dreams that work: The relation of dream incorporation to adaptation to stressful
events; Bulkeley & Kahan (2008). The impact of September 11 on dreaming.
*(The choice of subtopics related to dreaming is strongly influenced by my own
research interests [consciousness and cognition across the sleep/wake cycle] and areas
of expertise [cognition, perception, experimental methods]. Students are encouraged
to explore their own scholarly interests [within dream science] in their final paper).
In class, I deliberately acknowledge my own theoretical/methodological biases. I
encourage students to challenge any claims I might make concerning, for example, the
purported continuities between waking cognition and dreaming cognition and to ask
me (as I ask them) "what is the evidence." Students have reported greatly enjoying
these discussions—where my work is in the hot seat. Subtler "fruits" include enrichment of my own research activities as well as the opportunity for students to engage
in the kind of intellectual exchange that might occur among research colleagues.)*

Student Presentations JOURNALS DUE!
Sleep & Dreaming: Patterns, insights, and suggestions for future explorations/
course conclusions

FINAL PAPER:
*(For the section on dreaming, students develop a comprehensive paper [in APA style]
that integrates theory and evidence related to a topic of interest to the student. In this
paper, students incorporate several of the course readings and they select additional
resources, including research articles.)*

7) A final note to the student: Although we will consider a number of ways
that people have "worked" with dreams, this course is not devoted to methods

ASSESSMENT:	Points: % Due date:
Midterm Exam (in class)	280 points (28%)
Sleep & Dream Journal Project:	230 points (23%)
Final paper:	250 points (25%)
Class attendance, active (& informed) participation ongoing (including reading summaries, discussion questions, and end-of-quarter presentation)	240 points (24%)
	_____
	1,000 points (100%)

of dream interpretation (which are more art than science). Our focus is on
sleep science and contemporary research in dream psychology. The readings and
discussions draw upon neuropsychology, memory and cognition, cross-cultural

studies, developmental psychology, psychophysiology, and health psychology. There is no "perfect" preparation for this intellectual and experiential adventure. The ideal preparation is solid scientific reasoning skills, completion of two or more upper division psychology courses, experience in reading original journal articles, and a deep curiosity about sleep and dreaming. At the same time, the course is designed to be accessible to students who have not completed all prerequisites and/or are not psychology majors. The value you derive from this course is directly related to what you put into it. (If you have not completed the prerequisites, I encourage you to discuss their preparation with me.)

(A final note to you, the instructor: Teaching a course in dreaming [or sleep and dreaming!] can be daunting in view of the diversity of theories, approaches, common myths and misunderstandings, and backgrounds of both students and instructor. Studying our "night life" also is one of the most fascinating, personally revealing, and ultimately inspiring enterprises. There are many effective ways to "package" a course in dreaming [or, again, sleep and dreaming!]. My recommendation is to teach from your expertise and passion and you [and your students] will find the course experience hugely rewarding, perhaps even transformative!)

Dreaming AS3225A (3 cr)
The Corcoran College of Art and Design
Dept. of Art and Humanities
Prof. Bernard Welt
(with professor's commentary in italics)

> *Within each one of us there is another whom we do not know. He speaks to us in dreams and tells us how differently he sees us from how we see ourselves.*
>
> —Carl Jung

> *Dreams are real while they last. Can we say more of life?*
>
> —Havelock Ellis

In this course we take both a theoretical and an empirical approach to the study of dreaming—a phenomenon that, although universal in humans, occupying a considerable portion of our lives, and prominently celebrated in the beliefs and art of all societies, is nevertheless generally treated by scholarship as marginal to understanding humanity, culture, and the world. To study dreaming empirically, you'll receive training in recalling and recording your dreams, and exploring them in detail in your journal and in a supportive discussion group with fellow students. This is a journal-intensive course in which you'll develop your own well-founded view of the relation between your dreams and your inner life, work, and aspirations through weekly writing, dream-appreciation sessions, and readings. Our theoretical study of dreaming will be undertaken through readings, lectures, and videos on key issues, particularly the modern psychological thesis of the unconscious mind, with emphasis on the influence of Sigmund Freud and Carl Gustav Jung upon modern accounts of symbolism, art, and creativity. If dreams are, as Freud said, "the royal road to knowledge of the workings of the unconscious mind," then they are a key to comprehending a prominent feature of modern ways of understanding human life and culture.

Whether or not we end up agreeing on what dreams are, and on their place in individual psychology and social history, everyone in the class should find that they have dreams available to them to analyze, learn from, and appreciate as constructs of the imagination. The most essential work for the course, therefore, will be keeping a journal in which you record your own dreams and your own considered responses to them. Readings and requirements have been planned to give you time to focus on your own dreams and to enrich your understanding of them. Groups that have taken this course in the past have found that the experience has not only given them insight on their own dreams, but also has enhanced their general awareness of symbolic imagery and behavior, and has directly and positively affected their work and their lives.

(In introducing this course, I want students to be aware that it requires traditional mastery of information and concepts, while at the same time requiring attention to capacities not always cultivated in traditional academic work: introspection, intuition, associative and lateral thinking. In the context of the humanities, it is of some importance to emphasize that a focus on one's own subliminal thoughts and the productions of unconscious thought can dramatically increase one's sensitivity to symbolism and strengths in interpretation. In fact, by the end of the course, when students are asked to discuss a poem, story, or film "as if it were a dream," they are clearly more adept at volunteering interpretative views than when they started— when a call for interpretative comments might be thwarted by students' feeling that symbolism is an arcane and elite system, and that they'd "get it wrong.")

Goals and Requirements

Recall and explore your own dreams, assessing your capacity to inspect and articulate your own subjective, imaginative experience

- Keep your dream journal faithfully, making a sincere effort to recall and record dreams regularly.

- Comment on dreams in your journal daily, experimentally trying out methods derived from our major topics.

- Review your dream journal daily.

Report on the progress of your dream journal periodically and at the end of
the course

- Share and discuss dreams.

- Attend every session punctually, ready to listen and contribute.

- Consult your own experience as a dreamer and contribute examples
  when you feel comfortable doing so.

- Listen attentively and offer appropriate response to anyone who
  shares a dream.

Study and learn—psychological theories (emphasizing the contributions of Jung
and Freud), contemporary psychophysiological accounts, and cultural perspectives
Focus on the major issues raised in the course:

- The influence of the thesis of the unconscious on modern theories
  of mind

- The relation between theories of function and theories of interpretation in dream studies

- The relation of theories of dreaming and the unconscious to modern
  theories of culture, art, imagination, and creativity

- The distinction between accounts of objective physiological phenomena such as REM sleep and the subjective phenomenon of dreaming

- Dreaming as a topic in the history of religions, including accounts
  of dreaming as indicators of theories of the physical and spiritual
  worlds, and of the value accorded to subjective experience

- Dreaming as a topic in ontology, epistemology, and consciousness
  studies

- Dreaming as a topic in art movements and media, especially romanticism, surrealism, and the cinema

- The contemporary cultural phenomenon of widespread interest in
  dream sharing and interpretation

Complete assigned readings on time and raise questions for discussion as they
occur to you

Demonstrate mastery of assigned topics and independent critical thought in
writing assignments

(Students derive value not only from learning, but also from reaching clarity on just what it is they've learned. In a class in which discussions often focus on students' impression of the relation between dreams and behavior or cultural forms, it can be easy for them to feel that something interesting happened, but they're not quite sure what. It's helpful for students to see a clearly stated list of what they will be responsible for investigating, and it's only fair to them to assist them in judging the success of the course by stipulating its goals.)

Your most important project for this course is to keep your dream journal faithfully—an absorbing and rewarding exercise, but one that requires a special discipline unlike most "homework." Commit to establishing a routine for your dream journal the first day, whatever constraints or difficulties you encounter. In this course, the experience of the dream journal and dream sharing is given the kind of weight often given in other classes to readings and other external resources, and the assessment and articulation of your own experience the kind of emphasis often given to mastering research skills. Because the dream journal works best when privacy is secure, you will not be required to submit your journal, but to report on its progress and evaluate your experience.

Assignments and Grading

Writing assignments require you to read carefully and think independently. They should be thoroughly revised and proofread before submission. You are always welcome to submit written work by e-mail.

Grades are based on evaluation of written and other work done for the course in response to readings.

Dream journal report (two short reports)—40%

Essay on Freud or Jung—15%

Final essay—25%

Active participation in blog and class discussion—20%

A = Excellent: unified, coherent, well-reasoned, articulate, developed, and original work

B = Very good: coherent and well-founded presentation, demonstrating critical thought

C = Competent fulfillment of assignments

D = Failure to address issues or argue coherently

F = Failure to complete work for course

Essays and oral presentations are evaluated on the basis of four criteria:

- Observation and Accuracy (Analytic skill)

- Clarity and Precision (Language and style)

- Coherence and Development (Thesis and organization)

- Originality and Integrity (Intellectual distinction)

(The syllabus for this course also contains information and links to an online presence where students can find readings and assignments, submit work, and contribute to a blog, as well as some specifics on expectations and avoiding plagiarism, all of which I have omitted here. What remains is intended to emphasize that, when students' workload is divided among maintaining the journal and undertaking research essays, creative and analytic response, intuitive and critical faculties, it seems especially important to be quite clear about what is being evaluated, and by what criteria. This can alleviate a lot of students' underlying concerns about succeeding in the course and focus them on making the most of the dream journal as well as readings and other resources.)

Course Schedule—Fall 2008

Session 1
Introduction: The dream journal and the dream discussion group
Film: Warner Bros, *The Big Snooze*
(This course begins with careful explanation and discussion of keeping a dream journal, and an exemplary session on dream sharing—so that the relation between investigating one's own dreams, responding to the dreams of others, and studying the history of ideas about dreaming is a subject of discussion from the outset. In particular, the course focuses on the journey from private experience to shared expression, as discussed in Chapter 6.)

Session 2
Finding meaning: Are dreams private, subjective, and delusional experiences?
Read: Coleridge, The Pains of Sleep; Pu Songling, A Scholar of Feng-Yang
Film: Excerpts from Sherlock, Jr.
(This session uses fictional portrayals of dreams in literature and film to encourage students to discover their resources for dream analysis and interpretation by application to dreams that are not as charged for them as their own or those of their peers. It also focuses them on close attention to the identifiable characteristics of the dream experience as they know it, and as they see it represented and described in culture.)

Session 3
Finding meaning: Symbolism and unconscious thought; Dream art
Winsor McCay: An American Artist in Slumberland
Read: Winsor McCay, from Dreams of the Rarebit Fiend
*Report on progress of dream journal and write on a dream

(In this course, the dream journal is kept private and students are asked to report and reflect on their success and their reactions—in other words, to evaluate the ongoing experience of the dream journal, preparatory to assessing the value of recalling and investigating dreams. For this purpose, the assignment must pose very specific questions and evaluate for students' fulfillment of the goal of understanding dreams and dreaming more richly. Thus the student who has poor dream recall even when attempting to follow suggestions offered in the course must focus attention on older dreams, or literary dreams, or anything that will, frankly, avoid the possibility of using failure to recall dreams to excuse a failure to engage with the topic. Therefore the assignment requires answering questions such as these:

1. Describe and evaluate your method for recalling and recording dreams. (Are you satisfied that you have found a routine you can maintain? Do you recall enough dreams to allow you to observe your own dream life in some detail? If you don't recall dreams, how have you tried to catch them, and what could you change in order to do so? Do you imagine there's a particular reason you don't recall dreams?)

2. Describe and evaluate your practice in commenting on dreams. (Have you established a routine for reviewing your dream journal and commenting on your dreams? Do you analyze the dream into elements and consider them separately? Have you tried Gayle Delaney's suggestions? Do you identify and consider day residue, puns, metaphors, symbols?)

3. Do you note any prominent or recurring images, themes, or concerns in your dreams now?

4. Have you found a relation between your dreams and waking concerns that makes keeping the dream journal interesting or worthwhile?

5. Has keeping track of your dreams reminded you of any childhood memories or led you to think about your childhood?)

Session 4
Brain and mind: The objective phenomenon of REM and the subjective phenomenon of dreaming
Read: Jones, Dream Reflection
(The primary topics of this session are introduction to the roles of scientific method and empirical research in investigating REM sleep and the other physiological and neurological issues in dreaming; and establishing the range of validity in inferring basic assumptions about dreaming on physical evidence. These are considered in contrast to the methods for studying the subjective phenomenon of the dream as experienced by the dreamer.)

Session 5
A sociology of dreaming: Dreaming in the ancient world and Western tradition
Read: Artemidorus, from The Interpretation of Dreams; C. A. Meier, The Dream in Ancient Greece;
Aristotle on Dreams; Aristotle on Prophesying by Dreams

Session 6
A sociology of dreaming: Cultural functions and values
Read: Stewart, *Dream Theory in Malaya*; Hallowell, *The Role of Dreams in Ojibwa Culture*; Pelus, "That Which I Dream Is True": Dream Narratives in an Amazonian Community
(Two sessions are devoted to discussing the questions raised for anthropology and sociology by dreaming. Lecture material offers many more examples. The emphasis is on considering how the methods of anthropology focus our attention on issues in the relations of dreams to culture. For example, whether the cultural value accorded to dreams demonstrates the place of subjective experience in a culture's value system, or the view of the supernatural world, mortality, or sexual relations; whether the response to dreams indicates patterns of social authority; and how dreams may resolve cultural insecurities or crises.)

Session 7
Film: Werner Herzog, *Where the Green Ants Dream* (1984)
*Report on progress of dream journal and write on a dream

Session 8
Freud's Theory: Wish Fulfillment, Manifest and Latent Content
Read: Freud, *The Interpretation of Dreams*, Chapters 2–4 (128–195)
Film excerpts: *Freud-Analysis of a Mind*; *Secrets of a Soul* (G. W. Pabst, 1926); *Spellbound* (Alfred Hitchcock, 1945)

Session 9
Freud's Theory: The Dream-Work
Read: Freud, Chapter 5, sections A, B, D (196–253, 274–305); Chapter 6, sections A–E (311–439)
(Historically, this course began with my belief that undergraduate students should have some extended encounter with Freud and the impact of psychoanalysis on modern culture; and that that encounter should require close, critical acquaintance with Freud's most famous text. Although Freud's theory may no longer be central to psychology's understanding of dreaming, it remains highly significant in comprehending the history of modern ideas about dreaming, especially as they indicate popular and academic views of the unconscious and irrational, of sexuality, of symbolism, of personal development and the integrity of the self, and of the arts. As a literary text, The Interpretation of Dreams provides extraordinary opportunities to consider how dream accounts and dream analyses may be used for rhetorical purposes, ranging from support for fundamental assumptions about life and culture to a self-justifying autobiographical apologia.)

Session 10
Jung's Theory: The Functions of Dreams

Read: C. G. Jung, Symbols and the Interpretation of Dreams; Mary Ann Mattoon, The Nature of Dreams; The Jungian Approach to Dream Interpretation
Film excerpts: *Matter of Heart*

Session 11
Jung's Theory: Archetypes and the collective unconscious
Read: Jung, Aion: Phenomenology of the Self
Film excerpts: Lord Mountdrago, The Wizard of Oz
(Two sessions on Jung allow us to entertain such topics as individuation and archetypes of the self in sufficient detail to influence students' views of the functions of art and creativity; and to enlarge upon the study of Freud by considering the sociology of schools or movements in modern thought.)

Session 12
New Perspectives on Dreaming
Read: Blechner, The Analysis and Creation of Dream Meaning, Oneiric Darwinism; Revonsuo, The Reinterpretation of Dreams
Film excerpts: Meshes of the Afternoon; Fireworks
*Write on Freud or Jung
(Students are encouraged to explore the relevance of psychological dream theories to other elements of private and cultural life. Blechner suggests that one value of dreaming is in subverting basic assumptions or strategies in life that may be counter-functional—Is it illuminating to compare this to some modern accounts of the value of poetry or art?)

Session 13
Nightmares—Anxiety and Creativity
Read: Patrick McNamara, from *Nightmares*; Byron, *Darkness*
Film excerpts: The 5000 Fingers of Dr. T; Dead of Night; The Discreet Charm of the Bourgeoisie
(The special emphasis on the nightmare in this course responds to students' particular concerns about disturbing dreams, and pursues the thesis that nightmares offer special opportunities to confront profound existential concerns. The use of films that depict "trapped-in-a-dream" scenarios seeks to bring together narrative analysis, philosophical speculation, and psychoanalytic insights as a model for thinking about actual and fictional dreams. This theme is pursued in the final two sessions of the course with an attempt to reach outside accustomed accounts of dreaming and reality by offering examples from Eastern thought, Surrealism, and experimental film.)

Session 14
The Emptiness of Dreaming: Zen, Surrealism, and the Subversion of Daytime Thought

Read: Wai-Yee Li, Dreams of Interpretation in Early Chinese Historical and Philosophical Writings; Walt Whitman, The Sleepers
*Final essay: Dreaming on the Web; Dream and Art research topic; or topic in your dream journal

Session 15
Film: Richard Linklater, *Waking Life* (2001)

Appendix C

Establishing and Organizing Community Dream Groups

(with IASD Ethics Statements for Working with Dreams)

If you want to participate in a dream discussion group in your community, or organize one from scratch, here are some tips:

1. Search for existing groups. The Internet, community bulletin boards, and IASD are places to start.

2. If you find one, investigate whether it suits your needs. Is the group knowledgeable about dreams, to your satisfaction? Are its theoretical orientations and procedures compatible with yours? Does it adhere to ethical principles? Does it meet regularly, and with a frequency suitable to your needs? Do you find its members agreeable to you? Existing groups may differ considerably in orientation and level of sophistication. You may need to attend a meeting or two to get an adequate "feel" for the group.

If you are starting a group from scratch:

1. Recruit members. Do you already know people who will be interested in joining? Friends, neighbors, work colleagues, fellow church members, existing community groups, and relatives are good starting points. Alternatively, you could seek members from the community at large through public notices and word of mouth.

2. Once you have a core group, decide collectively basic matters of structure and procedure: group size, where and how often you want to meet, session length, leadership, assessment of fees as needed (for space rental, refreshments, etc.), rules for joining and retaining one's membership, theoretical orientation, requirements (if any) for ongoing education regarding dreams—including books to read. Be as explicit as possible about these matters without being rigid—ongoing experience may lead the group to change its initial decisions. Some groups will be quite informal and loosely structured, others less so. Either can work well. The nature of the group is less important than the clarity with which the members understand its precepts and agreements.

3. Adopt explicit ethical standards for dream work. The IASD ethics statement is an excellent framework; we reproduce it below along with ethical guidelines for dreamwork teaching education and training.

4. Determine a procedure for dream sharing. We recommend an explicit and somewhat formal procedure from which deviations may be made when appropriate. The problem with informal, conversational procedures is that they tend quickly to become chitchat and the focus on the dream is lost. We also recommend that members write or type their dream ahead of time and make enough copies for everyone, so that all members have the narrative to refer to and make notes on as they hear the dream spoken by the dreamer. However, some groups, especially those outside a course context, may prefer a looser and more informal process, and may find the typing and copying of their dreams too laborious. That's fine; "let a thousand flowers bloom!"

Here, as an example (but not a prescription), is the procedure used in Phil King's psychology class, which is a modified version of Montague Ullman's well-known method. King's version takes around 25 to 45 minutes per dream, depending on the dream's length and complexity. Ullman's method can take twice as long.

The group leader's job is not to be the expert but to move the process along. In established groups, the leader role may alternate from group to group. If the group is relatively new, the leader may be the member with the most experience in working with dreams or knowledge about dreams.

1. Select a volunteer dreamer to share a dream. If there is more than one volunteer, the person goes first who feels the most urgency or for whom it has been the longest since the last sharing.

2. The dreamer passes out copies of the (typed) dream narrative. The dreamer gives the dream story a title if one comes to mind. If not, the dreamer can give the dream a title at the end of the sharing process.

3. The dreamer reads the dream out loud, attempting to reflect in the voice the emotional timbre of the dream. Group members read the dream text while listening to the narration.

4. The dreamer reads the dream out loud a second time. Group members make notes about the possible feelings and meanings in the dream. (Hearing a dream a second time is much like seeing a movie for a second time—you already know the story, and are able to focus more on the details, subtleties, and nuances.)

5. Group members ask clarifying questions better to understand the dream, for example, "In the dream you were at University X. Did you attend it in waking life?" "Is the man in the room someone whom you actually know in waking? (In this stage, *don't* ask the dreamer about the feelings in the dream or about the dreamer's imputed meanings.)

6. Group members respond to the *feelings* of, in, and about the dream *as if it were their dream*. This is the "conscious projection" technique as popularized by Montague Ullman and Jeremy Taylor (e.g., "I felt sad when the . . ."; "the character of the father seemed joyful . . ."; "The overall tone I felt was one of wistfulness and regret . . ."). The dreamer listens but doesn't respond.

7. The dreamer reports which comments rang true and which (however intelligent and thoughtful) missed the mark.

8. Group members respond to possible *meanings* of the dream, *as if it were their dream*. Meanings include meanings of specific images or episodes, and overall thematic meanings of the dream as a whole (e.g., "If it were my dream, the blue rhinoceros would symbolize . . ." "If it were my dream, it would be about the frustration I feel when . . ."). The dreamer listens but doesn't respond.

9. The dreamer reports which comments rang true and which (however intelligent and thoughtful) missed the mark.

10. The dreamer sums up the feelings and meanings of the dream and what he or she learned from the process of sharing and comment. The dreamer may give the dream a title or change the one originally given.

The leader asks the dreamer if he or she feels done, if there is "closure" (noting that new feelings and insights may surface later and can be discussed then). If not, the dreamer is asked to continue talking, and the group responding, until the dreamer fells "done," for the time being.

This method has worked well in a classroom context and may be useful as a template in a community dream-sharing group setting. However, we are not promoting this particular procedure above equally worthy ones. Rather we emphasize the desirability of adopting *some* explicit procedure that fosters the solicitation of possible meanings from the group, dialogue between the dreamer and the group, and respect for the dreamer's ultimate authority over the dream.

A cautionary note here: Community dream-sharing groups are not therapy groups, and people should not use them as therapy. Personal growth, spiritual insight, self-knowledge, yes; clinical intervention, no. Groups should avoid, in Rita Dwyer's expression, opening up a dream they cannot close. If processing a dream engenders troubling feelings, the person should be encouraged to seek professional help for clarification and support. This is a bit tricky as (first) dealing with dreams will arouse feelings, and (second) some community dream groups will include psychology professionals. So the waters may get muddied.

IASD DREAMWORK ETHICS STATEMENT

"IASD celebrates the many benefits of dreamwork, yet recognizes that there are potential risks. IASD supports an approach to dreamwork and dream sharing that respects the dreamer's dignity and integrity, and which recognizes the dreamer as the decision-maker regarding the significance of the dream. Systems of dreamwork that assign authority or knowledge of the dream's meanings to someone other than the dreamer can be misleading, incorrect, and harmful. Ethical dreamwork helps the dreamer work with his/her own dream images, feelings, and associations, and guides the dreamer to more fully experience, appreciate, and understand the dream. Every dream may have multiple meanings, and different techniques may be reasonably employed to touch these multiple layers of significance.

A dreamer's decision to share or discontinue sharing a dream should always be respected and honored. The dreamer should be forewarned that unexpected issues or emotions may arise in the course of the dreamwork. Information and mutual agreement about the degree of privacy and confidentiality are essential ingredients in creating a safe atmosphere for dream sharing.

Dreamwork outside a clinical setting is not a substitute for psychotherapy, or other professional treatment, and should not be used as such.

IASD recognizes and respects that there are many valid and time-honored dreamwork traditions. We invite and welcome the participation of dreamers from all cultures. There are social, cultural, and transpersonal aspects to dream experience. In this statement we do not mean to imply that the only valid approach to dreamwork focuses on the dreamer's personal life. Our purpose is to honor and respect the person of the dreamer as well as the dream itself, regardless of how the relationship between the two may be understood."

(Prepared by the IASD Ethics Committee, Carol Warner, Chair, Association for the Study of Dreams, Spring, 1997)

ETHICAL CRITERIA FOR DREAMWORK TRAINING

"We, the Board of The International Association for the Study of Dreams (IASD), therefore adopt and recommend the following fundamental principles and elements as necessary for any adequate training program for professional work with dreams. We define dreamwork in the following way: any effort to discover, speculate about, and explore levels of meaning and significance beyond the surface of literal appearance of any dream experience recalled from sleep. This would include anyone serving in the role of psychotherapist, counselor, educator, or group facilitator in the interpretation or exploration of dreams for the purposes of providing psychotherapy, personal growth, or spiritual guidance for others. The ETHICAL CRITERIA FOR DREAMWORK TRAINING published herein are suggested basic criteria for those engaged in, or aspiring to undergo approved training in, working with dreams, and IASD assumes no responsibility in connection therewith.

These criteria are designed to apply to practitioners whose practice is exclusively or mainly focused on work with dreams. To the extent that other practitioners include work with dreams as part of their practice, these guidelines should also apply to them.

Formal human service work utilizing dreamwork, as defined above, should conform to all existing regional and national laws regulating the practice of health, mental health, pastoral counseling or spiritual direction. The publication of these criteria is not to be considered as an endorsement by IASD of a particular training paradigm, nor are they to be considered as qualifications or grounds for certification for serving the role of psychotherapist, counselor, educator, or group facilitator in interpretation of dreams for the purposes of providing psychotherapy, growth, or spiritual guidance for others."

    1. Any program training people to work with dreams should have a clearly stated ethical component. We recommend the "Statement

of Ethics for Dreamwork" adopted by the IASD as a foundation for ethical components of dreamwork training.

2. In accordance with this basic Statement of Ethics, any program training people to work with dreams should emphasize that all dreams may have multiple meanings and layers of significance. Programs that offer to train people to work professionally with dreams (i.e., responsibly, for pay) are free to emphasize one particular technique or theory over others, but in order to achieve minimum standards for adequate professional training, these programs must expose their students and trainees to a representative variety of different techniques and theoretical models that include an overview of current approaches in the field, and an historical and cross-cultural perspective of human studies and therapeutic approaches to dreams.

3. Any program training people to work with dreams should include a significant component of an adequately supervised practicum, face-to-face work with dreams, both one-to-one with individuals, and facilitating group experiences. As electronic media become increasingly more a feature of our lives, IASD wishes to encourage dreamwork training programs to extend this supervised practicum component to include telephonic, computer-linked, and other "media" as well, always making sure that these training experiences are carefully supervised by thoroughly skilled practitioners.

4. At the outset, any program training people to work with dreams should have clearly stated written goals, as well as clearly stated written policies regarding the evaluation of student/trainee progress and performance. Professional training programs should provide written evaluations of students' and trainees' progress and performance in a timely fashion. Evaluations of student/trainee work and progress should be applied equally to all students regardless of background. Written descriptions of educational goals and requirements, ethics, and evaluations policies should be made available to students prior to registration for the training program.

5. Any program training people to work with dreams should focus serious attention on the universal propensity of people to naively attribute their own less-than-conscious values, feelings, ideas, and judgments to others. Sometimes called "projection," or "transference" and "counter-transference," this universal tendency must be addressed directly and made more conscious in the process of professional work with dreams.

6. Any program training people to work with dreams should require its students to have done substantial work on their own dreams with qualified practitioners, and to commit themselves to ongoing personal dreamwork with qualified practitioners and supervisors.

7. A program should assure that the practitioner has at least some basic knowledge of related fields, such as group dynamics, psychology, psychiatry, medicine. These additional areas of knowledge should be detailed enough to ensure as far as possible that no harm is done to the dreamer or group member through errors of omission or commission by the practitioner. Additionally, any program training people to work with dreams should require its students or established practitioners to be alert to signs of and to obtain assistance for their personal problems at an early stage, in order to prevent significantly impaired performance. When students or established practitioners become aware of personal problems that may interfere with their performing work-related duties adequately, they should take appropriate measures, such as obtaining professional consultation or assistance, and determine whether they should limit, suspend, or terminate their work-related duties.

8. When dreamwork is done to help persons with any psychological problems, the practitioner should have an appropriate professional degree and license in addition to the dreamwork training.

9. Any program training people to work with dreams should offer and require a minimum familiarity with the history of dreamwork, not just as a preoccupation of Western culture, but as a worldwide phenomenon. Once again, professional dreamwork training and education programs are free to emphasize one element of this diverse history over others, (e.g., the Western medical/psychiatric tradition of dream exploration), but they must also present the student/trainee with a sufficiently diverse historical overview that includes exposure to at least some of the aboriginal and non-European traditions that view dreaming as means of communion with realms of spirit. It is recognized that the meaning and use of dreams may differ across and within cultures. When there are ethnic and/or cultural differences between the dreamer and the counselor, psychotherapist, dreamwork teacher, or spiritual guide these should be attended to and respected. Discussion of, sensitivity to, and respect for cultural differences both within and among cultures should not only be observed but considered an opportunity for greater communication and understanding.

10. Although dreamwork training for specialists (such as medical practitioners, therapists, social workers, etc.) will require further training beyond these basic areas, even specialized education and training in working with dreams should conform to the fundamental principles outlined here. Those who are licensed or regulated by regional or national requirements must follow those requirements for training and practice in specialty areas in addition to the guidelines described herein.

11. Those trained in dreamwork must demonstrate continued formal and informal study in their areas of expertise to refresh old skills and keep abreast with important developments in the field. It is recommended that a minimum of 15 hours per year be devoted to enhancing or reviewing areas of skills. Formal course work at accredited institutions, workshops with highly qualified practitioners, or continuing education offered by the IASD are ways to meet this requirement.

12. Professional practitioners of any skill have an ethical obligation to pass on to succeeding generations the substance of their specialized knowledge in a coherent and accessible fashion. This is as true for those who work with dreams as it is for any other professional group."

(Adopted by the 2001 IASD Board of Directors)

Appendix D

Outline for Short Presentations on Dream

One important type of dream education is the short talk given to a group whose purpose and reason for existing have nothing per se to do with dreams. Such exposure can introduce the subject, and can stimulate the latent interest that most people have in their own dreams. These presentations may range from 15 minutes to an hour or more. Talks to civic groups, such as Junior Chamber of Commerce breakfast meetings, or to workplace groups, likely will be shorter. Talks such as guest lectures to college classes will tend to be longer.

We provide here some suggestions and a topics outline for one-time-only presentations. In the limited time available, the speaker will want to focus on key points while keeping the group's interest. There won't be time to delve deeply into complex issues and controversies in the field. Nor generally should one discuss the dreams of audience members, as follow up is not possible. A light and engaging approach is advisable.

One effective way to introduce the subject is to liken dreams to movies that take place in our minds at night. The total time we spend dreaming storylike dreams in a typical night's sleep may be about the same as the length of a feature movie—90 minutes to 2 hours. These internal movies are broken up into segments of movie and segments of intermission. This is a way to introduce sleeping cycles and ground dreams in underlying sleeping processes. You might mention the imprecision of matching dreaming events to underlying sleeping and dreaming processes, although this is a complex topic for a short presentation. The dream–movie analogy is not exact, as *some* form of mental activity goes on throughout all sleep stages.

The movie analogy is nonetheless useful: The movie theater has the dreamer's name on it; admission is free; the dreamer is the screenplay writer, director, and props manager and usually has a primary role, if not always the lead one, in the dream "movie." The vividness and emotion-inducing qualities of movies parallel the immersion and emotion in dreams. One is swept up in a dream; it seems real, just as one can be swept up in a gripping movie.

There is a different movie playing most every night (although sometimes a movie is repeated if it is of special importance or if the audience didn't "get it" the first time around). Yet, many people do not even know that their personal movie theater exists because they don't remember their dreams. Here the speaker can segue into the question of dream recall, and provide suggestions for improving it.

It is good to leave time for questions. There may be more questions from a class of students than from a breakfast group of Jaycees. But in our experience, all sorts of groups are eager to share dream experiences—and to ask whether their dream lives are "normal," or perhaps extraordinary, in the view of an expert. Older audiences may wish to share dreams of absent loved ones; business groups may be most concerned about unlocking creative potential. Gauge your audience and be prepared to adapt to their needs.

We list 11 topics here. Right away, it is evident that these are too many for a short talk—a 20-minute presentation would allow less than 2 minutes per topic. One could perhaps cover all 11, briefly, in 60- to 90-minute college class. Better not to cram too much in. For shorter talks to general audiences, you may want to eliminate or truncate larger topics, or stay within your own special area of interest. Use these topics as a starting point for formulating your own talk, customized it for your interests and strengths, your audience, and the time available.

1. Introduction: Use the movie theater analogy or some other device to engage the audience, such as relating an intriguing dream.

2. Sleeping and dreaming processes, including sleep cycles and connections between REM and non-REM sleep and type of dream imagery.

3. Common conceptions and misconceptions—(common questions and answers) for example, how long do dreams last; do we dream in color, and so on.

4. Dream recall: average recall frequency, reasons for not remembering, how to improve recall. Some groups may be interested in a training session on how to recover dreams and keep a dream journal.

5. How people have viewed and used dreams in various cultures and times: spiritual and religious contexts of dreaming; common themes in beliefs about dreams and in practices of dream sharing and interpretation.

6. Theories of the sources and functions of dreams, and how one can interpret dreams. Some audiences will inevitably associate dream theory with Freudianism, so offering a more contemporary perspective on psychoanalytic dream theory and other theories can be very helpful.

7. Empirical research on dream content.

8. Dreams in art, literature, and film: the relation of dreaming to imagination, creativity, and theories of art; the artist's role in opening private dream experience to public expression. Sharing short passages or images is a great way to focus audience response to the topic of dreams.

9. Applications of dreams in clinical work and personal growth, including dream groups.

10. Paranormal and lucid dreams.

11. Spiritual dreams

We make special mention here of talks to churches, synagogues and other religious assemblies, and spiritual practice groups. These audiences can be among the most interested in dreams, and the best educated. Here are a few tips: It is important to tell this audience that you are not delivering a sermon, especially if you are speaking at a time normally used for religious services. Don't come across as a minister—unless of course you are one. Distinguish between religious dreams (that may be spiritual) and nonreligious but spiritual dreams. Examples of religious and spiritual dreams are more interesting to most audiences than histories of dreams in religious texts. For this reason, you may wish to focus on dream illustrations while mentioning historical matters only briefly. Be prepared for all sorts of questions about dreams. As an example, a talk on spiritual aspects of dreams by Phil King at a Universalist Unitarian Sunday meeting elicited more questions and comments about brain functioning in dreaming than about the talk topic.

The classes and community groups to whom we have spoken have been interested, responsive, and grateful that we have come to speak with them, almost without exception. We hope that you have equally rewarding experiences.

Appendix E

Using the DreamBank

The DreamBank is a large collection of dream reports and an Internet-accessible search engine (www.dreambank.net). Adam Schneider developed the DreamBank in 1999, under the direction of G. William Domhoff at the University of California at Santa Cruz. The genesis of the DreamBank is in Domhoff's work as a colleague of and successor to Calvin Hall and Robert Van de Castle, pioneer researchers in dream content analysis. The University is the repository, under Domhoff's care, of Hall's collection of dream reports buttressed by many other collections over the years. At any given time, many thousands of dreams from various sources are available on the DreamBank.

Domhoff extended and applied Hall and Van de Castle's content analysis system. His excellent book *Finding Meaning in Dreams—A Quantitative Approach* (1996) is a resource for dream educators interested in teaching content analysis or using the DreamBank for student projects. Clear instructions for DreamBank use are on the Web site. Domhoff's later book, *The Scientific Study of Dreams* (2003) also contains chapters on using the DreamBank and on the Hall–Van de Castle coding system.

The DreamBank amounts to a sociological and historical chronicle of people's dreams in different cultures, places and eras, and is an invaluable resource for dream education and research. As an example, one series of dreams in the DreamBank was that of an English girl, then a woman, ranging from the 1920s to the 1950s, encompassing World War II and the Blitz of London. What a window this is into the consciousness of this dreamer and the temper of the times.

The DreamBank includes sets of dreams gathered from multiple dreamers, and series of dreams recorded by individuals, some series numbering thousands of dreams over decades. Included are 16,000 dreams in English and another

6,000 in German. The DreamBank lends itself to any kind of analysis, quantitative or qualitative, using any organizing principles that the teacher or student wishes to pursue.

For example, a student may wish to investigate dreams about water, looking for regularities or themes that such dreams have in common. One can easily identify and extract "water dreams" by the use of key word searches—*water, lake, ocean, pool,* and the like. The DreamBank produces all dream reports containing the key word(s) in the particular collection(s) of dreams designated. The user can have key words highlighted in the dream narratives appearing on the screen, which he or she can then print for further scrutiny, study, and content coding.

On the other hand, a student may want to investigate how dream contents—for example emotions—change over time for an individual dreamer. The DreamBank will produce representative samples of a person's dreams for comparison—say, 10 (or 20, or any number—you choose) per year over many years.

A great thing about the DreamBank is that one can use it for quite basic analyses or for very sophisticated research. It simply produces the dream narratives of the kind that the user wishes to study. Therefore, it is potentially useful for students from intermediate school up to and including graduate-level researchers. Purely qualitative descriptions of themes noticed in multiple dreams can be instructive and interesting. For example, dreams including flowing water may have particular themes or emotional tones, such as friendliness among the dream characters.

For students doing quantitative analyses (e.g., in an undergraduate or graduate psychology course) the DreamBank provides an automatic way to compare two groups (e.g., men and women) on specific dream content elements (e.g., measures of friendliness and aggression). This requires use of the somewhat complex Hall–Van de Castle coding system. Moreover, the analysis is limited to comparisons between two groups.

One of us (King) has found this built-in statistical tool not as useful or versatile as standard statistical software such as SPSS, which permits simple coding of presence (1) or absence (0) of an element, and a large array of statistics including measures of association between and among variables as well as group differences. Even students who have not taken statistics can learn to use SPSS and learn enough statistics in the process to produce meaningful findings that they comprehend. We have included a procedural note for use of statistical software with data from the DreamBank at the end of this appendix.

The DreamBank is a valuable resource for dreams education in that it extends approaches to dreams from analyses of meanings of individual dreams to seeing patterns—commonalities, relationships, associations, and themes—among many dreams, for different dreamers and for individual dreamers over time. This involves a fundamental expansion pedagogically and disciplinarily, from "individual dream as narrative" to "aggregated dream content as data," and from interpretive skills in the humanities and applied clinical fields to data analytical skills in psychology and the social sciences. We believe that aggregate analyses of dream content are valuable educationally. They complement intriguing involvement in the meanings of the individual dream with a more detached perspective of the relations of dream-to-dream contents to dreamers' traits, experiences, and the social milieus in which dreamers are imbedded. Students at all levels can look to think and function as social scientists as well as empathic listeners to dream stories.

That aggregate analyses of dream themes are valuable does not mean necessarily that the Hall–Van de Castle categorization is the only, or always the best, system to use for the purpose. Domhoff makes a strong case for the measurement reliability of the Hall–Van de Castle categories. However, these categories are entirely decontextualized (i.e., removed from the narrative flow of the dreams that contain them) and instructors may want to consider other systems, including ones of their own or their students' devising, which take the dream story into account.

Student use of the DreamBank expands dream education beyond absorption of existing knowledge and perspectives by students to the generation of new knowledge. We believe student creation of new knowledge is important in education in all fields.

Bulkeley has found the resources of the DreamBank can be applied not only in psychology and anthropology but also in religious studies, insofar as dream content accurately reflects people's religious lives. There's a great deal of "low-hanging fruit" available on the DreamBank: simple, user-friendly research projects that can be adapted to many different educational purposes, including classes in the study of religion. Bulkeley's courses in universities and seminaries regularly feature a psychology-of-religion component in which the latest methods of content analysis are brought to bear on questions of religious meaning and spiritual insight. His most recent classroom assignment using the DreamBank gave the students in his "Psychology of Dreaming" course at JFKU an opportunity to test their interpretations of dreams at many levels—psychological, cultural, and religious. Some of the DreamBank series come from people who have provided extensive personal information about their waking lives. These extra data allow students to test their predictions from the word searches and deepen their understanding of how dreams are always rooted in a personal life context.

The assignment focused on two series gathered as part of a separate research project (originally published as *American Dreamers: What Dreams Tells Us About the Political Psychology of Conservatives, Liberals, and Everyone Else*). In that project several participants kept year-long sleep and dream journals, and they also agreed to a number of personal interviews about their dreams and their waking lives. The participants also were asked several questions about their religious beliefs, practices, and ideals. Many of the journals have been transcribed and

posted on the DreamBank, and in the JFKU class Bulkeley asked his students
to focus on either the "Will" series or the "Paul" series. To begin the process,
students were instructed to read through all the dreams (96 for Will, 17 pages of
written text; 136 for Paul, 13 pages of written text) and mark any reports that
qualify as either a nightmare or a bizarre dream, using the following definitions:

- A nightmare is a dream that is predominantly negative in its
  emotion with strong elements of aggression, misfortune, and/or
  loss.

- A bizarre dream is one in which highly improbable or physically
  impossible things happen, enough that it could not be taken as
  a report of an incident in waking life.

Of course, these are subjective judgments, and the students found some
ambiguous cases. The main goal was to enable the students to develop a general
overview of any instances of intensified, extraordinary dreaming—the kinds of
dream phenomena often associated with religious and spiritual beliefs. Next, the
students used word searches to formulate predictions about the following questions:
Who are the most important people in the dreamer's life? What are the dreamer's
biggest waking life concerns? What are the dreamer's feelings about religion/spiri-
tuality? According to Domhoff's continuity hypothesis, frequency of appearance in
dreams correlates with importance in waking life, so the students were encouraged
to anchor their predictions in this idea. After the students gave presentations to
the class explaining the evidence supporting their predictions, the instructor filled
them in on his knowledge of the biographical details of Will and Paul. Suffice
it to say that this exercise provided the students with a vivid illustration of the
continuities between waking and dreaming. With nothing but their dreams to go
on, the students were able to identify accurately Will's and Paul's most important
relationships, emotional concerns, religious beliefs, and life challenges.

Note on the use of statistical software with the DreamBank:
       Teachers can follow these general steps in helping their students use the
DreamBank to locate dreams of interest and to produce statistical findings:

1. Select samples of dreams from the DreamBank based on the topic
   or question, by using key word searches.

2. Choose the variables to measure, based on (a) *a priori* theoretical
   perspectives, (b) a reading of the dreams—what themes suggest
   themselves—or (c) existing elements in established content analysis
   systems, such as (but not limited to) Hall–Van de Castle.

3. Choose measurement categories: (a) presence versus absence of the element in a dream, (b) number of occurrences of the element, or (c) intensity or strength of the presence.

4. Code the variables into spreadsheets, with rows representing the dreams and columns representing the variables coded. Label the variables and the values coded (e.g. 1 = *present*, 0 = *absent*). It is helpful to have two or more students independently code each dream, as one can assess coding reliability in terms of identifying agreed–disagreed codings. Discrepancies can be discussed and resolved. (There will be less disagreement on presence vs. absence or number of occurrences than for intensity.) In a class context, teachers can assign projects to pairs of students, which facilitates this dual coding.

5. Analyze the data using the software program. First, generate frequency distributions and basic descriptive statistics. (Be sure not to do summary descriptive statistics on nominal or ordinal data—stick with frequency distributions.)

Do hypothesis tests if the level of instruction and skills of students permit. If doing hypothesis tests, specify them *a priori* as much as possible, rather than "cheating" based on a scrutiny of the descriptive results. This will reduce the number of tests done and will minimize interpretive problems stemming from multiple tests. If multiple tests are performed, use "multiplicity" adjustments of α or p, to avoid erroneous conclusions.

Consider teaching requisite statistical skills as part of the course project itself, if students do not already have statistical ability. For example, chi-square is a relatively straightforward statistic that students can use to test relationships between ordinal and/or nominal variables, such as gender versus presence/absence of a particular dream element—say success, or sadness. T tests and one-way analysis of variance can compare two, and more than two, groups of dreamers (respectively) on any number of interval–ratio variables, such as comparing ethnic groups on dream-recall frequency.

Of course, the more sophisticated the students are statistically, the more they can do with their data. We have found that students need not know the underlying logic of sampling distributions to be able to comprehend p values and to understand probability language in articulating their research results. Statistical training within the course can be "ad hoc."

In short, quantitative dream analysis projects can be springboards for students learning and developing statistical capabilities and confidence in an interesting and meaningful applied context. Several of our students who have done their first original statistical research on dream content have gone on to use statistical approaches profitably in subsequent graduate studies and careers.

We believe that steps should be taken to secure the DreamBank financially, providing for its upkeep, maintenance, expansion, and availability for public use. This could be done in conjunction with Domhoff's current oversight and its present physical location at the University of California at Santa Cruz, or at another location if and when appropriate. The bigger and more inclusive the DreamBank's holdings, the more useful it will become to future students and scholars.

Another Internet-based tool for dream research is the sleep and dream database (SDDB) developed by Kelly Bulkeley (http://sleepanddreamdatabase. org). This digital archive and search engine is similar to the DreamBank in enabling word searches and statistical analyses of dream content. The SDDB additionally includes a research-tested template of word search categories, extensive information about multiple demographic variables, and the ability to move quickly among different sets of dreams and levels of analysis.

Appendix F

Preserving Narrative Meanings in Dream Content Analysis

A Class Project

This was a class project in Phil King's undergraduate psychology course on dreams at Hawaii Pacific University. It may interest instructors who want to teach dream-content analysis and use quantitative methods, but who also want not to lose focus on the dream narrative. It was an attempt to bridge the gap, discussed in this book, between dream science (looking for patterns over many dreams), and dream experience (figuring out dream meanings). We encourage you to consider this project as a template for your activities in your own class. Adopt, adapt, and modify it to suit your purposes and needs.

"To personify statistics; to substantiate the dream narrative; to retain the person behind the numbers." These words from a student nicely state the thrust of our project.

Traditional content analysis is productive and interesting. It builds knowledge. Its weakness is that it abandons the dream as a story. We decided to keep (and explore) the story. We designed the project to teach content analysis to students while simultaneously teaching them how to explore the meanings of a dream series, by incorporating into content analysis the creation of a composite dream vignette. The vignette was based both on close readings of the dreams and the results of the content analysis. Students overlaid the vignette onto video footage selected and edited to capture appropriate visual imagery. We combined quantitative content analysis with narrative and presentational forms.

We grounded this project in a set of approaches, broadly termed *coopera-tive inquiry*, which emphasizes potentially transformative participation in the process, and on presentational forms other than conventional academic prose.

Participants consisted of five students and the professor. Dream material was a series of 40 dreams from one participant. All participants were "co-researchers." Although the professor facilitated the activity, we deemphasized the usual pro-fessor versus student and researcher versus subject dichotomy and hierarchy.

The focus was on dream motifs and themes within motifs. A dream motif is a recurring setting and initial situation. Dreams lodged in a common motif—sports—were selected. Motif dreams may represent dreams of particular importance to the dreamer. The recurring motif supplies an ongoing metaphoric context. Using dreams with a common motif was helpful to the dream vignette creation.

It is part of cooperative inquiry that the "subjects" of the study, in this instance the dreamers themselves, be participants in the project. The dreams that we analyzed were the professor's. This was *not* part of the intrinsic research design but rather was the only lengthy dream series of a common motif among the participants. It would have been preferable if the dream series had been from one of the student participants.

Where no project participant can provide a dream series with one motif and sufficient dreams (30 or more), there is an alternative. Each student could contribute dreams on a certain motif or theme. Examples include anxiety dreams, dreams of college, dreams that seemed subjectively important, dreams of family, dreams of nature, relationship dreams, and so on. If each student could muster several dreams, taken together they could make up a sufficient sample. The key point is that the providers of the dreams are participants in the analytical and creative activities.

We constructed a composite dream vignette to faithfully portray and evoke the content themes. We created a short film using existing footage with the vignette narrative recorded over it. This brought about a deeper appreciation of the dream themes.

The project therefore had three somewhat novel orientations and procedures. First was the use of a dream series with a common motif as a content domain. Second was the combination of quantitative content analysis with the creation of a composite dream narrative. And third was a cooperative inquiry process in which the dreamer was involved as a co-researcher, roles and hierarchies were deliberately mixed, and the effects of the experience on the participants was as much the point as was the creation of new knowledge or a product.

Steps in the Process

1. Select the dreamer(s) and the dreams. The point is to get interesting dreams with existential resonance, rather than a representative sample of dreams in general.

In our project, 40 dreams, all with sports themes, were dreamt between March 1998 and April 2005. Baseball themes and imagery appeared in 27 of the dreams, basketball in 7, tennis and golf each in 3, and football and boxing each in 1 dream.

2. Choose the variables. Project members combined variables of general interest with ones specific to the sports dreams themes: (a) Hall–Van de Castle variables, including striving (success and failure), good fortune and misfortune, and the five emotions; (b) variables chosen inductively based on close readings of the dream series; and (c) Eric Erikson's life-span developmental categories most age-appropriate to the dreamer: generativity versus stagnation, and integrity versus despair.

3. Perform content analyses. This involved three students acting as judges independently rating the series of 40 dreams. Discrepancies in ratings were reconciled in face-to face discussion among the judges. Reliabilities of the initial ratings among judges were determined. Students analyzed the consensus ratings quantitatively and compared the results to Hall–Van de Castle norms.

4. Construct a composite dream vignette based on the quantitative analysis findings as well as on multiple readings of the dreams. The dreamer was not involved in the vignette construction, but reviewed it and gave feedback. Participants revised the vignette based on dreamer feedback. They then repeated this process.

5. Select and edit visual footage (video), and revise it based on the dreamer's comments. None of the research group had any experience in film or movie-making, so we resisted the impulse to make a movie of the dream, taking the more modest tack of creating a narrative with visual images, using stock footage. Students then combined the video with the dream narrative as a sound track. There are other possible choices for how to create and present dream vignettes, from live readings and plays, to filming the vignette itself. We encourage teachers to try alternatives modes, while keeping the focus on enactment through presentation. (In fact this project, without the quantitative content analyses, could be adapted for use in humanities or arts courses, or with high school or elementary school students. Such adaptations could add the element of artistic creation—e.g., drawings or paintings of the dreams.)

6. Give feedback regarding their experience in the project. (See later.)

Logical argument, evidence, and "sympathetic resonance" in discussion among the participants all contributed to reliability of assessment, validation of dream themes, and the creation of the dream vignettes.

Teachers who are considering class projects based on this one can choose the extent to which they emphasize the quantitative content analysis. We made it equal in importance to the dream vignette creation and presentation. Here is a summary of the results of our analysis.

Ratings Reliability

We correlated ratings by the three judges by pairs, yielding for each variable three Pearson correlations, which were averaged to produce an overall reliability indicator. The mean of the average correlations over all variables was .909. These correlations were high enough for us to consider the ratings reliable, permitting further analyses. Rating reliabilities were quite similar for the different types of variables. Ratings of variables created inductively based on reading the dreams and those chosen from other psychological theories were just as reliable as on the established Hall–Van de Castle variables.

Hypotheses: Dream Series versus Hall–Van de Castle norms

We expected the sports dreams series content to differ from the Hall–Van de Castle male norms. Because the dreamer recorded his dreams in the first place because of their subjective importance, we predicted that the dreams would be longer, and richer—more saturated in feeling and striving—than the norms. That the dreams represented a sports motif, with winning and losing, led us to predict relatively high levels of both success and failure. We also predicted that this older dreamer would be more self-determining, and therefore have dreams in which he as a dream character is less subject to the whims of fate, than the young college students whose dreams comprised the male norms. Therefore, we predicted *lower* frequencies of both good fortune and misfortune for our dream sample.

The findings were all in the predicted direction. The sports motif dreams were significantly higher on success and failure for the dreamer character, other characters, and overall, and lower on good fortune and misfortune, and higher on all the emotions.

The sports dreams were longer than the normative dreams. We corrected for this by dividing frequency of occurrence of content by the average word length of the dreams. With this modification the sports motif dreams still differed significantly overall from the norms in the predicted directions—higher for success and failure, lower for good fortune and misfortune, and higher for sadness, anger, and happiness. Only for apprehension and confusion were the motif dreams not higher than the norms.

The dreamer related 88 codeable emotions, or 2.2 per dream, compared with 241 in 500 dreams, or 0.48 per dream, for the male norms. Correcting for dream length, the dreams from the dream series had a ratio of 1.8 to 1 emotions per word compared with the norms—an 80% difference. Subjectively important dreams were more densely laden with emotion than run-of-the-mill dreams.

Looking at the *patterning* of emotions, measured in terms of the percentage of all emotions claimed by a specific emotion, we found that sadness, anger, and happiness were almost twice as dominant for our sports dreamer, and apprehension and confusion roughly half as much. Our dreamer's emotions were less clouded by fear and confusion; anger, sadness, and happiness had freer rein.

Regarding Erikson's developmental stages of generativity versus stagnation, and integrity versus despair, the dreams fell decidedly, if modestly, on the positive side. We coded three instances of generativity, none of stagnation, eight of integrity, none of despair.

We then turned to the content variables selected inductively. Their intended use was to assist in the creation of a composite dream vignette representative of the series, and of the dreamer's existential concerns and personality. All variables referred to the dreamer as a character in the dream. Themes of centrality versus marginality, connection, belonging, leading, seeking recognition, confidence, eagerness, and frustration predominated.

Although the dreams were from an older man, two students, women in their early 20s, narrated the vignette in the first person. We could have used the dreamer himself or another venerable male voice. We chose the younger female voices to make the point that there is a universal quality to existential themes in dreams, transcending gender, age, and culture. We discovered through this project that anyone can narrate, in principle and with authority, anyone else's dream.

The student participants responded to questions about how well the process of combining content analysis with the dream narrative creation worked, and to how they were affected by their participation. Here are excerpts that convey the flavor of their comments:

Question: Did the quantitative content analysis and the qualitative dream vignette development inform and connect with each other, or were they essentially two parallel but separate activities?

Answer: There were times in the beginning that the activities felt separate, but in the end the interconnectedness became undeniably apparent. We were constantly using the content analysis variables that the other teammates had been working on to add elements that we realized in hindsight were prominent in the dream series. It was highly effective.

Answer: I believe that the two were connected to each other. Although it is definitely possible to compose a vignette without consulting the data analysis, such a vignette would only have been a summary of all of the dreams that only included what we thought was important. Having the numbers really helped to focus the vignette and point out important aspects of the dreams. Having the numbers available to inform the vignette helped to decrease and maybe even eliminate biases on the part of the researchers who created the vignette.

Answer: Statistical coders and vignette creators successfully blended the fruits of their labors. Statistics generated numerically significant material to include in the vignette, and the vignette gave statistics value beyond numbers. In the end, combining the vignette with statistical information created a powerful punch.

Question: What did you gain personally from this "cooperative inquiry"? Did the whole process affect you, and if so, how?

Answer: As a student I learned much about the universality of dreams, as I definitely could relate to some of the concerns and ideas expressed in the dreams themselves. This helped my teammates and me to even further connect the vignette with the content analysis.

Answer: I found a host of emotions that I could relate to in the dream series. The fact that this dream series happens to be from an older male does not affect my ability as a young female to relate to his experiences. Dreamer feedback was particularly useful. The cooperative approach fostered an atmosphere in which the members of the research team openly shared their feelings. Overall, it was a successful approach.

Answer: This experience has helped me to grow a lot personally and given me an opportunity to track that growth. Seeing the actual numbers and trying to understand why the results turned out the way they did, what they mean to the dreamer, and what they reveal about the dreamer has made me question my own dreams. This project was much different from the other research projects that I have worked on because it was less formal and much more personal.

Appendix G

Interdisciplinary Dream Course Template

What might a comprehensive interdisciplinary higher education course in dreams look like a few years from now? We speculate unconstrained by consideration of limits of resources, class contact hours or other factors in presenting what we intend to be an ideal model and prototype.

It is evident that enacting this template would exceed the practical limits of one standard course, and if developed fully would become a multicourse offering (or single course worth multiples of standard course credits). Our intent is not that this model or similar ones be adopted in toto, but that teachers could pick and choose elements that suit their interests and goals. Our assumption for this exercise is that technological developments would proceed, with innovations and abilities currently conceived mainly in terms of science fiction becoming realities and capacities available to teachers. Skills from many disciplines would be brought into play. Abilities ranging from artistic technique to statistical analysis can be brought up to levels adequate for meaningful course participation, for all students. For example, the students not favored with artistic talent could be taught to enjoy and learn from attempting to create and evaluate dream-based art, and the relatively innumerate student's quantitative skills trained to a level of being able to participate meaningfully in statistical analyses.

Elements

Elements across disciplines—(i.e., for entire course)

- Real or virtual laboratory experience in the measurement of sleep processes and underlying brain activity.

- Electronic re-creation and transmission of dream experience; inter-penetration of modalities from distinctly different disciplines—(e.g., arts and sciences).

- Use of students' dreams: feedback of dream studies into dreams (e.g., dreaming of writing about dreams; dreaming of imagery of being inside a data matrix.

- Re-creating and re-experiencing dream or aspects of it through appropriate narrative, dramatic, and artistic methods.

- A deliberate movement back and forth among experience immersion, reflection, and analysis.

Specific Topics and Activities

- Students (and instructor) dream sharing, toward personal reflection and psychological/spiritual development.

- Dream analyses regarding their social and cultural meanings.

- Immersion in dream series by the creation and enactment of a composite dream encompassing important settings, themes, and characters of the dream series (themes to be ascertained through dream content analysis).

- Quantitative analyses of dream series or sets, with comparisons of results against relevant reference group data. This can be done as a freestanding exercise or in conjunction with dream series immersion and enactment.

- Study of dream literature and the arts in historical and cultural context.

- Using dreams as both template and tool for creative writing projects and artistic creations.

Appendix H

Proposing a Course on Dreaming

Part-time and adjunct faculty—who often take the initiative in introducing dream studies courses—may not be familiar with the process and requirements of course proposal. For example, many schools, colleges, and other educational programs ask not only for a description of content, but for a rationale and a statement of learning objectives. Here are some suggestions for presenting your planned course and yourself to administrators and potential colleagues:

Establish the Need for Such a Course

- Show demand at other institutions, national interest in the topic.

- Write a one-paragraph rationale and description that explains the course concept accessibly, and within the larger field of study to which it contributes.

Prepare Sample Course Materials

- A very basic course outline indicating the major areas of study and learning experiences.

- A bibliography that can be handed directly to the institutional library to acquire texts quickly.

- Sample assignments and student projects, indicating how you'll expect students to work on the course, and even more importantly, how you'll communicate that to them.

- Other learning resources such as a guide to Web sites.

- If your course includes dream groups, include some written explanation of how they operate, to allay the fears of educators who are not familiar with them.

Show How Objectives Will be Met, and How "Learning Outcomes" Will be Evaluated

- Explain how in-class activities (such as dream groups, lectures, group projects) achieve identifiable learning goals and enhance students' educational experience. Don't assume administrators prefer quantifiable measures like testing. Use the approaches you think really work—for example, self-assessment, portfolio review, Web site or blog construction, peer-to-peer teaching or presentations. (See Appendix I for more on learning assessment and evaluation.)

Identify Yourself as a Teacher and Expert, Citing Experiences that Show Your Strengths and Exemplify Your Teaching Style and Philosophy

- Cite your publications and presentations of any relevant kind, not just academic teaching experience.

- If you can, emphasize active and hands-on learning and use of new educational technologies.

- Submit a CD with PowerPoint, or direct reviewers to a website that you maintain.

Research Your Target Schools. Find a School or Program That's a Good Fit for You

- What's their curricular philosophy?

- What's the student population like?

- Do they want to expand? Can you adapt to online learning, satellite programs, or an extension course overseas?

Get in the Door

- If you can discuss how to tailor your proposal to this school's needs, you may think of some entirely new approach. And the administrator will see you as a collaborator.

Appendix I

Assessment of Educational Effectiveness in Dream Studies

Dreams are such a fascinating, even dazzling, subject that there is a temptation to believe that teaching about them is self-justifying, and that the subjective sense of value gained is all one need to know about the effectiveness of the educational process. This was the impression we garnered from responses of dream educators to a question in a survey we conducted at the start of the project that led to this book. We asked: "How do you verify that your teaching is both accurate and valuable?" Answers focused on student satisfaction. Overall there was little evidence of systematic evaluation of the learning process and results.

Although student satisfaction is a good place to start—*dis*satisfaction would be an indicator of something amiss—it is far from sufficient. In this essay we offer some suggestions about ways in which dream educators at many levels and in many disciplines might consider evaluating the effects of what they do. All teachers are aware that much of what happens in learning—and much of the best—is unpredictable, unquantifiable, even intangible. But students expect and deserve to hear from the instructor where they are headed, and how they'll know when they've gotten there, even in a field as traditionally open-ended as the study of dreaming. Clearly stated learning objectives, although very far from covering all the growth we hope will happen in a course, give students confidence that their performance is being evaluated (and graded) fairly, and help instructors rethink and reinvent their courses and approaches over time. Like other educators, dream teachers value knowing that their instruction is effective, that this informs decisions about what and how to teach, and that outcomes are meaningfully assessed.

The easiest aspect of evaluation to do well is to assess cognitive learning in formal academic courses. A simple pretest at the first session, soliciting a few identifications of key concepts and figures, can gauge students' state of knowledge, stimulate interest, and provide focus in early sessions. Repeated at the end of the semester, it can provide vital documentation of the course's success in communicating vital information. Periodic examinations for the purposes of grading, learning reinforcement, and student motivation are tried and true methods of appraising students' mastery of course material. Instructors differ on their preferred kinds of exam questions. Essays (short and long) and explanations of terms have the simple advantage over multiple choice and "fill-in-the blank" questions that the more the student articulates his or her thoughts, the better.

Particularly useful in our experience are essays that pose a research question to students, asking them how they would go about designing and carrying through a study that would address the problem. An approach to dealing specifically with dream interpretation is to give students a dream narrative (real or invented), with some background information on the (purported) dreamer, asking them to interpret the dream from one or more theoretical perspectives. This example may show the complexities of evaluation of student learning about dreams, as well as the opportunities for developing a creative, individual approach. Some instructors would restrict their assessment to students' demonstrated mastery of competing theories of interpretation. Others might (conversely) argue for evaluating students' development of intuitive and sensitive attention to the details of a dream—which has to be accounted at least as much importance as demonstrating mastery of the details of theories. The choice depends on (and expresses) the instructor's personal philosophy of dream education.

Another evaluation tack of value, applicable in all disciplines, is to ask students to write essays on the impact of the dream course, or particular aspects of it, on their views of themselves, other people, and society. Instructors should be careful to couch such assignments in ways that provoke students' serious thinking and sincere opinions rather than eliciting "please-the-teacher" responses. Students must feel free to argue cogently against the instructors' expectations, including questioning basic assumptions about the value of sharing dreams. This approach effectively combines instructors' assessment of actual learning with students' self-assessment. (Welt requires an expository essay on the experience of recovering dreams, keeping the dream journal, participating in a dream group, and studying theories of dreaming, and often hears decades later from students who say it formed a model for their integration of academic learning into personal life and values.)

In fact, the unusual, if not unique, features of dream education that inspire so many instructors' and students' enthusiasm about their dream courses indicate how instructors in dreams courses can align themselves with the best contemporary practice in assessing student learning, rather than falling back on old models. Keeping a dream journal encourages self-observation and introspection, so it only makes sense to emphasize the value of self-assessment as a means of enhancing as well as documenting learning. A course journal kept along with a dream journal, including informal responses to readings and discussions, raising questions and testing theses, demonstrates learning (as well as effort) just as well as any quantified examination, if the instructor has the time and dedication to consider it in detail. Required blog entries perform the same function; for the purpose of grading, instructors may require a certain number per unit or semester without judging them in any other way.

As the dream journal encourages introspection, the dream discussion group enhances the quality of students' focus on their peers' contributions to the class. The practice of a higher level of sustained, sympathetic attention to others than is usual in classrooms may naturally evoke thoughtful and responsive criticism, in the best sense of the term. Students may be asked, for example, to write brief evaluations after in-class presentations of reports, projects, or papers. These not only provide a valuable assessment record, but also may lead you to think productively about why students' assessments might be different from your own.

Perhaps the most dramatic effect of keeping track of dreams for the first time is a new and profound awareness of the limitless creativity of one's own mind. Students who have never written poetry or stories before suddenly find themselves inspired to propose creative projects based on their dreams. The instructor's respect for this inspiration should not be overwhelmed by concerns about how to evaluate creative work fairly and effectively. If students are allowed—or encouraged—to submit paintings, poems, digital videos, or other artworks for course credit, it is important to clarify in advance the criteria and limits of evaluation, but also to welcome the idea that creative work can be as serious an indicator of real learning as any examination or research paper. Colleagues in departments of creative writing and the arts can be helpful in developing your own strategy for assessment of creative work. The portfolio approach to assessment of student learning—asking students to submit their own selection of their best work in response to a variety of assignments at the end of the semester—can embrace creative work effectively and help provide real perspective on the diversity of kinds of learning that may take place in one course. Like most of the other methods we have discussed here so far, it seems equally applicable to K–12 classes, particularly if the instructor intends to foster independent thought and mutual respect among students. Some methods appropriate to specialized and advanced training programs may not be suitable for secondary or undergraduate students.

In clinical fields such as psychiatry, clinical psychology, pastoral counseling, and psychosocial nursing, observing students work with patients or clients discussing their dreams would be most appropriate. A variant of this would be to have actors or fellow students simulate actual patients or clients. Replication of real-world situations not only tests a wide variety of skills and talents, but also sharpens them, and like many educators, we feel that evaluation contributes most when it is an opportunity in itself for synthesizing learning.

The evaluation imperative is still strong for brief courses and weekend workshops that generate continuing education credits for professional certification and licensure in clinical fields. Here the instructor who really cares about dream education must sometimes confront the widespread tendency to conduct pro forma evaluations, in which programs under various institutional pressures create the appearance of quantitative assessment without the substance. Rating questions such as "This course contributed to my mastery of the field" on a five-point scale is a standard form of specious evaluation, which invites the host program to pass off a survey of opinion as the documentation of acquisition of skill. In such instances no evaluation would be better than a pseudo-evaluation that can obscure the fact that meaningful assessment was not done. In a field as unfamiliar to outsiders as dream studies almost always is, instructors are well advised to create their own assessment documents, at least as an adjunct to the ones required by their sponsoring program.

Assessment of learning about dreams becomes more difficult, and in certain contexts less relevant, as one moves out from college courses into other venues and with other groups. Teachers in freestanding institutes and community dream certificate programs face much the same task as those in universities, which is to demonstrate that the students have learned content, points of view, and skills commensurate with program goals and instructor intentions. This may take on an extra dimension of importance to the extent that such institutions and programs wish to ascertain for themselves their effectiveness, and to demonstrate to others the academic merit of their dream teaching for transferable course credit, certification, or APA or other professional imprimatur.

Evaluation of the effectiveness of dream education is important. Equally important is that it be done in approaches that are not heavy-handed and which do not interfere with the creative freedom and intuitive grace which infuse excellent teaching about dreams. Evaluation activities should not be intrusive; nor should they drive what is taught. As dream teachers we must not "teach to the evaluation," but we should evaluate in careful ways.

We cannot claim that there exists a body of material substantiating some of the claims we make informally in this book, based on our own experiences and those of the many colleagues we have surveyed. However, as the field of dream education continues to grow, instructors will no doubt become increasingly cognizant of the value of demonstrating the benefits of dream courses—and their characteristic methods such as the dream journal and dream group—not only through testimony and argument, but through widespread documentation of results. We believe, for example, in the long-term impacts of "dream appreciation," in Montague Ullman's phrase, such as increased openness to considering the unconscious factors in one's own and others' behavior, which can positively affect learners' professional and personal lives. If we wish to prove the case, however, we must provide some serious long-term studies based on instruments of assessment widely accepted by consensus among dream educators. Such evaluations would require prospective longitudinal studies (monies for which are essentially not available, as heart disease and human physical growth are among the few areas—if not the only ones—that have enjoyed significant funding for multidecade longitudinal research). Retrospective studies are possible, but they are similarly costly and methodologically problematic. So although much of the value of working with dreams may reside in long-term effects in an interaction with other developmental processes, the prospects for this being a focus of assessment depend on dream educators like ourselves, and you, our readers, to become as creative and innovative in testing the veracity of our intuitions and conclusions as we are in our teaching.

Appendix J

Why I Teach Dreams
in Freshman Composition

Barbara Bishop

Four years ago, I began teaching college writing courses using dreams as the primary subject. I began with some trepidation: What would the administration say when students reported back that the entire class was about dreams? Would freshmen, 18 and 19 years of age, be remotely interested in studying dreams? Could I introduce enough grammar and rhetorical skills alongside the material on dreams so that students would have sufficient exposure to both topics? Would students with still-developing egos be willing to interpret each others' dreams with openness and sensitivity? Could a college classroom be turned into a safe space for such an endeavor? In the 4 years I have been engaging in this wild experiment, the course has evolved and my confidence about it as a worthwhile endeavor has increased. I am now prepared to describe what I have learned and encourage others to bring dreams into the undergraduate classroom in meaningful ways. I believe that teaching students to pay attention to their dreams holds numerous benefits: They have the opportunity to develop more than just their intellectual capacities, as universities have done traditionally; dream study holds the promise of developing their emotional, spiritual, and social selves as well. Paying attention to their dreams can help students become independent and self-aware as they make important life decisions. Finally, group dreamwork brings students together in a playful, fun way at a time when they are feeling most alone, frightened, and vulnerable.

First, some background about my experience as a writing teacher: I began teaching freshmen writing classes as a graduate student at UCLA 20-plus years ago. As beginning teachers, we were encouraged to experiment with different textbooks and approaches. There was the "Dead White Guys" approach, using a text with essays by Plato, Aristotle, St. Thomas Acquinas, Augustine, Dante, and others. The underlying assumption of the text was that by introducing students to great philosophers and theorists, the students themselves would begin to think in profound, interesting ways. The essays proved difficult for 18-year-olds. I spent much of my time "translating" the ideas into language they could understand. Other texts focused on race relations in America, gender issues, and education. I experimented with numerous possibilities, but remained dissatisfied with every approach. Essays on gender, for example, caused students to ask why a writing class had to be about "women's lib." A focus on race relations caused similar resentment. I believed, and continue to believe, that an effective writing class must include a clear subject or subjects for students to write about. At one juncture I decided that my writing classes would focus on literary texts exclusively rather than essays across the curriculum. Nothing satisfied and when I left teaching to get a graduate degree in counseling psychology, I thought that I would never return.

My hiatus from teaching taught me many things, once of which was how much satisfaction I got from teaching. I missed it. I had become interested in dreams while writing my dissertation several years before, and I thought that I would focus on dream work in therapy. But during the years I worked as a therapist, I recognized that I wanted to *teach* dreams, not just facilitate dreamwork with clients. My dream group during these years introduced me to the "If it were my dream" methodology of Jeremy Taylor and Montague Ullman and I began to think about designing a course that would include the subject of dreams as well as the methodology of working with dreams in groups.

I was hired as an adjunct professor 3 days before the fall semester was to begin at a small, private Catholic school. The English Department was desperate to find an instructor at the last minute. Their desperation gave me the courage to order texts outside of anything I had tried before. That first semester, along with a traditional writing text and a novel, I added *Where People Fly and Water Runs Uphill* by Jeremy Taylor; in subsequent semesters I adopted as a writing text *Dreams and Inward Journeys* by Marjorie and John Ford and added *An Introduction to the Psychology of Dreaming* by Kelly Bulkeley. I have experimented with various novels that include dreams in them: *Wuthering Heights, Till We have Faces* by C.S. Lewis and *The Kin of Ata are Waiting for You.* One key to keeping the course interesting is that I have introduced new essays, new ideas about dreams and techniques for dreamwork as I have learned them. However, some core elements of the initial course remain.

I teach students how to recall their dreams at the beginning of the course. The first day, I tell students that my writing course will focus on dreams and one of the requirements for the course is to keep a dream journal; I invite students who find such a topic threatening to withdraw and find another course. Some do. One semester, a student came up to me after the first class and explained that she had suffered from schizophrenia for much of her adolescence and she had to withdraw from the class. I accepted her assessment and signed the withdrawal form. She took a literature course from me a year later and I concluded again that for her, exploring the world of the unconscious vicariously through literature was probably a safer alternative than the more direct, "royal road" of dreams, at least outside of a therapist's office.

This brings up the topic of safety. I needed to make certain that my classroom remained a safe space for the study of dreams. Because they emerge from the unconscious, dreams almost always reveal more than the dreamer intends. Given that adolescence can be a time of great vulnerability, I wondered if it would even be possible to create a safe enough space to study students' dreams in a college classroom. Another consideration concerned my grading and assessment of student writing and its impact on dream analysis in the classroom. I happened on a few rules: Students never have to write about their own dreams in their essays outside of class. When I check to see that they are keeping journals, I flip through the pages quickly to see that they have the number of entries required, but I do not read their private journals, no matter how tempting a dream title is. A student can always write about his or her own dream in the third person, without revealing that the dreams belong to him or her. I never discuss dreams from papers in class unless I have a student's permission. I may consider a dream innocuous that is sensitive to the writer. I give students a variety of paper topics to choose from; some offer them a chance to meet with others to discuss dreams before writing a paper on their own dreams; others allow them to write about a family member's dream or a friend's. In this way, they choose how much to reveal about themselves. I have found that most students eventually want to explore their own dreams and write about them, although many have gained important insights about family members from writing about their dreams.

Another way that I attempt to create a safe classroom is to bridge the gap between the two subjects of dreams and writing strategies although I cannot say that I have been completely successful. Assessing student writing is a tricky business. It can impose an external, even foreign representation upon a paper in such a way that the paper is wrenched away from the original writer. Clearly, this is not the goal. I often use the "If this were my dream" approach in my assessment of the student's writing. A graded paper to students seems like merely pointing out to them all of the things they have done wrong. But when I begin my assessment of a paper (in my mind) with "If this were my paper," I find that I'm less critical and more attuned to what works in the paper instead of only what does not work. Could this be because I'm considering it as if *I* might have written it, and I'm less harsh about my own writing than someone else's? I still point out gaps in communication between writer and reader. But I find myself writing, "What examples might support this concept?" instead of pointing the finger in an accusatory way: "You need more examples to support this idea." This approach is not always possible when explaining grammatical errors or sentence structure problems. But I believe that the notion of projection behind the respectful, "If it were my dream" approach can be applied to other arenas besides dreams. I cannot say truthfully that assessment of student writing is ever completely fair or stress free, for student *and* professor. Still, I think the study of dreams has softened my critical edge.

Students are required to write six out-of-class essays. Each day that a paper is due, we explore dreams from volunteers using the "If it were my dream" method. When students forget to preface their remarks with that phrase, I remind them. I model it as well as explaining the problems with "you" directed remarks. I point out to them the multiple meanings that emerge from this type of dream exploration. In attempts to keep the discussions safe for the dreamer, I check in with him or her regularly. If the dreamer wants to stop at any point, we move on to another dream. Or, if the dreamer wants to continue exploring a dream that I believe may potentially embarrass him or her, I steer the discussion to areas in the dream which would be safe to explore. If I notice that students are becoming silly about someone's dream, I remind them of our agreement, which I cover the first day, that they always treat other people's dreams in a respectful, courteous manner. They can be curious; they can find puns and word plays; they can notice odd phrases and strange behaviors; they can cuss and use slang if such language addresses potential meanings of a dream. But they cannot belittle someone's dream or the person who dreamed it.

Students develop friendships and support by discussing dreams together. A recent graduate told me that all of his close friends at college were either in his first English class (mine) or had taken a class from me another semester and did dream work. Some students take my class because a roommate or friend recommends it after hearing about the person's frequent nightmares or dream questions. I cannot properly describe the thrill of observing students unpack a recurring dream that has haunted a dreamer for years, or the satisfaction from hearing a student say, after learning about a particular theoretical concept, "This is really great stuff. Where can I read more about this?" I have had students bring a parent's recurring dream into a class discussion, because the parent has said, "Hey, ask your teacher what this dream means." One semester another professor experienced sudden health problems and had to stop teaching 2 days after the beginning of the semester. I was called to take over the class. When I entered the classroom, a student raised her hand and said, "We heard that you study dreams in your classes. We've been talking and that's what we want to do." It did not take much arm-twisting to change from the original professor's curriculum to my own.

Techniques in group dreamwork apply to writing strategies. Breaking down a dream into its various parts, for example, corresponds to analytical writing. Students who previously have had trouble analyzing a topic in depth gain greater confidence in their ability to do so as they analyze dreams orally as part of a class discussion. I point out to them after our discussions what they have been doing—as a way of linking the discussion to my expectations for out-of-class essays. Discussion of other rhetorical strategies emerges from oral dreamwork as well. I explain how to write comparison and contrast essays, for example, in the context of discussing the Jungian notion of "compensation" dreams. I discuss the differences between Freud and Jung when I assign the comparison/contrast essay as well. The process essay is assigned at the same time the students read Chapter 4 of *Where People Fly*, which models process-type writing. The students learn about problem-solving dreams before writing a cause-and-effect essay.

One of the great benefits to discussing dreams in the classroom is its inherent interdisciplinary, multicultural nature: Topics of social and political significance emerge naturally, without any effort on my part, from the dreams themselves. For example, during the semester that the Iraq war began, students reported several nightmares on war. A thoughtful discussion on war emerged from the analysis of a young woman's dream, allowing students to consider how they felt about the impending war. Another student's 60-year old father, who had retired from the military, was being called back into service and would go, in the weeks following our discussion, to Iraq. Without my ever saying so, our dreamwork together made it poignantly clear that dreams have political and ethical relevance that invites students to broaden their understanding of social issues. Dreams, as Jeremy Taylor points out, "reflect society as a whole as well as the dreamer's relationships to it."

Sexuality, race, and gender issues emerge regularly in our class discussion of dreams. Students voice their opinions about these topics, as they analyze the dream, without overt instruction from the teacher. In the past, I felt I was imposing my feminism upon students when I asked them to read essays having a feminist bias. Now, discussions of gender and race equality emerge from dreams which students bring to class. Because dreamwork encourages multiple approaches to one dream, many viewpoints emerge about a single topic. Students begin to develop opinions about social issues as they consider how their own points of view differ from parents, fellow students, and teachers. A dream may seem to invite a "liberal" approach, but because each student projects his or her perspective onto the dream, the discussion is less likely to be totally hijacked by the teacher's perspective. The student whose father went to Iraq not only explored his feelings about this very personal event via someone else's dream, he experienced the concern and support of other students throughout the semester. Because this student was a shy young man, he probably would have had no opportunity to reveal the information about the fears for his father had we not been discussing someone else's dream about this very charged topic. By discussing dreams, the real concerns of students come into the classroom, rather than only the topics of interest to the teacher.

Additionally, the classic texts continue to find their way into class discussions every semester. Plato's "ideal forms," Aristotle's discussion of happiness, Jonah's unfortunate residence in the belly of the whale, Dante's call to travel—discussion of all of these began when a student shared a dream that reminded me of biblical stories, philosophical ideas, or characters from literary texts. In this way, I have the opportunity to introduce students to the notion of archetypes by showing them that ancient ideals and philosophies still inform our world and find their way into their psyches.

Students dealing with a particular problem have the opportunity to research that topic in depth. One student was gang-raped the summer before beginning college. She suffered from PTSD nightmares and decided to write her research paper on that topic. Another student had many explicit sexual dreams. She decided to research the topic of sexual dreams. Students have written on dreams in films, if that is their particular interest, dreams of divorce, addiction, and education. Many students write about dreams in the context of their particular religious and/or ethnic heritage. One student interviewed her Cherokee grandmother and discovered a whole family heritage on dreams that had previously been unknown. Some Hispanic students have grandmothers, or aunts with a particular "gift" for dream work that is part of the family tradition. Students have the opportunity to bring their heritage into the classroom, explore and honor it, instead of always having to leave it behind as they become acculturated and "educated" in the American way. These research projects educate *both* student and professor.

Exploring one's dreams invites the dream world to address waking-life problems in creative and expansive ways. I teach students how to direct their dreams toward a particular problem or concerns. Not all students succeed, but many report and write about their surprising, amazing successes in receiving a dream about a particular concern. Students have received dreams about what to major in, what to do about a boyfriend or girlfriend, and how to solve roommate problems. One student's parents wanted her to major in business so that she could "make a decent income." She knew that business did not interest her, and asked for a dream about what to do. In the dream, she is walking toward a tall office building. She is wearing a business suit and her long hair is up, contained in a sort of bun. Then she notices that her hair is being held up with crayons, the big fat kind that kindergarteners use. Beneath her fancy white business blouse is a bright orange bra that shows clearly. The student's dream confirmed for her what she already knew about herself: She loved young children and wanted to major in elementary education. She said the bright orange bra symbolized the notion that even if she went ahead and "dressed herself" for the business world by majoring in business, her true colors would shine through, like the bra does in the dream. The crayons represent her real passion: developing children's creativity. The student *LOVED* this dream. She felt validated in her hesitation to commit to something of no interest to her. The dream gave her courage to tell her parents in a direct way that she was majoring in elementary education.

I do not have time to introduce my students to all that I want them to know about dreams. I keep my focus on teaching them enough about the dream world so that the students can make their dreams work for them. Lucid dreaming and asking for solution dreams to problems are two ways students can access the rich resources inside of them. Still another approach is to allow students to express dream content in ways other than writing in connection with one of their paper assignments. Some students have written poems; others have written music; many draw their dreams. Then they explore the difference between the two forms of interpretation. Many people are surprised at the new information that emerges from expressing a dream in a nonlanguage medium. "I didn't know this dream had anger in it until I started pounding on the piano," one student reported. One student's dream journal contained more poems than prose. Another's had multiple drawings. One student included a poem about the dream he analyzed in every essay he turned in. He claimed that it clarified for him what the dream was about.

Not all dreams lead to creative expression. Some require therapeutic intervention. I have confronted students (in the privacy of my office) about drug use, bulimia, anorexia, and depression—all from listening to their dreams. Dreams do not lie, even when students continue to deny a problem. Typically, students seem relieved that someone else knows about their (secret) problem. One student had life-threatening bulimia. She wrote a paper about the problem in the past tense, but I sensed that she continued to struggle. A dream that she shared unwittingly as part of a class discussion confirmed my suspicions. Although I did not share those projections with the class during our discussion, I did tell her afterward of my fears, and she began sobbing as she confessed. College-age young adults often engage in a variety of self-destructive behaviors. Their dreams will reveal those often-covert activities and the students expose them inadvertently. When they share those types of dreams in class, fellow students prove especially helpful in providing solutions.

For example, one student revealed a dream about a teenage cousin who was pregnant. The student's parents did not know, and the student did not want to tell them for fear that they would no longer allow her to associate with the cousin. In addition to being a professor, I'm a mother and as a mother, I had some opinions about this dream and the situation it reflected. What to say? As I was trying to figure that out, a student said, "If that were my dream, I'd tell my mom about my cousin. 'Cause things get bad when I try to hide stuff." At this point, the dreamer revealed that she was beginning a sexual relationship with a married man. That confession in turn led to an extended discussion of hiding sexuality from the family and the dreamer's underlying self-esteem problems. I was an anguished listener that day. Certainly I could have delivered a sound lecture on the problems of teenage parenthood and how low self-esteem causes girls to get involved in bad relationships. It was on the tip of my tongue. But the discussion's effectiveness derived from fellow students delivering the advice, via the projections onto her dream.

I feel lucky to do something I love. I like college students. I feel gratified beyond expression when I receive letters from parents thanking me for teaching their son or daughter's favorite class. Students like my class because they get to explore themselves by examining the wonderful world of dreams. When students discover that their dreams provide useful information, to make them laugh and cry, to stop them from heading down a self-destructive path, to confirm something they intuitively sense or to help them appreciate the uncanny, spiritual aspect to their lives, they feel a greater confidence about attempting the difficult task of maturing and becoming and independent, contributing adults.

Notes

Introduction

1. Globus, G. (1991). Dream Content: Random or Meaningful? *Dreaming* 1: 27–40. Cited in Van de Castle, R. (1994). *Our dreaming mind.* New York: Ballantine, 278.

2. Hunt, Harry T. (1989). *The multiplicity of dreams: memory, imagination and consciousness.* New Haven: Yale University.

3. Hartmann, E. (1998). *Dreams and nightmares.* New York: Plenum, 13–15.

Chapter 1

1. Parker, J. and D. Parker. (1998). *The complete book of dreams.* New York: Dorling Kindersley Publishing, 28–29, 40–44.

2. Delaney, G. (1998). *All about dreams.* New York: HarperCollins, Chapters 4 and 5.

3. Moss, R. (1996). *Conscious dreaming.* New York: Three Rivers Press, 43–47.

4. Kottler, J. (1991). *The compleat therapist.* San Francisco: Jossey Bass, 1–23.

5. Boss, Medard. (1958). *The analysis of dreams.* New York: Philosophical Library.

6. Ullman, M. & Zimmerman, N. (1979). *Working with dreams.* Los Angeles: Jeremy. P. Tarcher, 315–320.

7. Roger Knudson, comments in a panel discussion "Key issues in higher education courses on dreams," International Conference of the Association for the Study of Dreams, Sonoma State University, July 1, 2007.

8. Ullman and Zimmerman, op. cit., 317

Chapter 2

1. Elbow, P. (1975). *Writing without teachers.* New York: Oxford University Press; Elbow, P. (1995). *Writing with power.* New York: Oxford University Press.

2. Bishop, B. "Why I Teach Dreams in Freshman Composition." (Unpublished paper.) See Appendix J for the full text of this insightful account of Bishop's experiences.

3. Bishop, "Why I Teach Dreams in Freshman Composition."

4. Jason Tougaw interview.

5. All three of these stories of artistic inspiration from dreams along with many others are told in van de Castle's *Our Dreaming Mind*, op. cit. Aside from its general value as a survey for the teacher of any cross-disciplinary course on dreams, it offers perhaps the most extensive collection of examples of "Dreams That Have Changed the

World," as the author puts it, available in one book. Van de Castle points out that Coleridge's story of the composition of "Kubla Khan" is reputed to be an instance of self-mythologizing.

6. Ruth Lingford interview.

7. Allucquere Rosanne Stone interview. A description of the "Dream/Delirium" course can be found at http://home.actlab.utexas.edu/dream.shtml.

8. Blogs from "English 399W: Dreams" at Queens College of the City University of New York can be found at: http://blogs.qc.cuny.edu/blogs/0906N_1432/. Web projects posted by the students are at: http://blogs.qc.cuny.edu/blogs/dreams/.

9. Tougaw, J. (2009). Dream Bloggers Invent the University, *Computers and Composition, 6*(4), 260.

Chapter 3

1. Foulkes, D. (1991). Why study dreaming: One researcher's perspective. *Dreaming, 1, 5,* 247.

2. See Seligman, M, (1998), *Learned optimism,* 19. In Seligman's view—and relevant to dreams—Freud asked the right questions but his method of generalizing from a few case studies was inadequate for answering them.

3. Excerpts from Yalom's seminal texts *Existential psychotherapy* and *The theory and practice of group psychotherapy,* and selections from *Love's executioner, When Nietzsche wept,* and *Lying on the couch,* can be found in a volume of his selected works, Yalom, I. (1998), *The Yalom reader.* New York: Basic Books. Included are essays on literature informing psychology, and psychology informing literature, which have implications for the dream narrative as a text and how we engage it.

4. See Part 3, "Dreams and Interpretation," in Bulkeley, K. (1994), *The wilderness of dreams* (Albany: State University of New York Press), in which the author engages perplexing questions of how one might encounter the dream text in ways that will yield valid interpretations—(i.e., the dream's meanings).

5. Note Domhoff, G. W. (1996), *Finding meaning in dreams: A quantitative approach* (New York: Plenum), 153–189. Among the persons whose dreams Domhoff compares with established norms are those of Freud and Jung themselves. Although in this study their individual dreams are aggregated and not interpreted, the overall amounts and patterns of dream elements reflect what is known about their biographies and personalities, and the differences in their views that make up an important chapter in the history of psychology, and of dream theory.

6. See Ullman, M, and Zimmerman, N. (1979), *Working with dreams* (London: Jeremy P. Tarcher) and Taylor, J. (1993), *Where people fly and water runs uphill: Using dreams to tap the wisdom of the unconscious* (Clayton, VIC, Australia: Warner Books). Both books set forth the view, now relatively commonplace but then novel, that there is no such thing as a dreams "expert" when it comes to definitively knowing meaning(s) of someone's else's dream. One can propose, but the dreamer herself must dispose. Hence, the modesty of the interpretive offering couched as "if it were my dream . . ."

7. Rainville, R. (1988), *Dreams across the life span* (Boston: American Press) briefly describes the laboratory component of his course.

8. See http://www.dreambank.net. Becoming familiar with this Web site is a "must" for all dream teachers. Even for those not interested in having their students pursue content analyses, multiple dreams of any themes lending themselves to "word-search" procedures can be collected easily for class use.

9. See Delaney, G. (1998), *All about dreams* (New York: HarperSanFrancisco), 88–101.

10. Ullman and Zimmerman, op. cit., 315–320.

11. Hewett, Michael C. (2001), doctoral dissertation: "A ripple in the water: the role of organic inquiry in developing an integral approach in transpersonal research" presented as a one-act play and video. Institute of Transpersonal Psychology, Palo Alto, CA., 133. The Heron reference is to Heron, J. (1966) *Co-operative inquiry.*

12. Hewett, op. cit., 54.

13. Domhoff, G. W. (2003). *The scientific study of dreams.* Washington, D.C.: American Psychological Association.

14. Solms, M. *The neuropsychology of dreams.* Mahwah, NJ: Erlbaum, 225–236.

15. Pagel, J. F. (2008). *The limits of dream.* Boston: Elsevier, 171–194.

16. Pagel, op. cit., 195–201.

17. Foulkes, D. (1978), *A grammar of dreams* (New York: Basic Books), 99, quoted in Van de Castle, R. (1994), *Our dreaming mind* (New York: Ballantine), 274.

18. Van de Castle, op. cit., 278.

19. Kramer, M. (2008). The dream experience: A systematic exploration. Address given at the 25th annual conference of the International Association for the Study of Dreams, Montreal, Quebec, Canada, July 11, 2008.

20. Schwartz, J. M. and Begley, S. (2002). *The mind and the brain.* New York: HarperCollins.

21. Schwartz and Begley, op. cit., 38–46.

22. Rainville, op. cit., iii–iv.

23. This information about Hobson's course comes from Deirdre Barrett.

Chapter 4

1. Lincoln, J.S. (1935). *The dream in primitive cultures.* London: University of London Press.

2. Kracke, W. (2001). Kagwahiv mourning: Dreams of a bereaved father. In *Dreams: A reader on the religious, cultural, and psychological dimensions of dreaming,* edited by K. Bulkeley. New York: Palgrave Macmillan. Herdt, G. (1977). The Shaman's "Calling" Among the Sambia of New Guinea. *Journal de la Société des Océanistes* 33:153–167. Hollan, D. (2003). Selfscape Dreams. In *Dreaming and the self: New perspectives on subjectivity, identity, and emotion,* J. M. Mageo, ed. (2003). Albany: State University of New York Press.

3. Kracke, op.cit., 184.

4. Kracke, op.cit., 176.

5. Eggan, D. (1955). The Personal Use of Myth in Dreams. *Journal of American Folklore* 68:452.

6. For an example of an anthropologist using Hall and Van de Castle methods, see Gregor, T. (2001), A content analysis of Mehinaku dreams. In *Dreams: A reader on*

the religious, cultural, and psychological dimensions of dreaming, edited by K. Bulkeley. (2001). New York: Palgrave Macmillan.

7. Stewart, K., in Tart, Charles (1969). *Altered States of Consciousness*. San Francisco: HarperCollins, 194.

8. Stewart in Tart, op.cit, 193.

9. Stewart in Tart, op.cit., 195.

10. One of the co-authors (Bulkeley) wrote a paper in graduate school many years ago comparing Freudian and Senoi methods of dream interpretation, with much criticism of the former and a very favorable conclusion about the latter. The paper received an A.

11. Tedlock, B., ed. (1987). *Dreaming: Anthropological and psychological interpretations*. New York: Cambridge University Press, 25.

12. Tedlock, op.cit, 128–129.

13. It is worth noting that both Gregor and Herdt have focused on masculinity issues in their studies of the Mehinaku and Sambia, respectively. For more on dream content and gender, see also Domhoff, G. W. (1996), *Finding meaning in dreams*, chapters 4–6.

14. Wallace, A. F. C. (1958). Dreams and Wishes of the Soul: A Type of Psychoanalytic Theory among the Seventeenth-Century Iroquois. *American Anthropologist* 60:234–248.

15. Mageo, J. M., ed. (2003). *Dreaming and the self: New perspectives on subjectivity, identity, and emotion*. Albany: State University of New York Press, 7.

16. A similar kind of cross-cultural exchange of dream theories in the classroom is described by Jayne Gackenbach (1996) in a Canadian context.

17. Mageo, op.cit., 78.

18. Mageo, op.cit., 93, emphasis in original.

19. Gackenbach, J. (1996). Reflections on dreamwork with Central Alberta Cree: An essay on an unlikely social action vehicle. In *Among all these dreamers: Essays on dreaming and modern society*, edited by Kelly Bulkeley. Albany: State University of New York Press, 51.

20. Gackenbach, op. cit., 67.

21. Edgar, I. R. (1995). *Dreamwork, anthropology and the caring professions*. Aldershot, England: Avebury, ix.

22. More recently Edgar has done field investigations in Pakistan to study the role of dreaming in Islamic jihad movements. See Edgar, I. R. (2004), The dream will tell: Militant Muslim dreaming in the context of traditional and contemporary Islamic dream theory and practice. *Dreaming* 14 (1):21–29.

23. Bulkeley, K. (2008). *American dreamers: What dreams tell us about the political psychology of conservatives, liberals, and everyone else*. Boston: Beacon Press. See also Bulkeley, K., ed. (1996), *Among all these dreamers: Essays on dreaming and modern society*. Albany: State University of New York Press; Ullman, M. and Zimmerman, N. (1979), *Working with dreams*. Los Angeles: Jeremy Tarcher; Shulman, D. and Stroumsa, G., eds., (1999), *Dream cultures: Explorations in the comparative history of dreaming*. New York: Oxford University Press; Von Grunebaum, G.E. and Callois, R., eds., (1966), *The dream and human societies*. Berkeley: University of California Press; Jedrej, M. C. and Shaw, R. eds., (1992), *Dreaming, religion, and society in Africa*. Leiden: E.J. Brill.

Chapter 5

1. Nagel, Thomas. (1987). *What does it all mean?: A very short introduction to philosophy*. New York: Oxford University Press, 10, emphasis in original.

2. Plato. (1961). *The republic*. In *Plato: Collected dialogues*, edited by E. Hamilton and H. Cairns. Princeton, NJ: Princeton University Press, 155.

3. Plato, op. cit.,150.

4. Descartes, René. (1960). *Discourse on method and meditations*. Lafleur, L. J., trans. Indianapolis: Bobbs-Merrill, 76–77.

5. On Descartes and dreaming, see chapter 1 in Bulkeley, K. (2005), *The wondering brain: Thinking about religion with and beyond cognitive neuroscience*. New York: Routledge.

6. *Upanisads*. (1996). P. Olivelle, trans. Oxford: Oxford University Press, 25 ff., 59 ff.

7. Tzu, Chuang (1997). *The inner chapters*. D. Hinton, trans. New York: Counterpoint, 18, 32, 34, italics in original. Zhuangzi and Chuang Tzu are two different transliterations of the same name.

8. All following quotes in this section are from Christopher Dreisbach interview.

9. Dreisbach, C. (2000). *Dreams in the history of philosophy*. Dreaming 10 (1):31–42.

10. Christopher Dreisbach interview.

11. Plato, op. cit., IX 571c.

12. Augustine. (1991). *Confessions*. H. Chadwick, trans. Oxford: Oxford University Press, 10:30.

13. See Lamoreaux, J. C. (2002). *The early Muslim tradition of dream interpretation*. Albany: State University of New York Press; Hermansen, M. (2001). Visions as "good to think": A cognitive approach to visionary experience in Islamic Sufi thought. *Religion* 27 (1): 25–44; Von Grunebaum and Callois, eds. (1966). *The dream in human societies*. Berkeley: University of California Press; Bulkeley, K., Adams, K. and Davis. P. M. (2009). *Dreaming in Christianity and Islam: Culture, conflict, creativity*. New Brunswick: Rutgers University Press.

14. The Dalai Lama. (1997). *Sleeping, Dreaming, and Dying*. Boston: Wisdom Publications, 107–108.

15. Patton, K. (2004). "A great and strange correction": Intentionality, locality, and epiphany in the category of dream incubation. *History of Religions* 43 (3): 194–223.

16. Malcolm, N. (1959). *Dreaming*. London: Routledge & Kegan Paul, 7. Emphasis in original.

17. LaBerge, S (1985). *Lucid dreaming: The power of being awake and aware in your dreams*. Los Angeles: Jeremy Tarcher; Kahan, T. and LaBerge, S. (1994). Lucid dreaming as metacognition: Implications for cognitive science. *Consciousness and Cognition* 3 (246–264); Kahan, T. (2001). Consciousness in dreaming: A metacognitive approach. In *Dreams: A reader on the religious, cultural, and psychological dimensions of dreaming* (2003), K. Bulkeley, ed. New York: Palgrave Macmillan; Gackenbach, J. and LaBerge, S., eds. (1988). *Conscious mind, sleeping brain: Perspectives on lucid dreaming*. New York: Plenum Press; Gackenbach, J. (1991). Frameworks for Understanding Lucid Dreaming: A Review. *Dreaming* 1 (2):109–128.

18. Eleanor Rosch interview.

19. See Patton, K. and Ray, B. C., eds. (2000). *A magic still dwells: Comparative religion in the postmodern age.* Berkeley: University of California Press.

20. Barnard, G. W. (1997). *Exploring unseen worlds: William James and the philosophy of mysticism.* Albany: State University of New York Press. Parsons, W. B. (1999). *The enigma of the oceanic feeling: Revisioning the psychoanalytic theory of mysticism.* Oxford: Oxford University Press. Kripal, J. J. (2001). *Roads of excess, palaces of wisdom: Eroticism and reflexivity in the study of mysticism.* Chicago: University of Chicago Press.

21. Good sources of information include Van de Castle's *Our dreaming mind* (1994), Krippner, Bogzaran, and Carvalho's *Extraordinary dreams and how to work with them* (2002), and Bynum's *Families and the interpretation of dreams* (1993). Geoff Nelson's Doctor of Ministry dissertation (2007) also includes important insights into effectively working with paranormal phenomena within the context of dream-sharing groups based in Christian church congregations.

Chapter 6

1. Rupprecht, C. S., ed. (1993). *The dream and the text: Essays on literature and language.* Albany: State University Press of New York,1–2.

2. Garber, M. (1974). *Dream in Shakespeare: From metaphor to metamorphosis.* New Haven: Yale University Press.

3. Foucault, M. (2001). *The order of things: An archeology of the human sciences.* (2nd ed.) New York: Routledge.

4. Rupprecht, C. S., op. cit.

5. Coleridge, S. T. (2003). *Coleridge's poetry and prose.* Halmi, N., Magnuson, P., and Modiano, R., eds. New York: Norton. Reliable versions of classic poems may almost always be found online.

6. Coleridge's view of dreams was the topic of two special issues of the journal *Dreaming*, Vol. 7, Number 1 and 2, 1997 as well as Ford, J. (1998). *Coleridge on dreaming: Romanticism, dreams, and the medical imagination*, New York: Cambridge University Press.

7. Shakespeare, W. (2000). *Shakespeare's sonnets.* S. Booth, ed. New Haven: Yale University Press.

8. Milton, J. (1999.) *The complete poems.* (J. Leonard, ed.) New York: Penguin.

9. Ample selections are available in McCay, W. (1973). *Dreams of the rarebit fiend.* New York: Dover.

10. Clampett, R. [director] (1946). *The Big Snooze* [Animated cartoon]. United States: Warner Bros.

11. Gamwell, op. cit.

12. An excellent guide to the influence of psychoanalysis on culture is Zaretsky, E. (2004). *Secrets of the soul: A social and cultural history of psychoanalysis.* New York: Knopf. Invaluable cultural perspectives on the origins and development of depth psychology and the idea of the unconscious are provided by Ellenberger, H. (1970). *The discovery of the unconscious.* New York: Basic.

13. Hartmann, E. (1998). *Dreams and nightmares.* New York: Plenum; Lakoff, G. and Johnson, M. (1980). *Metaphors we live by.* Chicago: University of Chicago Press.

14. As explored in Hogan, P. (2003). *Cognitive science, literature, and the arts: A guide for humanists.* New York: Routledge; Fireman, G. D., McVay, T. E., and Flanagan, O. J., eds. (2003*). Narrative and consciousness: Literature, psychology and the brain.* New York: Routledge; and Zunshine, L. (2006). *Why we read fiction: Theory of mind and the novel.* Columbus: Ohio State University Press.

15. Blechner, M. (2001). *The dream frontier.* London: The Analytic Press, esp. pp. 15–30. In addition to the theory outlined in Hartmann, E., 1998, op. cit., "hyperassociativity" is a key concept in an exchange between Hobson, J. A. (1998), Dreaming as delirium: A reply to Bert States, *Dreaming* 8(4), 211–222 and States, B. O. (1998), Dreaming as Delirium: A Response to Allan Hobson, *Dreaming,* 8 (4), 223–228.

16. States, B. O. (1988). *The rhetoric of dreams.* Ithaca, NY: Cornell University Press; (1993). *Dreaming and storytelling.* Ithaca, NY: Cornell University Press.

Also helpful is States, B. O., (2003). Dreams, Art and Virtual Worldmaking. *Dreaming* 13(1). Retrieved from http://iasdreams.org/journal/articles/13-1_states.htm.

17. Kilroe, P. (2000). *Dreaming* 13(1). Retrieved from http://iasdreams.org/journal/articles/10-3_kilroe.htm.

18. Ropp, C. C. (2000). A Hermeneutic and a Rhetoric of Dreams. *Janus Head* 3 (1). Retrieved from http://www.janushead.org/3-1/cropp.cfm.

19. In a special issue of *Dreaming* in 1999 devoted to "Dreaming and Interdisciplinarity," guest editors Carol Schreier Rupprecht and Dennis Schmidt argued that the future of dream studies depends on pushing beyond the traditional boundaries of academic disciplines and developing new research methods that can adequately account for the complexities and multiplicities of dreaming experience. Two of the articles offer particularly useful guidance for teachers in the humanities. Sarah White's study of "Dreamwork as Etymology" explores the many points of contact between studying dreams and studying the origins of words. Although she questions Freud's overreliance on dubious etymological theories, White agrees with his insight that the history of language holds great benefit for both personal dreamwork (of which she gives an example with one of her own dreams) and dream research generally: "[A] modest, conscientious, and creative etymology deserves a place among the tools of those who study dreams. Like dreamwork, it tracks the continuous evolution of words and experience, noting antitheses, connections, shifts, and breaks, allowing for ambiguous meaning in the present as well as the past. Like any historical consciousness, etymology enhances our sense of present complexity and deepens our respect for the generative power of language and dreaming." (White 1999, 20).

Rupprecht's article on "Dreaming and the Impossible Art of Translation" explores the long-used metaphor of dreamwork as a kind of translation process. Like White, she critiques Freudian, Jungian, and other psychological theories for outdated assumptions about human languages and the actual practice of translating words and meanings from one language to another. Rupprecht includes an extensive account of classroom practices she used in her comparative literature classes at Hamilton College in upstate New York. One of the exercises she gave her students (who were native French speakers and knew English as a second language) was to first record their dreams in English, and after a period of time translate the dream reports into French. The different versions then were compared and analyzed in terms of their linguistic precision and adequacy to the dream content. Rupprecht's efforts in these courses were guided by what she calls "an axiom at the heart of my pedagogy: If you want to gain the deepest possible understanding of a text, translate it or teach it. Do both these things in tandem with dream work and your liberal arts education will take on an intellectual and imaginative depth rare in the undergraduate academic experience" (Rupprecht 1999, 90). Together, White and Rupprecht show that studying dreams can be a plausible means of enabling students to gain greater sensitivity to the creative workings of human language, and also of bringing the insights and methods of comparative literature to help dream researchers in future investigations.

Chapter 7

1. Langer, S. (1977). *Feeling and form.* New York: Prentice Hall.
2. Tyler, P. (1967). *The three faces of the film: The art, the dream, the cult.* New York: T. Yoseloff.
3. McGinn, C. (2005). *The power of movies.* New York: Pantheon.
4. Metz, C. (1986). *The imaginary signifier: Psychoanalysis and the cinema.* Bloomington: Indiana University Press.
5. Baudry, J-L. (2004). The apparatus: Metapsychological approaches to the impression of reality in cinema. In Braudy, L., and Cohen, M., eds., *Film theory and criticism: Introductory readings* (6th ed.), 760–777. New York: Oxford University Press.
6. Eberwein, R. (1985). *Film and the dream screen.* Princeton, NJ: Princeton University Press.
7. Carroll, N. (1991). *Mystifying movies: Fads and fallacies in contemporary film theory.* New York: Columbia University.
8. Petric, V. (1981). A theoretical-historical survey: Film and dreams. In Petric, V., ed. *Film & dreams: An approach to Bergman.* South Salem, NY: Redgrave.
The volume also contains a fascinating rarity: an essay on Ingmar Bergman's films by the dream psychologist J. Allan Hobson, which shows his extraordinary gifts as a film critic.
9. *Secrets of a Soul* has finally been made available in a restored version by Kino Video (2008), as an outstanding example of German Expressionist cinema between the two world wars.
10. Tyler, P. (1967), op. cit.
11. Many classic Surrealist and experimental short films may be found online in the archives at www.ubuweb.com.
12. Jones, E. (1951). *On the nightmare.* New York: Liveright.
13. Mack, J. E. (1970). *Nightmares and human conflict.* New York: Columbia University Press; McNamara, P. (2008). *Nightmares: The science and solution of those frightening visions during sleep.* Santa Barbara, CA: Praeger.

Chapter 8

1. Keller, J. W., Brown G., Maier, K. et al. (1995). Use of dreams in therapy: A survey of clinicians in private practice. *Psychological Reports,* 76: 1288–1290.

2. Schredl, M., Bohusch, C., Kahl, J., Mader, A., and Somesan, A. (2000). The use of dreams in psychotherapy. *Journal of Psychotherapy Practice and Research*, 9:2, 81–87.

3. See, for example, Kazdin, A.E. (2010). *Single-case research designs: Methods for clinical and applied settings* (2nd ed.). New York: Oxford University Press; Goodheart, C.D., Kazdin, A.E. & Sternberg, R.J. (Eds.), (2006). *Evidence-based psychotherapy: Where practice and research Meet.* Washington, DC: American Psychological Association; and Kazdin, A.E. (Ed.), (2003). *Methodological issues and strategies in clinical research* (3rd. ed.). Washington, DC: American Psychological Association.

4. Hill, C. E., ed. (2003). *Dream work in therapy.* Washington, D.C.: APA.

5. Hill, C. E. and Coates, M. K. Research on the Hill cognitive-experiential dream model. In Hill, ed., op. cit., 273.

6. Montague Ullman developed the "conscious projection" technique in which dream group members respond to another's dream as if it were their own. Jeremy Taylor has promulgated and popularized the practice and the phrase.

7. Hunt, H. L., *The multiplicity of dreams*, op. cit.

8. Yalom, I. and Leszoz, M. *The theory and practice of group psychotherapy* (5th ed.). New York: Basic Books.

9. Bonime, W. (1962). *The clinical use of dreams.* New York: Basic Books.

10. Mahrer, A. (1989). *Dreamwork in psychotherapy and self-change.* New York: Norton.

11. Hill, C. (1996). *Working with dreams in psychotherapy.* New York: Guilford.

12. Barrett, D., ed. (1996). *Trauma and dreams.* Cambridge, MA: Harvard University Press.

13. van Deurzen, E. (2002). *Existential counselling and psychotherapy in practice.* London: Sage.

14. Bulkeley, K. (1997). *An introduction to the psychology of dreaming*, op. cit.

15. Bulkeley, K. (1994). *The wilderness of dreams*, op. cit.

16. Delaney, G. (1998). *All about dreams*, op. cit., 88–101

17. Kantrowitz, J. L. Brief communication: A comparison of the place of dreams in institute curricula between 1980–1981 and 1998–1999. *Journal of the American Psychoanalytical Association*, 43, 3, 985–997.

18. Myers, W. (1993). *Shrink dreams.* Oneonta, NY: Touchstone. In addition to being a telling critique of the abandonment of therapy in psychotherapist training, the book also contains an excellent example of using clients' dreams in therapy (Chapter 5, 107–127).

19. Van de Castle, R. *Our dreaming mind*, op. cit., Chapter 13, "Somatic Contributions to Dreams," 361–404.

20. Pannier, W. and Lyons,T. (2008). Tapping the healing potential of dream imagery and new developments in dream work with cancer patients: An IASD Project. Presentations at the annual conference of the International Association for the Study of Dreams, Montreal, Quebec, Canada, July 2008.

21. King, P. (1994). *Healing the healer (Self-healing in nurses' dreams).* Address given at the International Conference of the Association for the Study of Dreams, Leiden, The Netherlands, 1994.

22. Dombeck, M. (1991). *Dreams and professional personhood.* Albany, New York: SUNY Press.

23. Kingsley, G. (2007). Contemporary group treatment of combat-related post-traumatic stress disorder. In *Journal of American Academy of Psychoanalysis,* 35: 51–69

24. Brockway, S. (1987). Group treatment of combat nightmares in post-traumatic stress disorder. *Journal of contemporary psychotherapy,* v. 17, n. 4, 270–284.

25. Coalson, R. (1995). Nightmare help: Treatment of trauma Survivors with PTSD. *Journal of Psychotherapy,* 32, 3, 381–388.

26. Hartmann, E. (1996). Who develops PTSD nightmares and who doesn't. In Barrett, D, ed. *Trauma and dreams,* op. cit., p.108.

27. Hartmann, E., in Barrett, *Trauma and dreams,* op. cit., 100–113.

28. Kelsey, M. (1991). *God, dreams and revelation: A Christian interpretation of dreams.* Minneapolis: Augsburg Publishing.

29. Sanford, J. (1982). *Dreams: God's forgotten language.* New York: Crossroads.

30. Taylor, J. (1983). *Dream work: Techniques for discovering the creative power in dreams.* Mahwah, NJ: Paulist Press

31. Bulkeley, K. (2000). Dream interpretation: Practical methods for pastoral care and counseling. *Pastoral Psychology* 49.2,: 95–104.

32. Bulkeley, K. (2002) *Dreams of healing: Turning nightmares into visions of hope.* Mahwah, NJ: Paulist Press.

33. Bulkeley, K. and Bulkley, P. (2005). *Dreaming beyond death: A guide to pre-death dreams and visions.* Boston: Beacon Press.

34. Bulkeley, K., Adams, K., and Davis, P. M., eds. (2009). *Dreaming in Christianity and Islam: Culture, conflict, creativity.* (2009). Piscataway, NJ: Rutgers University Press.

Chapter 9

1. Stanley Krippner survey responses and Saybrook University Web site at www.saybrook.edu.

2. See the Web site at http://dream-institute.org.

3. The Internet is a great vehicle for locating dream education programs. Finding them is relatively easy; ascertaining their value in advance of participation difficult. As with seeking psychotherapists, physicians, plumbers, and roofers, we advise getting recommendations from persons you trust that have gone through the programs. Also we advise reviewing the educational credentials and experiences of the practitioners, and talking with them about the nature of the program and what you want to gain from it. Is the program accredited, and if so by which accrediting body? Find out as much as you can. An experience ideally suited for one learner (or prospective dreams teacher) might not be as good a fit for the next. Ultimately there are no guarantees; be careful. With due diligence, it is very likely that you will find a good (and ethical) program.

4. Reed, H. (2005). *Dream medicine: Learning how to get help from our dreams.* Rancho Mirage, CA: We Publish Books.

5. Ullman and. Zimmerman, op. cit., 20–33

6. For this and other IASD programs and activities, see their Web site at http://asdreams.org

7. Kerlinger, F. (1986). *Foundations of behavioral research.* Orlando: Holt, Rinehart & Winston.

Chapter 10

1. Siegel, A. and Bulkeley, K. (1998). *Dreamcatching.* New York: Three Rivers Press.

2. Bulkeley, K. (1993). Dreaming is play. *Psychoanalytic Psychology* 10 (4):501–514; (2004). Dreaming is play II: Revonsuo's threat simulation theory in ludic context. *Sleep and Hypnosis* 6 (3):119–129.

3. This list adapted from Bulkeley (2004), op. cit., 125–126.

4. Reklaw, Jesse (2000). *Dreamtoons.* Boston: Shambhala; (2008). *The night of your life.* Milwaukie, Oregon: Dark Horse Books.

5. Van de Castle, R. (1994). *Our dreaming mind,* 309: "The percentage of animal figures decreases as the dreamer's age increases. This finding is theoretically significant: animal imagery may represent an immature, less developed or less-differentiated form of cognitive structure."

6. www.sleepfoundation.org.

7. White-Lewis, J. (1996). Dreams and social responsibility: Teaching a dream course in the inner-city. In *Among all these dreamers: Essays on dreaming and modern society,* Bulkeley, K., ed. Albany: State University of New York Press. 6–7.

8. Jean Campbell interview.

9. Jean Campbell interview. Campbell has recently developed the "Dream Scouts International" program for children's dream education via the Internet.

10. Adams, K. (2003). Children's dreams: An exploration of Jung's concept of big dreams. *International Journal of Children's Spirituality* 8 (2): 105–114.

11. Adams, K. (2009). Dreams of Muslim and Christian Children. In *Dreaming in Christianity and Islam: Culture, conflict, and creativity.* New Brunswick, NJ: Rutgers University Press, 224–225.

Chapter 11

1. Dreams teachers, especially those focusing on dream interpretation and less inclined toward critical assessment of the claims of various dream theories, should read and consider Domhoff, G. W. (1996), *Finding meaning in dreams.* New York: Plenum; and (2003), *The scientific study of dreams,* Washington, DC: American Psychological Association, for a useful countervailing perspective.

2. Domhoff, G. W. (2003). op. cit., 157–163.

3. See Bulkeley, K. (1994). *The wilderness of dreams.* Albany: State University of New York Press, 111–118

4. Gadamer, H.-G. (1975). *Truth and method.* Trans. by Barden, G. and Cumming, J., trans. New York: Seabury Press. Discussed in Bulkeley, K. (1994), op. cit., 99–129.

5. Bulkeley, K. (1994) op. cit., 115.

6. Johnson, M. *The meaning of the body.* (2007). Chicago: University of Chicago Press.

7. Johnson, M. (2007), op. cit., xi

8. Johnson, M. (2007), op. cit., 2.

9. Johnson, M. (2007), op. cit., 7.

10. Johnson, M. (2007), op. cit., 14–15

11. Morewedge, C. and Norton, M. (2009). When dreaming is believing: the (motivated) interpretation of dreams. *Journal of Personality and Social Psychology*, 2009, 96(2): 249–264.

12. Morewedge and Norton (2009), op. cit., 249.

13. See Asch, S. E. (1951). Effects of group pressure upon the modification and distortion of judgment. In H. Guetzkow (ed.) *Groups, leadership and men*. Pittsburgh, PA: Carnegie Press, Asch, S. E. (1955); Opinions and social pressure. *Scientific American*, 193, 31–35; Asch, S. E. (1956). Studies of independence and conformity: A minority of one against a unanimous majority. *Psychological monographs*, 70 (Whole no. 416); Milgram, S. (1963). Behavioral Study of Obedience. *Journal of Abnormal and Social Psychology* 67: 371–378; Milgram, S. (1974). *Obedience to Authority: An Experimental View*. HarperCollins.

14. The American Psychological Association Monitor: May 1997, 14.

15. See, for example, http://movies.aol.com/trailer_clip_movie_preview_video/archive; www.Britishpathe.com; www.fotosearch.com.

16. www.cyberdreamwork.com.

17. The American Heritage Dictionary of the English Language, 3rd edition, Houghton Mifflin, 1992, pp. 940, 1186.

18. See the "academics" sections of the school's websites at www.grinnell.edu and www.macalester.edu.

Bibliography

Adams, K. (2003). Children's dreams: An exploration of Jung's concept of big dreams. *International Journal of Children's Spirituality, 8*(2), 105–114.

Adams, M. V. (1996). *The multicultural imagination: "Race," color, and the unconscious.* New York: Routledge.

Anderson, L., & Krathwohl, D. (Eds.). (2000). *A taxonomy for learning, teaching, and assessing: A revision of Bloom's taxonomy of educational objectives.* (Abridged ed.) Boston: Allyn & Bacon.

Artemidorus of Daldis. (1975). *The interpretation of dreams.* (R. J. White, Ed. & Trans.). Park Ridge, NJ: Noyes Press.

Asch, S. E. (1951). Effects of group pressure upon the modification and distortion of judgment. In H. Guetzkow (Ed.), *Groups, leadership and men.* Pittsburgh, PA: Carnegie Press.

Asch, S. E. (1955). Opinions and social pressure. *Scientific American, 193,* 31–35.

Asch, S. E. (1956). Studies of independence and conformity: A minority of one against a unanimous majority. *Psychological Monographs, 70* (Whole no. 416).

Augustine. (1991). *Confessions* (H. Chadwick, Trans.). Oxford: Oxford University Press.

Barnard, G. W. (1997). *Exploring unseen worlds: William James and the philosophy of mysticism.* Albany: State University of New York Press.

Barrett, D. (Ed.). (1996). *Trauma and dreams.* Cambridge, MA: Harvard University Press.

Baudry, J-L. (2004). The apparatus: Metapsychological approaches to the impression of reality in cinema. In L. Braudy & M. Cohen (Eds.), *Film theory and criticism: Introductory readings* (6th ed., pp. 760–777). New York: Oxford University Press.

Blechner, M. J. (2001). *The dream frontier.* London: The Analytic Press.

Bosnak, R. (1986). *A little course on dreams.* Boston: Shambhala Publications.

Bonime, W. (1962). *The clinical use of dreams.* New York: Basic Books

Boss, M. (1958). *The analysis of dreams.* New York: Philosophical Library

Brickman, C. (2003.) *Aboriginal populations in the mind: Race and primitivity in psycho-analysis.* New York: Columbia University Press.

Brockway, S. (1987). Group treatment of combat nightmares in post-traumatic stress Disorder. *Journal of Contemporary Psychotherapy, 17*(4), 270–284.

Bulkeley, K. (1993). Dreaming is play. *Psychoanalytic Psychology, 10*(4), 501–514.

Bulkeley, K. (1994). *The wilderness of dreams.* Albany: State University of New York Press.

Bulkeley, K. (1996). *Among all these dreamers: Essays on dreaming and modern society.* (R. V. d. Castle, Ed.). Albany: State University of New York Press.

Bulkeley, K. (1997). *An introduction to the psychology of dreaming.* Westport, CT: Praeger.

Bulkeley, K. (2000). Dream interpretation: Practical methods for pastoral care and counseling. *Pastoral psychology, 49*(2), 95–104.

Bulkeley, K. (Ed.). (2001). *Dreams: A reader on religious, cultural, and psychological dimensions of dreaming.* New York: Palgrave Macmillan.

Bulkeley, K. (2002). *Dreams of healing: Turning nightmares into visions of hope.* Mahwah, NJ: Paulist Press.

Bulkeley, K. (2004). Dreaming is play II: Revonsuo's threat simulation theory in Ludic context. *Sleep and Hypnosis, 6*(3), 119–129.

Bulkeley, K. (2005). *The wondering brain: Thinking about religion with and beyond cognitive neuroscience.* New York: Routledge.

Bulkeley, K. (2008). *American dreamers: What dreams tell us about the political psychology of conservatives, liberals, and everyone else.* Boston: Beacon Press.

Bulkeley, K., and Bulkley, P. (2005). *Dreaming beyond death: A guide to pre-death dreams and visions.* Boston: Beacon Press.

Bulkeley, K., Adams, K., & Davis, P.M. (Eds.). (2009). *Dreaming in Christianity and Islam: Culture, conflict, creativity.* New Brunswick, NJ: Rutgers University Press.

Burroughs, W. (1996). *My education: A book of dreams.* New York: Penguin.

Caillois, R. (Ed.). (1963). *The dream adventure.* New York: Orion.

Carroll, N. (1991). *Mystifying movies: Fads and fallacies in contemporary film theory.* New York: Columbia University.

Cixous, H. (1994). *Three steps on the ladder of writing* (S. Sellers, Trans.). New York: Columbia University Press.

Clampett, R. [director] (1946). *The big snooze* [Animated cartoon]. United States: Warner Bros.

Coalson, R. (1995). Nightmare Help: Treatment of trauma survivors with PTSD. *Journal of Psychotherapy, 32*(3), 381–388.

Cole, J. R. (1992). *The Olympian dreams and youthful rebellion of René Descartes.* Urbana: University of Illinois Press.

Coleridge, S. T. (2003). The pains of sleep. In N. Halmi, P. Magnuson, & R. Modiano (Eds.), *Coleridge's poetry and prose* (pp. 182–183). New York: Norton. (Original work published 1816)

Cooper, M. (2008). *Essential research findings in counseling and psychotherapy.* London: Sage.

Dalai Lama. (1997). *Sleeping, dreaming, and dying.* Boston: Wisdom Publications.

Delaney, G. (1998). *All about dreams.* New York: HarperSanFrancisco.

Derrida, J. (1998). *Of grammatology* (G. C. Spivak, Trans.). Baltimore, MD: Johns Hopkins University Press.

Descartes, R. (1960). *Discourse on method and meditations* (L. J. Lafleur, Trans.). Indianapolis: Bobbs-Merrill.

Dodds, E. R. (1951). *The Greeks and the irrational.* Berkeley: University of California Press.

Domhoff, G. W. (1985.) *The mystique of dreams: A search for Utopia through Senoi dream theory.* Berkeley: University of California Press.

Domhoff, G. W. (1996). *Finding meaning in dreams—a quantitative approach.* New York: Plenum.

Domhoff, G. W. (2003). *The scientific study of dreams.* Washington, D.C.: American Psychological Association.

Dombeck, M. (1991). *Dreams and professional personhood.* Albany: State University of New York Press.

Dreisbach, C. (2000). Dreams in the history of philosophy. *Dreaming,10*(1), 31–42.

Eberwein, R. (1985). *Film and the dream screen.* Princeton, NJ: Princeton University Press.

Edgar, I. R. (1995). *Dreamwork, anthropology and the caring professions.* Aldershot, England: Avebury.

Edgar, I. R. (2004.) The dream will tell: Militant Muslim dreaming in the context of traditional and contemporary Islamic dream theory and practice. *Dreaming, 14*(1), 21–29.

Eggan, D. (1952). The manifest content of dreams: A challenge to social science. *American Anthropologist, 54,* 469–485.

Eggan, D. (1955). The personal use of myth in dreams. *Journal of American Folklore, 68;* 445–463.

Eggan, D. (1957). Hopi dreams and a life history sketch. *Primary Records in Culture and Personality, 2*(1), 1–147.

Elbow, P. (1975). *Writing without teachers.* New York: Oxford University Press.

Elbow, P. (1995). *Writing with power.* New York: Oxford University Press.

Ellenberger, H. (1970). *The discovery of the unconscious.* New York: Basic Books.

Epel, N. (1993). *Writers dreaming: 25 writers talk about their dreams and the creative process.* New York: Carol Southern Books.

Fireman, G. D., McVay, T. E., & Flanagan, O. J. (Eds.). (2003). *Narrative and consciousness: Literature, psychology and the brain.* New York: Routledge.

Flanagan, O. J. (2000). *Dreaming souls: Sleep, dreams, and the evolution of the conscious mind.* New York: Oxford University Press.

Fontana, D. (1994). *The secret language of dreams.* San Francisco: Chronicle Books.

Foucault, M., & Binswanger, L. (1993). *Dream and existence* (F. Williams & J. Needleman, Trans.). Atlantic Highlands, NJ: Humanities Press International.

Foucault, M. (2001). *The order of things: An archeology of the human sciences* (2nd Ed.). New York: Routledge.

Fonagy, P. (2005). *What works for whom? A critical review of psychotherapy research.* New York: Guilford.

Foulkes, D. (1978). *A grammar of dreams.* New York: Basic Books.

Foulkes, D. (1982). *Children's dreams: Longitudinal studies.* New York: Wiley.

Freud, S. (1965). *The interpretation of dreams* (J. Strachey, Trans.). New York: Avon.

Freud, S. (1966). *Introductory lectures on psychoanalysis* (J. Strachey, Trans.). New York: W. W. Norton.

Freud, S. (1980). *On dreams* (J. Strachey, Trans.). New York: W. W. Norton.

Fromm, E. (1951). *The forgotten language.* New York: Grove Press.

Gackenbach, J. (1991). Frameworks for understanding lucid dreaming: A review. *Dreaming, 1*(2), 109–128.

Gackenbach, J. (1996). Reflections on dreamwork with Central Alberta Cree: An essay on an unlikely social action vehicle. In K. Bulkeley (Ed.), *Among all these dreamers: Essays on dreaming and modern society.* Albany: State University of New York Press.

Gackenbach, J., & LaBerge, S. (Eds.). (1988). *Conscious mind, sleeping brain: Perspectives on lucid dreaming.* New York: Plenum Press.

Gadamer, H.-G. (1975). *Truth and method* (G. Barden & J. Cumming, Trans.). New York: Seabury Press.

Gaiman, N. (1993–1997). *The sandman* (10 vols.). New York: Vertigo.

Gamwell, L. (Ed.). (2000). *Dreams 1900–2000: Science, art and the unconscious mind.* Ithaca, NY: Cornell University Press.

Garber, M. (1974). *Dream in Shakespeare: From metaphor to metamorphosis.* New Haven, CT: Yale University Press.

Garfield, P. (1991). *The healing power of dreams.* New York: Simon & Schuster.

Garfield, P. (1997). *The dream messenger.* New York: Simon & Schuster.

Gerona, C. (2004.) *Night journeys: The power of dreams in Transatlantic Quaker culture.* Charlottesville: University of Virginia Press.

Ginzburg, C. (1992.) *The night battles: Witchcraft and agrarian cults in the sixteenth and seventeenth centuries* (J. Tedeschi & A. Tedeschi, Trans.). Baltimore: Johns Hopkins University Press.

Goodheart, C.D., Kazdin, A.E. & Sternberg, R.J. (Eds.), (2006). *Evidence-based psychotherapy: Where practice and research meet.* Washington, DC: American Psychological Association.

Goodheart, K., & Sternberg, R. J. (Eds.). (2006). *Evidence-based psychotherapy: Where practice and research meet.* Washington, DC: APA.

Gregor, T. (2001). Content analysis of Mehinaku dreams. In K. Bulkeley (Ed.), *Dreams: A reader on the religious, cultural, and psychological dimensions of dreaming* (pp. 133–166). New York: Palgrave Macmillan.

Hannah, B. (1976). *Jung—His life and work.* New York: Capricorn/Putnam.

Hartmann, E. (1984). *The nightmare: The psychology and biology of terrifying dreams.* New York: Basic Books.

Hartmann, E. (1996). Who develops PTSD nightmares and who doesn't. In D. Barrett (Ed.), *Trauma and dreams* (pp. 100–113). Cambridge, MA: Harvard University Press.

Hartmann, E. (1998). *Dreams and nightmares.* New York: Plenum.

Herdt, G. (1977). The shaman's "calling" among the Sambia of New Guinea. *Journal de la Societé des Océanistes, 33*, 153–167.

Hermansen, M. (1997). Visions as "good to think": A cognitive approach to visionary experience in Islamic Sufi thought. *Religion, 27*(1), 25–44.

Hermansen, M. (2001). Dreams and dreaming in Islam. In K. Bulkeley (Ed.), *Dreams: A reader on the religious, cultural, and psychological dimensions of dreaming* (pp. 73–91). New York: Palgrave Macmillan.

Hill, C. E. (1996). *Working with dreams in psychotherapy.* New York: Guilford.

Hill, C. E. (Ed.). (2003). *Dream work in therapy.* Washington, DC: APA.

Hobson, J. A. (1988). *The dreaming brain.* New York: Basic Books.

Hobson, J. A. (1998). Dreaming as delirium: A reply to Bert States. *Dreaming, 8*(4), 211–222.

Hogan, P. (2003). *Cognitive science, literature, and the arts: A guide for humanists.* New York: Routledge.

Hollan, D. (2003). Selfscape dreams. In J. M. Mageo (Ed.), *Dreaming and the self: New perspectives on subjectivity, identity, and emotion* (pp. 61–74). Albany: State University of New York Press.

Hunt, H. L. (1989). *The multiplicity of dreams*. New Haven, CT & London: Yale University Press.

Jacobi, J., & Hull, R. F. C. (Eds.). (1970). *C. J. Jung: Psychological reflections*. Princeton, NJ: Princeton/Bollingen.

Jedrej, M.C., & Shaw, R. (Eds.). (1992). *Dreaming, religion, and society in Africa*. Leiden: E.J. Brill.

Johnson, M. (2007). *The meaning of the body*. Chicago: University of Chicago Press.

Jones, E. (1951). *On the nightmare*. New York: Liveright.

Jones, R. M. (1968). *Fantasy and feeling in education*. New York: New York University Press.

Jones, R. M. (1978). *The new psychology of dreaming*. New York: Pelican.

Jones, R. M. (1980). *The dream poet*. Cambridge, MA: Schenkman.

Jung, C. G. (1974). *Dreams* (R. F. C. Hull, Trans.). Princeton, NJ: Princeton University Press.

Jung, C. G. (2008). *Children's dreams: Notes from the seminar given in 1936–1940* (E. Falzeder & T. Woolfson, Trans.). Princeton, NJ: Princeton University Press.

Kahan, T. L. (2001). Consciousness in dreaming: A metacognitive approach. In K. Bulkeley (Ed.), *Dreams: A reader on the religious, cultural, and psychological dimensions of dreaming* (pp. 333–360). New York: Palgrave Macmillan.

Kahan, T. L., & LaBerge, S. (1994). Lucid dreaming as metacognition: Implications for cognitive science. *Consciousness and Cognition, 3*, 246–264.

Kahn, M. (2002). *Basic Freud*. New York: Basic Books.

Kazdin, A.E. (Ed.). (2003). *Methodological issues and strategies in clinical research* (3rd ed.). Washington, DC: American Psychological Association.

Kazdin, A.E. (2010). *Single-case research designs: Methods for clinical and applied settings* (2nd ed.). New York: Oxford University Press.

Keller J. W., Brown G., Maier, K., et al. (1995). Use of dreams in therapy: a survey of clinicians in private practice. *Psychological Reports, 76*, 1288–1290

Kelsey, M. (1991). *God, dreams and revelation: A Christian interpretation of dreams*. Minneapolis: Augsburg Publishing.

Kerlinger, F. (1986). *Foundations of behavioral research*. Orlando, FL: Holt, Rinehart & Winston.

Kerouac, J. (2001). *Book of dreams*. San Francisco: City Lights.

Kilroe, P. (2000). The dream as text, the dream as narrative. *Dreaming, 10*(3). Retrieved from http://iasdreams.org/journal/articles/10-3_kilroe.htm.

King, P. (1994) *Healing the healer (Self-healing in nurses' dreams)*. Address given at the International conference of the Association for the Study of Dreams, Leiden, The Netherlands.

Kingsley, G. (2007). Contemporary group treatment of combat-related posttraumatic stress disorder. *Journal of American Academy of Psychoanalysis, 35*, 51–69.

Kottler, J. 1991. *The compleat therapist*. San Francisco: Jossey-Bass.

Kracke, W. (2001.) Kagwahiv mourning: Dreams of a bereaved father. In K. Bulkeley (Ed.), *Dreams: A reader on the religious, cultural, and psychological dimensions of dreaming* (pp. 175–187). New York: Palgrave Macmillan.

Kramer, M. (2008, July). *The dream experience: A systematic exploration*. Address presented at the 25th annual conference of the International Association for the Study of Dreams, Montreal, Canada.

Kruger, S. F. (1992). *Dreaming in the middle ages.* Cambridge: Cambridge University Press.

Kripal, J. J. (2001). *Roads of excess, palaces of wisdom: Eroticism and reflexivity in the study of mysticism.* Chicago: University of Chicago Press.

Krippner, S., Bogzaran, F., & de Carvalho, A. P. (2002). *Extraordinary dreams and how to work with them.* Albany: State University of New York Press.

Krippner, S., & Dillard, J. (1988). *Dreamworking.* Buffalo, NY: Bearly Limited.

LaBerge, S. (1985). *Lucid dreaming: The power of being awake and aware in your dreams.* Los Angeles: Jeremy Tarcher.

Lakoff, G., & Johnson, M. (1980). *Metaphors we live by.* Chicago: University of Chicago Press.

Lamoreaux, J. C. (2002). *The early Muslim tradition of dream interpretation.* Albany: State University of New York Press.

Langer, S. K. (1977). *Feeling and form.* New York: Prentice Hall.

Lansky, M. (Ed.). (1992). *Essential papers on dreaming.* New York: New York University Press.

Leiris, M. (1988.) *Nights as day, days as night* (R. Sieburth, Trans.). New York: Marsilio.

Levin, C. (2008). *Dreaming the English Renaissance: Politics and desire in court and culture.* New York: Palgrave Macmillan.

Lincoln, J. S. (1935). *The dream in primitive cultures.* London: University of London Press.

Lohmann, R. (Ed.). (2003). *Dream travelers: Sleep experiences and culture in the South Pacific.* New York: Palgrave Macmillan.

Lohmann, R. (2001). The role of dreams in religious enculturation among the Asabano of Papua New Guinea. In K. Bulkeley (Ed.), *Dreams: A reader on the religious, cultural, and psychological dimensions of dreaming* (pp. 111–132). New York: Palgrave Macmillan.

Mack, J. E. (1970). *Nightmares and human conflict.* New York: Columbia University Press.

Mageo, J.M. (Ed.). (2003). *Dreaming and the self: New perspectives on subjectivity, identity, and emotion.* Albany: State University of New York Press.

Mahfouz, N. (2005.) *The dreams* (R. Stock, Trans.). Cairo: The American University in Cairo Press.

Mahoney, M. F. (1966). *The meaning in dreams and dreaming.* Secaucus, NJ: Citadel Press.

Mahrer, A. (1989). *Dreamwork in psychotherapy and self-change.* New York: Norton.

Malcolm, N. (1959). *Dreaming.* London: Routledge & Kegan Paul.

Marzano, R. J., & Kendall, J. S. (Eds.). (2008). *Designing and assessing educational objectives: Applying the new taxonomy.* Thousand Oaks, CA: Corwin Press.

Mattoon, M. A. (1984). *Understanding dreams.* Dallas, TX: Spring Publications.

McCay, W. (1973). *Dreams of the rarebit fiend.* New York: Dover.

McCay, W. (2005). *Little Nemo in slumberland.* Palo Alto, CA: Sunday Press

McGinn, C. (2005). *The power of movies.* New York: Pantheon.

McNamara, P. (2008). *Nightmares: The science and solution of those frightening visions during sleep.* Santa Barbara, CA: Praeger.

Metz, C. (1986). *The imaginary signifier: Psychoanalysis and the cinema.* Bloomington: Indiana University.

Milgram, S. (1963). Behavioral study of obedience. *Journal of Abnormal and Social Psychology, 67,* 371–378.

Milgram, S. (1974). *Obedience to authority: An experimental view.* HarperCollins.

Milton, J. (1999.) *The complete poems* (J. Leonard, Ed.). New York: Penguin.

Morewedge, C., & Norton, M. (2009). When dreaming is believing: The (motivated) interpretation of dreams. *Journal of Personality and Social Psychology 96*(2), 249–264.

Moss, R. (1996). *Conscious dreaming.* New York: Three Rivers Press.

Nagel, T. (1987). *What does it all mean? A very short introduction to philosophy.* New York: Oxford University Press.

Norbu, N. (1992). *Dream yoga and the practice of natural light.* Ithaca, NY: Snow Lions Publications.

O'Flaherty, W. D. (1984). *Dreams, illusion, and other realities.* Chicago: University of Chicago Press.

Pagel, J. F. (2008). *The limits of dream.* Boston: Elsevier.

Pannier, W. with T. Lyons. (2008, June). *Tapping the healing potential of dream imagery and new developments in dream work with cancer patients: An IASD project.* Presentations at the annual conference of the International Association for the Study of Dreams, Montreal, Quebec, Canada.

Parker, J., & Parker, D. 1998. *The complete book of dreams.* New York: Dorling Kindersley.

Parsons, W. B. (1999). *The enigma of the oceanic feeling: Revisioning the psychoanalytic theory of mysticism.* Oxford: Oxford University Press.

Patton, K. (2004). "A great and strange correction": Intentionality, locality, and epiphany in the category of dream incubation. *History of Religions, 43*(3), 194–223.

Patton, K. C., & Ray, B. C. (Eds.). (2000). *A magic still dwells: Comparative religion in the postmodern age.* Berkeley: University of California Press.

Petric, V. (1981). A theoretical-historical survey: Film and dreams. In V. Petric (Ed.), *Film & dreams: An approach to Bergman* (pp. 1–48). South Salem, NY: Redgrave.

Plato. (1961). The Republic. In *Plato: Collected dialogues.* (E. Hamilton & H. Cairns, Eds.). Princeton, NJ: Princeton University Press.

Plato. (1961). Theaetetus. In *Plato: Collected dialogues.* (E. Hamilton & H. Cairns, Eds.). Princeton, NJ: Princeton University Press.

Potocki, J. (1996). *The manuscript found at Saragossa* (I. MacLean, Trans.) New York: Penguin.

Pu Songling. (2006). *Strange tales from a Chinese studio* (J. Minford, Trans. and Ed.). New York: Penguin.

Rainville, R. (1988). *Dreams across the life span.* Boston: American Press.

Rascaroli, L. (2002). Like a dream: A critical history of the oneiric metaphor in film theory. *Kinema,* Fall 2002. Retrieved from http://www.kinema.uwaterloo.ca/rasc022.htm.

Reklaw, J. (2000). *Dreamtoons.* Boston: Shambhala.

Reklaw, J. (2008). *The night of your life.* Milwaukie. Oregon: Dark Horse Books.

Richardson, J. (2000). The dream of reading. *The Yale Review, 88*(4), 80–108.

Richardson, L. (1966). Writing: A method of inquiry. In N. Denzin & Y. Lincoln (Eds.), *Handbook of qualitative research* (pp. 516–529). Thousand Oaks, CA: Sage.

Ropp, C. C. (2000). A hermeneutic and a rhetoric of dreams. *Janus Head, 3*(1). Retrieved from http://www.janushead.org/3-1/cropp.cfm.

Rupprecht, C. S. (Ed.). (1993). *The dream and the text: Essays on literature and language.* Albany: State University Press of New York.

Rycroft, C. (1979). *The innocence of dreams.* London: The Hogarth Press.

Sanford, J. (1982). *Dreams: God's forgotten language.* New York: Crossroads.

Schredl, M., Bohusch, C., Kahl, J., Mader, A., & Somesan. A. (2000). The use of dreams in psychotherapy. *Journal of Psychotherapy Practice and Research, 9*(2), 81–87.

Schredl, M., & Erlacher, D. (2007). Self-reported effects of dreams on waking-life creativity: An empirical study. *Journal of Psychology, 14*(1), 35–46.

Schwartz, J. M., & Begley, S. (2002). *The mind and the brain.* New York: HarperCollins.

Segaller, S., & Berger, M. (1990). *The wisdom of the dream.* Boston: Shambhala.

Seligman, M. (1998). *Learned optimism.* New York: Simon & Schuster.

Shafton, A. (1995). *Dream reader.* Albany: State University of New York Press.

Shakespeare, W. (2000). *Shakespeare's sonnets* (S. Booth, Ed.). New Haven, CT: Yale University Press.

Shelley, M. (2000). *Frankenstein.* New York: Signet.

Shulman, D., Stroumsa, G. A., & Stroumsa, G. G. (Eds.). (1999). *Dream cultures: Explorations in the comparative history of dreaming.* New York: Oxford University Press.

Sivanada, R. (1994). *Realities of the dreaming mind.* Spokane, WA: Timeless Books.

Sobel, M. (2000). *Teach me dreams: The search for self in the Revolutionary era.* Princeton, NJ: Princeton University Press.

Solms, M. (1997). *The neuropsychology of dreams.* Mahwah, NJ: Erlbaum.

Stephen, M. (1995). *A'Aisa's gifts: A study of magic and the self.* Berkeley: University of California Press.

Stewart, K. (1951). Dream theory in Malaya. *Complex, 6,* 21–33.

States, B. O. (1988). *The rhetoric of dreams.* Ithaca, NY: Cornell University Press.

States, B. O. (1993). *Dreaming and storytelling.* Ithaca, NY: Cornell University Press.

States, B. O. (1998). Dreaming as delirium: A response to Allan Hobson. *Dreaming, 8*(4), 223–228.

States, B. O. (2003). Dreams, art and virtual worldmaking. *Dreaming, 13*(1), Retrieved from http://iasdreams.org/journal/articles/13-1_states.htm.

Sumegi, A. (2008). *Dreamworlds of shamanism and Tibetan Buddhism.* Albany: State University of New York Press.

Tart, C. T. (1969). *Altered states of consciousness.* San Francisco: HarperCollins.

Taylor, J. (1983). *Dream work: Techniques for discovering the creative power in dreams.* Mahwah, NJ: Paulist Press.

Taylor, J. (1993). *Where people fly and water runs uphill: using dreams to tap the wisdom of the unconscious.* Clayton, VIC, Australia: Warner Books.

Tedlock, B. (Ed.). (1987). *Dreaming: Anthropological and psychological interpretations.* New York: Cambridge University Press.

Tedlock, B. (2005). *The woman in the shaman's body: Reclaiming the feminine in religion and medicine.* New York: Bantam.

The American Heritage Dictionary of the English language (3rd ed.). (1992.) Boston: Houghton Mifflin.

Tougaw, J. (2009). Dream bloggers invent the university. *Computers and Composition, 6*(4), 260.

Townley, R. (1998). *Night errands: How poets use dreams.* Pittsburgh: University of Pittsburgh Press.

Tyler, P. (1960). *The three faces of the film: The art, the dream, the cult.* New York: T. Yoseloff.

Tzu, C. (1997). *The inner chapters* (D. Hinton, Trans.) New York: Counterpoint.

Ullman, M., & Zimmerman, N. (1979). *Working with dreams*. Los Angeles: Jeremy. P. Tarcher.

Ullman, M. (1996). *Appreciating dreams: A group approach*. Thousand Oaks, CA: Sage.

Upanisads. (1996). (P. Olivelle, Trans.). Oxford: Oxford University Press.

Van de Castle, R. (1994). *Our dreaming mind*. New York: Ballantine.

van Deurzen, E. (2002). *Existential counselling and psychotherapy in practice*. London: Sage.

Vedfelt, O. (1999). *The dimensions of dreams*. New York: Fromm International.

Von Grunebaum, G. E., & Caillois, R. (Eds.). (1966). *The dream and human societies*. Berkeley: University of California Press.

Wallace, A. F. C. (1958). Dreams and wishes of the soul: A type of psychoanalytic theory among the seventeenth century Iroquois. *American Anthropologist, 60*, 234–248.

Watterson, B. (2005). *The complete Calvin and Hobbes*. Kansas City, MO: Andrews McNeel.

White-Lewis, J. (1996). Dreams and social responsibility: Teaching a dream course in the inner-city. In K. Bulkeley (Ed.), *Among all these dreamers: Essays on dreaming and modern society* (pp. 3–12). Albany: State University of New York Press.

Wollheim, R. (1971.) *Sigmund Freud*. New York: Cambridge University Press.

Yalom, I. (1998). *The Yalom reader*. New York: Basic Books.

Young, S. (1999). *Dreaming in the lotus: Buddhist dream narrative, imagery, and practice*. Boston: Wisdom.

Yourcenar, M. (1999). *Dreams and destinies* (D. F. Friedman, Trans.). New York: Palgrave Macmillan.

Zaretsky, E. (2004). *Secrets of the soul: A social and cultural history of psychoanalysis*. New York: Knopf.

Zunshine, L. (2006). *Why we read fiction: Theory of mind and the novel*. Columbus: Ohio State University Press.

Index